D0023175

PSYCHOLOGICAL FOUNDATIONS
OF MUSICAL BEHAVIOR

PSYCHOLOGICAL FOUNDATIONS
OF MUSICAL BEHAVIOR
Second Edition

By

RUDOLF E. RADOCY

*Professor of Art and Music Education
and Music Therapy
The University of Kansas
Lawrence, Kansas*

and

J. DAVID BOYLE

*Professor of Music Education
and Music Therapy
The University of Miami
Coral Gables, Florida*

C H A R L E S   C   T H O M A S • P U B L I S H E R
Springfield • Illinois • U.S.A.

Published and Distributed Throughout the World by

CHARLES C THOMAS • PUBLISHER
2600 South First Street
Springfield, Illinois 62794-9265

© *1988 by* CHARLES C THOMAS • PUBLISHER

ISBN 0-398-05514-9

Library of Congress Catalog Card Number: 88-16050

With THOMAS BOOKS *careful attention is given to all details of manufacturing
and design. It is the Publisher's desire to present books that are satisfactory as to their
physical qualities and artistic possibilities and appropriate for their particular use.*
THOMAS BOOKS *will be true to those laws of quality that assure a good name
and good will.*

Printed in the United States of America
SC-R-3

Library of Congress Cataloging-in-Publication Data

Radocy, Rudolf E.
    Psychological foundations of musical behavior / by Rudolf E.
Radocy and J. David Boyle.
        p. cm.
    Includes bibliographies and index.
    ISBN   0-398-05514-9
    1. Music-Psychology.   I. Boyle, J. David.   II. Title.
ML3830.R15 1988
781'.15—dc19   88-16050
                                                                                        CIP
                                                                                        MN

PREFACE TO THE SECOND EDITION

Since publication of the first edition in 1979, research and other writings related to the psychological foundations of musical behavior have increased many fold. The research and writing have come not only from individuals who might be considered music psychologists, but also from individuals whose primary interests are psychology, music theory, and/or music education. The authors believe that this is good for the discipline, because these researchers and writers bring varying perspectives to the study of musical behavior.

To the extent that individuals studying musical behavior are open and objective in their evaluations of research and writing from the varying perspectives, there can be true cross-disciplinary interchange, thus facilitating even better knowledge of the variables influencing musical behavior. Such knowledge is important in and of itself, but its ultimate value comes when musicians, psychologists, and teachers apply it to enhance the development of children's and older students' musical abilities, as well as to enrich all people's lives individually and collectively through musical experience.

Much recent research and writing has been concerned with understanding music cognition. A particular focus of research in music cognition has been on pattern perception, both melodic and rhythmic, with special emphasis on identifying the cognitive processes underlying perception. Research designed to gain better understanding of the cognitive processes involved in music perception is an important approach to understanding musical development and behavior, and it has had significant effects on the authors' revisions.

However, the psychological foundations of musical behavior are much more broadly based than in perceptual and cognitive processing. Examination of research and writings on other pertinent variables is essential. Research related to musical behavior is conducted under a variety of

v

rubrics, which may or may not include research on cognitive processing. Systematic musicology, i.e., the study of various systems that function in music, has much to offer students of musical behavior. Its subfields of psychoacoustics, psychomusicology, and sociomusicology examine music from particular perspectives. Psychological aesthetics, focusing on variables underlying the affective or feeling response to music, also has much to offer. Philosophical aesthetics also provides valuable insights into musical meaning and response. Much music education research provides data relevant to understanding musical behavior, particularly musical development and musical learning. With increased sophistication of physiological recording equipment and development of new techniques for examining neurological and other physiological reactions to music, there is a renewed interest in psychophysiological research as an avenue for understanding musical behavior.

While music throughout history has been an integral part of society, the emerging development of sociology of music as a discipline suggests an increased recognition of societal and cultural influences on musical behavior. Music's constant availability via various electronic media, both alone and with accompanying film or video, either as background music or music intended specifically for listening, may directly influence musical responsiveness, as well as have effects on many nonmusical behaviors. (Research on music's effects on nonmusical behaviors also constitutes an important dimension of research in music psychology.)

The authors recognize that the psychological foundations of musical behavior are increasingly complex and that research from many disciplines can contribute to understanding musical behavior. The various areas of research, however, are not discrete; results and conclusions from areas and approaches to research on musical behavior must be considered in relation to those from other areas and approaches. Further, disciplines not concerned directly with musical behavior, but which seek to develop understanding of general cognition and behavior, may offer many insights into musical behavior. In short, individuals seeking to understand musical behavior must draw from many disciplines. Such an eclectic viewpoint is essential for the eventual understanding of musical behavior.

Constraints of time, space, and resources necessarily limited the scope and breadth of the revision. Consequently, the authors have exercised their professional judgments, based on teaching psychology of music and conducting related research and scholarly inquiry, regarding content.

Naturally, some arbitrary decisions were necessary, and the authors' scholarly biases are reflected. Time and events inevitably will make some material obsolescent or trivial. Given their chosen content, however, the authors have tried to make this book comprehensive, comprehensible, and contemporary. Traditional areas of study are represented, but the authors have attempted to incorporate recent research and contemporary psychological perspectives, while not losing sight of the book's primary concern: To facilitate the readers' understanding of variables underlying musical behavior.

ACKNOWLEDGMENTS

Preparing a second edition of an existing text is facilitated by experience with the first. The authors are grateful to their students at The University of Kansas, the University of Miami, and The Pennsylvania State University, and, indirectly through their instructors, to many students elsewhere for feedback regarding comprehending and applying the text since the first edition appeared in 1979.

Manuscript preparation is time consuming, and long-range projects must be completed within the opportunities and limitations of the academic world. The authors appreciate the encouragement and patience of George Duerksen, Chairman of the Department of Art and Music Education and Music Therapy at the University of Kansas, William Hipp, Dean of the University of Miami School of Music, and Payne Thomas, our managing editor.

Life is more than the pursuit of scholarship. The authors are grateful for the loving support of their wives, Judith Radocy, RMT–BC, and Arlene Boyle, Ed.D., who understood the authors' priorities on numerous occasions.

R.E.R.
J.D.B.

CONTENTS

PSYCHOLOGICAL FOUNDATIONS
OF MUSICAL BEHAVIOR

Chapter One

INTRODUCTION

Purpose

This book provides the reader with a comprehensive overview of human musical behavior, as viewed from a psychological perspective. Music has been a cultural component since a time prior to recorded history. Organizing sound for functional and aesthetic purposes provides many fascinating (if not always answerable) questions. Description, prediction, and explanation of composition, as well as performance, and listening behavior are challenging and unfinished tasks. This book focuses questions and general interest in such description, prediction, and explanation for the benefit of psychologists, musicians, educators, and anyone else with a serious interest in music.

An understanding of human musical behavior has utility for the musician in the studio, on the stage, in the classroom, or in a commercial setting. Why are there preferences for certain sounds? How relevant is acute pitch discrimination? What psychophysical processes underly musical perception? Are there specialized cognitive processes for dealing with musical stimuli? Are some individuals "naturally" musical? Why is a deviation from stereotyped performance practice a "stroke of creative genius" when done by a well-known conductor but "failure to understand the literature" when done by an amateur? Can business people employ music in successful marketing strategies? Knowledge of human musical behavior in its many manifestations is essential for addressing these and numerous other questions.

Contemporary musicians and educators, struggling to balance conflicting philosophies and societal demands, may find utility in developing understanding and familiarity with human musical behavior. Does music really motivate and/or sedate students? What physiological changes may occur in listening to music? Why are children more receptive to "different" music in the primary grades than in later years? How related is musical

3

capacity or ability to intellectual and manual abilities? Again, although this book does not promise definitive answers, the information provided can focus relevant inquiry.

Scope

Music psychology's traditional domains include psychoacoustics, measurement and prediction of musical ability, functional music, cultural organization of musical patterns, music learning, and the affective response to music. Music cognition recently has emerged as a more contemporary domain. The chapter organization reflects the traditional domains. However, relevant research on music cognition is incorporated into discussions of the traditional domains, particularly in the chapters examining psychacoustics, musical preference, learning, and the psychological foundations of rhythm, melody, and harmony. Further, contemporary interest in the sociocultural underpinnings of musical behavior is reflected in the chapter on music as a phenomenon of man, society, and culture.

Musical behavior is one aspect of human behavior; consequently, it must be subject to the same genetic and environmental controls which govern all human behavior. A concern for what people do with musical stimuli, in natural as well as laboratory situations, is expressed throughout the book.

Behavior, as used herein, means the activity of living dynamic human beings. Such activity is directly observable and is of interest either in itself or as external evidence of some internal state. Cognition, the internal processes of memory and "thinking," may be behavior in a covert sense, but the only way to study objectively such covert behavior is to study overt manifestations thereof. Perception is a process of sensing the environment; it obviously is essential for behavior. Perception may be studied only through evidence of its results. Musical behavior includes performance, listening, and creative activity involved in composition. The study of musical behavior thus necessarily includes related cognitive and perceptual processes. That which people do with music is musical behavior. So, too, is that which music does to people.

As Gaston (1968, p. 7) indicates, musical behavior is studied through psychology, anthropology, and sociology. This book primarily reflects a psychological study, as psychology is the study of human behavior. Nevertheless, the authors have not hesitated to look beyond the general body of psychological literature. Sociology, anthropology, philosophy, and acoustics are germane areas from which the authors have drawn valuable material.

Preview

In planning this book, the authors have considered the dynamic (in the sense of moving and ever-changing) aspects of musical performance and listening as well as important influences of prior experiences on present behaviors. No human musical activity is solely the result of willful individual interaction with music. Cultural influences, learning, and biological constraints are as crucial as motivation, reward, and any "inherent" properties of the musical stimulus.

As Gaston (1957, p. 26) has stated:

> To each musical experience is brought the sum of an individual's attitudes, beliefs, prejudices, conditionings in terms of time and place in which he has lived. To each response, also, he brings his own physiological needs, unique neurological and endocrinological systems with their distinctive attributes. He brings, in all of this, his total entity as a unique individual.

Chapter two examines the question of why people have music. There are varying opinions; the chapter considers philosophical, functional, and cultural issues. Music is examined in terms of its functions for individuals, its social values, and its importance as a cultural phenomenon. While the focus is on Western music, certain ethnomusicological research suggests that there are commonalities of musical function among different cultures.

Without certain psychoacoustical phenomena related to the perception and processing of pitch, loudness, and timbre, music would not exist, at least as it is presently known. The third chapter discusses basic descriptions and relationships involving those phenomena. Considerable attention is given to perception, judgment, and measurement, as well as physical and psychophysical events.

Music, a dynamic art form, exists in time; some organization of tonal durations is present in all music. The fourth chapter discusses rhythmic behaviors and what is involved in producing and responding to rhythms. The authors believe that the rhythmic response is a learned one; no person "has rhythm" on an absolute inherent basis.

Definitions and opinions regarding melody and harmony differ; it is debatable whether they exist in all music. Nevertheless, they are vital considerations in much Western music, and the terms are used freely by musicians and nonmusicians. Research in cognitive psychology suggests that the mental organization of "real" music depends, in part, on structural aspects involving melody and harmony. The fifth chapter considers horizontal and vertical pitch organization, tonality, scales, and value judgments, as well as related pedagogical issues.

Chapter Six is concerned with the "chills up the spine" effect and other indications of an affective response to music. There is no question that physiological changes can occur with music. But what is their nature? What is the influence of training? What is meant by "beautiful" music? The chapter discusses several approaches to studying the affective response to music, with particular emphasis on recent developments in psychological aesthetics.

Musical preference is the subject of the seventh chapter. Attention is given not only to what appear to be existing preferences and tastes but also to musical and social variables of which preference is a function.

Music's utility as a stimulator, tranquilizer, and reward, of particular concern to music therapists as well as music educators, is discussed in the eighth chapter. Ceremonial and industrial aspects also receive attention, as does the use of music to influence consumer behavior.

Measurement and prediction of musical ability have been stressed in psychology of music. Construction and publication of aptitude and "talent" measures suggest a concern for student selection, but such measures also reflect assumptions regarding the nature and manifestations of musical ability. Although this is not a measurement book, the ninth chapter considers several approaches to measuring musical ability and underlying rationales.

Music teachers obviously must be concerned with music learning—not just in the traditional sense of memorization, but also in the sense of learning to perform, analyze, and organize musical ideas. The tenth chapter presents basic learning considerations and offers practical applications to music learning.

The final chapter examines some future research directions. As more knowledge regarding neural circuitry, dual sensory responses, and social pressures is accumulated and assimilated, there may be profound effects upon the study of musical behavior.

Throughout the chapters is the authors' bias that music is a human phenomenon. Individuals bring their prior experiences to the performance and listening situations, where such experiences interact with all the dynamic aspects of human intercourse. There is much to be learned regarding musical behavior. Its complexities can overwhelm the student, teacher, and researcher. Seemingly far-fetched and distantly related ideas may begin to appear with surprising frequency. One must believe that musical behavior is, in the last analysis, another form of human behavior —it is no more, and no less. As Gaston (1968, p. 21) said, "Music is not mystical nor supernatural—it is only mysterious."

REFERENCES

Gaston, E.T. (1957). Factors contributing to responses in music. In E.T. Gaston (Ed.), *Music therapy 1957.* Lawrence, KS: The Allen Press.

Gaston, E.T. (1968). Man and Music. In E.T. Gaston (Ed.), *Music in therapy.* New York: MacMillan.

Chapter Two

MUSIC: A PHENOMENON OF
MAN, SOCIETY, AND CULTURE

Music has been examined from many perspectives, including historical, psychological, philosophical, sociological, and cultural anthropological, as well as from the more specialized domains of ethnomusicology, sociomusicology, and sociology of music.* There appears to be consensus that society and culture have much influence on the musical behaviors of individuals within given societal and cultural groups, including subgroups.

Ethnomusicologists tell us that music is present in all cultures, primitive and civilized (Nettl, 1956, p. 6).

> The importance of music, as judged by the sheer ubiquity of its presence, is enormous and when it is considered that music is used both as a summatory mark of many activities and as an integral part of many others which could not be properly executed, or executed at all, without music, its importance is substantially magnified. There is probably no other human cultural activity which is so all-pervasive and which reaches into, shapes and often controls so much of human behavior. (Merriam, 1964, p. 218)

The preceding statement, while made by an individual concerned with the study of music outside Western traditions, accurately reflects music's place in contemporary society. The ever-presence of music, be it in the concert hall, supermarket, discotheque, home, church, school, radio, television, etc., provides evidence that the statement is equally as true for "sophisticated" as for primitive societies.

For the most part musical behavior is interhuman, interpersonal, or

---

*Sociomusicology focuses primarily on any aspect of music or musicmaking that influences or is influenced by society (Lundquist, 1982, p. 107). Sociomusicology's interests and concerns are ultimately *musical*. Sociology of music, however, "is not about music but about society" (Dasilva, Blasi, & Dees, 1984, p. 1). Nevertheless, each field of study offers insights into the effects of society on musical behavior.

social (Mueller, 1963). According to Dasilva, Blasi, & Dees (1984, pp. 3–5), music may be considered social in several senses: (a) Performing, creating, hearing, and interpreting music involves the use of shared social constructs—grammars and symbols, (b) music involves composers, interpreters, and listeners, and (c) music is communal in nature; that is, it takes place in "communities," limited circles in which particular interpersonal and intergroup relationships exist. Dasilva et al. argue that musical behavior, or "conduct" as they prefer, cannot be understood without examination of the social processes involved. Sloboda (1985, p. 240), while primarily concerned with music cognition, also maintains that social influences are essential to any full explanation of human conduct.

The authors agree that understanding music in its social and cultural contexts can provide insights regarding musical behavior. The present discussion, therefore, examines music from several perspectives: its functions, its differences from other sounds, theories of its origins, and its role as a cultural phenomenon.

Why Music?

Underlying this discussion is the recognition of music as human behavior: "Music is the essence of humanness, not only because man creates it, but because he creates his relationship to it" (Gaston, 1968, p. 15). Gaston maintains that the human brain, which distinguishes man from other animals by making possible speech, communication, and abstract thinking, also enables "significant noverbal communication in the form of music." Sloboda (1985, p. 268) and Dowling and Harwood (1986, pp. 236–237) also recognize that biological development has been essential to music becoming such a vital part of society and culture. Artistic creativity and appreciation are unique to human beings (Roederer, 1975, p. 11).

Most readers probably will agree that music is behavior unique to mankind, but there may be less consensus regarding why music exists. While philosophical inquiry into this question has been concerned with examination of music as an art form that has aesthetic value, anthropologists and ethnomusicologists agree that music exists because of its enculturational function (Johnson, 1985, p. 54; Nettl, 1985, p. 69). Merriam's (1964, pp. 209–227) insightful discussion of music's functions explicates the enculturation function and provides a perspective to the question "Why music?"

Merriam's Functions of Music

Merriam distinguishes between *uses* and *functions* of music. *Uses* refer to ways or situations in which people employ music; *functions* concern the reasons, particularly the broader purposes, for which it is used. Merriam notes that, while nonliterate societies might *use* music in minute and directly applied ways more frequently than "sophisticated" societies, such use is by no means necessarily more *functional.* Music appears to serve essentially the same functions in most cultures. Merriam recognizes ten major musical functions:

1. Emotional expression
2. Aesthetic enjoyment
3. Entertainment
4. Communication
5. Symbolic representation
6. Physical response
7. Enforcing conformity to social norms
8. Validation of social institutions and religious rituals
9. Contributions to the continuity and stability of culture
10. Contributions to the integration of society

Music as *emotional expression* provides a vehicle for expression of ideas and emotions which might not be revealed in ordinary discourse. It can convey either individual or group emotions. The social protest songs of the sixties allowed young people a socially tolerable outlet for expressing displeasure with the world situation. Teenagers with guitar in hand publicly will express feelings toward the opposite sex which otherwise might not be expressed, at least in socially acceptable fashion. By serving as a means for expressing feelings toward subjects which are taboo, music allows the release of otherwise unexpressible thoughts and ideas and provides an opportunity to "let off steam" with respect to social issues.

Music as *aesthetic enjoyment* will be examined in Chapter Six. Suffice it to say here that the creating and contemplating of beauty in music is evident in Western culture as well as many other major cultures, including those of China, Japan, Arabia, India, and Indonesia. Gaston (1968) contends that aesthetic experience is ultimately physiological, a function of man's need to create and enrich the sensory environment. Roederer (1975, p. 164) relates musical experience to dispensation of reward and punishment by the limbic system. The making of beauty and sensitivity to beauty presumably comprise a basic need for man's well-being.

Music functions as *entertainment* in all societies. Musselman (1974, p. 140) notes that *entertainment* "engages the attention agreeably" and "amuses or diverts" while *art* is concerned with aesthetic principles. To say that music cannot serve both an entertainment and aesthetic function is difficult and would probably depend on how aesthetic experience is defined. In Western culture, it appears that "popular" music in its broadest sense serves an entertainment function while art music seems to serve an aesthetic function; this is not to say, however, that popular music cannot function as aesthetic nor that art music cannot serve as entertainment. What appears to interest, amuse, or divert one individual might provide an aesthetic experience for another. The crux of the matter, discussed in Chapter Six, is the nature of the response to or involvement with the music. Music as entertainment also can be combined with other functions, particularly in nonliterate societies where the function of music is more directly related to its uses.

Merriam suggests that music's function as *communication* is perhaps the least understood of the ten major functions. He notes that music is *not* a universal language; rather it is shaped in terms of the culture of which it is a part. It may convey emotion or something similar to emotion to those who understand the culture's musical idioms, although it is doubtful that all individuals within a given culture will receive the same emotional meaning. Farnsworth (1969, p. 80) notes that the mood or emotion conveyed depends on a variety of factors external to the music itself. A listener's personality structure, the mood he or she holds just prior to the listening period, the word meanings of the libretto if there is one, and the listener's attitudes toward music in general and the particular composition in question all affect the mood or emotion perceived. On the other hand, Gaston (1968) maintains that music's ability to provide *nonverbal* communication reflects its potency and value. He maintains that feelings or emotions can be conveyed nonverbally through music and that attempts to express such feelings verbally often are totally inadequate. That which is communicated, however, does not necessarily have common meanings to any large group of people.

Music functions in all societies as a *symbolic representation* of other things, ideas, and behaviors. Merriam cites two essential attributes of a symbol: First, a symbol must be different in kind from that which it symbolizes; otherwise it is an *icon*. Second, a symbol must have ascribed meaning. According to Merriam, symbolism in music can be considered at four levels: (1) the symbolizing evident in song texts, (2) the symbolic reflection of affective or cultural meaning, (3) the reflection of other cultural behavior and values, and (4) the deep symbolism of universal principles.

Music's function as a *physical response* is based on the fact that music does elicit physical response. The use of music with dance is a part of all cultures. Music elicits, excites, and channels crowd behavior, although the type and extent of the behavior also is shaped culturally.

Enforcing conformity to social norms is one of music's major functions. Merriam notes that songs of social control play an important part in many cultures by providing either direct warnings to erring members of the society or by indirectly indicating what is considered proper behavior. Related to this function is the function of *validation of social institutions and religious rituals.* Social institutions are validated through songs which emphasize the proper and improper in society, as well as through songs which tell people what to do and how to do it. Religious systems are validated through recitation of myth, legend, or doctrine in song.

By providing a construct through which emotion can be expressed, aesthetic experience and entertainment can be received, communication can occur, physical response is elicited, social norms are reinforced, and social institutions and religious rituals are validated, music also *contributes to the continuity and stability of culture.* Merriam maintains that "music is in a sense a summatory activity for the expression of values, a means whereby the heart of the psychology of a culture is exposed" (p. 225).

Perhaps music's most important function is its *contribution to the integration of society.* Music is truly a social phenomenon, inviting, encouraging, and in some instances almost requiring individuals to participate in group activity. Music is used as a signal to draw people together or as a rallying point around which individuals gather to engage in activities which require group cooperation and coordination.

Music's ability to function in all of the above ways depends, of course, on a commonality of experience with music in the appropriate functional contexts. Emotional expression of taboo subjects is less meaningful to those for whom the subjects never have been taboo. Music with powerful religious significance may lack any validation or ritualistic function for persons who do not practice the religion.

Gaston's Fundamental Considerations of Man in Relation to Music

Gaston's (1968) "fundamental considerations" are in essence another view of music's functions, and while some considerations express functions similar to Merriam's, some are sufficiently different to warrant separate discussion. The eight considerations include:

1. Need for aesthetic expression and experience
2. The cultural matrix determines the mode of expression
3. Music and religion are integrally related
4. Music is communication
5. Music is structured reality
6. Music is derived from the tender emotions
7. Music is a source of gratification
8. The potency of music is greatest in the group

Gaston views the *need for aesthetic expression and experience* as essential to the development of hum_____ uty and the making of beauty a_____guishing characteristics. Individu_____ beauty—whether in music or some other me_____ may not be achieving their full potential as human beings; Gaston goes so far as to suggest that they may be handicapped.

While perhaps not a function per se, the view that *the cultural matrix determines the mode of expression* is fundamental to all functions of music. While music serves similar functions in nearly all cultures, individuals respond only to functional music within their own culture; i.e., they learn the music of their own culture and generally react to it in terms of the way their particular society reacts to it.

The *integral relationship of music and religion* is evident in virtually every culture. Gaston believes the primary reason for this is that there are some common purposes to religious services and music performances, the greatest of which is their valence for drawing people together. Music and religion go hand in hand to defend against fear and loneliness. Music also seems to be a particularly appropriate mode for reaching for the supernatural, which is a concern of many religious services.

As mentioned above, Gaston views *music as communication* as nonverbal communication, which provides music its potency and value. Gaston maintains that there would be no need for music if it were possible to communicate verbally that which is easily communicated musically. Even the best verbal descriptions of feelings elicited by music fail to communicate adequately. Perhaps it is because of music's wordless meaning that philosophical explanations of music's meaning are inadequate.

That *music is structured reality* should become evident from discussions in Chapters Four and Five. Just because music is temporal does not suggest that it is any less tangible sensorily than objects which we touch, see, feel, or smell. Gaston maintains that music therefore is a particularly valuable therapeutic medium through which reestablishment of contact with reality can be accomplished by individuals who have withdrawn from society. (This will be discussed further in Chapter Eight.)

Gaston's contention that *music is derived from the tender emotions* is clearly evident in the uses made of today's popular music, as well as in religious music, folk songs, art songs, and patriotic music. All such music reflects a concern for other individuals, and the predominant theme is love in one of its various manifestations—love of one another, love of country, love of God, etc. Music also provides a feeling of belonging, thus providing a sense of closeness to others and the alleviating of loneliness.

In our culture, as well as in others, *music is nearly always an expression of good will, a reaching out to others,* and is so interpreted. Music, then is a powerful expression of the interdependence of mankind, and from the lullaby to the funeral dirge, an expression of the tender emotions. (Gaston, 1968, p. 25)

The recognition of *music as a source of gratification* is particularly apparent in children and adolescents, although it also is apparent in adults. Gratification is a by-product of achievement per se rather than competition. Music provides opportunities for achievement in noncompetitive situations. The self-esteem which results from music accomplishment contributes greatly to an individual's state of well-being.

That *the potency of music is greatest in the group* should be self-evident. Music is a social phenomenon which invites and encourages participation. Music provides group activities which bring together individuals who otherwise might not come in contact with one another. It provides them opportunities to interact in intimate yet ordered and socially desirable ways.

The functions of music recognized by Merriam and Gaston in many respects are overlapping, but with different labels attached to them. Further, the various functions are not discrete; given musical experiences may serve different functions for different individuals and more than one function for a given individual. The important point is that music is human behavior that serves a variety of functions in virtually every culture. While some cultures, particularly Western ones, place greater emphasis on the aesthetic function, all functions contribute to the importance of music in society.

Another Perspective

Merriam's and Gaston's answers to "Why music?" essentially reflect the perspective of ethnomusicologists and cultural anthropologists, and most students of musical behavior would agree that the functions they recognize are plausible reasons for music having become such an important aspect of virtually all cultures and societies. However, some recently proposed views on the functions of music in society and culture suggest that biological development (Sloboda, 1975, pp. 260–268) and music's *biological adaptive value* (Dowling and Harwood, 1986, pp. 236–237) have been instrumental in making music so valuable for the human species.

In raising the question "Does man *need* music?" Sloboda (p. 266) notes that individuals can go without music for very long periods without showing any noticeable ill effects. He suggests that perhaps *cultures* rather than individuals need music and that the *need* might be more direct in nonliterate cultures than in our complex contemporary societies.

> Primitive cultures have few artifacts, and the organization of the society must be expressed to a greater extent through transient actions and the way people interact with each other. Music, perhaps, provides a unique framework with which humans can express, by the temporal organization of sound and gesture, the structure of their knowledge and social relations. Songs and rhythmically organized poems and sayings form the major repository of human knowledge in non-literate cultures. (Sloboda, 1985, p. 267)

Sloboda goes on to speculate that human mental processes, which he views as a product of evolution, have led to a natural propensity to behave in adaptive ways, including a propensity to use language and music. He maintains that evolution supplied a *motivation* for music, making it "natural" and enjoyable for people to indulge in it.

Dowling and Harwood (1986, pp. 236–237) advocate a similar position, suggesting that evolution should be considered in terms of the *gene pool* of groups rather than in terms of adaptations of *individuals*. They agree that music is valuable to human groups and note that as humans evolved over hundreds of thousands of years in small groups, singing and playing music served as a "cohesion-facilitating group activity—an expression of social solidarity" (p. 236). They recognize music as a powerful symbol of cultural identity, especially since musical style tends, like language, to reflect a highly stable set of shared behaviors that are culturally transmitted. They maintain that music's *biological adaptive value* is reflected in its value to human societies. Furthermore, they maintain that, even with changes in social structures and other developments that have come with industrialized societies, including some division of labor between "musicians" and "consumers," music's sociocultural values and the underlying distribution of musical abilities are essentially the same as in more primitive societies.

The answer to "Why music?" continues to be in terms of the many important functions music serves in society and culture. Perhaps understanding the role of biological evolution in the development of human adaptive behaviors provides at least a partial answer as to "how" music became so important to human society and culture.

What Makes Some Sounds Music?

Studies of the development of musical behavior suggest that differential responses to musical sounds and other sounds become evident during infancy (Michel, 1973; Moog, 1976; Fridman, 1973; Dowling, 1984). Virtually every child and adult "knows" what music is. The enculturation process assures that early in life children develop a concept of music, albeit vague, ill-defined, and nonverbalized. That individuals' concepts reflect cultural bias is readily apparent, although the authors believe that most individuals will recognize another culture's music as music even though it may sound "strange."

Music of all cultures involves the organization of sounds with varying pitches, loudness levels, and timbral qualities within a rhythmic framework. When one considers the range of perceptually just noticeable differences in pitch, loudness, and timbre, it would appear that the variety of sounds and sound combinations which could comprise music is infinite.

It also can be argued that all sound has the attributes of pitch (perhaps indefinite and transient), loudness, and timbre and that these sounds are temporal. Further, while the claim is usually made that musical sounds have organization, it also is apparent that many "nonmusical" sounds have discernible organization, e.g., speech, sounds of machinery, and many natural sounds. Also, some contemporary music, *musique concrete*, records and incorporates sounds of nature into a recognized musical style.

The question of why some sounds (but not others) are music has been studied by philosophers, musicologists, psychologists, and theorists, resulting in a variety of explanations, ranging from physical explanations in terms of the harmonic structure of musical sounds to elaborate metaphysical theories to psychological characteristics. Others (Gaston, 1968, Beament, 1977) even suggest that the basic difference in what is recognized as music is ultimately a function of man's physiological or biological nature.

Blacking (1973, p. 10) argues that music could not exist if human beings had not developed a capacity for structural listening, that is, the ability to perceive *sonic order.* He goes on to argue that understanding music involves both sound (the object) and man (the subject); for Blacking, the key to understanding music is in the relationships existing between subject and object, the activating principle of organization (p. 26).

Perhaps there is no acceptable answer for everyone, but there appears to be one basic difference in the sounds of nature and the sounds of music. Sounds of nature are "constantly changing from instant to instant in the frequencies present and in the amplitudes of the frequencies" (Beament, 1977, p. 7). Beament notes that music primarily involves sounds with sustained constant frequencies (heard as fixed pitches) without which melodic and harmonic music could not exist. He maintains that fixed pitches "are virtually an *artefact* [sic] *of man.*"

The use of fixed pitches in music is virtually universal. Further, psychophysiological explanations of the processing of music support the need for using fixed pitches. Roederer (1975, pp. 161–163) maintains that fixed pitches are essential for perception of music. A tone has to last a minimum period of time for it to be processed by the brain. Sounds continually changing in frequency do not allow sufficient processing time. In everyday terms, it is easier to identify pitches of sounds which have a certain duration than pitches of sounds which pass by quickly.

Roederer (pp. 161–162) suggests that recurring patterns of a relatively small number of fixed pitches have come to be used for music within given cultures because

> it is easier for the brain to process, identify, and store in its memory a melody that is made up of a time sequence of discrete pitch values that bear a certain relationship to each other . . . rather than one that sweeps continuously up and down over all possible frequencies.

While the use of fixed pitches appears to be an attribute of sound that is used in most music, it should be noted that the range of sounds used in music has other attributes for which adequate "reasons for being" have not been offered. For example, Sloboda (1985, pp. 253–259) recognizes other musical universals. He notes that virtually all music takes place with respect to fixed *reference* pitches such as a drone or tonal center. He also notes that the octave is a "privileged" interval in that it is a frequently used interval in nearly all music and that scales in virtually all cultures do not divide into equal sized intervals. A fourth universal involves the use of pulse or meter to provide *time reference* points. Sloboda argues that both pitch and time reference points are essential for people to coordinate their behaviors in such a way as to make music the structured social phenomenon that it is.

Perhaps consensus never will be achieved in the answer to "Why music?" It appears, however, that any answer must encompass more than the objective ordering of sounds. The answer also must recognize that music is a human construct, with certain psychophysical, perceptual, cognitive, and behavioral potentials for interacting with sound constructs. Finally, the answer must consider that musical sounds vary from culture to culture, yet serve many similar functions within all cultures.

The ultimate answer to the question under consideration must be in terms of the *function* of sounds within a given cultural context. If sounds are (a) created or combined by a human being, (b) recognized as music by some group of people, and (c) serve some function which music has come to serve for mankind, then those sounds are music.

Origins of Music

If music is viewed as human behavior, explanations of its origins must be in terms of how man came to use sounds for musical functions; metaphysical and ethereal explanations, while perhaps of interest to those examining music from a philosophical perspective, are inadequate.

Unfortunately, music's temporal character does not afford anthropologists the same opportunities for studying its beginnings as do many other artifacts of human behavior. While the study of music in primitive societies offers some insight, the origins of music and musical behavior are primarily a matter of conjecture. The value of such conjecture has been questioned (Blacking, 1973, p. 56), but some of the theories are reviewed here for the benefit of the interested reader.

Nettl (1956, pp. 134–137) and Revesz (1953, pp. 224–235) have summarized the prominent theories regarding music's origins; in addition, each has offered another theory. The present discussion reviews their discussions as well as a theory implicit in Gaston's writings. The discussion concludes with an examination of music's origins as they relate to biological man and music's role in primitive society.

The *Darwinian theory* of music's origins holds that music developed in conjunction with sexual instincts and was originally a mating call. Proponents of this theory cite the mating calls of some animals and bird songs which often serve a sexual function. The song was used in seeking a mate. Although most music today is related to the tender emotions, there is little evidence to support the Darwinian theory. Both Nettl and Revesz criticize the theory, although from different perspectives. Revesz notes that birds "sing" outside of the mating season and suggests that music in primitive cultures today should be preponderantly love songs (which it is not) if the theory were true. Nettl says that perhaps the weightiest argument against the theory is the absence of music-like mating calls among apes.

A *theory of rhythm* suggests that music evolved from its close relationship to dance. That dance ordinarily is accompanied by music in most cultures is indisputable. Revesz acknowledges that dance provides motives and occasions for singing and musicmaking, but maintains that because they are used together offers little or no support for the argument that music evolved from dance or vice versa. "It does not make us see how man came to combine movements with words and notes, to choose a number of fixed intervals in the continuous tone-series, and to link the intervals together in larger combinations" (Revesz, p. 228).

A *work song theory,* attributed to Karl Buecher, holds that work songs provide the impetus for music. Buecher's study of Western folksongs revealed a number of such songs, and he postulated that primitive people must have devised songs to coordinate their work efforts. Nettl criticizes this theory, noting that the world's simplist cultures do not have work songs, and even when they do work in groups, they do not recognize rhythmic efficiency.

Revesz recognizes a *theory of imitation* which suggests that music originated as a result of man's imitation of bird songs. Support for this theory generally is based on the tendency of some birds' songs to use some fixed pitches and the same relative intervals. Perhaps the strongest argument against this theory is the fact that no primitive cultures have songs which are imitative of bird calls. Revesz also asserts that the supporters of this theory have overlooked the fact that the vocal utterances, even when serving as mating calls or alarm cries, are merely direct and automatic reactions of biological states. Instinct dominates bird songs and animal sounds; man's music is guided by purposive, conceptual, and aesthetic behaviors.

The *theory of expression* reflects the view that music evolved from "emotional" speech. The argument made for this theory is that, as an individual becomes emotional in his or her speech, the speech patterns acquire the characteristics of fixed pitches. Revesz notes, however, that the speech-sounds manifesting emotion have nothing in common with music or song; neither do they serve a musical function. They are reflexive and invariable expressions of momentary emotion which lack any sort of musical significance.

What Nettl calls a *theory of impassioned speech* appears to be somewhat similar to the above theory of expression and to what Revesz calls the *theory of melodic speech*. The basic view is that music evolved from the accentuation and intonation of human speech. These melodic characteristics arise in excited speech and during recitation, and they gradually evolved into music. Revesz recognizes that recitative-like speech is present in most cultures, but questions whether such speech had any formative influence on music's development. He further argues that it cannot be assumed that recitative speech developed in advance of the most primitive form of music.

Revesz notes that parallels have been drawn between the beginnings of music and the *lalling melodies of children*. The assumption of this view is that primitive people created melodies in a manner similar to the ways young children's earliest melodies are created. However, he quickly discounts this theory on the basis that young children's melodies are conditioned by the singing and other music they hear in their environment. Obviously, music's originators would have had no such models to condition their efforts.

Several versions of a *communication theory* have been offered. Revesz is a proponent of the communication theory, labeling his the *calling signal theory*. The basic view is that individuals desiring to communicate a message from a distance use shouting or calling signals. Such signals, maintains Revesz, acquire musical characteristics in that they use fixed pitches and varying loudness levels. Nettl, while noting that Carl Stumpf also advocated this theory, disregards it because his study of primitive cultures reveals that calling signals with fixed pitches are not used.

Nettl also cites Siegfried Nadel's *theory of communication with the supernatural* as one view of music's origins. Nettl recognizes the theory's logic in view of the close connection between music and religion, but suggests that it is supported by little more than circumstantial evidence. Further, he maintains that "the high degree of complexity of many contemporary primitive religious songs discourages assuming that they are survivals of the earliest musical style" (p. 135).

Nettl's theory of music's origins assumes that an undifferentiated method of communication existed in the earliest primitive cultures. Such communication was neither speech nor music, but possessed three attributes common to both: pitch, stress, and duration. There were no fixed pitches nor definite vowels and consonants; rather, the sounds were grunts, cries, and wails which sounded like neither speech nor music. Nettl hypothesizes that, through a long, gradual stage of differentiation and specialization in culture, language acquired the characteristics of vowels and consonants while music acquired the characteristic of fixed pitches. In summary, there are three stages to Nettl's theory: (1) undifferentiated communication, (2) differentiation between music and language, and (3) differentiation among various musical styles. Nettl acknowledges that it is only for the last stage that any data are available.

Gaston's view on music's origin holds that music developed along with the beginning of family and society, thus giving music "a biological as well as a cultural basis" (p. 11). With development of the brain's cortex, primitive man was able to suppress rage and hostility, a necessity for the development of society. Cortical development also freed the primitive female from blind, instinctive behavior that would cause her to accept just any male at each period of estrus. The cortical became dominant over the endocrine factor. These two aspects of development fostered the beginnings of family with its resulting division of labor, modified aggressive behavior between male and female, and increased communication. "All this leads to a uniqueness in humans, among all animals, of the mother-child relationship, without which there would be no culture as we know it" (Gaston, p. 11). The human infant is highly dependent on the mother for a long period of time. While the primitive father provided food and protection, the mother devoted time to the care of her baby. It could be hypothesized that, as the primitive mother sought to soothe her child and express feelings for it, her soothing efforts assumed the rhythmic character of lullabies. Further, the kinds of sounds which are most effective in soothing are repetitious, sustained, and legato. (See Chapter Eight.) These early lullabies, developed for functional purposes, could have been one of the earliest forms of music.

Sloboda (1985, pp. 265–268) also recognizes the importance of man's biological development to the origins of music, but he does not focus on the family and mother-child relationship as does Gaston. As noted previously in this chapter, Sloboda suggests that as primitive cultures developed music served a *need* in that it provided a mnemonic framework through which society could express and communicate the structure of its social relations. Because of the *appeal* of musical structure, which provided further motivation for musicmaking, music came to be "natural" and enjoyable for people. It served a cohesion-building function in early societies and cultures and became a deeply rooted part of man's humanness. Even in today's complex technological and electronic society, the essence of music is still rooted in the infancy of humanity, particularly through the human voice and rhythmic movement of the human body.

designed to assist memory

Perhaps "the truth" regarding the origins of music will never be known. Whatever its beginnings, the authors submit that the earliest music, just as all music today, including art music, ultimately was functional to the well-being of its creators.

Music in Society and Culture

Whatever its origins, music is human behavior that occurs within a cultural context. Through the enculturation process each social order develops its institutions and artifacts for perpetuation of itself, and music is one of the few things common to all cultures (Nettl, 1975, p. 71). Previously in this chapter it was noted that music serves some common functions in most societies even though the musical styles and forms vary from culture to culture. Through its functionality to society, music has become an integral cultural component, serving both as a cohesive and perpetuating force. On the other hand, music itself also reflects cultural values and temperaments. Max Weber's (1958, p. xxvi) analysis of the rational and social foundations of music even suggests that the difference between Western music and that of other (particularly Eastern) cultures is rooted in Western people's temperament and their drives to rationalize and understand environmental phenomena. Nettl (1975, p. 93) concurs that the character of a society and its quality of life greatly influence its music, but he notes that other factors, e.g., technological level of the society, types of raw materials available for instrument construction, amount of contact with other cultures, and attitudes toward cultural change or continuity, also influence the development of a culture's music.

Even the recognition of cross-cultural "universals" (Dowling & Harwood, 1986, pp. 238–239) does not negate the fact that sociocultural context influences musical behavior. While music may have some similarities and serve similar functions in different cultures, it is also obvious that musical behaviors of individuals vary greatly from culture to culture. It is difficult to generalize regarding why this is so, but Sloboda makes a strong case for the use of notation as a primary variable (1985, pp. 244–248). Sloboda notes that oral and literate cultures are different. In the oral culture learning is inextricably bound to fundamental human interactions; individuals gain knowledge through custom and ritual. In literate societies the knowledge is not limited to what can be remembered; rather, they allow storage of knowledge, thus putting psychological *distance* between the individual and the accumulated knowledge of a culture. Also, individuals must *select* certain aspects of knowledge and may examine such knowledge more objectively than in an oral culture where learning and knowledge are an integral part of one's self.

Sloboda points out how this might affect the musical traditions and behaviors of the two types of cultures. In oral cultures music, like verbal knowledge, is subject to mutation over time; thus exact knowledge of particular pieces of music that might be gained through repeated examination of scores and hearings of records (which are considered an extension of notation) is virtually impossible. Sloboda suggests several implications of the oral/literate differences for musical behavior: (a) memory processing strategies and structures of individuals in the two cultures will be different, (b) the "architectural" complexity of an oral culture's music will necessarily be limited, (c) nature of the musical *content* of literate cultures may be examined in isolation from musical *context,* and (d) notation leads to the *selection* of some aspects of sound for preservation and discards others.

While culture affects musical behavior, music, conversely, may influence the culture. Perhaps Lomax (1968, p. 133) best summarizes music's cultural role when he suggests that music is man's vehicle for expressing what is most basic in his relationships with others. Lomax's examination of music in different cultural settings revealed that a culture's favorite music "reflects and reinforces the kinds of behavior essential to its main subsistence efforts and to its central and controlling social institution" (p. 133).

Nettl (1975, pp. 71–100), studying music's role in Iranian culture, examined three distinct musical traditions: folk music of rural areas, popular music of the cities, and the traditional classical music. While the three musical traditions reflected different walks of Iranian life, it was apparent that each also reflected the values and attitudes of the respective subculture. For example, a dominant mood of traditional Iranian classical music is sadness. Nettl notes that Iran (Persia) has a long tragic history of warfare, struggle, and divisiveness and that its music reflects the bitterness and other feelings resulting from such a history.

The work of Nettl (1956), Hamm, Nettl, and Byrnside (1975), Merriam (1964), Lomax (1968), and Blacking (1973) alone supports the hypothesis that music is an integral part of culture. Lundin (1967) and Farnsworth (1969) premise their psychology of music texts on the view that music is a cultural and social phenomenon.

The emergence of music sociology, psychomusicology, ethnomusicology, and anthropology of music as fields of study also attests to the increasing recognition of musical behavior as integral to society and culture. Students of musical behavior, therefore, must be cognizant of the context in which the behavior occurs.

Summary

Following are the major points of this chapter:
1. Music is present in all cultures.
2. Music is unique to human beings.
3. Merriam's ten functions of music include
   a. emotional enjoyment
   b. aesthetic enjoyment
   c. entertainment
   d. communication
   e. symbolic representation
   f. physical response
   g. enforcing conformity to social norms
   h. validation of social institutions and religious rituals
   i. contributions to the continuity and stability of culture
   j. contributions to the integration of society
4. Gaston's fundamental considerations of man in relation to music include
   a. need for aesthetic expression and experience
   b. the cultural matrix determines the mode of expression
   c. music and religion are integrally related
   d. music is (nonverbal) communication

    e. music is a source of gratification

    f. music is derived from the tender emotions

    g. the potency of music is greatest in the group

5. There is increasing recognition that music's importance in society and culture is dependent in part on man's biological evolution that made possible adaptive behaviors such as language and music.

6. Music of all cultures involves the organization of sounds with varying pitches, loudness levels, and timbral qualities within a rhythmic framework.

7. Fixed pitches are an attribute of music.

8. Sounds which are created or combined by a human being, are recognized as music by some group of people, and serve some function for man may be considered music.

9. Some theories regarding music's origins include the

    a. Darwinian theory

    b. theory of rhythm

    c. work song theory

    d. theory of imitation

    e. theory of expression

    f. theory of melodic speech

    g. communication theory

    h. Nettl's theory of an undifferentiated method of primitive communication

    i. Gaston's view that music developed with the beginning of family

    j. view that music served a *need* for primitive societies by providing a mnemonic framework through which the structure of social relations could be communicated.

10. The music of a culture is affected by the characteristics of the culture, particularly whether it is an oral or literate culture.

11. Music reflects the values, attitudes, and temperment of a culture.

REFERENCES

Beament, J. (1977). The biology of music. *Psychology of Music,* 5 (1), 3–18.

Blacking, J. (1973). *How musical is man?* Seattle: University of Washington Press.

Dasilva, F., Blasi, A., & Dees, D. (1984). *The sociology of music.* Notre Dame, IN: University of Notre Dame Press.

Dowling, W.J. (1984). Development of musical schemata in children's spontaneous singing. In W.R. Crozier & A.J. Chapman (Eds.), *Cognitive processes in the perception of art* (pp. 145–163). Amsterdam: North-Holland.

Dowling, W.J., & Harwood, D.L. (1986). *Music cognition.* Orlando, FL: Academic Press.

Farnsworth, P.R. (1969). *The social psychology of music* (2nd ed). Ames: The Iowa State University Press.

Fridman, R. (1973). The first cry of the newborn: Basis for the child's future musical development. *Journal of Research in Music Education, 21,* 264–269.

Gaston, E.T. (1968). Man and music. In E.T. Gaston (Ed.), *Music in therapy.* New York: MacMillan.

Hamm, C., Nettl, B., & Byrnside, R. (1975). *Contemporary music and music cultures.* Englewood Cliffs, NJ: Prentice-Hall.

Johnson, G.T. (1985). Learning from music. In *Becoming human through music.* Reston, VA: Music Educators National Conference.

Lomax, A., et al. (1969). *Folk song style and culture.* Washington, D.C.: American Association for the Advancement of Science.

Lundin, R.W. (1967). *An objective psychology of music* (2nd ed.). New York: Ronald Press.

Lundquist, B.L. (1982). Sociomusicology: A status report. *College Music Symposium, 22* (1), 104–111.

Merriam, A.P. (1964). *The anthropology of music.* (n.p.): Northwestern University Press.

Michel, P. (1973). Optimal development of musical abilities in the first years of life. *Psychology of Music, 1* (2), 14–20.

Moog, H. (1976). The development of musical experience in children of preschool age. *Psychology of Music, 4* (2), 38–45.

Mueller, J.H. (1963). A sociological approach to musical behavior. *Ethnomusicology, 7* (3), 216–220.

Musselman, J.A. (1974). *The uses of music.* Englewood Cliffs, NJ: Prentice-Hall.

Nettl, B. (1985). Montana and Iran: Learning and teaching in the conception of music in two contrasting cultures. *Becoming human through music.* Reston, VA: Music Educators National Conference.

Nettl, B. (1975). Music in primitive cultures: Iran, a recently developed nation. In Hamm, C., Nettl, B., & Byrnside, R., *Contemporary music and music cultures.* Englewood Cliffs, NJ: Prentice-Hall.

Revesz, G., (1973). *Introduction to the psychology of music* (G.I.C. de Courcy, trans.). London: Longmans, Green.

Sloboda, J. (1985). *The musical mind: The cognitive psychology of music.* New York: Oxford University Press.

Roederer, J.G. (1975). *Introduction to the physics and psychophysics of music* (2nd ed.). New York: Springer-Verlag.

Weber, M. (1978). *The rational and social foundations of music* (D. Martindale, J. Riedel, G. Neuwirth, trans. and ed.). (n.p.): Southern Illinois University Press.

Chapter Three

PSYCHOACOUSTICAL FOUNDATIONS

Psychoacoustics is a branch of psychophysics, the study of sensory responses to physical stimuli. When one studies auditory sensations, one studies psychoacoustics. Questions regarding comparative pitches and loudness, assigning pitch and timbre sensations to tonal clusters and, indeed, perceptions of all tonal properties essentially are psychoacoustical questions. Without psychoacoustical phenomena, music (as we know it) could not exist. After presenting brief overviews of the production and transmission of musical sounds (which may be omitted by anyone familiar with elementary acoustics of music), this chapter considers reception of musical sounds and psychoacoustical phenomena organized around the basic psychological tonal properties of pitch, loudness, and timbre. The organization and cognitive processing of basic *musical* properties are considered later in the text.

Production of Musical Sounds

Vibration—something moving back and forth—is basic to any sound. If the vibration is generally periodic, i.e., vibrates with a more-or-less regularly recurring motion, people are likely to sense the vibration as a musical tone. Sources of musical sounds include vibrating strings, air columns, metal plates, metal bars, membranes, and electrical circuits.

Consider a vibrating pendulum, one of the simplest illustrations of vibration and related properties. The pendulum, once displaced and thereby set into motion, will swing back and forth. Although the distance it swings will decrease gradually, the pendulum will swing long enough for an observer to note that it regularly returns to the point at which it began to swing. Every so often, with regularity, it completes a cycle. A cycle is the complete journey of a vibrating object from an original point through both extremes of displacement and back to the original point. The time required for the cycle's completion is the period. The number of cycles completed in a given amount of time is the frequency. The distance between a vibrating object's original location and its point of maximal displacement is the amplitude. One readily can observe and describe a cycle, period, frequency, and amplitude in relation to a vibrating pendulum.

Although their individual cycles cannot be seen, in the ordinary sense, vibrating objects producing musical sounds also vibrate in cycles and with a certain period, frequency, and amplitude. Musical sounds generally are a complex of individual vibrations; they contain numerous frequencies. Musical sounds can be analyzed into their individual component frequencies, but one usually hears a given musical sound as having just one frequency.

Not all vibrations are perceivable as sound, of course. A minimal amount of power (intensity) is necessary, and human ears normally respond to an approximate frequency range of 20 to 18,000 cycles per second [called Hertz, abbreviated Hz, in honor of Heinrich Hertz (1857–1894), who conducted early research with electromagnetism]. Individuals vary in their frequency sensitivity, particularly regarding the upper limit. Sounds considerably lower than 20 Hz may be heard under artificial conditions.

The production of musical sounds, then, requires that something be set into periodic vibration. If it vibrates with acceptable frequency and intensity, and those vibrations somehow can be transmitted to a listener, music is possible.

Transmission of Musical Sounds

Transmission, as used here, refers to the propagation or spread of a disturbance through the air from a sound source to a listener. We are not considering electrical or electronic transmission or sound's travel through media other than air.

Consider a row of upright dominoes. If they are placed at a critical distance from each other, a person can produce an amusing ripple effect by pushing the first domino into its neighbor. This is somewhat analogous to what happens when a disturbance spreads through the air from a sounding musical instrument to a listener. The vibrating body disturbs air particles around it. Those particles bump other particles, which in turn bump others. Unlike the dominoes, each particle can move back and forth as long as the source of the disturbance continues to vibrate. However, just as the first domino does not travel to the end of the row, no one air particle travels from the musical source to the listener. The *disturbance* travels.

A disturbance spreading through air is a *longitudinal* disturbance, i.e., the overall disturbance travels in the same direction as the slight movement of each particle. (In *transverse* disturbances, the overall disturbance travels in a direction perpendicular to the slight movement of each particle. Transverse disturbances do not occur in a gas.) A travelling disturbance or a chain of travelling disturbances often is called a wave. A sound wave is a series of disturbances travelling through a medium.

Waves may travel directly from a sound source to a listener. They may encounter a surface which represents a sudden change in properties of the medium; then, the wave will be *reflected*, although some of its energy will be absorbed by the reflecting surface. Reflection represents a sudden direction change for the wave; a gradual change in direction often results from *refraction*, a gradual "bending" of the waves owing to a gradual change in medium properties such as temperature or density. We can sense sounds from sources not aligned directly with our ears or obscured from view because of *diffraction*, the ability of a wave to "go around corners" or pass through a small opening.

A travelling wave represents changing locations of particles as they undergo bumping and the resulting displacements. Accompanying the continual changes in particle location are changes in pressure. When particles are compressed more closely together than they are in an undisturbed state, the pressure increases. When particles are spread further apart (rarefacted) than they are in an undisturbed state, the pressure decreases. This means that a periodic pressure fluctuation occurs at any point in a travelling wave in air. Such periodic pressure fluctuations, minute though they are, are the form in which Beethoven symphonies, Handel oratorios, rock tunes, and third-grade recorder ensemble sounds reach our ears.

Reception of Musical Sounds

From Air to Inner Ear

The periodic pressure fluctuations accompany the travelling wave as it enters the ear. The obvious external or cosmetic portion of the ear is the pinna; the "hole in the head" is the entrance to the auditory canal or meatus. The travelling wave passes through the auditory canal and encounters the eardrum or tympanic membrane, which separates the outer and middle ear. Resonance, particularly in the approximate frequency range of 2000–7000 Hz, may increase the sound pressure exerted by the wave as it travels through the auditory canal (Pickles, 1982, pp. 12–13).

The eardrum responds to the pressure fluctuations by moving in and out. (Incredibly tiny amounts of pressure change are sufficient to move the eardrum.) Eardrum motion is more efficient when the air pressure is equal on both sides of the eardrum, and the air supplied through the Eustachian tube, connected to the back of the throat, assists in the equalization. Three tiny middle ear bones or ossicles (hammer, anvil, and stirrup or malleus, incus, and stapes) connect the eardrum to another membrane separating the middle and inner ears, the oval window. The ossicles transmit motion to the oval window. The acoustic reflex, resulting from the contraction of two muscles (tensor tympani and stapedius) connected to the ossicles, may increase the bones' stiffness and thereby help protect the inner ear from damage due to strong sounds.

The oval window's motions create wavelike movements in fluid contained in the snail-shell-shaped inner ear or cochlea. The basilar membrane, which is one part of the cochlear duct, an appendage connected to the cochlear wall near the oval window, detects the fluid movements and in turn moves up and down in a manner which depends on their frequencies. Higher frequencies elicit maximal membrane movement closer to the oval window end or base; lower frequencies elicit maximal movement closer to the "far" end or apex of the basilar membrane. Combinations of frequencies, such as most musical tones, excite the membrane at several locations. Where, when, and how much the basilar membrane is excited provides basic information for perception and organization of the psychological sensations basic to music.

From the time the original vibrating body disturbs the surrounding medium until the resulting disturbance reaches the basilar membrane, the form of energy expended is mechanical. It is a matter of movement. Lying alongside the basilar membrane are hair cells, collectively known as the organ of Corti, which sense the membrane's movements and function as transducers. A transducer is a device which converts one form of energy to another (microphones and loudspeakers are common examples); the hair cells convert mechanical energy to electrochemical energy and start auditory signals on their way to the brain.

From Inner Ear to Brain

The basilar membrane's characteristic vibration innervates (excites) the hair cells, particularly as the membrane moves toward the center of the cochlear duct. Estimates vary regarding the exact number of hair cells, but 30,000 probably is a good approximation. According to Moore (1982, p. 24), there are about 25,000 outer hair cells, each containing about 140 hairs and arranged in three rows, and about 3500 inner hair cells, each containing about 40 hairs. (Outer and inner refer to location in relation to the outside of the cochlea.) The outer cells are more sensitive and respond at lower sound levels than the inner cells. The hair cells differ functionally, as evidenced by the guinea pig's inner cells producing a cochlear microphonic (an electrical discharge obtained by inserting an electrode into the cochlea) proportional to the *velocity* of basilar membrane movement while the outer cells produce a cochlear microphonic proportional to the amount of basilar membrane *displacement* (Dallos et al., 1972).

Even a single-tone stimulus activates a large portion of the cochlear neural fibres; two tones which are very slightly different activate respective areas along the basilar membrane which overlap considerably. The boundaries between activated and unactivated areas apparently help signal the stimulus frequency(ies). Intensity apparently is signalled in terms of the number of activated fibres and the frequency of neural discharge (Whitfield, 1967). The basic information regarding frequency, intensity, and waveform properties is passed to and through the neural pathways to the auditory cortex, in rough accordance with the schematic diagram in Figure 3-1 (Whitfield; Roederer, 1975). Although the auditory cortex is the "ultimate destination," neural processing occurs prior to the cortex; some perception necessary for basic musical decision making is completed at subcortical levels. Frequency discrimination, for example, probably is complete at the collicular level (Whitfield, p. 163). Research with cats and monkeys suggests that neurons in the auditory pathway respond preferentially to various stimulus aspects, such as frequency, duration, and various rapid transient properties such as those which characterize beginnings of tones; so, although details are sketchy, a subcortical mechanism for clarifying and enhancing tonal features apparently exists (Moore, 1982, pp. 35–37).

Most hair cells innervate the fibers of the auditory nerve and send signals along the *afferent* neural pathway to the brain. There also is a "descending" or *efferent* neural pathway through which the brain can modify the excitability of the hair cells, especially the inner cells (Davis, 1962; Pickles, 1982, pp. 31–32). The afferent pathway includes the spiral ganglion, the dorsal and ventral cochlear nucleus complex, the superior-olivary complex, the nuclei of the inferior colliculus and lateral lemniscus, the medial geniculate body, and the auditory cortex. The efferent pathway includes higher descending neurons and the olivo-cochlear bundle (Gacek, 1972). While the neuroanatomy may be obscure, the afferent pathway is important musically, because that is how information goes to the place where it can be organized. The efferent pathway is important because, despite its relatively low information handling capacity, it provides a way for the brain to "alert" the cochlea for particular sounds.

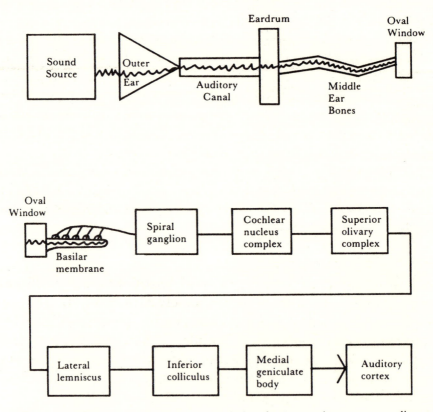

Figure 3-1. Diagram of auditory transmission from sound source to auditory cortex.

The purpose of the above abbreviated description of the travel of a sound encoded in a pressure fluctuation at a musical source to its encoding as an electrochemical discharge directed toward the auditory cortex is to enable the reader to have some idea of the structures involved. Readers interested in more detailed knowledge may consult Stevens and Warshofsky (1965) for a highly readable and profusely illustrated description; more technical and physiologically-oriented descriptions are available in hearing texts such as Whitfield, Moore, and Pickles.

Pitch Phenomena

While pitch pervades most music, it often is ill-defined and confused with other phenomena. A tone's pitch in the usual sense of the term is the tone's apparent location on a high-low continuum. Placement on that abstract continuum in relation to other pitches is learned. In the usual sense, pitch is a metathetic (place) variable, rather than a prothetic (magnitude or strength) variable (Stevens, 1975).

There are some prothetic aspects of pitch. Sounds vary in their definity or obviousness of pitch; it usually is easier to match the pitch of a flute than the pitch of a bass drum. Rakowski (1979) calls this definity pitch strength and suggests measuring it by the variability of the subjects' attempts at matching pitches to standards. When individual pitches occur in a sequential tonal context, the intimacy or similarity of any two pitches varies in accordance with tonality (Krumhansl, 1979).

The following discussion of pitch phenomena is organized around clarification of its relationship to frequency, various kinds of pitch processing, phenomena resulting from pitch combinations, absolute pitch, and attempts to measure pitch.

Frequency-Pitch Relationship

In general, people may experience a pitch sensation from any sufficiently periodic sound in the range of approximately 20 to 18,000 Hz. The upper limit fluctuates widely with individuals; under special conditions even the lower limit can be exceeded: Whittle, Collins, and Robinson (1972) successfully presented highly intense frequencies as low as 3.15 Hz to subjects seated in a cabinet in such a manner that their entire bodies were immersed in uniform sound pressure.

Pitch varies largely as a function of frequency variation, but each minute frequency change does not elicit a pitch change. Classical psychophysics developed the concept of the just noticeable difference (jnd) or difference limen, an amount by which a stimulus must be changed in order for an observer to detect a difference a certain criterion percentage of the time. The jnd for frequency discrimination (and hence potential detection of discrete pitches) varies greatly with methodology as well as people (Woodworth and Scholsberg, 1965); the size of the jnd varies with the stimulus frequencies such that it is smaller (in terms of Hz) for lower frequencies (Nordmark, 1968; Moore, 1974). Despite its fluctuation, the jnd usually lies well within the limits necessary for functional musical discrimination, and its exact size is rarely of any musical importance.

The pitch assigned to a particular frequency may vary without any change in the physical vibration rate. A tone which increases in intensity while remaining at a constant frequency may be heard as rising or falling in pitch while also becoming louder (Stevens, 1935; Terhardt, 1974b). The shift-of-pitch-with-intensity effect, however, appears rather idiosyncratic and more likely to occur with tones containing just one frequency than with typical musical tones.

Another example of the changing pitch of a constant frequency is binaural diplacusis, in which one tone is heard with a different pitch in each ear. This bizarre condition is difficult to research because it fluctuates in the listener; its relation to music processing appears to be noncritical (Sherbon, 1975), although in some clinical instances it must play a role in music perception.

Frequency is a physical property of musical tones; pitch is a psychological property. They are not perfectly related, and they are not the same thing.

Pitch Processing of Single Pure Tones

A "pure" tone is a tone of just one frequency. Except for some of the sounds produced by electronic means, there are no pure tones in music, although certain flute and organ tones come close to being pure. Musical tones are complex; they contain a mixture of frequencies. Nevertheless, much has been learned about the behavior of the auditory system with the aid of pure tones. Furthermore, all complex tones may be analyzed into pure tone components, so knowledge of pure tone processing is useful.

Pure tones, being of one frequency, actually are less clear in pitch than complex tones. For a given duration of sound, a high frequency tone can be determined with greater accuracy than can a low one. A certain minimal amount of time is necessary for pitch perception of a given frequency; the greater the frequency, the shorter the time period may be (Kock, 1935).

Stevens, Davis, and Lurie (1935) used the remarkable similarity of guinea pig cochleas to those of humans to study the relationship of particular membrane stimulations to pitch perception. Using the output of an electrode placed in contact with a guinea pig's cochlea, they saw, via an oscilloscope, that higher tones were localized among the membrane near the oval window end, tones around 2000 Hz near the middle, and lower tones closely near the far (helicotrema) end. They noted throughout that two tones could be differentiated provided that areas of the membrane differing by .025 mm were stimulated. This study illustrates what is basically responsible for particular pure tone perceptions: the place of greatest stimulation along the basilar membrane.

The stimulation areas (or resonance maxima) on the membrane have been mapped (Von Bekesy, 1960). For example, 5000 Hz stimulates the membrane maximally about 10 mm from the base (oval window end). Two thousand Hz has its resonance maximum at approximately 16 mm; the relatively low frequency of 200 Hz has its resonance maximum about 300 mm from the base (apex end).

Detection of a difference between two pure tones requires that the location of resonance maxima for the two tones be different. In terms of frequency difference (Δf), this translates in one study to from 3 to 0.5 percent of the initial frequency for pure tones of a constant intensity (Zwicker, Flottorp, and Stevens, 1957); at 100 Hz, a change to 103 or 97 Hz is necessary, while at 2000 Hz, the frequency must change to 1990 or 2010 Hz. These figures are for a continuous sounding, slowly changed tone; the subject's task sometimes is called frequency resolution. The jnd for any sort of frequency distinction is not a precise unchanging value; it varies with frequency, intensity, duration, and rate of change (Roederer, 1975).

Pitch Processing of Combined Pure Tones

Tones which contain only one frequency when they leave their respective sound sources may combine in the air and reach the ear in the form of a tonal superposition; a sound wave is determined by the interaction or interference of both waves. Any sound wave, in the sense of a pattern of displacements, is determined at any given time by the frequency and intensity of each component. When there is only one component, as in the case of a pure tone, the wave is simply dependent upon that tone's frequency and intensity, but a combination of pure tones makes a superposed waveform, which depends not only on the two vibrations' frequencies and combined intensity but also on their relative phase.

Phase refers to the part of a regularly recurring cycle which is complete at a particular time. The moon may appear as new, a quarter crescent, full, or elsewhere at various predictable times of the month—one can speak of phases of the moon. So too may a vibration cycle be at varying degrees of completion or phase—the vibrating particle is at its original position or displaced in varying amounts in one direction or another. Two vibrations' cycles may or may not be at the same phase. Both may be starting and completing cycles at identical times, in which case they are in zero phase or the same phase relative to each other. One may be behind the other; for example, one vibration cycle may be at a point of maximal displacement while the other is at the original position of rest. In this case, they are out of phase. The superposed waveform will be influenced by relative phase. It is even possible to have, for two tones of identical frequency, a combined waveform which shows less amplitude than either individual waveform because of the destructive interference resulting from the individual waves, in effect, working against each other. Of course, the combined waveform may be stronger than either component, which will happen when the tones are in phase and constructive interference results.

The combination of pure tones, which in a way is similar to a complex tone, will stimulate the basilar membrane strongly at more than one location. If the frequency difference (Δf) between the two tones is of sufficient size, which could be as low as 6 percent but is more likely to be from 12 to 20 percent or more (Cardozo, 1974), there is a clear discrimination of two separate tones. If Δf is insufficient, a sensation of roughness, beating, or unison will result. The distance along the membrane that must be exceeded to promote a clear two-tone sensation is known as the *critical band width;* according to Roederer (1975), it has a value of approximately 1.2 mm. In terms of Hz, it varies with frequency from about 25 to over 2000 Hz; different studies give somewhat different results (Plomp, 1976; Moore, 1982).

The concept of a critical band width as a minimal distance between points of stimulation and the corresponding sensation may be illustrated easily through the sense of touch, as suggested by Roederer (1975), borrowing the analogy from Von Bekesy (1960). One person touches another's underarm skin or back with two pencil points simultaneously, *(analogy "touch")* and the person being touched must indicate whether he or she is being touched in one place or two. It will be found that a certain minimal distance must be exceeded for it to become obvious that a person is being touched in two places rather than one.

Thus, frequency discrimination of two simultaneous pure tones also is primarily dependent on the location of basilar membrane stimulation. The jnd for frequency discrimination of two simultaneous tones is considerably larger than the jnd for detecting changes in a single pure tone (Roederer, 1975). However, musicians rarely deal with pure tones.

Pitch Processing of Complex Tones

A complex tone contains more than one frequency. It differs from a combination of pure tones in that the waveform from one sound source is complex. A bowed violin string, a plucked guitar string, a blown trumpet, and a human voice all output a complex waveform which is a mixture of individual frequency components.

The individual frequency components include a *fundamental* frequency (generally the lowest frequency) and higher frequencies which may be in a harmonic or inharmonic relationship. In a harmonic relationship, the higher frequencies are in an integral multiple relationship with the fundamental, i.e., nondecimal whole numbers multiplied by the fundamental frequency will give the frequencies of the higher components or *harmonics.* In an inharmonic relationship, the higher components are related in a nonintegral multiple manner. Musical complex tones show varying *degrees of harmonicity.* The more nearly harmonic the relationship, the more obvious is the pitch sensation.

The relative strengths of the particular frequency components vary. Diagrams of complex tones, made via spectrum analyzers or other analytic electronic equipment, show, within limits, the particular component frequencies and their intensity levels. Curiously, the fundamental frequency is not always the strongest component, despite the fact that the

---

*The terms partial, harmonic, and overtone sometimes are used interchangeably. This is unfortunate because they have different meanings. A *partial* is any component of a complex tone, regardless of any mathematical relationship or lack thereof. A *harmonic* is any frequency (not necessarily a component of a particular tone) which is in an integral multiple relationship with the fundamental frequency. (The fundamental itself is the first harmonic, f × 1 = f.) An *overtone* is any harmonic *other than* the fundamental which is in a particular complex tone. Any component of a complex tone is a partial; it may or may not be a harmonic. Any integral multiple of the fundamental frequency is a harmonic; it may or may not be a partial or an overtone (Backus, 1977).

pitch associated with the complex tone almost always is the pitch elicited by the fundamental.

A complex mixture of frequencies may stimulate the basilar membrane at eight or more locations; such stimulations often exceed the critical band width. Yet a complex tone is heard with one distinct pitch. Why? The answer lies in the fact that the basilar membrane serves as an analyzer and information passer for complex tones—the pitch assignment primarily occurs higher in the auditory pathway.

Pitch perception of complex tones is based on the auditory system's ability to use information regarding the pattern of stimulation—placewise, timewise, or both. Sounds to which people are able to assign a definite pitch sensation are periodic, or nearly so: Motions of sound waves are regularly recurring.* The simplest kind of wave (a sine wave) arises from a pure tone; one is diagrammed in Figure 3.2. (Wave diagrams such as this, similar to oscilloscope traces, should be conceived as a particular displacement pattern frozen in time.) A complex wave appears in Figure 3.3. In each case, there will be recurring pattern. Sooner or later the wave-form will *repeat* itself; it has *periodicity*. The particular structure of the recurring pattern and the rate at which it repeats are extremely important musically.

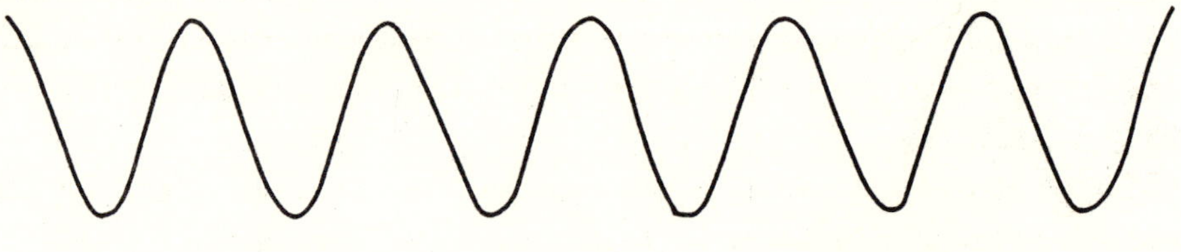

Figure 3-2. Displacement pattern arising from a pure tone.

Place information, where and to what degree the particular stimulations occur, and temporal information, the rate at which the stimulations recur, are the two categories of information gleaned from basilar membrane activity. Place information is available over the entire auditory range. Temporal information is available only to about 5000 Hz and would seem to be especially important for musical pitch because musical pitch generally is lost for pure tones beyond 5000 Hz: Sequences of really high tones are difficult to organize as melody (Moore, 1982, pp. 121–122).

---

*A more restrictive definition of a periodic vibration is that all the frequency components are in a harmonic (integral multiple with the fundamental) relationship.

Figure 3-3. Displacement pattern arising from a complex tone.

The usually obvious pitch sensation of a complex tone (some people can hear out individual frequency components) is known as low pitch, periodicity pitch, virtual pitch, residual pitch, and subjective pitch. Low pitch probably is the term which is most free of semantic difficulties arising from particular theories or other phenomena. Low pitch perception is not understood thoroughly; two broad classes of explanatory models are the *pattern recognition* and *temporal* models.

In pattern recognition models, low pitch is derived from neural signals which correspond to the primary basilar membrane stimulations, such as the individual partials' pitches. Resolution of the separate components of the tonal *spectrum* (the combination of particular frequencies and their relative strengths) is crucial. Pattern recognition models cannot account for situations where harmonic relationships are especially complex and frequency components are too high to be resolved (Moore, 1982, pp. 123–140).

Models where low pitch is based on the time interval between recurring aspects of the overall pattern, perhaps the time between waveform peaks, are temporal models. Through a process known as *fundamental tracking,* a wave's repetition frequency can yield a low (or periodicity) pitch sensation. For example, a complex tone with component frequencies of 50, 100, 150, 200, and 250 Hz will make a wave with a repetition frequency of 50 Hz, as will a complex tone with components of 400, 450, and 500 Hz. In each case, the pitch sensation corresponding to 50 Hz is assigned.

According to Moore (1982, p. 140), temporal models cannot account for situations in which tonal components do not interact in either ear. Such noninteraction is illustrated by the Houtsma and Goldstein (1972) study, where, using earphones, the investigators presented randomly chosen paired upper harmonics, without the fundamental, monotically (two harmonics to one ear) and dichotically (one harmonic to each ear) to three experienced musicians. The musicians were able to recognize melodies which the missing fundamentals would have formed in both conditions, even though the harmonics could not combine in either ear in the dichotic condition. Fundamental tracking evidently is a central (in the neural network) rather than a peripheral (in the cochlea) process.

Moore (1982, pp. 140–144) offers a five-stage model incorporating features of pattern recognition and temporal models which, in the authors' opinion, probably is about as comprehensive and logical an accounting of low pitch perception as yet exists.

The first stage is analogous to a series of overlapping filters which pass through and modify certain aspects of stimulus information. Filters responding to low frequency components output simple waveforms and resolve individual components. Filters responding to high frequency components output complex waveforms, which are based on the interaction of several components and have repetition rates corresponding to the stimulating waveform.

The second stage is the transduction process. Neurons fire in accordance with basilar membrane motions to reflect the temporal structure of the waveform. Particular neurons are "driven" by the waveform's frequency components which are near the neurons' "characteristic frequencies" or frequencies at which the neurons are most likely to fire.

In Moore's third stage, the times between the firings of each neuron are analyzed; the model assumes comparisons of the time intervals and a search for a common interval during the fourth stage.

In the final stage, a decision mechanism selects one time interval. The perceived pitch of the complex tone then is the pitch elicited by the frequency of the reciprocal of the selected time interval. (Frequency, the number of vibration cycles in a designated time, and period, the time required to complete one vibration cycle, are related as reciprocals. A frequency of 100 Hz and a period of 1/100 sec are reciprocals of each other.)

Moore's model predicts dominance of lower frequency components because of less ambiguous temporal information for lower than for higher components. Research (Plomp, 1967b; Ritsma, 1970) suggests a certain *spectral dominance*, in which the components mainly determining a complex tone's pitch vary with the fundamental frequency. In general, the lower the fundamental, the higher the component numbers of the important components. The degree of dominance of any component may vary as a function of the component's strength in relation to neighboring components (Moore, Glasberg, & Peters, 1985).

Curious effects involving a shift in periodicity pitch for two-component complex tones may be demonstrated under laboratory conditions. With adjacent harmonic frequencies, such as 480 and 600 Hz (fourth and fifth harmonics of 120 Hz), the pitch corresponds to that elicited by the missing fundamental, which is the waveform repetition frequency. Shifting frequencies away from a harmonic situation while maintaining a constant frequency difference, to an *anharmonic complex* such as 520 and 640 Hz, results in a pitch shift upward. Exactly why this happens is unclear (Smoorenburg, 1970).

The pitch perception of a complex tone need not be a unitary sensation. Individuals can learn to "hear out" some of the partials in a complex tone when the frequency separation exceeds the critical band width (Plomp, 1964).

Of profound musical importance, complex tone pitch perception is related to waveform pattern and periodicity, although not simply so. Music as it is currently known could not exist without low pitch.

Combination Tones

When two different frequencies are sounded together, such as in a violin double stop or in a harmonic interval on an organ, a third, generally lower, pitch sometimes may be heard in addition to the pitches associated with the two primary frequencies. This is a combination tone. Combination tones with frequencies equivalent to the differences between the two primary tones (f_2-f_1, "difference" tones) usually are the easiest to hear. Higher-order combination tones, as in $2f_1$-f_2 and $3f_1$-$2f_2$, also are audible; theoretically, many other combinations resulting from multiples of the lower tone (f_1) and upper tone (f_2) are possible.

A true combination tone is not present in the external sound stimulus, although it is perceived as if it were present (Rasch and Plomp, 1982). A combination tone should not be confused with the very strong third sound which may be obtained by feeding two inputs into one speaker, as with a synthesizer, electronic organ, or two audio oscillators. The third frequency in those cases is an electronic artifact resulting from heterodyning, in which two signals mix and fluctuate in amplitude (Strange, 1972, p. 10), and is physically present in the soundwave which reaches the ear.

A true combination tone results from cochlear distortion. Such a tone requires a minimal intensity level of the primary frequencies which is well beyond threshold. Plomp (1965) found that subjects heard more combination tones at higher sound pressure levels; 51–57 db marked the detectability threshold, i.e., the sensation level at which combination tones just become audible. At customary listening levels for many people combination tones are avoided because the ear does not distort sufficiently, although there are large interindividual differences. Audibility also may vary with the particular combination tone (Plomp, 1976).

What is being referred to here as distortion is a tendency of the basilar membrane to move more than it should in simple response to a given amount of stimulation. Excess movement could cause hair cell stimulation at extra places, thereby creating extra sound sensations. Contemporary evidence shows that such distortion is genuine. Sweetman and Dallos (1969) showed that guinea pig cochleas evidence distortion; the question is not whether there is distortion, but whether it is electromechanical or just mechanical. Dallos and Sweetman (1969) demonstrated that harmonics of a low-frequency fundamental, which could give rise to combination tones, are more prominent at the low-frequency end of the guinea pig cochlea than they are at the regions which their particular frequencies would suggest. Goldstein (1970) showed that a "cancellation tone" of identical frequency as a combination tone, adjusted for proper amplitude and relative phase, could cancel the combination tone. By taking advantage of the Mossbauer effect, which entails using an implanted radioactive substance to trace basilar membrane displacements, Rhode and Robles (1974) observed nonlinearity, i.e., distortion, in the cochlea of a squirrel monkey. Rasch and Plomp (1982) refer to cochlear distortion as "nonlinear transmission." Given such evidence, it seems reasonable that tonal sensations can arise through cochlear distortion.

Combination tones can interact with other components to increase tonal complexity; they can alter the way a tonal stimulus is heard. As such, they may have some musical utility.

Intervals

An interval is a simultaneous or successive sounding of two tones, pure or complex. Some musicians call a simultaneous interval harmonic and a successive interval melodic. Psychology of music has been concerned with apparent consonance, pitch, and size of intervals.

Consonance-Dissonance. Study of consonance historically has been confused by varying uses of the label as well as different views of what causes a consonance classification. Peterson and Smith (1930) asked subjects to evaluate mistuned intervals and report "unnatural" ones, thereby equating certain tunings with consonance. Bugg (1933) reported that subjects were confused when asked to classify intervals as consonant on the basis of fusion, blending, smoothness, and purity (all of which have nonauditory connotation), as if they were synonymous terms. He felt that a problem with consonance was that it is not necessarily a pleasantness-unpleasantness dimension; affective reactions somehow must be removed from consonance. Terhardt (1974a) divorced psychoacoustic consonance (the absence of roughness) from any musical interval sensations: Psychoacoustic consonance is a matter of frequency distance, whereas musical intervals are ratio phenomena. Difficulties with consonance theories and judgments obviously are related to psychologists' and musicians' inabilities to agree regarding a definition.

Musicians generally regard consonance as a relatively restful and passive state of auditory sensation while dissonance is a relatively agitated and active state. Seconds, the augmented fourth, and sevenths currently are considered dissonant in an abstract sense, while unisons, thirds, fourths, fifths, sixths, and octaves are considered consonant. Since such judgments can change with time and context, Lundin (1947) proposed what probably is the most espoused explanation of consonance: It is a matter of cultural conditioning. Prior physical theories, resorting to numerical relationships, beats, fusion, and genetics, all are lacking because of incorrect interpretations of physiology or failure to consider mistuned consonances.

Musicians may merely use the terms consonance and dissonance as qualifying adjectives for interval names: Consonance and dissonance then are simply extra labels. Van de Geer, Levelt, and Plomp (1962) found that nonmusicians evaluated (rather than named) intervals in terms of consonance-dissonance, euphonious-diseuphonious, and beautiful-ugly. Plomp and Levelt (1965) used nonmusical subjects in establishing evidence that consonance-dissonance may be a matter of how partials from the tones comprising a simultaneous interval align along the basilar membrane: Basilar membrane stimulations which are identical, *or* are separated by critical band width, promote consonance; nonidentical stimulations *within* a critical band width promote dissonance. (This is the theory of "colliding harmonics" (Roederer, 1975).) Siegel and Siegel (1977) found musicians tending to categorize intervals very accurately but to make few distinctions in interval size within categories; although

77 percent of the intervals were out-of-tune, the six musicians judged only 37 percent as such.

Perhaps the concept of consonance and dissonance should be reevaluated in terms of musical context. Bharucha (1984) suggests that the establishment of a tonal context at the beginning of a work generates certain expectancies regarding stable and unstable tones in a melodic context. Unstable tones tend to resolve or be assimilated into stable tones or anchors; consonance and dissonance then may have meaning in accordance with melodic structure. This may be far more salient than the labelling or evaluating of isolated intervals.

Apparent Pitch. An interval is two tones which, when sounded together, *may* have a unitary pitch sensation. For many listeners there is no such tonal fusion, and the concept of intervallic pitch is vague.

Farnsworth (1938, 1969) studied the applicability of Stumpf's principle, which, in its original form, states that any simultaneous interval has an intervallic pitch equivalent to that of the lower tone. He concluded that the upper tone is more likely to dominate any intervallic pitch sensation for most musicians other than some basses while the lower tone is dominant for the musically untrained.

A concept of intervallic pitch probably is too elusive: Harmony is not a unitary pitch sensation. One mystery in psychology of music is why two simultaneous sound sources, like two violin strings, usually produce an interval while a tone from single sound source, or even a noise which is more complicated acoustically than the interval, produces a unitary pitch sensation. The answer probably lies in the brain's ability to use various cues related to localization and transient waveform characteristics (Roederer, 1975). Deutsch (1982, p. 108) notes that von Helmholtz, a pioneering psychoacoustician, suggested in 1885 that a complex tone sounds as one tone because all the components start and stop together.

Apparent Size. Musical intervals usually are specified by the scale degree (third, fifth, sixth, etc.) of their upper tones in relation to the lower tones, subject to modification by accidentals (minor, major, augmented, etc.). Another way is to specify the interval ratio; each interval has in its simplest (just) form a characteristic ratio. An octave's upper frequency is related to its lower frequency as 2 is to 1. A perfect fifth's upper frequency is in a 3:2 ratio with its lower frequency. Other characteristic ratios are 16:15 for a minor second, 9:8 for a major second, 6:5 for a minor third, 5:4 for a major third, 4:3 for a perfect fourth, 7:5 for an augmented fourth, 5:3 for a minor sixth, 8:5 for a major sixth, 9:5 for a minor seventh, and 15:8 for a major seventh. In performance practice there is considerable deviation from the simple ratios; the tempered scale, even when perfectly tuned, lacks the characteristic ratios except for the octave. The most specific way to indicate physical interval size is in cents (one cent = 1/1200 of an octave). For example, an octave is 1200 cents; a perfect fifth (3.2 ratio) is 702 cents; the less-than-perfect fifth of the tempered scale is 700 cents. The number of cents in an interval may be computed via the formula

$$n = 3986.31 \, [\log(f_2/f_1)],$$

where n is the number of cents of the desired interval, f_2 is the frequency of the upper tone, and f_1 is the frequency of the lower tone (Backus, 1977).

All identically named intervals have a degree of perceptual similarity, regardless of particular frequency components, which aids in identification and musical utility. But if an interval, particularly a successive interval, is evaluated rather than simply categorized, its apparent size may vary with frequency range. There is conflicting evidence regarding the direction of change. Some maintain that physically equal intervals appear to increase in size with increasing frequency (Stevens, Volkmann, and Newman, 1937; Stevens, 1975); others say that intervals in lower frequency ranges have greater "melodic distance," which implies that they appear to become smaller with increasing frequency (Winckel, 1967). Radocy (1978) found apparent interval size to vary with the interaction of the particular interval, musical experience, interval direction, and frequency range; he concluded that perceived interval size is highly idiosyncratic.

Beating

A perceptible rise and fall in apparent loudness is associated with the simultaneous sounding of two slightly different frequencies. The beat frequency for a mistuned unison is equivalent to the difference between the two frequencies; the further away the frequencies are from each other, the faster is the beating. With sufficient frequency separation, the beating becomes a roughness. Once the separation corresponding to the critical band width is reached, a sensation of two tones results.

Beating is caused by periodic changes in the superposed waveform. Beating of a mistuned unison is first order beating; it is a result of peripheral, i.e., cochlear, auditory processing. Beating of a mistuned interval other than a unison, particularly an octave, fourth, or fifth, is

second order beating (Roederer, 1975), which may result from the peripheral interference of combination tones or, especially at lower frequencies,
from central neural processing (Plomp, 1976). Binaural beating, a special
kind, may occur when a separate input is provided to each ear.

First order beating may be useful in tuning. Piano tuners often count
beats to obtain the proper tempered tuning of designated intervals.
Instrumentalists are confident that they are in tune when the first order
beats disappear. However, tuning by eliminating the beats between a
reference tone and a tone to be tuned may be ambiguous to the tuner
because of uncertainties regarding the direction of deviation. Corso
(1954) had a violinist, a bassoonist, an alto saxophonist, and two clarinet-
ists tune to a piano and a variety of electronic tone sources. In one
experimental condition the performer played alone, then with the reference tone to enable a comparison using beating. In the other condition
the performer first listened to the reference tone, then played alone.
Neither procedure produced more accurate tuning than the other. Corso
suggested that unison tuning is more dependent on pitch-matching than
on beat elimination. One should not regard tuning by beat elimination
as a necessarily superior method.

Second order beating, also known (unfortunately) as the beating of
mistuned consonances, is more ambiguous than first order beating. It is
not obvious just what is fluctuating. Second order beats are strong when
the beating interval, such as a mistuned fourth or fifth, is below 500 Hz.
The beats become progressively weaker above 1000 Hz. The beats, when
audible, do not disappear when noise is introduced to cover (mask)
possible peripheral effects such as combination tones; evidence strongly
suggests central processing of second order beats (Plomp, 1967a).

If a different sound is presented to each ear in such a manner that the
sounds cannot possibly mix until they reach the neural pathways, binaural beats may result. In an intensive study regarding detection limits for
binaural beats, Perrott and Nelson (1969) found that beat detection was
most likely around 500 Hz. Likelihood of detection decreased with higher
frequencies; beyond 1500 Hz, there were no binaural beats. The stimulus
conditions varied regarding the difference in Hz between the tones; with
higher standard frequencies greater interear frequency differences produced more obvious binaural beats. For smaller frequency differences,
subjects reported a "fused" auditory image, waxing and waning. For
larger frequency differences, a rapid flutter was reported while each
individual pitch retained its identity in its particular ear.

Perception of binaural beats may have some nonauditory implications. According to Tobias (1972), women normally hear binaural beats at lower frequencies than men, but the frequency levels increase at the onset of menstruation, then decline, then increase slightly fifteen days later.

Beating is of obvious musical importance. One reason that one French horn amplified to ten times its output cannot sound like ten horns is that the complex beating among the ten horns' outputs adds a quality of "richness" to which listeners have become accustomed. (This is the so-called chorus effect (Backus, 1977).) Beating in exposed orchestral passages that is not dismissed as vibrato may make listeners cringe. Binaural beats require high quality headphones and are not usually exploited musically, but they may offer interesting possibilities for those who wish to experiment with new musical effects.

Absolute Pitch

The phenomenon of absolute pitch is often astounding to those who do not possess it and may be viewed as quite ordinary and a bit of a nuisance by those who do. Also known as perfect pitch, absolute pitch exists when one can correctly identify a tone by letter name without reference to any external standard. To correctly label a sound as "C" when only a C is heard is quite different from being presented with a tone labelled as F, and then being asked to label C in relation. Many a musician acquires relative pitch, the ability to name tones in relation to a known external standard by utilizing interval relationships, but the acquisition of absolute pitch is no simple matter.

The presence of absolute pitch in persons who have not had extensive musical training suggests some extra perceptual ability, possibly even genetically transmitted. It has been suggested that "tonal chroma," cylical tonal characteristics with octave-octave consistency, are responsible for absolute pitch (Bachem, 1954).

For some authorities, absolute pitch is a matter of deliberate learning. Meyer (1956) believed in the memorization of tone height with practice. Corso (1957) found that some tonalities were easier to judge than others; ascending scales were more conducive to tonality recognition than random scale patterns or chord sequences. Such differences were believed related to learned habit as well as technical considerations. Cuddy (1968) suggested that internalizing A440 as a reference tone was more effective than trying to learn each tone individually. She noted that judgments of pure tones were related to musical training and that judgments of piano tones were specifically related to piano training. Internalizing a particular reference would enable one to display absolute pitch, but differential degrees of accuracy with different performance media suggest learning a pseudoabsolute pitch by using auditory cues other than frequency, e.g., timbre characteristics.

A somewhat more contemporary view of absolute pitch development relates learning tonal identification to a critical age period, roughly four to seven years, when pitch has a greater salience, in speech and in music, than it does in later life. Jeffress (1962) noted that some supposedly tone-deaf individuals were from India and spoke a language in which pitch is insignificant. Sergeant (1969) showed that a majority of surveyed adults possessing absolute pitch experienced intensive musical training during the critical period. De Gainza (1970) indicated that isolated sounds attracted her small children, but with maturity form, structure, and tonal relations replaced individual pitch saliency. The ear can observe and perceive details, but it also can perceive structure, which, in music, may become more important than the details which foster absolute pitch development. The critical period view is called imprinting, in analogy with the maternal connection a hatched duckling makes with the first moving object it encounters. During the critical period a label is highly associable with a tonal sensation.

In investigating absolute pitch, it is important to use varied stimuli and avoid relative pitch cues. It is not enough to "come within a third" or label only certain tones produced by instruments with which the individual is familiar. Many individuals probably can learn to identify certain tones some of the time, but to insist that they can identify any tone all of the time is misleading. In their detailed discussion of absolute pitch, Ward and Burns (1982) recognize that frequency-pitch relations are acquired early in life and that, despite many attempts, only one person has been able to develop proficient absolute pitch as an adult. If absolute pitch is desirable, more consideration of the means whereby the *labels* are attached to the pitch sensations is necessary, particularly during early childhood.

Pitch Measurement

Pitch may be measured in various ways, but any technique must use a human observer (or an apparatus built to simulate one). The stroboscope and digital frequency counter measure frequency, not pitch.

Pitch matching often is used as a measure. Intonation problems are pitch-matching problems; to say that someone is "out-of-tune" is to say that, in some observer's subjective judgment, a produced sound does not match a standard.

A judgment that one tone is higher or lower than another may suffice, but quantitative comparisons of pitch require more detail. There is an interesting quantitative pitch scale known as the mel scale (scale in the measurement, not the musical sense). On the mel scale 1000 Hz of frequency, 40 db above the hearing threshold, are equivalent to 1000 mels of pitch sensation. The changes in mels for given frequency changes are not equivalent, e.g., a pitch sensation of 2000 mels, "twice as high" as 1000 mels, is elicited by 3120 Hz, not 2000 Hz. A frequency of 500 Hz is 602 mels; 500 mels requires a frequency of approximately 390 Hz. A lucid table of frequency-mel equivalents appears in Stevens (1975).

The mel scale was established by the psychophysical method of fractionation (Stevens, Volkmann, and Newman, 1937). Five observers set variable frequencies to sound half as high as standards of 125, 200, 300, 400, 700, 1000, 2000, 5000, 8000, and 12000 Hz, and the resulting average values were developed into the mel scale. It was noted that there was considerable variability. For 1000 Hz, the frequency equivalent to half pitch was set at 391, 485, 590, 622, and 640 Hz, and the observer, who was a trained musician, had trouble disregarding octave sensations and could not conceive of a "zero" pitch.

In a practical sense, particularly to musicians, the mel scale suggests pitch relationships which just do not hold. For a musician, an octave is "twice as high." This may be an artifact of musical training; Allen (1967) had ten musical and ten nonmusical subjects rate the similarity of twenty-three test tones to a 1000 Hz standard. The musical subjects rated the test tones forming an octave with the standard as significantly more similar than did the nonmusical subjects. Perhaps the mel scale relationships cannot hold for musical subjects because of indoctrination to the octave.

Radocy (1977) had musicians and nonmusicians listen to successive intervals at five different frequency levels. Some intervals were in a 2:1 mel relationship; some were physical octaves, and the others were neither. Subjects simply classified each interval as to whether its upper tone was less than twice as high, twice as high, or more than twice as high as the lower tone. In general, nonmusicians heard all intervals as larger, but in no instance did a majority of listeners, musicians, or nonmusicians, classify a 2:1 mel relationship as twice as high. Octaves generally were considered twice as high, but not always.

The search for a quantitative pitch measure continues. The mel scale obviously has problems. An octave, a 2:1 frequency relationship, is not always a 2:1 pitch relationship, but then what is?

Loudness Phenomena

Loudness is an obvious but complex property of sound. Musical performances may be evaluated readily as "too loud" or "too soft" by very unsophisticated listeners. Considerable pedagogical effort is directed by music educators toward improving a student's sensitivity or musicality by using more effective dynamic contrasts in performance.

Curiously, although human ears are sensitive to a range of sound intensity of about one trillion to one, minute loudness distinctions have not attained the importance of minute pitch distinctions in Western music. Loudness notation generally is entrusted to symbols for dynamic levels and words indicating a gradual change. Furthermore, although six basic dynamic levels—pp, p, mp, mf, f, ff—have been used for approximately 200 years, few instrumentalists have a dynamic range capable of attaining those six discrete levels. This generally is not due to limitations of musical instruments. Restricted musical dynamic ranges and solo passages equal in loudness to full orchestral passages, characteristic of films and television, may be partly responsible, but the general artistic demand for a range and variation seems restricted (Patterson, 1974).

Our loudness discussion is organized around distinguishing loudness from other properties, measurement of loudness and systematic relations emerging therefrom, masking, loudness summation, and dangers of prolonged exposure to high loudness levels.

Intensity-Loudness Relationship

Intensity and loudness are not interchangeable terms. Intensity is an objectively measured physical property, an amount of power. It often is expressed in power units per unit area, as in watts per square meter. Loudness is a subjective sensation of the magnitude or strength of sound. It requires an animate perceiver (or a machine built to simulate one).

The amount of sound intensity is the major physical determinant of loudness, but the intensity-loudness relationship is not on a simple-one-to-one basis. A minimal perception time is necessary for a sound to build to its maximal loudness: Experimental results, varying with stimuli and subjects, yield critical durations from 10 to 500 msec and beyond (Scharf, 1978, pp. 205–206). Prolonged steady sounds may diminish in loudness due to auditory fatigue or habituation (Roederer, 1975). Loudness may vary with a sound's "rise" time, i.e., the time it takes a sound to reach its maximal intensity, particularly at lower frequencies and for pure tones (Gjaevenes & Rimstad, 1972). The fact that the intensity-loudness relationship is confounded by frequency is especially important for music: Because the ear's sensitivity varies with frequency, equal intensities do not elicit equal loudness across all audible frequencies.

Volume

It is most unfortunate that volume, which implies an amount of space or capacity, commonly is used as a synonym for loudness, which is an amount of strength or a magnitude. Volume is the apparent size or extensity of a sound; most would say that a tuba tone is more voluminous than a flute tone of equal intensity.

People generally are not trained to judge volume. Their criteria are unstable, and more conspicuous differences between tones may obscure volume differences. Nevertheless, in an early study (Stevens, 1934b), five observers matched paired tones in volume by changing intensities. Tones judged equivalent in volume were compared for frequency and intensity differences. It was noted that volume differences were greater at lower intensity levels for all frequencies. However, an increase in intensity level brought a more rapid volume increase at higher than at lower frequencies.

That volume depends in a complex way on frequency and intensity was demonstrated with forty-six observers by Terrace and Stevens (1962). They plotted frequency-intensity combinations necessary for equal volume judgments and formed a "vol" scale of measurement in which 1 vol equals the apparent volume of 1000 Hz at 40 decibels of sound pressure level. They found that regardless of frequency, at around 140 db all tones sounded equal in volume. In general, higher frequencies required greater intensities for equivalent volume, and the rate of growth in volume (as intensity increased) varied with frequency.

Volume's existence as an independent tonal attribute is questionable. Volume has no quasi-parallel relationship with any single physical attribute in the way that loudness is related to intensity or pitch is related to frequency. Nevertheless, the ability of observers to make reliable volume judgments which relate lawfully to frequency-intensity combinations, independently of loudness, suggests that the volume concept is more than fanciful thinking.

Density

Density, the apparent compactness of a sound, is another tonal attribute which lacks one distinct quasi-parallel physical relationship. It also is questioned regarding its independent existence, and it may be merely the opposite pole of volume.

Stevens (1934a) had four observers equate different paired frequencies in density by varying one tone in intensity. Differences in settings between equal density and equal loudness judgments were noted. Opposite to volume judgments, judgments of equal density required that lower frequency tones be louder than higher frequency tones. For a given frequency, the louder the tone, the more dense it appeared.

Guirao and Stevens (1964) later found that density grows in a lawful way with increases in intensity, but the rate of growth is slower at higher frequencies.

Observation that volume decreases while density increases with increasing frequencies and that lawful relationships apparently exist between increasing intensity and corresponding increases in volume and density suggested a relationship between *loudness* and some *combination* of volume and density. It indeed was found that loudness judgments are proportional to the products of volume and density judgments, and, furthermore, that softness judgments are proportional to the products of smallness and diffuseness judgments. Such proportionality was more clearcut for noise than tone, but the concept of loudness as a synthesis of volume and density is intriguing (Stevens, Guirao, and Slawson, 1965).

Annoyance and Noisiness

In research by Hellman (1982, 1985), subjects listened to a series of tones embedded in varying degrees of background noise. In addition to estimating loudness, the subjects estimated how much they were bothered by the sounds (annoyance) and the sounds' quality or clarity (noisiness). Besides identifying properties about which subjects could agree, the research is important because it showed that the dominant of the three properties varied with overall intensity and with the ratio of tone to noise. Furthermore, annoyance corresponded more closely to loudness than to noisiness. Perhaps people who complain about "loud" music are occasionally reacting to something other than or in addition to perceived strength of the musical sounds.

Measurement of Loudness

Quantification of loudness, a challenging and controversial task because of the many complications, may be approached in terms of quantifying the tonal stimulus, in which case one is not really quantifying the loudness sensation, or in terms of quantifying the response to the stimulus magnitude.

Stimulus Measures. Since intensity is defined as an amount of power per unit area, it must be quantified in terms of a power unit per area unit. Watts per square meter are common units for sound intensity. Most sound intensities are rather small values; one watt per square meter is a rather intense sound which approaches the upper limit of hearing. The threshold of hearing at 1000 Hz is around .000000000001 w/m². Negative powers of ten often are utilized in expressing such tiny numbers; the above threshold is 10^{-12} w/m².

Sound intensity usually is expressed in terms of intensity level rather than pure intensity. Intensity level implies a comparison of a particular intensity to some baseline value, just as the fourth floor of a building is the fourth floor in comparison to the ground. The comparisons implied by intensity levels of sound are ratio comparisons which use the unit known as the *decibel*.

Decibels are measures of power ratios. They are not limited to measure of sound; light and electric current also may be measured in decibels. Decibels are best defined in terms of the formula by which they are computed. For sound intensity,

$$D = 10 \left[\log \left(I/I_0 \right) \right],$$

where D is the number of decibels, I is the particular intensity which the decibel value places on a level, and I_0 is the baseline value. A logical baseline is the intensity at the threshold of hearing; hence 10^{-12} w/m² often is used.

It is important to recognize two consequences of a decibel value being a shorthand way to express a ratio comparison. One, a relative small range of decibels encompasses a relatively large range of acoustic powers. Two, one cannot simply combine decibels to obtain an intensity level for tonal combinations.

An intensity of 10^{-6} w/m² (.000001 w/m²) has an intensity level of 60 db. An intensity of 10^{-5} w/m^2 (.00001 w/m^2) has an intensity level of 70 db. That 10 db difference represents a tenfold (10:1) increase in power—.00001 is ten times .000001. An intensity level of 80 db is attained by an intensity of .0001 w/m^2 (10^{-4}); the difference between 80 and 60 db represents a one hundredfold (100:1) increase in power—.0001 is 100 times .000001. *Any* 10 db difference means that one sound has ten times the intensity of the other. A 20 db difference always represents one hundred times the intensity; 30 db, one thousand times; 40 db, ten thousand times, etc. The decibel scale is logarithmic; equal decibel amounts stand for equal ratios.

Two decibel values may not be summed directly in any acoustically meaningful way. Two intensity levels of 60 db do not total 120 db—they total approximately 63 db. Each intensity corresponding to a 60 db level is .000001 w/m^2; .000001 w/m^2 + .000001 w/m^2 = .000002 w/m^2, not .00001 w/m^2, which has a level of 70 db, and *obviously not* 1.0 w/m^2, which has a level of 120 db. By working backwards in the decibel formula, adding the intensities themselves, and finding the level for the sum of intensities (a formidable task unless a calculator with logarithmic functions is available), one can show that any intensity level increases by approximately 3 db when combined with an equivalent level. If the combined intensity levels are not equal, the result will be something less than 3 db added to the higher level: 60 db + 59 db ≈ 62.2 db, e.g.

Sound pressure level is a more common stimulus measure than intensity level because it is easier to measure and it relates logically to the concept of pressure variations being responsible for sound. Sound pressure level (SPL) is expressed in decibels which are computed differently in relation to a different baseline. The formula is

$$D = 20\,[\log\,(P/P_0)],$$

where D is the number of decibels, P is a particular pressure value, and P_0 is a baseline pressure. A common baseline is .00002 newtons per square meter. With SPL decibels, a difference of 20 decibels represents a tenfold increase in sound pressure level; 40 decibels represents a one hundred-fold increase, etc. Most decibel measures in psychoacoustic literature are indicators of SPL; investigators should specify clearly the baseline and the property, intensity level or SPL.

Response Measures. One way to measure the loudness sensation is to refer individual loudness sensations for particular frequency and intensity combinations to a reference frequency. Fletcher and Munson (1933) made so-called equal loudness contours (sometimes called Fletcher-

Use this.

Munson curves today) by having eleven observers make 297 observations of comparative loudness. Schneider et al. (1972) derived equal loudness contours by noting different rates of loudness growth with intensity at different frequencies. Molino (1973) showed that the spacing between equal loudness contours varied with the standard frequency to which judgments must be related, although overall curvatures were consistent across differing standards. Whittle, Collins, and Robinson (1972) extended equal loudness contours to 3.15 Hz under laboratory conditions. Scharf (1978) described differences in curvature patterns between equal loudness contours obtained through earphones and those obtained under "free-field" listening conditions. Although there are individual differences, studies yielding equal loudness contours, a sample of which appears in Figure 3-4, show several things about the ear's behavior.

Understanding equal loudness curves (or contours) is facilitated by realizing that any point on an equal loudness curve is equally as loud as any other point on the same curve. Furthermore, each point on any curve represents a particular frequency-intensity combination. In Figure 3-4, the horizontal axis represents frequencies and the vertical axis represents intensity levels.

Frequency's confounding influtionship is evidenced by the fact that the curves indeed are *curved.* If a given intensity elicited a given loudness sensation regardless of frequency, the curves would appear as straight lines. One can note that the curves "go down" as frequency increases to around 2000 Hz, thereby indicating increasing auditory sensitivity. Beyond about 3000 Hz, sensitivity decreases and the curves "go up." The amount of change is less at higher loudness levels.

Each curve has a phon value. Phons are arbitrarily equivalent to decibels at 1000 Hz; e.g., a 1000 Hz tone of 60 db also is 60 phons. Any other frequency judged as equal in loudness to the 1000 Hz—60 db standard also is 60 phons. Phons, the measurement unit for loudness level (not loudness), thus are measures of equivalency to the intensity level of some standard.

Equal loudness curves, based on observed averages, will vary with individual sensitivities and stimulus conditions. The curves represent characteristic auditory behavior well, but they enable loudness comparisons only at the less than, equal to, or greater than level.

Laboratory attempts to measure loudness in terms of how much louder one sound is than another have used observers' productions and/or

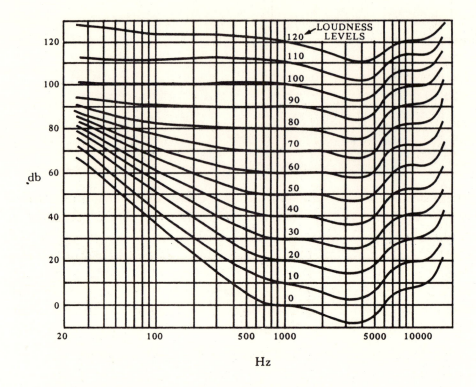

Figure 3-4. Sample equal loudness curves. The curves connect frequency-intensity level combinations which are judged to be equally loud as a 1000 Hz standard of a given intensity level.

estimations of various loudness distances or ratios. A sone scale of loudness, based on estimates of apparent ratios, and a lambda scale, based on equal-appearing intervals and ratios, are alternative ways of describing apparent loudness relationships (Beck and Shaw, 1967). Methodology influences the results of loudness estimates and production. The Method of Constant Stimuli, in which predetermined tones are presented in random order, biases responses toward the middle of the stimulus ranges; the extreme loudnesses are under- or overestimated. The Method of Adjustment, in which the subject adjusts a tonal stimulus to match a conceptualization of another stimulus, biases responses in relation to the stimulus range and the starting position of the adjustment apparatus. The Method of Limits, using ascending and descending series of stimulus tones, biases in relation to range and direction (Warren, 1970). Despite procedural difficulties, a large body of evidence suggests that equal stimulus ratios produce equal response ratios. This is known as the *power law*, and it merits separate and detailed treatment.

The Power Law

The power law, one form of the psychophysical law, was developed largely through the work of S.S. Stevens and his students and advocates. Symbolization of the power law varies; in Stevens's text, published posthumously with his widow's assistance, it is stated as

$$\psi = \kappa\phi^\beta,$$

where ψ is the sensation magnitude, ϕ is the stimulus magnitude, and β is an exponent which indicates the growth rate of the sensation in relation to stimulus growth (Stevens, 1975). (The κ is an experimental constant depending on units of measurement; Attneave (1962) says that it depends on the reference stimulus.) The β value varies with the stimulus; when β is greater than 1.00, the sensation grows faster than the stimulus. When it is less than 1.00, the sensation grows more slowly than the stimulus. Values for β, called power functions, which Stevens reported include:

0.67, for the loudness sensation elicited by a 3000 Hz tone.
0.50, for the brightness sensation elicited by a brief light flash.
1.00, for the apparent visual length of a projected line.
1.40, for the apparent taste of salt.
0.80, for the hardness experienced in squeezing rubber.
3.50, for the sensation of electric shock experienced from a current applied to the fingers.

The power law is believed to result from a general tendency of human sensory systems to perceive equal sensation ratios for equal stimulus ratios. Perceptual invariance, as when something which looks twice as large as something else appears that way under varying lighting conditions, may enable encoding the environment in a maximally useful way (Yilmaz, 1967). The size of the sensation ratio is expressed as a power function of the stimulus ratio by the power law. For example, it works out, in accordance with the loudness power function of .67, that any increase of 9 db (remember, decibels are ratio comparisons) of SPL increases loudness in sones by a factor of two for the standard condition. (One sone is the loudness of a band (frequency spread) of noise centered on 3150 Hz sounding at an SPL of 32 db.) (Stevens, 1972; 1975).

Many investigations of the power law as it applies to loudness and other prothetic continuua employed *magnitude estimation* to obtain mea-

surements of sensation. Measurement in this way is a matching operation in which one sensory continuum is matched to another. As it is
usually practiced, the observer assigns numbers to stimuli on a propor-
tionate basis: The sensory continuum being measured is matched with
the continuum of apparent numerosity. For example, if a tone is judged
as "100" and the next tone is half as loud, the observer will call it "50."
Stevens (1956b) described recommended magnitude estimation procedures regarding stimulus ranges, session lengths, presentation orders,
and numbers of subjects. It is *not* necessary to give an observer a common standard; he or she may use any numbers which seem to represent
his or her sensations.

In his text, Stevens reports (p. 28) data from an early magnitude
estimation experiment. Eight 1000 Hz tones, with SPLs ranging from 40
to 110 db in increments of 10 db were presented. Subjects assigned
numbers in accordance with their individual standards; the numbers
were converted to a common scale and averaged.* The stimulus SPLs
and their corresponding average magnitude estimations were:

(SPL)	(Average Magnitude Estimate)
40	1.1
50	2.1
60	5.0
70	10.0
80	18.0
90	40.0
100	90.0
110	200.0

Power law relationships have been criticized because of the averaging
of individual magnitude estimations and productions and a belief that
such sensory judgments are a part of learning and indoctrination. In
defense, two studies are particularly interesting. Stevens and Guirao
(1964) obtained magnitude estimates and productions for a 1000 Hz tone
from eleven observers individually. Each observer yielded an approximately similar function. Bond and Stevens (1969) had five five-year-old
children adjust a lamp's brightness to match the apparent loudness to a
500 Hz tone set at eight different levels. If stimulus-sensation relations

---

*Averaging of magnitude estimations is via the median or the geometric mean of each set of
estimations. The median is the middle value; the geometric mean is the nth root of a geometric
series of n terms, i.e., $\sqrt[n]{(X_1)(X_1)(\ldots)(X_n)}$.

for loudness depend on learning, the children's results should have differed from those of adults. But they did not differ. Predicted relations were obtained.

Experimental arrangements have troublesome influences on results obtained with magnitude estimation. Stimulus range, location of the first stimulus presented within the range, and the standard and its associated number cause variation. Poulton (1968) cites these difficulties and insists that Stevens's impressive results are artifacts of using trained observers and restricted experimental conditions. Zwislocki and Goodman (1980), however, found that subjects tended to pair numbers with sounds (and line lengths) on absolute scales; they believe that numbers generally acquire absolute psychological magnitudes before age six. Their subjects seemed to "match impressions" spontaneously, not "assign numbers."

Investigation of any psychological phenomenon may alter that phenomenon, and measuring loudness via magnitude estimation is no exception. Furthermore, individuals will vary in their sensations and in their abilities to express them with numbers. The power function for loudness will vary with the stimulus condition; loudness generally grows more rapidly with lower frequencies. In spite of complexities, criticisms, and contradictions, implications of the power law, as demonstrated through magnitude estimation, for the musician are:

1. Loudness grows systematically with intensity as a function of natural perceptual processes.
2. Individuals are capable of making far more subtle loudness judgments than traditional dynamic markings suggest.

Masking

As is obvious from ordinary experience, one sound, normally perfectly audible by itself, can become inaudible in the presence of a louder sound. This phenomenon is called *masking.* That which is made inaudible is the masked tone (or noise); that louder sound which makes the softer sound inaudible is called the mask*er.* Orchestral woodwind players sometimes will disregard certain passages because they are not "exposed." Such players feel that other instruments will mask the sound of the disregarded passage, so it need not receive special attention in practice sessions.

A quantitative relationship between loudness and masking was noted by Fletcher and Munson (1937), who related it to early attempts to measure loudness. Egan and Hake (1950) conducted a classic study of the masking effects of a pure tone of 400 Hz and a 365–465 Hz band of noise centered on 410 Hz. The threshold of hearing in quiet was determined at various frequencies for the five subjects, then the masker was introduced. Subjects adjusted the masked tones to make them audible again; the amounts of adjustments required were plotted to show the *masking curve* for each masker. Egan and Hake noted that noise was a more efficient masker because it lacked the problems with beating and combination tones experienced with certain masking tone-masked tone frequency relationships.

Masking curves diagram attempts to mask a variety of tones with a given tone or noise. Masking curves, a sample of which appears in Figure 3–5, characteristically show maximal masking effect near the frequency of the masker. At lower intensity levels of the masker, the curve declines symmetrically; masking effects below the masking frequency are about as extensive as masking effects above the masking frequency. However, the masking curve is asymmetrical at higher masker intensity levels; masking is more extensive for frequencies above the masker. Dips and ambiguous regions often appear in masking curves for tones at places near a harmonic relationship between the masking and masked tones. It is important in interpreting masking curves to recognize that the curve's height represents a *difference* in the strength of a sound between (1) when the masked sound was just audible in the masker's absence and (2) the point to which the masked sound must be raised to make it audible in the masker's presence.

A newer technique for studying masking holds the masked tone (sometimes called a probe frequency) constant and varies the masking tone. This apparently permits closer investigation of areas where the masking and masker frequencies coincide (Vogten, 1974). The levels to which the masking tone must be altered to mask the constant masked tone may be plotted to form a *tuning* curve, which is opposite (inverted and extended to the left) in shape to conventional masking curves (Zwicker, 1974).

In addition to simultaneous masking, forward and backward masking are possible in the laboratory. In forward and backward masking, the masking sound respectively precedes or follows the masked by a very brief time period. Forward masking probably is a matter of reduced auditory sensitivity or prolonged neural stimulation from the masker.

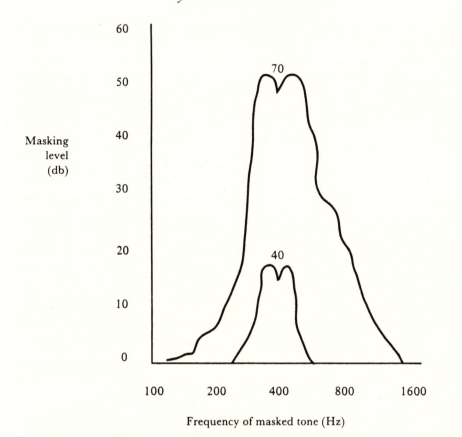

Frequency of masked tone (Hz)

Figure 3-5. Typical masking curves, drawn for 400 Hz masking tones at 40 and 70 db. The height of each curve shows the increase in db necessary in order to "unmask" a masked tone. These curves are hypothetical, but they are similar to published curves.

Backward masking* is mysterious; it must result in some way from incomplete processing of the masked sound (Moore, 1977).

Loudness Summation

Individual loudnesses sum to form combined loudness. This obvious mathematical fact is perceptually complex and of musical importance because sounds summate differently under different conditions.

Fletcher (1946), using an early tone synthesizer, demonstrated that complex tones sound louder than pure tones. Stevens (1956a) noted that

---

*In this context, backward masking refers to inability to hear a sound which occurred earlier in time. It is not related to the use of "backward masking" to refer to incomprehensible or inaudible messages becoming clear when a tape is played backwards.

separate noise bands (and, by analogy, groups of frequencies) are not simply additive. Even frequencies widely separated from each other can have a mutually inhibitive effect.

Zwicker, Flottorp, and Stevens (1957) showed that loudness summation for pure tones depends on frequency separations in relation to the critical band width. When the frequency spacing (Δf) between simultaneous pure tones is increased to a critical point (Δf $\approx$ 100 Hz for a 500 Hz standard, $\approx$ 180 Hz for a 1000 Hz standard, $\approx$ 350 Hz for a 2000 Hz standard), the loudness sensation increases. A similar loudness increase was noted when the width of a noise band was increased beyond a certain point. At low SPLs, with wide frequency spacing, there is no summation; the total loudness is equivalent to the loudest individual tone. Loudness summation appears greatest for tones at a loudness level of 50 to 60 phons; uniform spacing of frequency components produces greater loudness than nonuniform spacing.

When a stimulus with designated SPL is presented binaurally it sounds louder than when it is heard with only one ear. In one study (Reynolds and Stevens, 1960), monaural loudness grew with a power function of .54, while binaural loudness grew with .60. The ratio between monaural and binaural loudness for corresponding stimuli grew as a function of SPL with an exponent of about 0.066. The superiority of two-eared hearing thus becomes greater as the stimulus magnitude increases.

The critical frequency difference for loudness summation vanishes under conditions of dichotic presentation—separate frequencies to each ear. For between ear differences of 0 to "several thousand" Hz, Scharf (1969) noted that dichotic pairs remained equally loud. Dichotic summation occurred even when the tonal sensation was of two separate localized tones, one in each ear. This is logical in relation to previous studies showing ordinary loudness summation related to the basilar membrane's critical band widths, because dichotic presentation prevents phenomena which are dependent on the critical band width.

In one of his last published works, Stevens (1972) outlined a computational procedure, based on careful laboratory observations, for the perceived loudness of a noise divided into one-third octave bands. By analogy, it may apply to mixtures of complex tones. The procedure uses a standard reference of a one-third octave band centered on 3150 Hz, the sone as defined above, the power law for loudness, equal loudness contours for noise, and the summation rule

$$S_t = S_m + F(\Sigma S - S_m),$$

Dangers
To Hearing

where S_t is the total loudness, S_m is the loudness of the loudest sound, ΣS is the sum (in sones) of the loudness of all bands, and F is a tabled value which varies as a function of the loudest band.

Individuals demonstrating loudness summation must be cognizant of relative phase, particularly with two individual loudnesses. Destructive interference can produce a tonal superposition which has a waveform of smaller amplitude than either component waveform.

Dangers to Hearing

Exposure to sound at high intensity levels can cause a temporary threshold shift; i.e., a greater amount of intensity is necessary in order for the listener to just perceive a sound. Temporary threshold shifts may depend on the amount of SPL in the critical bands around the affected frequencies as well as the exposure time (Yamamoto et al., 1970). Under conditions of prolonged exposure such threshold shifts may become permanent.

Musicians and others have questioned effects of high intensity levels on rock-and-roll musicians, whose characteristic styles often demand high loudness levels. Jerger and Jerger (1970) measured the hearing sensitivity of nine rock-and-roll performers just prior to a performance and within an hour of the performance's conclusion. Eight performers showed a threshold shift of at least 15 db for at least one frequency in the 200–8000 Hz range; some losses were as high as 50 db. The shift influenced frequencies which may appear high for many musical purposes, but intelligibility of speech suffers with a loss of high frequency sensitivity because consonants become blurred.

Rintelmann, Lindberg, and Smitley (1972) exposed twenty females with normal hearing to taped rock-and-roll at an SPL of 100 db on two occasions. One tape contained 60 minutes of continuous music; the other had one minute of ambient (chance, random, background) discotheque noise at an SPL of 80 db inserted after each three minutes of music. The temporary threshold shift was significantly less for the intermittent listening condition, although recovery (return to normal hearing threshold) time was about the same for both conditions. The authors noted that 50 percent of the subjects in the intermittent condition and 80 percent in the continuous condition were "endangered" in accordance with published standards restricting daily exposure to high sound levels.

Rock-and-roll is not the only culprit, of course, and hearing loss is not the only implication. Stephens and Anderson (1971) determined the "threshold of discomfort" or uncomfortable loudness level for a 1000 Hz tone and also administered personality measures to a group of British subjects. The higher the hearing threshold, the lower was the uncomfortable loudness level. There were significant negative correlations, i.e., a tendency for a group to be high on one trait and low on another between uncomfortable loudness level and introversion, test anxiety, and motivation to avoid failure.

Personal radio headsets provide individual listeners with opportunities to expose themselves to preferred sounds at high SPL's. These devices are not protecting their wearers against outside sounds while they produce their "inside" sounds; hearing protection is not provided in any significant way (Skrainar et al., 1985).

Just as not everyone who smokes will develop lung cancer, not everyone who listens to music at high sound levels will destroy hair cells excessively, but the likelihood of serious damage is increased by loud sounds, just as the likelihood of disease is increased by cigarette smoke. The danger to hearing is not just propaganda from people who do not like particular musical styles or are unduly bothered by noisy environments. Musicians who plan rehearsals of large groups in small rooms, stand near powerful speakers while they perform, or feel that they must be "totally bathed" in sound must consider the risks they may be creating for themselves and others.

Timbre Phenomena

Timbre or tone quality is the tonal attribute that distinguishes sounds of identical pitch, loudness, and duration. An oboe and a viola can play an A of identical frequency and sound pressure level for an identical time period, but they sound different. Timbre, because of its multidimensionality and the difficulty of separately controlling separate dimensions, lacks the amount of research literature characteristic of pitch and loudness. Considered here are timbre's relationship to waveform, timbre recognition, and measurement.

Waveform-Timbre Relationship

Waveform, the pattern of displacements associated with a soundwave, is the closest quasi-parallel physical property to the psychological property of timbre. A complex waveform depends on the particular component frequencies, the number of frequencies, the relative strengths of the frequencies, and the relative phases among the frequencies (Backus, 1977). Different musical instruments sound differently to a large extent because of their different frequency combinations and interactions. As will be discussed below, however, waveform is not a sufficient control of timbre sensations.

It once was believed, in accordance with Ohm's acoustical law, that the ear was "phase deaf." While sounds containing components of identical frequencies and amplitudes but differing relative phases would look different in waveform, they would not sound different. Research now shows that although phase sensitivity is relatively weak, there are subtle effects of relative phase on timbre, particularly when changing phase relationships occur within a continuously sounding tone (Patterson, 1973; Plomp & Steeneken, 1969; Raiford & Schubert, 1971; Risset & Wessel, 1982).

Influences Other than Waveform

A musical tone is a dynamic ever-changing entity; no static waveform can represent a sound and its associated timbre adequately. Timbre is significantly a function of a tone's onset (initial transient, attack, rise time, initial frequency smear) and transient fluctuations within the tone.

A vibrating system cannot attain a reasonably steady vibration pattern instantaneously. A brief amount of time characterized by "extra" frequency components and differing rise times for the components that eventually will be part of the steady vibration exists as the onset period, during which more and more energy is supplied to the vibrating system.

Winckel (1967) has discussed extensively onset effects from theoretical and experimental standpoints. Onset times vary with different instruments; the trumpet has a rapid onset of about 20 milliseconds while the flute requires 200 to 300 milliseconds. Individual complex tone partials have their own rates of growth. Every tonal attack includes a very rapidly decaying "smear" of inharmonic and harmonic frequencies. Sharper, more staccato, attacks have relatively wide frequency "smear" ranges and short onset times. Mellower, more legato, attacks have relatively narrow frequency "smear" ranges and long onset times. Onset behavior inherent in the vibrating system is modified by idiosyncrasies of the player, the instrument (or voice), and the acoustical environment. It is clear that attempts to compare "good" and "bad" sounds via the oscilloscope or to imitate orchestral instruments with organs and economy-model synthesizers are unlikely to be fruitful because of inability to duplicate onset behavior.

A millisecond (.001 sec.) is a rather short period of time to most people; 300 milliseconds is less than a split second. Anyone who questions the importance of the brief onset for timbre, however, needs only to experiment with removing the initial portions of taped musical tones. In studies such as that of Elliott (1975), experienced musicians had considerable difficulty in identifying common orchestral instruments when the onset portions of the tones were absent.

The relative distribution of energy among the partials may vary with overall sound pressure level. In general, higher partials have proportionately more energy at greater SPL's than they do at weaker levels (Risset & Wessel, 1982). This appears particularly true for wind instruments, and the band director who asks the band to play with exactly the same timbre in loud and soft passages may be asking for an impossibility.

In the free-field listening situation characteristic of a concert hall, reverberant sound dominates for the greater part of the audience. The waveform's makeup differs from point to point, so even steady-state tones have different timbres at different locations (Plomp and Steeneken, 1973).

Tone Source Recognition

The basilar membrane stimulation pattern resulting from a particular complex waveform's characteristics probably is the physiological basis for timbre perception, at least in the case of a steady-state waveform (static case) (Plomp, 1970).

Roederer (1975) discusses dynamic ("in context") tone source recognition as a matter of timbre perception, resulting from neural processing of waveform information, storage in memory with a learned label, and comparison with prior information. The sensation of a clarinet sound as opposed to a trumpet sound may be experienced by anyone with normal hearing, but the distinction between the two in terms of labels requires learning, which likely results in actual neural modifications of cortical structures.

Measurement of Timbre

Timbre is a multidimensional property. As a result, there is not and cannot be a measurement unit analogous to the mel for pitch or the sone for loudness. Qualitative descriptions of timbre may use words, similar to those found in orchestration texts, such as "rich," "mellow," "thin," "buzzy," "comical," "noble," etc.

Modern attempts to measure timbre often use subjects' verbal descriptions or judgments of tonal similarity to uncover underlying dimensions along which timbre perceptions may be ordered. For example, von Bismarck (1974a;b) had eight musicians and eight nonmusicians classify twenty-five 200 Hz complex tones with varying waveforms, five steady-state vowel segments, and five noise bands along thirty seven-point scales formed by bipolar adjectives (semantic differentials). His statistical analysis yielded four factors, which collectively explained 91 percent of the variability in classification. The most important factor was sharpness (as in one pole of "dull-sharp," not high in pitch), which seemed to depend on the upper frequency in a complex sound and the comparative progressive reduction in upper partial strengths, i.e., slope of the spectral envelope. By demonstrating that sharpness may be doubled or halved, just as loudness, von Bismarck suggested another basic tonal property.

Grey (1977) presented subjects with tones synthesized by computer to match natural oboe, clarinet, saxophone, English horn, French horn, flute, bassoon, trumpet, and string tones. The subjects judged tones of equal pitch, loudness, and duration for perceived similarity. Using the sophisticated mathematical technique of multidimensional scaling, Grey found that the similarity ratings could be organized along three dimensions in geometric space. One dimension was the spectral energy distribution which resulted from the particular waveform. Another was related to the low and high frequencies in the onset. The third was related to spectral fluctuations.

Plomp showed that multidimensional analyses of physical spectra of organ tones gave a similar dimensional configuration to analyses of subjects' similarity. While dimensional research is time-consuming and complex, there is no way to order sounds on any unidimensional scale with respect to timbre (Rasch & Plomp, 1982), so quantitative measurement of timbre beyond the most general and global level inevitably must employ multidimensional methodology.

Summary

Chapter Three has presented considerable information related to music's psychoacoustical foundations. It is difficult to simplify that which is inherently complex, but the main points in the chapter include the following:

1. Musical sounds depend on rapid atmospheric pressure fluctuations resulting from physical vibration, generally of a periodic nature.

2. Pressure fluctuations are transmitted as mechanical vibrations to the inner ear, where they are processed and converted to electro-chemical signals directed to the brain.

3. Pitch, a tone's apparent relative location on a high-low continuum, is dependent on the physical property of frequency, but the pitch-frequency relationship is not perfect.

4. In addition to the highness-lowness dimension, pitch includes dimensions of definity, which refers to how obvious the pitch sensation is, and similarity, intimacy, or circularity, which refers to how a particular pitch relates to other pitches.

5. Pitch assignment for a pure tone depends upon the area of basilar membrane stimulation.

6. A combination of pure tones forms a sensation of unison, beating, roughness, or two tones in accordance with the frequency separation of the tones.

7. The amount by which a frequency must be changed in order to elicit a pitch difference varies with the individual, the occasion, and the frequency range.

8. The pitch of a complex tone depends on the low pitch resulting from the waveform's spatial pattern and repetition frequency, detected through the central neural process of fundamental tracking.

9. Low pitch may shift away from waveform repetition frequency under certain conditions.

10. Combination tones result from cochlear distortion; they are distinguished from low pitch in that they require more than minimal intensity level for perception and are peripheral rather than central effects.

11. Consonance or dissonance usually is considered as another label for various intervals by musicians and as an evaluated tonal phenomenon by nonmusicians.

12. Consonance and dissonance judgments depend heavily on training and experience, but there may be some physical basis for

consonance as a tonal phenomenon because of the basilar membrane alignment of tonal components.

13. Why complex tones from separate sound sources generally result in harmony while individual complex tones yield a unitary pitch sensation is unclear.

14. The apparent size of a musical interval of constant ratio may vary with frequency range and other conditions in an idiosyncratic manner.

15. First order beating, an apparent rise and fall in loudness of a mistuned unison, is a peripheral effect.

16. Second order beating, an apparent waxing and waning or fluttering of a mistuned nonunison interval, is a central pitch processing effect.

17. Binaural beats and fusion may be created by feeding separate sounds to each ear.

18. Absolute pitch, the ability to name a tone without reference to any external pitch standard, may be related to learning label-sensation associations at a critical age.

19. Attempts to measure pitch as distinct from frequency via the mel scale have been somewhat disappointing.

20. Loudness, the apparent strength or magnitude of a tone, depends largely on intensity, but the intensity-loudness relationship is not perfect.

21. Loudness is distinct from volume, the apparent size or extensity of a tone, and density, the apparent tonal compactness, but loudness may be a product of volume and density interactions.

22. Decibels are measures of the physical dimensions of intensity level and sound pressure level, not of loudness.

23. Equal loudness curves connect frequency-intensity combinations which produce loudness levels equivalent in phons.

24. Equal loudness curves show how frequency confounds the intensity-loudness relationship; a given intensity does not lead to an equal loudness sensation across all frequencies.

25. Loudness may be measured via various estimation and production techniques; the sone scale has been derived therefrom.

26. The power law shows that loudness grows in a lawful manner in relation to growth in sound intensity; the growth rate varies with stimulus conditions.

27. One sound may mask another and particular masking behaviors may be quantified through masking curves.

28. Loudness summation depends on the particular component frequencies, their degrees of separation, and relative phase as well as individual loudness; there is no simple additive process.

29. Exposure to music at high intensity levels can degrade hearing sensitivity.

30. Timbre, apparent tone quality or color, depends on the factors influencing waveform as well as onset and transient waveform characteristics.

31. Tone source recognition depends on learning as well as timbre perception.

32. As timbre is a multidimensional property, its measurement beyond qualitative descriptions depends on uncovering dimensions along which perceptual judgments of timbre may be placed.

REFERENCES

Allen, D. (1967). Octave discriminability of musical and non-musical subjects. *Psychonomic Science, 7,* 421–422.

Attneave, F. (1962). Perception and related areas. In S. Koch (Ed.), *Psychology: A study of a science* (Vol. 4) (pp. 619–654). New York: McGraw-Hill.

Bachem, A. (1954). Time factors in relative and absolute pitch determination. *Journal of the Acoustical Society of America, 26,* 751–753.

Backus, J.W. (1977). *The acoustical foundations of music* (2nd ed.). New York: W.W. Norton.

Beck, J., & Shaw, W.A. (1963). Single estimates of pitch magnitude. *Journal of the Acoustical Society of America, 35,* 1722–1724.

Beck, J., & Shaw, W.A. (1967). Ratio-estimations of loudness intervals. *American Journal of Psychology, 80,* 59–65.

Bharucha, J.J. (1984). Anchoring effects in music: The resolution of dissonance. *Cognitive Psychology, 16,* 485–518.

Bond, B., & Stevens, S.S. (1969). Cross-modality matching of brightness to loudness by 5-year olds. *Perception and Psychophysics, 6,* 337–339.

Bugg, E.G. (1933). An experimental study of factors influencing consonance judgments. *Psychological Monographs, 45* (2). (Whole No. 201).

Cardozo, B.L. (1974). Frequency discrimination at the threshold. In E. Zwicker and E. Terhardt (Eds.), *Facts and models in hearing* (pp. 164–177). New York: Springer-Verlag.

Corso, J.F. (1954). Unison tuning of musical instruments. *Journal of the Acoustical Society of America, 26,* 746–750.

Corso, J.F. (1957). Absolute judgments of musical tonality. *Journal of the Acoustical Society of America, 29*, 138–144.

Cuddy, L.L. (1968). Practice effects on the absolute judgment of pitch. *Journal of the Acoustical Society of America, 43*, 1069–1076.

Dallos, P.S., & Sweetman, R.H. (1960). Distribution pattern of cochlear harmonics. *Journal of the Acoustical Society of America, 45*, 37–45.

Dallos, P., Billone, M.C., Currant, J.D., Wang, C.Y., & Raynor, S. (1972). Cochlear inner and outer hair cells: Functional differences. *Science, 177*, 356–360.

Davis, H. (1962). Advances in the neurophysiology and neuroanatomy of the cochlea. *Journal of the Acoustical Society of America, 34*, 1377–138.

DeGainza, V.H. (1970). Absolute and relative hearing as innate complementary functions of man's musical ear. *Council for Research in Music Education, 22*, 13–16.

Deutsch, D. (1982). Grouping mechanisms in music. In D. Deutsch (Ed.), *The psychology of music* (pp. 99–134). New York: Academic Press.

Egan, J.P., & Hake, H.W. (1950). On the masking pattern of a simple auditory stimulus. *Journal of the Acoustical Society of America, 22*, 622–630.

Elliott, C.A. (1975). Attacks and releases as factors in instrument identification. *Journal of Research in Music Education, 23*, 35–40.

Farnsworth, P.R. (1938). The pitch of a combination of tones. *American Journal of Psychology, 51*, 536–539.

Farnsworth, P.R. (1969). *The social psychology of music* (2nd ed.). Ames: Iowa State University Press.

Fletcher, H. (1946). The pitch, loudness, and quality of musical tones. *American Journal of Physics, 14*, 215–225.

Fletcher, H., & Munson, W.A. (1933). Loudness. *Journal of the Acoustical Society of America, 5*, 82–108.

Gacek, R.R. (1972). Neuroanatomy of the auditory system. In J.V. Tobias (Ed.), *Foundations of modern auditory theory* (vol. 2) (pp. 241–262). New York: Academic Press.

Gjaevenes, K., & Rimstad, E.R. (1972). The influence of rise time on loudness. *Journal of the Acoustical Society of America, 51*, 1233–1239.

Goldstein, J.L. (1970). Aural combination tones. In R. Plomp & G.F. Smoorenburg (Eds.), *Frequency analysis and periodicity detection in hearing*. Leiden: Sijthoff.

Grey, J.M. (1977). Multidimensional perceptual scaling of musical timbres. *Journal of the Acoustical Society of America, 61*, 1270–1277.

Guirao, M., & Stevens, S.S. (1964). The measurement of auditory density. *Journal of the Acoustical Society of America, 36*, 1176–1182.

Hellman, R.P. (1982). Loudness, annoyance, and noisiness produced by single-tone-noise complexes. *Journal of the Acoustical Society of America, 72*, 62–73.

Hellman, R.P. (1985). Perceived magnitude of two-tone complexes: Loudness, annoyance, and noisiness. *Journal of the Acoustical Society of America, 77*, 1497–1504.

Hellman, R.P., & Zwislocki, J.J. (1968). Loudness determination at low sound frequencies. *Journal of the Acoustical Society of America, 43*, 60–64.

Houtsma, A.J.M., & Goldstein, J.L. (1972). The central origin of the pitch of complex tones. *Journal of the Acoustical Society of America, 51*, 5520–5529.

Jeffress, L.A. (1962). Absolute pitch. *Journal of the Acoustical Society of America, 34,* 987.

Jerger, J., & Jerger, S. (1970). Temporary threshold shift in rock-and-roll musicians. *Journal of Speech and Hearing Research, 13,* 221–224.

Kock, W.E. (1935). On the principle of uncertainty in sound. *Journal of the Acoustical Society of America, 7,* 56–58.

Krumhansl, C.L. (1979). The psychological representation of musical pitch in a tonal context. *Cognitive Psychology, 11,* 346–374.

Lundin, R.W. (1947). Toward a cultural theory of consonance. *Journal of Psychology, 23,* 45–49.

Meyer, M. (1956). On memorizing absolute pitch. *Journal of the Acoustical Society of America, 28,* 718–719.

Molino, J.A. (1972). Pure-tone equal-loudness contours for standard tones of different frequencies. *Perception and Psychophysics, 14,* 1–4.

Moore, B.C.J. (1974). Relation between the critical bandwidth and the frequency difference limen. *Journal of the Acoustical Society of America, 55,* 359.

Moore, B.C.J. (1982). *An introduction to the psychology of hearing* (2nd ed.). London: Academic Press.

Nordmark, J.O. (1968). Mechanisms of frequency discrimination. *Journal of the Acoustical Society of America, 44,* 1533–1540.

Patterson, B. (1974). Musical dynamics. *Scientific American, 231* (5), 78–95.

Patterson, R. (1973). The effects of relative phase and the number of components on residue pitch. *Journal of the Acoustical Society of America, 53,* 1565–1572.

Perrott, D.R., & Nelson, M.A. (1969). Limits for the detection of binaural beats. *Journal of the Acoustical Society of America, 46,* 1477–1481.

Peterson, J., & Smith, F.W. (1930). The range and modifiability of consonance in certain musical intervals. *American Journal of Psychology, 42,* 561–572.

Pickles, J.O. (1982). *An introduction to the physiology of hearing.* London: Academic Press.

Plomp, R. (1964). The ear as a frequency analyzer. *Journal of the Acoustical Society of America, 36,* 1628–1636.

Plomp, R. (1965). Detectability threshold for combination tones. *Journal of the Acoustical Society of America, 37,* 1110–1123.

Plomp, R. (1967a). Beats of mistuned consonances. *Journal of the Acoustical Society of America, 42,* 462–474.

Plomp, R. (1967b). Pitch of complex tones. *Journal of the Acoustical Society of America, 41,* 1526–1533.

Plomp, R. (1970). Timbre as a multidimensional attribute of complex tones. In R. Plomp & T.G. Smoorenburg (Eds.), Frequency analysis and periodicity detection in hearing (pp. 397–411). Leiden: Sijthoff.

Plomp, R. (1976). *Aspects of tone sensation.* London: Academic Press.

Plomp, R., & Levelt, W.J.M. (1965). Tonal consonance and critical bandwidth. *Journal of the Acoustical Society of America, 38,* 548–560.

Plomp, R., & Steeneken, H.J.M. (1969). Effect of phase on the timbre of complex tones. *Journal of the Acoustical Society of America, 46,* 409–421.

Plomp, R., & Steeneken, H.J.M. (1973). Place dependence of timbre in reverberant sound fields. *Acustica, 28,* 50–59.

Poulton, E.C. (1968). The new psychophysics: Six models for magnitude estimation. *Psychological Bulletin, 69,* 1–19.

Radocy, R.E. (1977). Pitch judgments of selected successive intervals: Is twice as frequent twice as high? *Psychology of Music, 5* (2), 23–29.

Radocy, R.E. (1978). The influence of selected variables on the apparent size of successive pitch intervals. *Psychology of Music, 6* (2), 21–29.

Raiford, C.A., & Schubert, E.D. (1971). Recognition of phase changes in octave complexes. *Journal of the Acoustical Society of America, 50,* 559–567.

Rainbolt, H.R., & Schubert, E.D. (1968). Use of noise bands to establish noise pitch. *Journal of the Acoustical Society of America, 43,* 316–323.

Rakowski, A. (1979). The magic number two: Seven examples of binary apposition in pitch theory. *Humanities Association Review, 30,* 24–45.

Rasch, R.A., & Plomp, R. (1982). The perception of musical tones. In D. Deutsch (Ed.), *The Psychology of Music* (pp. 1–24). New York: Academic Press.

Reynolds, G.S., & Stevens, S.S. (1960). Binaural summation of loudness. *Journal of the Acoustical Society of America, 35,* 1337–1344.

Rhode, W.S., & Robles, L. (1974). Evidence from Mossbauer experiments for nonlinear vibration in the cochlea. *Journal of the Acoustical Society of America, 55,* 588–596.

Rintelmann, W.R., Lindberg, R.F., & Smitley, E.K. (1972). Temporary threshold shift and recovery patterns from two types of rock and roll music presentation. *Journal of the Acoustical Society of America, 51,* 1249–1254.

Risset, J.C., & Wessell, D.L. (1982). Exploration of timbre by analysis and synthesis. In D. Deutsch (Ed.), *The Psychology of Music* (pp. 26–58). New York: Academic Press.

Ritsma, R.J. (1970). Periodicity detection. In R. Plomp & G. Smoorenburg (Eds.), *Frequency analysis and periodicity detection in hearing* (pp. 250–263). Leiden: Sijthoff.

Roederer, J.G. (1975). *Introduction to the physics and psychophysics of music* (2nd ed.). New York: Springer-Verlag.

Scharf, G. (1969). Dichotic summation of loudness. *Journal of the Acoustical Society of America, 45,* 1193–1205.

Scharf, G. (1978). Loudness. In E.D. Carterette & M.P. Friedman (Eds.), *Handbook of perception* (vol. 4) (pp. 187–242). New York: Academic Press.

Schneider, B., Wright, A.A., Edelheit, W., Hock, P., & Humphrey, C. (1972). Equal loudness contours derived from sensory magnitude judgments. *Journal of the Acoustical Society of America, 51,* 1951–1959.

Sergeant, D. (1969). Experimental investigation of absolute pitch. *Journal of Research in Music Education, 17,* 135–143.

Sherbon, J.W. (1975). The association of hearing acuity, diplacusis, and discrimination with musical performance. *Journal of Research in Music Education, 23,* 249–257.

Siegel, J.A., & Siegel, W. (1977). Categorical perception of tonal intervals: Musicians can't tell *sharp* from *flat. Perception and Psychophysics, 21,* 399–407.

Skrainar, S.F., Royster, L.H., Berger, E.H., & Pearson, R.G. (1985). Do personal radio headsets provide hearing protection? *Sound and Vibration, 19* (5), 16–19.

Smoorenburg, G.F. (1970). Pitch perception of two-frequency stimuli. *Journal of the Acoustical Society of America, 48,* 924–942.

Stephens, S.D.G., & Anderson, C.M.G. (1971). Experimental studies on the uncomfortable loudness level. *Journal of Speech and Hearing Research, 14,* 262–270.

Stevens, J.C., & Guirao, M. (1964). Individual loudness functions. *Journal of the Acoustical Society of America, 36,* 2210–2213.

Stevens, S.S. (1934a). Tonal density. *Journal of Experimental Psychology, 17,* 585–592.

Stevens, S.S. (1934b). The volume and intensity of tones. *American Journal of Psychology, 46,* 397–408.

Stevens, S.S. (1935). The relation of pitch to intensity. *Journal of the Acoustical Society of America, 6,* 150–154.

Stevens, S.S. (1956a). Calculation of the loudness of complex noise. *Journal of the Acoustical Society of America, 28,* 807–832.

Stevens, S.S. (1956b). The direct estimation of sensory magnitudes-loudness. *American Journal of Psychology, 69,* 1–25.

Stevens, S.S. (1966). Matching functions between loudness and ten other continua. *Perception and Psychophysics, 1,* 5–8.

Stevens, S.S. (1972). Perceived level of noise by Mark VII and decibels (E). *Journal of the Acoustical Society of America, 51,* 575–601.

Stevens, S.S. (1975). *Psychophysics.* New York: Wiley.

Stevens, S.S., & Warshofsky, F. (1965). *Sound and hearing.* New York: Time, Inc.

Stevens, S.S., Davis, H., & Lurie, M.H. (1935). The localization of pitch perception of the basilar membrane. *Journal of General Psychology, 13,* 297–315.

Stevens, S.S., Guirao, M., & Slawson, A.W. (1965). Loudness, a product of volume times density. *Journal of the Acoustical Society of America, 39,* 503–510.

Stevens, S.S., Volkman, J., & Newman, E.B. (1937). A scale for the measurement of the psychological magnitude pitch. *Journal of the Acoustical Society of America, 8,* 185–190.

Strange, A. (1972). *Electronic music.* Dubuque, IA: W.C. Brown.

Sweetman, R.H., & Dallos, P. (1969). Distribution pattern of cochlear combination tones. *Journal of the Acoustical Society of America, 45,* 58–71.

Terhardt, E. (1974a). Pitch, consonance, & harmony. *Journal of the Acoustical Society of America, 55,* 1061–1069.

Terhardt, E. (1974b). Pitch of pure tones: Its relation to intensity. In E. Zwicker & E. Terhardt (Eds.), *Facts and models in hearing* (pp. 353–360). New York: Springer-Verlag.

Terrace, H.S., & Stevens, S.S. (1962). The quantification of tonal volume. *American Journal of Psychology, 75,* 596–604.

Tobias, J.V. (1972). Curious binaural phenomena. In J.V. Tobias (Ed.), *Foundations of modern auditory theory* (vol. 2) (pp. 465–486). New York: Academic Press.

Van den Brink, G. (1974). Monotic and dichotic pitch matchings with complex sounds. In E. Zwicker & E. Terhardt (Eds.), *Facts and models in hearing* (pp. 170–188). New York: Springer-Verlag.

Van der Geer, J.P., Levelt, W.J.M., & Plomp, R. (1962). The connotation of musical consonance. *Acta Psychologica, 20,* 308–319.

Vogten, L.L.M. (1974). Pure-tone masking: A new result from a new method. In E. Zwicker & E. Terhardt (Eds.), *Facts and models in hearing* (pp. 142–155). New York: Springer-Verlag.

Von Bekesy, G. (1960). *Experiments in hearing.* New York: McGraw-Hill.

Von Bismarck, G. (1974a). Timbre of steady sounds: A factorial investigation of its verbal attributes. *Acustica, 30,* 146–149.

Von Bismarck, G. (1974b). Sharpness as an attribute of the timbre of steady sounds. *Acustica, 30,* 159–172.

Ward, W.D., & Burns, E.M. (1982). Absolute pitch. In D. Deutsch (Ed.), *The psychology of music* (pp. 431–452). New York: Academic Press.

Warren, R.M. (1970). Elimination of biases in loudness judgments for tones. *Journal of the Acoustical Society of America, 48,* 1397–1403.

Whitfield, I.C. (1967). *The auditory pathway.* London: Arnold.

Whittle, L.S., Collins, S.J., & Robinson, D.W. (1972). The audibility of low-frequency sounds. *Journal of Sound and Vibration, 21,* 431–448.

Winckel, F. (1967). *Music, sound and sensation* (T. Binkley, trans.). New York: Dover.

Woodworth, R.S., & Schlosberg, H. (1965). *Experimental psychology* (rev. ed.). New York: Holt, Rinehart, and Winston.

Yamamoto, T., Takagi, K., Shoji, H., & Yoneada, H. (1970). Critical band with respect to temporary threshold shift. *Journal of the Acoustical Society of America, 48,* 978–987.

Yilmaz, H. (1967). Perceptual invariance and the psychophysical law. *Perception and Psychophysics, 2,* 533–538.

Zwicker, E. (1974). On a psychophysical equivalent of tuning curves. In E. Zwicker & E. Terhardt (Ed.), *Facts and models in hearing* (pp. 132–140). New York: Springer-Verlag.

Zwicker, E., Flottorp, G., & Stevens, S.S. (1957). Critical band width in loudness summation. *Journal of the Acoustical Society of America, 29,* 548–557.

Zwislocki, J.J., & Goodman, D.A. (1980). Absolute scaling of sensory magnitudes: A validation. *Perception and Psychophysics, 28,* 28–38.

Chapter Four

RHYTHMIC FOUNDATIONS

The foundations of musical behavior examined in Chapter Four contrast somewhat with those foundations or perspectives of Chapters Two and Three. Chapter Two reflects the *social approach* to understanding musical behavior. It recognizes music as a sociocultural phenomenon, suggesting that musical behavior is much influenced by the social and cultural contexts in which it occurs. The Lundin (1967) and Farnsworth (1969) psychology of music texts tended to place primary focus on sociocultural determinants of musical behavior. Any attempt to understand or account for musical behavior without adequate recognition of social and cultural influences is, in the authors' opinion, incomplete and inadequate. *Musical behavior is socially and culturally dependent.*

Chapter Three focused on human response to tonal stimuli; the basic concern was to understand response to various attributes of a tonal stimulus as a result of human psychophysiological makeup. Sloboda (1985, p. 239) terms this approach the *biological approach* to music psychology, because it tends to stress the physiological variables that underlie human interaction with music. The learning mechanism and basic neurological pathways for processing tonal stimuli appear to be biologically determined and as such reflect inherent human limits for processing tonal stimuli.

Chapters Four and Five, with due recognition of musical behavior's dependence on sociocultural and biological influences, examine the contributions of *cognitive psychology* to the understanding of musical behavior. A superficial dichotomy may appear between the study of musical *behavior* and music *cognition,* but the authors, as do many other educators and psychologists, recognize that behavior and cognition are integrally related and mutually interdependent. Reasons for various educators, psychologists, and other writers appearing to focus either on *behavior* or *cognition* to the neglect of the other often are deep-rooted,

79

philosophical, complex, and perhaps irrelevant to the present discussion. Suffice it to say here that research from both perspectives has resulted in invaluable contributions to the understanding of musical behavior, and the authors have drawn on research from both perspectives. However, because of recent interest in music cognition (e.g., Deutsch, 1982; Dowling & Harwood, 1986; Hargreaves, 1986; Howell, Cross, & West, 1985; Sloboda, 1985; Taylor, 1981), Chapters Four and Five seek to explicate such contributions to the understanding of rhythmic, melodic, and harmonic foundations of musical behavior.

Why Study Rhythm?

Rhythm is an essential component of all musics, whether of primitive societies, traditional Western styles, or contemporary popular styles. Despite its musical importance, Cooper and Meyer (1960, p. v) note that the study of rhythm in performance "has been almost totally neglected in the formal training of musicians since the Renaissance."

This is not to suggest, however, that rhythm as a phenomenon has not been studied. To the contrary, it has been studied both intensively and extensively from many perspectives. Winick's (1974) annotated bibliography of rhythm in music includes nearly 500 sources. Innumerable definitions and explanations of rhythm and its various attributes have been offered. Theorists have examined music's rhythmic structure, and through their analyses have developed and/or theorized underlying organizational schema for Western music (e.g., Cooper & Meyer, 1960; Yeston, 1976; Lerdahl & Jackendoff, 1983). Philosophers have offered theories of rhythm. Psychologists also have developed theories to account for rhythmic response. In addition, they have studied rhythm both as a stimulus and response (Lundin, 1967) and in recent years have become increasingly concerned with examining the processes underlying the perception of rhythm. Other writers have been concerned with exploring developments in rhythm from the time of the ancient Greeks to the present, while still others have sought to examine musical rhythms in relation to rhythms in nature. A smaller group of writers has been concerned with notation systems. Persons concerned with influencing human behavior through music have recognized and studied rhythm's role in music used to modify nonmusical behaviors. Performing musicians, in addition to depending on rhythm to lend structure and hold performances together, use rhythm as one means of enhancing expression or creativity. Music teachers have examined rhythm from a pedagogical perspective.

In spite of such interest in rhythm, it has traditionally been less studied than melody and harmony. Dowling and Harwood (1986, p. 179) argue that the neglect of rhythm has been especially unfortunate for the psychology of music because "rhythmic information is, if anything, more fundamental to music cognition than pitch information." In recent years theorists, psychologists, and educators have devoted increasing efforts to understanding its role in music and how people interact with rhythm in music. However, approaches to the study of rhythm and rhythmic behavior are diverse, and persons concerned with understanding the psychological foundations of rhythmic behavior are faced with the perplexing problem of synthesizing a vast body of diverse literature into a conceptual framework that will provide a basis for dealing with rhythmic behavior. Such a framework necessarily requires an examination of (a) rhythm's function in music, (b) rhythmic structures in music, (c) perceptual processes underlying rhythmic behaviors, (d) the development of rhythmic behaviors, (e) teaching and learning rhythmic behaviors, (f) analyses of rhythmic performance, and (f) evaluation of rhythmic behaviors.

Functions of Rhythm in Music

"When the musics from all cultures of the world are considered, it is rhythm that stands out as most fundamental. *Rhythm is the organizer and the energizer.* Without rhythm, there would be no music whereas there is much music that has neither melody nor harmony" (Gaston, 1968, p. 17). Cooper and Meyer (1960, p. 1) also view rhythm as fundamental to music: "To study rhythm is to study all of music. Rhythm both organizes and is itself organized by all the elements which create and shape music processes." Mursell (1956, pp. 254–257), whose study and writings concerning rhythm spanned forty years, notes that rhythm (a) gives life, sparkle, reality, and expressiveness to musical performance, (b) adds immensely to the pleasure of listening, (c) greatly facilitates musical performance and music reading, and (d) is the best and most natural starting point for musical creation.

Benjamin (1984) recognizes three particular functions that musical meter serves in the perception of music. Meter's primary function is to provide a way for measuring time in terms of a specific work being heard. It also facilitates the perception of group structure by providing an underlying framework for the rhythm of the melodic phrase. Benjamin's third function of meter essentially is an aesthetic function. Music's metric hierarchy provides structural time-points which greatly expand the functional range of interplay between time and pitch.

Sloboda (1985, p. 188) also argues that rhythm provides an important organizational basis in music and maintains that rhythm and tonality are mutually interactive systems. He notes that "knowledge of the tonal structure can help determine the rhythmic structure, and *vice versa.*"

Clearly, rhythm's primary function in music is to give order. Music is a temporal art which must be organized in such a way that it is comprehensible. Rhythm, in its broadest sense, *"is everything pertaining to the temporal quality (duration) of the musical sound"* (Apel, 1944, p. 640). It is the organization of sound's durational attributes which indeed allows sound to become music. When comprehensible organization is lacking, the listener does not perceive the sound as music.

Gabrielsson (1982, pp. 159–163), however, maintains that rhythm in music involves more than the performed musical sound and proposes a general model for what is involved in musical rhythm. For Gabrielsson, musical rhythm involves *musical performance* which produces *sound sequences* which in turn may elicit psychological and physiological responses in the listeners. He notes that listeners' responses may be of three types: (a) *experiential,* including various perceptual, cognitive, and emotional variables, (b) *behavioral,* including more or less overt movements such as tapping the beat with one's foot, swaying of the body, or dancing, and (c) *physiological,* such as changes in breathing, heart rate, or muscular tension.

Rhythm provides the forward movement of music, thus making music a dynamic (in the sense of motion and change), energizing force. Music with little rhythmic movement elicits lower dynamic responses than music in which rhythmic movement is active. Rhythm gives "life" to music, and a "feel" or "sense" of rhythm as the dynamic force within music facilitates a person's interactions with music, both as a performer and a respondent.

Whether as a performer or respondent, an individual's interaction with rhythm in music can result in aesthetic experience (Sachs, 1953, p. 18). The increasing importance of rhythm as an aesthetic device is readily apparent when one compares its prominence and complexity in twentieth-century music with its role in renaissance, baroque, classical, and romantic music.

Most traditional definitions of rhythm allude in some way to rhythm as the organizational and dynamic force in music.* Even with a general agreement regarding rhythm's basic function in music, there is, as Creston (1964, p. v) notes, a need "to separate the chaff from the wheat." Discussions of rhythm and its attributes yield little consensus, but a clear understanding of the attributes of rhythm in music is essential to understanding the psychological foundations of rhythmic behavior. The next section examines the various attributes of rhythmic structure in music.

Rhythmic Structure in Music

Descriptions of the attributes of musical rhythm are many and varied. There is some commonality of terms employed in these descriptions, but common meanings are not always applied to the terms. Mursell (1937, p. 190), for example, recognizes two attributes of musical rhythm: (a) the underlying beat and (b) the phrase rhythm. Cooper and Meyer (1960, p. 3) recognize three basic modes of temporal organization: (a) pulse, (b) meter, and (c) rhythm. Gordon (1971, pp. 67–69), in a departure from traditional terminology, maintains that rhythm is comprised of three basic elements: (a) tempo beats, (b) meter beats, and (c) melodic rhythm. Relations resulting from combinations of these three basic elements comprise "rhythmic patterns" that "elicit musical meaning...in the mind of the listener" (Gordon, 1971, p. 69). Creston (1964, pp. 1–44), writing from a composer's vantage point and considering rhythm in terms of "the organization of duration in ordered movement," a view consistent with the authors' perceptions of the function of rhythm in music, identifies four basic aspects of rhythm: (a) meter, (b) pace, (c) accent, and (d) pattern. Creston views the terms *time* and *tempo* as somewhat indefinite and inaccurate and replaces them with *meter* and *pace* respectively. Most current writers also use meter in place of time, but substitution of pace for tempo is not so common. Tempo is still the prevalent term. *Accent* is used in the traditional sense (emphasizing a beat), while *pattern* refers to any subdivision of a pulse or beat into smaller units.

Benjamin (1984, p. 359), however, maintains that *accent* and *grouping*

---

*For discussions of various definitions of rhythm, see Creston, 1964; Behrens, 1984.

"are the basic, if not neatly separable, modes of partitioning musical time and that meter is a secondary construct, imposed on the interaction of group structure and accent in response to certain practical and aesthetic needs." Gabrielsson (1973), based on analysis of data from several experiments, recognizes the following properties of rhythm: (a) meter, (b) the level of accent on the first beat, (c) the type of "basic pattern," (d) the prominence of a basic pattern, and (e) the "uniformity-variation" or "simplicity-complexity" of a rhythm.

As may be apparent, the examination of rhythmic structure in music is somewhat confounded by the fact that discussions of structure, particularly recent ones such as those by Benjamin (1984), Lerdahl and Jackendoff (1983), Gabrielsson (1973;1982), Clynes and Walker (1982), and Dowling and Harwood (1986), necessarily reflect *perceived structure*, albeit in as objective a manner as possible. To varying degrees, such discussions treat rhythmic structure as a psychological phenomenon as well as an objective physical (acoustical) phenomenon. Consequently, discussions of structure reflect various writers' personal and research-based experiences with both the physical structure of notated and performed rhythm and the perception of rhythm, a psychological phenomenon. Recognizing that these limitations also apply to the present discussion, a somewhat traditional overview of rhythmic structure is included here for the reader who may be interested. Discussion of the perceptual bases of rhythm follows in a subsequent section of this chapter.

Pulse, commonly referred to as *beat*, underlies rhythm's structural components. The beat is the basic unit of duration and divides duration into equal segments. Lerdahl and Jackendoff (1983 p. 18) point out that beats do not have duration; rather beats are points on a duration continuum, and the durational intervals between the points are termed *time-spans*, which do have duration.

A problem arises in discussion of beat with respect to meter. Meter signatures specify which unit of notation receives a beat (i.e., fills the time-span from one beat to the next); in practice, however, the unit designated by a meter signature as receiving the beat is not always the same as the beat which is felt in response to the music (as in, for example, a 3/4 "Viennese" waltz or a 6/8 march at a customary march tempo). Mursell (1937, pp. 189–198) uses the German term *Takt* to indicate the felt beat; Farnsworth (1969, p. 233) refers to it as the *true beat*. For this discussion, the beat indicated by a meter signature will be referred to as the *metrical beat*, and the beat felt in response to music will be referred to as the *true beat.* Instances in which the true beat coincides with the metrical beat will simply be referred to as beat. Metrical beat will be used only when referring to a beat indicated by a meter signature that does not coincide with the true beat.

Meter involves the grouping of beats, usually metrical beats. Just as are beats, meter is periodic in that its function is "to mark off the musical flow, insofar as possible, into equal time-spans" (Lerdahl & Jackendoff, 1983, p. 19). Meter usually is considered in terms of notation and is commonly indicated by bar lines. The idea is that the first beat of each measure should receive an accent, thus delineating the meter. Obviously, music does not always conform mechanically to this pattern; departure from the norm allows music to be an expressive medium rather than confining it to being mechanical or arithmetical.

Most theories of meter recognize that there may be more than one level of meter operating within a musical work, but because meter involves grouping of beats this is more a matter of perception than structure and therefore will be discussed later under the discussion of meter perception. It is sufficient to note here, however, that when the tempo of music is quick, the effect on the listener often is to make the notated measure, rather than the metrical beat, the unit of the beat. These true beats are often grouped into several measures, thus creating the effect of a superimposed meter.

In other instances neither the metrical beat nor the measure are the same as the true beat; e.g., 6/8 meter in moderate or faster tempo is felt in twos, with the ♩ functioning as the unit of the true beat. Jaques-Dalcroze (1921, Musical Supplement, p. 1) suggested a plan whereby meter signatures would be more meaningful and which would avoid the confusion between the metrical beat and the true beat. The note that is to be the unit of the beat would be substituted for the lower number of the meter signature. (See Figure 4-1.)

Tempo, or *pace* as Creston terms it, refers to the speed at which beats recur. Tempo in music notation is indicated in general terms by use of the traditional Italian terms, including (from slowest to quickest) *grave, largo, adagio, lento, andante, moderato, allegro,* and *presto.* More precise tempo indications are given in terms of metronome markings which indicate the number of times a given note value or unit of time recurs in one minute. The note value indicated may coincide with either the metrical beat or the true beat. A typical metronome indication is ♩ = M.M.80. This means that the quarter note is the beat unit, and the beat

$$\frac{3}{4} = 3 \; \mid \; \frac{6}{8} = 2 \; \mid \; \frac{12}{8} = 4 \; \mid \; \frac{9}{8} = 3 \; \mid \; \frac{6}{4} = 6 \qquad \text{or} \qquad 3 \text{ or } 2$$

$$C = \frac{4}{4} \; \mid \; \mathtt{C}\!\!\!\mid \, = \frac{2}{2} \quad \text{etc.}$$

Figure 4-1. Jaques-Dalcroze's rationalized meter signatures. While Jaques-Dalcroze's suggestion has received some following in recent years, it is far from common practice, and musicians must continue to cope with distinguishing between the metrical beat and the true beat.

would recur at the rate of 80 per minute. (Maelzel constructed the metronome in 1816, and M.M. is a standard abbreviation for Maelzel Metronome.)

Accent is the aspect of rhythm which makes prominent or emphasizes a beat. Creston recognizes eight types of accents: dynamic, agogic, metric, harmonic, weight, pitch, pattern, and embellished. A *dynamic accent* emphasizes a beat by means of tone intensity; i.e., the tone is louder than others. An *agogic accent* emphasizes by means of duration, i.e., the tone is longer than those preceding or following it. A *metric accent* basically reflects the particular grouping of true beats or metrical beats and often is a dynamic accent. A *harmonic accent* emphasizes a beat by use of dissonance or harmonic change on the beat. A *weight accent* expresses emphasis through change in texture. A *pitch accent* denotes emphasis on the highest or lowest tone of a group. *Pattern accents* occur on the initial tone of a melodic figure that is repeated. *Embellished accents* emphasize a beat through the use of melodic embellishments, e.g., mordents, trills, or grupetti. Creston views accent as the "very life of rhythm" without which meter becomes monotonous, pace (his term for tempo) has no sense of motion, and pattern becomes a nebulous elaboration.

Lerdahl and Jackendoff (1983, pp. 30–35) and Benjamin (1984) also provide in-depth discussions of types and functions of accents. They focus more on the role and function of various accents in *grouping* durational events within the total musical structure. They are careful, however, to delineate between *metrical* accents, which reinforce grouping of beats, and other types of accents, which facilitate other groupings within the musical context as well as serving various other musical and aesthetic functions.

Beat, meter, tempo, and accent are the most agreed upon aspects of rhythmic structure. Phrase rhythm, melodic rhythm, rhythm pattern, or rhythm grouping are some names given to the rhythm of the melody and harmony parts that overlie and/or are entwined with beat, meter, tempo, and accent. These "overlying" aspects of rhythmic structure constitute an area in which it is quite difficult to separate discussion of physical structure from rhythm as a perceptual phenomenon. Whereas beat and meter essentially provide reference points in musical time, tempo refers to the speed at which beats recur, and accent provides a means for emphasizing a beat, phrase or melodic rhythm patterns may be grouped at various levels. Because grouping is a function of both the musical structure and the perceiver's experience, most of the discussion regarding it is under the section below on the perception of rhythm. However, some descriptions of the basic structural units of melodic rhythm are included here.

Mursell (1937, pp. 176–185) and Cooper and Meyer (1960, p. 6) recognize rhythmic groupings or units, derived from ancient Greek poetic meter, which involve grouping unaccented beats around an accented beat as the basic structural level for melodic rhythms. The five basic units include *iamb* (∪–), *anapest* (∪∪–) *trochee* (–∪), *dactyl* (–∪∪), and *amphibrach* (∪–∪); the dash indicates an accent. The theory is that these units underlie the melodic rhythms of music, but Yeston (1976, pp. 27–34) notes several problems in attempting to reduce rhythm to such basic units, particularly when laws of perception are considered. He maintains that attempts to analyze rhythm in these terms are overly reductive and not reflective of the realities of rhythmic variety.

Gordon (1971, pp. 67–71; 1976, pp. 31–58) and Creston (1964, pp. 34–43) view subdivisions of beats as the underlying structural units for melodic rhythms. Both Gordon and Creston agree that beats are subdivided into basically twos or threes. When the beat is divided into two equally spaced subdivisions (which he calls *meter beats*), Gordon labels this duple meter; when the beat is subdivided into three meter beats he labels it triple meter.* Creston refers to subdivisions as *patterns*, which may be classified as *regular* or *irregular* and *simple* or *compound*. Regular patterns reflect subdivisions suggested by meter signatures; irregular patterns are subdivisions not suggested by meter signatures. Repeated patterns are called simple patterns, and changing patterns are considered compound.

Hymeola?

---

*The reader should keep in mind that for Gordon, "duple" and "triple" meter are based on groupings of *subdivisions* of beats; conventional references to duple and triple meter are based on whether accented beats are grouped in twos or threes. More recently Gordon's terminology has been modified and the terms *macrobeats* and *microbeats* are used respectively in place of *tempo beats* (Gordon's term for a conventional beat) and *meter beats*.

Regardless of how one analyzes rhythm patterns, there is common agreement that melodic rhythms overlay and entwine themselves around the beat. Melodic rhythms may vary infinitely; they may be even, uneven, use subdivision of beats, or involve durational values extending over many beats. It is the very freedom of melodic rhythm that provides a primary means for making music a dynamic energizing force.

While melodic rhythm with its free organization in relation to the substructure of beat, accent, and meter provides both variety and unity for musical structure, it must be recognized that many additional extensions of rhythmic structure are used to provide even greater interest. The potentials of polyrhythms, multimeters, changing meters, changing tempi, and ametrical rhythms, in combination with the potential for rhythmic variety within conventional rhythmic structure, make rhythmic structure a truly dynamic, integral, and essential part of all music.

Perceptual Bases of Rhythmic Behavior

Until recent years efforts to understand the perceptual bases of rhythmic behavior have been more a matter of speculation and theory than research. Traditional psychology of music literature recognized three classes of theories intended to account for human interaction with musical rhythm: (a) instinctive, (b) physiological, and (c) motor. Lundin (1967, pp. 116–122) proposed a fourth theory, which emphasized the role of learning in the development of rhythmic behaviors. The instinctive theory, of which Seashore (1938) was a major proponent, held that "there are two fundamental factors in the perception of rhythm: an instinctive tendency to group impressions in hearing and a capacity for doing this with precision in time and stress" (p. 138). This theory reflects the position that rhythmic potential is an inherited trait, not a learned one. A number of studies, however, provide data suggesting that rhythmic potential, or capacity as Seashore preferred, can be improved with training, thus disconfirming the theory (e.g., Nielson, 1930, p. 78; Lundin, 1967, p. 114; Whitson, 1951, p. 56; Coffman, 1949, p. 74).

Physiological theories suggest that rhythmic responses depend upon recurring physiological processes. The idea that the human heart rate serves as a basis for rhythm and tempo in music has been the most prevalent view, of which Jaques-Dalcroze (1921, pp. 79–82) was an avid supporter. However, evidence to support the heart rate theory is entirely lacking. Mursell (1937, p. 155) criticizes the heart rate notion on the basis that there is no mechanism known to psychology by which the heart beat gives us our sense of time. Lund's (1939) classic study of the true beat in music also refutes the theory. Lund reported no significant relationships between college students' preferred tempi for selected popular songs and the rate of any of their objectively measured physiological processes. Recent research on tempo perception, which is discussed below, also offers little or no support for physiological theories. While the "natural" rhythms of human physiology, including the menstrual cycle and cyclic changes in body temperature, wakefulness, and biochemistry, may influence a person's *receptivity* to musical stimuli, they are too lengthy, complex, and variable to explain rhythmic responses to relatively short-term musical stimuli.

The motor theory holds that rhythm depends on the action of the voluntary muscles. Schoen (1940, p. 21) notes that nearly all investigations concerning the nature of rhythmic experience find a motor or muscular factor, thus lending support to motor theory advocates. Mursell (1937, p. 162) and Lundin (1967, p. 106) both recognize the motor theory as the most plausible of the traditional theories, but neither accepts it without reservation. Mursell argues that neuromuscular movement does not function in isolation from the human brain, but must function in conjunction with the brain and central nervous system which control voluntary movements. Lundin, although essentially an S–R psychologist, views rhythmic behavior as both a perceptual and behavioral response. The complex interactions between motor activity and cognition, as evident in all of psychology but particularly with respect to their relative influences on rhythmic behavior, will be examined below.

Lundin's (1967, pp. 106–113) account of rhythm response recognizes the importance of learning, which involves both perception and motor response. Perception of rhythm requires observation of rhythmic stimuli and may or may not involve overt behaviors. It involves both perceptual *organization* of rhythmic stimuli and *discrimination* among stimuli, and Lundin contends that the ability to organize and discriminate among rhythmic stimuli is dependent on learning. Hebb's (1949, pp. 22–37) classic discussion of the role of experience in perception lends strong support to Lundin's position. Lundin goes on to argue that overt motor rhythmic responses have a perceptual base and that the overt motor rhythmic responses reflect the *clarity* of an individual's perceptions. Anyone who has taught music recognizes that students' rhythmic behaviors can be modified. To say that rhythmic behaviors can be explained independently of learning, therefore, is to ignore the evidence.

In recent years there has been a growing body of research related to the psychological bases of rhythmic behavior. Much of the research has focused on perception of various aspects of rhythm. Although most rhythmic behavior involves interaction with music as a more or less holistic, integral part of musical behavior, the present discussion examines the research and related writings as they pertain to (a) the role of movement in the perception of rhythm, (b) tempo perception, (c) meter perception, and (d) perception of rhythm groups.

Movement and Perception

Tradition and conventional wisdom of music teachers tend to support the view that movement somehow interacts with and facilitates the perception and performance of rhythm, but Behrens (1984) questions the "long-assumed relationship between rhythm and movement." Whether the present discussion will clarify the issue is doubtful, but examination of certain general psychological theories that address the issue of mental/motor interactions may be helpful.

Piaget, who devoted a lifetime to epistemology, placed much importance upon early sensorimotor learning as the basis of intellectual development.*

> In his scheme of things, a sensorimotor intelligence, not perception, provides the foundation for later intellectual development (and, . . . it is the matrix from which and in which perception itself originates and evolves). (Flavell, 1963, p. 472)

The studies of early sensorimotor experiences of chimpanzees reported by Hebb (1958, p. 116) corroborate Piaget's view. Chimpanzees whose sensorimotor experiences were limited greatly during infancy were much slower at learning simple tasks than were other chimpanzees who had been allowed normal sensorimotor experiences during infancy.

Views that motor activity aids in thinking are not new. Indeed, the motor theory served as an impetus from which modern views concerning the effect of movement on thinking have evolved. The motor theory of thought was originally devised in order to avoid postulating ideation to explain thinking. Hebb (1958, p. 58) states:

---

*A discussion of Piaget's views regarding learning appears in Chapter Ten.

It proposed that, when a man is thinking, what is really going on is that he is talking to himself, or making movements with his hands and fingers that are too small to be seen. Each word or movement of the hand produces a feedback stimulation that produces the next one, in a chain reaction: instead of ideation, therefore, what we have is a series of S–R reactions. The theory is no longer entertained as a complete explanation ... but the conceptions which it developed concerning sensory feedback remain valid and important for the understanding of serial behavior.

Sensory feedback is usually of two kinds: exteroceptive and proprioceptive. Exteroceptive sensory cells are excited by events external to the body. Proprioceptive sensory cells are excited by *movements* of the body, and it is the proprioceptive feedback that is of particular relevance in understanding rhythmic behavior.

Proprioceptive feedback usually is equated with kinesthetic feedback. Feedback from movement is now called proprioception rather than kinesthesis, because the concept of kinesthesis generally is associated with introspection, whereas proprioception emphasizes receptor and sensory nerve action which can be determined neurophysiologically (Osgood, 1953, p. 29).

That proprioceptive pathways to the thalamus, cerebellum, and cortex exist is an established fact (Morgan, 1965, p. 258). There are three types of neural receptor cells for proprioceptive sensations: (a) "spray type" cells at different positions in the joints, (b) Golgi and organs, and (c) Pancenian corpuscles. These cells are actually in the joints rather than in the muscles.

Proprioceptive stimuli may travel to the cortex via either of two routes. The direct route is through the thalamus. The other, more diffuse and indirect, is through the reticular activating system. Morgan (1965, p. 41) reports that the various sensory inputs and outputs are not clearly separated in the reticular system.

Thus, neurophysiological findings support the contentions that sensory feedback from movement is related to higher mental processes. However, the precise role that proprioceptive impulses play in higher mediating processes is not known. It is, though, subject to much speculation.

Osgood (1953, p. 651) says "it may be that motor tone merely serves as a facilitative agent for mental activity in general." Hebb (1958, p. 69) maintains that thinking cannot be accounted for by central processes alone or by muscular feedback alone: Both mechanisms are involved.

At least two theories of perception have movement as one of their bases. These theories primarily are concerned with visual perception, but the principles involved also apply to perceptions through other sensory media.

Hebb maintains that eye movements are essential to visual perception. He does not, however, insist that perceptual integration is wholly the result of such motor activity. Eye movements "contribute, constantly and essentially, to perceptual integration, even though they are not the whole origin of it" (Hebb, 1949, p. 37).

The sensory-tonic field theory of perception postulates that both proprioceptive and exteroceptive feedback are essential to perceptual integration (Allport, 1955, pp. 183–207). This theory holds that it can be shown experimentally that sensory, i.e., exteroceptive, and tonic, i.e., proprioceptive, factors are equivalent with respect to their contributions to the dynamic outcome.

Perhaps the following statement best summarizes the status of the motor versus mental controversy:

> Actually the interrelation of motor and mental activity is one of cyclic and reciprocal interdependence. However, the nature of the problem and current trends in thinking make it necessary at this time to emphasize particularly the dependence of the mental upon motor activity. (Sperry, 1964, p. 429)

In the last decades of the nineteenth century and the early decades of this century, the perception of rhythm was investigated frequently. Introspective analysis was the accepted experimental technique of the times; thus, when evaluating the findings concerning the value of movement (or kinesthesis as it was called) as an aid in the perception of rhythm, this factor must be taken into consideration.

Boring (1942, p. 586) reports that all investigators during this time discovered that auditory rhythms tend to be accompanied by kinesthetic accentuation. Bolton, McDougall, Stetson, Miner, and Kofka were prominent among investigators reporting such findings.

Ruckmick (1913, pp. 305–359) attempted to answer once and for all the question concerning the role of kinesthesis in the perception of rhythm. In his much quoted study, he presented subjects with both auditory and visual rhythm patterns. The subjects were to give their impressions of the groupings verbally. His conclusions were that (a) the perception of rhythm may take place without accompanying kinesthesis, (b) there are individual differences in the amount of kinesthesis involved in the perception of rhythm, and (c) generally kinesthesis is connected most prominently with the initial clear perception of the type and form of rhythm.

In 1945 (p. 84), Ruckmick explained that the last conclusion meant that "kinaesthesis was essential for the establishment of a rhythm pattern" (Ruckmick, 1945, p. 84). It was only after a rhythm pattern had been established that kinesthesis ceased to be necessary for the perception of a rhythm.

From his review of Ruckmick's and other early studies concerning rhythmic perception, Boring (1942, p. 587) concluded that many perceptions are grouped by concomitant kinesthesis and many are not. "Kinesthesis is not a *sine qua non* of rhythm."

Moog's (1979) comparison of rhythmic discrimination of physically handicapped, mentally handicapped, and normal children supports the contention that movement facilitates perception. He notes that both children who had limitations of movement due to physical handicaps and children of lower intelligence scored significantly lower than normal children on an investigator-constructed measure of rhythmic discrimination. He concludes that children with limitations of movement since early childhood do not develop their rhythmic perception skills to the same extent as normal children.

Because perception, as cognition, is essentially a covert process, investigators of perception generally study perception in terms of some overt manifestation of perception.[*] As Rainbow (1977, p. 56) notes, perception in music historically has been measured by asking subjects to *perform* a given task. Studies of rhythmic perception have asked subjects to demonstrate perception by reproducing a pattern through clapping or in the case of perception of beat or meter by stepping or marching in time to music. Rainbow suggests, however, that vocally chanting rhythms might be a more appropriate measure of rhythmic perception, particularly for young children.

Thackray's (1968) investigation of rhythmic abilities sought to clarify the distinction between rhythmic perception and rhythmic performance and to investigate the extent to which the two are related. A factor analysis of the correlation coefficients among his seven rhythmic percep-

---

[*]For a particular examination of the relationship between covert conceptual or perceptual activity and overt instrumental (movement) or symbolic (verbal) musical behaviors, the reader should consult Woodruff (1970, pp. 51–54) and Regelski (1975, pp. 11–15).

tion subtests revealed a fundamental factor in rhythmic perception: *The ability to perceive and memorize a rhythmic structure as a whole, and to analyze it consciously* (Thackray, 1968, p. 15). Thackray's rhythmic perception test battery essentially involved *discrimination tasks,* and the responses required were symbolic, i.e. verbal, rather than instrumental, i.e., movement. Thackray concluded that there are three essentials for rhythmic perception: (a) ability to count, (b) time discrimination, and (c) loudness discrimination.

Thackray also devised a five-part rhythmic performance test which required subjects to reproduce rhythmic patterns through movements. He found a "positive but not especially high" (.65) correlation between subjects' score on the rhythmic perception and rhythmic performance tests. A factor analysis of the combined batteries revealed a substantial factor of general rhythmic ability running through the tests. His results suggest that this general rhythmic factor is measured appreciably better by the performance test than by the perception test. The best individual measure is the reproduction of the rhythm of a melody.

Thackray's (1968, p. 45) general conclusion regarding the relationship between rhythmic perception and rhythmic performance is stated thusly:

> Although rhythmic ability is complex, there is a common factor running through all the forms of rhythmic activity which we have considered, which might be defined as the ability to perceive rhythmic structures in respect to the three elements of timing, duration and intensity, and to perform rhythmic movements in which these qualities are clearly defined.

Researchers' use of terminology has not always been consistent with Thackray's distinction between perceptual behaviors and performance behaviors, but there appears to be consensus that movement and rhythmic perception are integrally related. Gabrielsson (1973; 1982) and Fraisse (1982), apparently in an effort to avoid such a dichotomy, suggest that it might be more appropriate to speak of rhythmic *experience* rather than rhythmic perception. Fraisse states that "it is necessary not to dissociate motor *behaviors* linked to rhythms from . . . perceptions" and that "the play of music is always based on movements" (p. 175). He goes on to note that because of the motor component rhythmic perception is in effect "plurisensorial."

Tempo Perception

Beats and meter provide the underlying structure upon which rhythm patterns are superimposed. Perception of tempo, the rate at which beats recur in music, is important, because beats divide time into a series of reference points around which listeners and performers organize their rhythmic responses and performances. Dowling and Harwood (1986, p. 186) maintain that beats serve as "cognitive frameworks" for perception of rhythm. If listeners and performers cannot perceive the rate at which the beats are recurring, their perceptions (and behaviors) related to rhythmic patterns may be impaired.

Fraisse (1982, p. 149) also argues that rhythmic perception depends on tempo, "because the organization of succession into perceptible patterns is largely determined by the [Gestalt psychology] law of proximity." If a tempo becomes too slow, the forms of both rhythm and melody become difficult for a listener to discern. When a performer is unable to feel (i.e., perceive) the tempo of a piece, the rhythm patterns being performed become disjointed from the overall temporal structure. In short, it appears that rhythmic response and performance are seriously deficient for individuals who are unable to perceive an underlying tempo.

Sink's (1984) analysis of the psychological dimensions underlying the auditory processing of monotonic and melodic rhythmic patterns supports the contention that tempo perception is basic to rhythmic processing. Her analysis of data from 38 university music students' rhythmic dissimilarity judgments revealed that duration and tempo were the underlying dimensions of rhythmic processing.

Perhaps because of the increased cognizance of tempo's importance to the rhythmic experience in music, research on tempo perception has increased in recent years. Kuhn (1974) observed that professional musicians could identify decreases in the tempo of beats produced by a metronome more easily and more quickly than increases in tempo. Subsequent studies by Geringer and Madsen (1984) and Wang (1984), which examined tempo perception in a musical context, yielded results that were consistent with Kuhn's finding that tempo decreases were easier to perceive than tempo increases. A surprising sidelight of both of these studies was that there were no significant differences in the responses of music majors and nonmusic majors.

Wapnick (1980) examined the perception of tempo change in terms of subjects' *magnitude estimations* of tempo deviation from given standards. He observed that 48 undergraduate music students' responses were systematically affected by the standard/repetition speed ratio. He observed an apparent propensity to estimate repetitions as either twice or half as fast as the standard.

Duke (1987) asked college music majors to tap the perceived beat of periodic monotonic stimuli presented at various speeds ranging from 40 to 200 tones per minute. His results revealed that rates above 120 beats per minute were apparently "too fast" to be perceived as beat notes; rates slower than 60 beats per minute appeared "too slow" to be perceived as beat notes. In response to stimuli presented at faster than 120 or slower than 60, subjects tended to tap rates that were half or double the rates of the respective stimulus tones. Duke concluded that there is a relatively narrow tempo range within which periodic stimulus tones are perceived as beats by trained musicians.

Several studies have examined the effects of selected variables on tempo perception and preference. Kuhn (1977) observed that, contrary to conventional wisdom, dynamic level during performance had no effect on the tempo of 20 university students' performance of a well known Beethoven melody. However, subjects did tend to perform both the second half of the melody and the second performance of it faster than the tempo established for the initial performance, leading Kuhn to conclude that there is a tendency for musicians to increase tempo during solo performance of easy-to-perform melodies.

Wang (1980) examined the effects of rhythm pattern, texture, beat location of tempo change, and direction of tempo change on the amount of time college students need to perceive tempo change. Besides the result noted above that tempo decrease is easier to perceive than tempo increase, she observed that significantly more time was needed to perceive tempo change for uneven rhythms than for even rhythms and for melody alone than for melody with accompaniment. Her data also suggest that differential rhythmic groupings may influence tempo perception.

Wang and Salzburg (1984) examined the influence of music training and age on 116 string students' ability to perceive tempo change. Subjects were asked to identify the direction of tempo change or whether there was no change. Their data revealed a statistically significant curvilinear relationship between tempo perception and music training and between tempo perception and age. Subsequent regression analysis indicated that musical style, initial tempo, and direction of change also contributed significantly to tempo perception, leading the investigators to conclude that tempo perception is a complex phenomenon for which all parameters have yet to be identified.

Killian (1985) sought to determine college music majors' (a) tempo performance accuracy across repeated trials under differing feedback conditions, (b) tempo perception accuracy after performing and hearing a recording of the performance, and (c) the relationship between verbal perception and tempo performance. The three feedback conditions included performance results only, performance plus a prerecorded metronome standard before the next trial, and control. Data revealed no statistically significant effects of condition on tempo performance, but significant results were observed for subjects' perceptions of accuracy. Subjects receiving feedback improved accuracy of tempo perception. The relationship between performance and perception accuracy was analyzed by examining frequency of agreements between performance and perception, and overall there was a low percentage of agreement between performance and perception scores (32.5%).

To summarize, tempo perception is basic to rhythmic processing. The perception of regular recurring beats provides a cognitive framework for rhythmic perception and performance. However, perceptual accuracy does not guarantee performance accuracy. Tempo perception and performance are complex phenomena and are influenced by, or at least related to, a number of stimulus and perceptual variables.

Trained musicians appear to have a propensity for perceiving periodic rhythmic stimuli in terms of a limited range of tempi. Duke's study regarding the propensity to double or halve rates of periodic stimuli so that they fall within the 60 to 120 beats per minute range needs replication. Such grouping of beats may be more a matter of meter perception than tempo perception.

Meter Perception

Musicians, educators, and psychologists generally agree that meter perception involves grouping beats, usually in relation to an accented beat. In traditional Western music, meter is periodic, and while some may argue that the measured grouping of beats provides a rigidity leading to metronomic, unmusical performance and response, Benjamin (1984) makes an eloquent case for just the opposite view. He argues that metric structure, especially when considered at multiple levels, in larger units, and in greater depth, "is at times supple and, far from being anti-musical, at all times enriches the musical experience by giving the listener a measured grip on the time in which music's events happen."

As noted in the discussion of rhythmic structure, notation creates some problems relative to meter perception in that beats and meter indicated by notation may not conform to the beats and meter perceived or "felt" by listeners. Creston (1964, p. 3) suggests that tempo is a primary variable in determining whether a perceived or felt grouping of beats conforms to a notated grouping, i.e., the grouping indicated by the meter signature.

Jones (1985) notes that, while various definitions and accounts of meter frequently fail to distinguish clearly between notation and perception of meter, perhaps a more important concern is in the contradictions regarding how metric patterns are perceived or subjectively organized. To provide at least a partial resolution to some of the contradictions, he conducted a dialectic analysis of five theories or approaches to defining meter. Theories examined include what he termed a traditional music theory definition and those offered by Cooper and Meyer (1960), Yeston (1976), Gordon (1971; 1980), and Serafine (1975). The traditional music theory definition tends to focus on groupings of beats in terms of notated measures, and as discussed above, there frequently are inherent differences between what is notated and what is perceived.

Cooper and Meyer (1960) and Yeston (1976) both recognize that metrical groupings may occur at more than one level. Cooper and Meyer emphasize "architectonic" levels of meter and suggest that meter usually is present at three levels. Their "primary level" of meter is the level on which beats are felt and counted. Subdivisions of the primary level are considered lower level meter; units of the primary level meter may be combined to form higher level meter. Jones views their theory as an elaboration and extension of the traditional definition. He criticizes the theory for not considering tempo's influence on the selection of levels. Also, the theory appears to focus on visual perception and analysis to the neglect of aural perception and analysis.

Yeston's theory recognizes that meter is periodic and depends on at least two rates of rhythmic motion that interact relative to each other. The fastest level, termed the *foreground,* is grouped by the slower motion, termed the *background.* Any intermediary levels are called *middlegrounds.* Yeston's complex system of analysis allows melody and harmony to play a major role in determining which level of meter is considered dominant. Jones notes that this allowance for pitch relationships to influence how meter is determined is a unique contribution of Yeston's theory. However, the system is essentially an analytic tool and as such offers only limited insight into the aural perception of meter.

Gordon's theory, aspects of which were outlined under the discussion of rhythmic structure, places primary emphasis on subdivisions of the traditional beat. The subdivisions, which are called *meter beats (micro beats)*, are the primary basis for his hierarchy of meter and rhythm. The hierarchy, which is theoretically rather than empirically-based, has two main categories, *usual* and *unusual;* classifications into the categories depend on various groupings of *tempo beats (macro beats)* and *meter beats.* The system has value for those who follow Gordon's particular instructional system and are willing to disregard traditional terminology and concepts of meter. Many musicians, however, are unwilling to think of duple and triple meter primarily in terms of subdivisions of the basic beat that is felt or perceived. Jones (1985) and Brink (1983) criticize the theory from several other perspectives: its theoretical rather than empirical basis, its failure to accommodate adequately higher levels of metric groupings, and some inconsistencies of the theory with musical practice.

Serafine (1975, p. 32) defines meter as essentially the equivalent of beat, apparently in an effort to avoid any cultural bias as reflected in the proclivity of traditional Western music to be grouped in two's or three's. Jones (1985) argues that there is little value in such a theory for conceptualizing metric music and maintains that equating pulse with meter adds unnecessary semantic confusion to the research literature.

Jones's synthesis of his analysis of the theories is that there is general agreement that "metric grouping" occurs at the level of the basic beat, as well as at levels of subdivision and multiples of that beat" (p. 54). He notes virtually unanimous agreement about the frequent inconsistency of meter signatures with meter and rhythm perception and performance. He suggests that the relationship between tempo and meter perception should be explored.

Madsen, Duke, and Geringer (1986) examined 100 musicians' note preferences for excerpts of eight relatively familiar orchestra works in which dotted notes, which ordinarily are subdivided into three, were presented at original tempi and at tempi either 12 percent faster or slower. Excerpts were purposely ambiguous with whether they "could be felt, perceived, or conducted in either a 'slower one' or a 'faster three'" (p. 103). Generally, when tempi were faster, subjects tended to select the dotted note as the unit of the beat, and when tempi were slower, they tended to select the subdivision of the dotted note as the unit of the beat, suggesting that tempo is a primary variable in determining the units of the beat and metric groupings.

Boyle's (1987) exploratory investigation of meter perception also supports the contention that tempo is a primary variable in musician's categorizations of melodies into different meters. Twenty college musicians were asked, without more specific instructions, to classify 20 unfamiliar melodies into metric groupings of two's, three's, or four's. Tempi for beat notes ranged from 70 to 200 beats per minute. Although the computer generated melodies were constructed with no accents, they were designed to reflect idiomatic rhythm patterns in duple and triple meter and included only duplet and triplet subdivisions of the beat. Subjects clearly categorized meter into two's, three's, and four's according to the intended beat note rather than in terms of duplet or triplet subdivisions. Furthermore, at faster tempi, melodies designed to reflect 4/4 meter tended to be categorized in two's rather than four's.

Data from both the Madsen, Duke, and Geringer study and the Boyle study raise questions regarding the tempo at which musicians begin to group periodic stimuli at higher levels. While neither theory nor research has yet provided definitive answers to the meter perception dilemma, it appears that tempo is a basic structural variable in determining the level at which periodic stimuli are grouped. Perhaps even more important variables, which have been little explored by psychologists, are those related to the musical experience and training of the perceiver.

Rhythm Groups

While grouping of periodic stimuli such as beats into meter and lower levels of meter into higher levels appears to be primarily dependent on tempo, grouping of nonperiodic musical duration events into rhythm patterns appears to be influenced by many other variables, some of which relate to the musical structure and others of which relate to the listener's experiences. As Davies (1978, p. 197) puts it, rhythm groups "are properties of people, as well as of musical sounds." While the musical stimuli may be grouped objectively in a given way, they are never really grouped until perceived as such, because groupings are ultimately a psychological phenomenon.

Sloboda (1985, pp. 28–30) maintains that perceptions of durational patterns are *categorical*; i.e., experienced listeners tend to perceive aurally presented rhythm patterns (as well as pitch patterns, which will be discussed in Chapter Five) into *categories* consistent with previously experienced rhythmic (and pitch) groupings. He draws an analogy to the manner in which people, apparently universally, perceive basic speech sound classes called "phonemes" in categories. Although the sounds of a given phoneme may vary slightly from one time it is heard to the next, they are perceived as the same and are functionally equivalent.

To support this view, Sloboda cites data indicating that accurate perception of slight deviation from musical rhythms is quite difficult and notes that performers are rarely able to *exactly* imitate another's performance (p. 30). He also cites data provided by Sternberg, Knoll, and Zukofsky (1982) showing that highly trained professional musicians were unable to reproduce nonstandard divisions of a beat accurately, although they were very accurate in reproducing traditional subdivisions of a beat. He goes on to suggest that while training will enable musicians to discriminate subtle rhythmic differences, most people do not experience them as such; they perceive the rhythms in terms of previously experienced categories and most likely subconsciously experience the subtle rhythm differences as differences in the quality or style of performance.

Lerdahl and Jackendoff (1983, p. 13) note the importance of rhythmic grouping by stating that once a listener "has construed a grouping structure for a piece, he has gone a long way toward 'making sense' of the piece." They go on to argue that grouping is the "most basic component of musical understanding."

Rhythm groups, just as metrical groups, are hierarchical in that given "surface structures" or patterns are subsumible into larger "deep" structures based on combinations of durational structures, as well as melodic, harmonic, textural, and extramusical information. (There are some similarities between this line of reasoning and the seminal work of Chomsky (1957, 1965, 1968) regarding deep structures in language and Schenker's (1935/79) theoretical system for conceiving musical structures as outgrowths of an underlying musical core or *Urtext.*) Sloboda's (1985) text is both an introduction to and a detailed treatment of the cognitive organization of music on the basis of abstracted structures.

Many attempts to model hierarchical perceptual structuring of music exist; West, Howell, and Cross (1985) provide an excellent review. No model yet appears completely adequate either from a practical or theoretical standpoint. West, Howell, and Cross (pp. 45–48) make five general observations and offer three specific principles for developing models of perceived structure. Their observations and principles are reviewed here because they provide an overview of what such models are trying to accomplish and demonstrate their relevance to perception and cognitive organization of music.

Their first observation is that anything in the music that can be perceived should be able to influence perceptual groupings. Neither pitch nor rhythm alone determines grouping and hierarchical organization; different sorts of musical information may conflict and interact. Second, listeners bring prior experiences to the musical encounter. Whatever organizational components emerge for listeners must be in terms of scales, idioms, rhythms, and other aspects that have meaning for the listeners. Thirdly, not all music will immediately be perceived, organized, and classified in a detailed, well-ordered hierarchy, even by sophisticated listeners. The distinctive features of a composition may change with repeated listening. West, Howell, and Cross's fourth observation is that the organizational structure resulting from applying a model to a particular piece should be verifiable in terms of the behavior of particular listeners. Particular structural preferences should be predictable. Finally, extramusical or historical context may influence structural grouping, as when lyrics demand linguistically sensible phrasing or when instrumental characteristics restrict possible performance options.

Their first specific principle is that models must account for both vertical and horizontal structures, because music often involves a string of concurrent events across time. Good continuation, proximity, similarity, regularity, symmetry, and common fate, grouping principles encompassed by Gestalt psychology, could be a significant part of a model. Grouping is suggested at various sounds' locations, repetitions, and sequential movements. Lastly, groups formed from Gestalt principles may form larger groups at higher hierarchical levels. "Dominant" events within a group, such as accents, dynamics, or prominent pitches, may subsume other events and be "dominant" or be subsumed by other events in a higher-order group. A lengthy sequence of sounds may be just one grouping at the highest level, while more and more subgroupings exist at increasingly lower hierarchical levels.

One of the most elaborate models, inspired in part by psycholinguistics and grammar, is that of Lerdahl and Jackendoff (1983). They propose four hierarchical components (rather like conceptual skeletons) in the structure of a musical composition. Essentially, the components differ in their organizational bases. Two components, *metrical structure* and *grouping structure,* are concerned primarily with durational structure, whereas the other two components, *time-span reduction* and *prolongational reduction,* focus on pitch structures. Of relevance to the present discussion, *grouping structure* suggests that the continuous stream of musical events is segmented, from three- or four-event (note) motives into phrases and into larger sections. Certain "rules" of the Lerdahl and Jackendoff theory, *well-formedness rules*, which specify possible structures, and *preference rules*, which designate the probable structures that are likely to conform to the way experienced listeners organize the music, govern grouping structures. The preference rules specify principles that appear to govern the establishment of group boundaries and include (a) principles of proximity and change, (b) a principle of parallelism, which states that musical segments construed as parallel should hold equivalent level in the grouping structure, and (c) a principle of symmetry, which suggests preferred subdivisions and groupings of segments into two parts of equal length. In essence, Lerdahl and Jackendoff's rules recognize that both nondurational aspects of musical structure, such as attack, articulation, dynamics, and registration, and more global considerations, such as symmetry and motivic, thematic, rhythmic, and harmonic parallelism, may influence grouping structure (Lerdahl and Jackendoff, pp. 43–55).

Barela (1979) recognizes three elements of a rhythm group: upbeat or anacrusis, accent, and afterbeat. Lerdahl and Jackendoff prefer the term anacrusis over upbeat and define it broadly to include the "span from the beginning of a group to the strongest beat of a group" (p. 30). An accent, often termed a structural accent because it results from some nonmetrical event such as pitch, dynamics, or texture, reflects the focal point of a rhythm group to which the events of the anacrusis point. Following the accent are the afterbeats of the rhythm group, which Lerdahl and Jackendoff prefer to call the extension of the group.

Empirical testing of theories of rhythmic grouping such as that offered by Lerdahl and Jackendoff is virtually nonexistent, and if the recent interest in cognitive theories of musical processing are to gain and maintain credibility, they must be validated empirically. Although the bulk of the research on cognitive processing is music has been concerned with melodic rather than rhythmic processing, a limited amount of research concerning perception of rhythm groups has been conducted, and studies providing data relevant to some of the variables underlying rhythmic grouping are examined here.

Povel and Essen (1985) examined university psychology students' perception and reproduction of temporal patterns in a nonmusical context. They sought to validate a theory of cognitive processing in which it is assumed that listeners attempt to generate an "internal clock" to facilitate accurate perceptions of given patterns. They maintain that the selection of the internal clock is based primarily on the distribution of accents perceived in the pattern, although it also might be influenced by another concurrent pattern or by the perseveration of a clock induced through previously presented patterns. The investigators maintained that when no internal clock was induced, a temporal pattern was poorly reproduced or judged as complex.

The temporal order in which sounds occur may be overridden in perceptual organization of rhythm patterns. *Auditory stream segregation,* in which auditory input is organized into two simultaneous patterns on the basis of common elements rather than strict temporal order, and rhythmic or melodic *fission,* in which alternating tones form two separate melodic rhythms, are interesting cases of rhythm perception which are not uncommon in music.

When Bregman and Campbell (1971) presented a short cycle of six tones (three high and three low) at a rapid rate, their subjects invariably divided the sequences into two streams on the basis of frequency. The patterns actually perceived were only those which related elements in the same subjective stream. The perceptual split depended on the frequency difference and presentation rate; faster presentation rates required less difference between high and low tones in order to induce the streaming effect.

Auditory stream segregation on the basis of frequency differences is more likely when the tones are short and discrete. Frequency glides between the tones and longer tones result in a continuity which makes the temporal order easier to follow and discourages stream splitting (Bregman & Dannenbring, 1973).

Rhythmic fission was illustrated by Dowling (1968), who presented tone sequences, at about ten tones per second, which were constructed so that frequency difference between *successive* tones was *large* while the difference between *alternate* tones was *small.* Melody was detected among alternating tones of the same intensity and frequency range, especially when observers were directed in their listening. The rhythmic fission was intensified by intensity differences or stereophonic separation between the patterns.

In a later study, Dowling (1973) showed that two familiar melodies formed by alternating successive tones ("interleaved" melodies) are easily identified as the result of melodic fission when the two melodies' frequency ranges do not overlap. When frequency ranges do overlap, the task is more difficult, although listeners can track a familiar melody if it is prespecified, i.e., they know the melody in advance. All melodies were altered to a rhythm of alternating quarter notes and quarter rests, and the combined tonal sequences ("interleaved" melodies) were presented at a rate of eight tones per second.

The organization of auditory streams is context dependent; e.g., widely separated frequencies may be in one stream if other stimulus elements are noises. Two organizational principles, one of element similarily and one of temporal proximity, may conflict. Basically, auditory streams appear to form in such a manner that elements within a stream are maximally similar (McNally & Handel, 1977).

Whether rhythm patterns are more easily perceived in isolation or in a total musical context has been subject to much speculation and a limited amount of research. Individuals vary in their claims regarding which presentation mode is easier, and research apparently is inconclusive. Sink's (1983) summary of research on the effect of context yields no clear-cut conclusion regarding the effects of context. Petzold (1966) reported no significant differences in children's ability to perform rhythm patterns presented in melodic or monotonic contexts, but Gabrielsson (1973) and Moog (1979) both reported data suggesting that melodic information interfered with the processing of rhythmic information. Boisen (1981), however, reported no statistically significant effects of melodic context on 2,207 seventh, ninth, and eleventh graders' perceptual judgments of rhythmic completeness or incompleteness, while Schellenberg and Moore (1986) reported that memory for rhythm patterns by 57 music majors and 57 nonmusic majors was significantly better when patterns were presented in a melodic context.

Obviously, data could vary for many reasons, but it appears that the matter of context is not a simple one. In an effort to examine the issue systematically, Sink (1983) studied the effects of rhythmic and melodic alterations on rhythm dissimilarity judgments of university music students. The melodic alterations included monotony, M-shaped melodies, and V-shaped melodies; nine rhythmic alterations were used. Her results indicated that both melodic and rhythmic alterations affect dissimilarity judgments.

To gain further information regarding rhythmic judgments, Sink (1984) investigated the psychological dimensions underlying the auditory processing of monotonic melodic-rhythmic patterns and the influences of selected musical experiences on the dimensionality of 38 university music students' rhythmic processing. Rhythm was recognized as a multidimensional structure within music's broader multi-dimensional structure. Dimensions identified as possible organizers of rhythmic information in music included tempo, meter, rhythmic patterning, and melodic patterning. Subjects' experiential variables examined included ensemble experience, listening habits, and musical preferences.

Sink's data suggest that tempo, duration and pitch characteristics, melodic and rhythmic phrase patterning, and monotony are organizers of rhythmic processing. Major performing instrument and classification of major performing instrument also significantly affect the dimensionality. Analyses of variance data revealed a slight effect of "generic style" music listening preference, music course experience, and hours of music listening. Sink concluded that "the importance of each organizer for subjects depended in part on the objective ordering of rhythmic and tonal information, and in part on past music experiences, particularly instrumental training" (p. 190).

An earlier multidimensional analysis of the dimensionality of rhythmic patterning by Gabrielsson (1973) also revealed that tempo was a primary dimension in similarity and dissimilarity ratings. His analysis also suggested that density of patterns, which he labeled "rapidity," was another underlying dimension for the processing of melodic-rhythmic patterns.

To summarize, the perception of rhythm groups in music is both categorical and hierarchical. There are three basic components of a rhythm group: an anacrusis, a structural accent, and its extension. Theory suggests that certain perceptual laws, including Gestalt laws, operate in rhythmic processing. Multidimensional analyses and other research suggest that the extent to which rhythm groups are perceived as groups is a function of both the musical structure, particularly tempo but including all of its interacting rhythmic, melodic, harmonic, dynamic, textural, and articulation events, and the experience of the listener. Theories such as that offered by Lerdahl and Jackendoff attempt to encompass the effects of such structural and experiential variables, but systematic, empirical validation of such theories is lacking, perhaps because isolating the effects of the myriad of variables that underlie how a listener groups rhythm patterns is a difficult and complex process.

Development of Rhythmic Behaviors

Rhythmic behaviors include a broad spectrum of behaviors, ranging from simply tapping the toe in time with the beat to sightreading intricate rhythms. The development of rhythmic behaviors has been the subject of much speculation, research, and trial and error. This section examines research findings and music teachers' views regarding the development of rhythmic behaviors. In addition, it reviews approaches to measuring rhythmic behaviors.

Research on the development of rhythmic behaviors basically is developmental or experimental. Developmental research can be either longitudinal or cross-sectional. Longitudinal studies investigate one group's rhythmic abilities (or whatever trait one wishes to study) over an extended period of time, whereas cross-sectional studies compare a trait in different groups at various age or developmental levels. Although longitudinal studies usually are the preferred methodology, nearly all studies of the development of rhythmic behaviors are cross-sectional. Few involve the study of a given group for more than one year.

Developmental Research

Although there are some exceptions, nearly all developmental research regarding rhythmic behaviors examines one of the following two behaviors: (a) the ability to keep time with the beat of music and (b) the ability to repeat a given rhythm pattern. The variables in the different studies are numerous, thus making it difficult to understand clearly the status of rhythmic behaviors at different age or developmental levels. Some studies examine rhythmic behaviors in isolation from any melodic behaviors, while others examine rhythmic behaviors in conjunction with behaviors related to pitch organization.

Studies of infants' rhythmic development, however, necessarily involve a research strategy different from the types just mentioned. The investigator must observe the infants' rhythmic behaviors, either freely emitted or in response to rhythmic stimuli.

Several studies (Demany, McKenzie, & Vurpillot, 1977; Chang & Trehub, 1977; Allen, Walker, Symends, & Marcell, 1977) indicate that infants respond to differences in rhythm patterns. Infants apparently tend to habituate to a recurring pattern, but when a change occurs, they respond. One study used eye movement as a measure of response to change; the other two used heart rate as a measure of change.

Moog (1976, pp. 39–40) observed that between the ages of four and six months is the stage at which infants begin to respond to music with overt movement. He noted that the infants do not move in disorganized clumsy ways; rather, they use clear repetitive movements which are related to the rhythmic aspects of the musical stimulus. As the child develops, the movements increasingly are coordinated with both the musical rhythm and dynamics. The movements of the four- to six-month-old infant often involve movements with the whole body, but as the child develops the movement responses to rhythm also change, particularly to include more movements with individual body parts. Moog reports that by the age of eighteen months about 10 percent of children are able, for short stretches of time, to match their movements to the rhythm of the music.

Sloboda (1985, p. 200), however, questions whether infants during the first year of life are actually able to demonstrate overt rhythmic behaviors. He particularly questions some of Moog's results and suggests that much of what is considered rhythmic behavior reflects a high degree of inference on the part of the adult observer. He argues that observers should look for some indication of rhythmic intention before interpreting infants' movements as rhythmic. Before he would accept infant movement as rhythmic behaviors he would expect it to clearly reflect one or more of the following: (a) moving or beating in time to music, (b) imitating a given rhythm pattern, (c) subdividing a beat, or (d) omitting a beat and then resuming it in correct time after a pause (pp. 200–201).

Studies of rhythmic behavior in early childhood, childhood, and into adolescence show a general refinement in rhythmic skills with increasing age. Jersild and Bienstock (1935) examined two- to five-year-old children's ability to beat time to music. Seventy-four children's responses were analyzed, and a large increase in scores was evident between two and five year olds. Of 400 possible beats (administered in smaller segments), the number of correct beats for the two year olds was 84.5, three year olds, 109.4, four year olds, 159.9, and five year olds 192.8.

Rosenbusch and Gardner (1968, pp. 1271–1276) studied five to thirteen year olds' abilities to reproduce four different rhythm patterns. Responses were compared for four age groups: five to seven, seven to nine, nine to eleven, and eleven to thirteen. Results showed a significant decrease in errors with increase in age.

Gardner (1971, pp. 335–360) studied first, third, and sixth graders' abilities to reproduce given rhythm patterns. Each child was asked to duplicate twenty rhythm patterns which included from four to eight taps each. The mean numbers of correctly tapped patterns for the three groups were 7.35, 13.00, and 16.00, respectively. These differences were statistically significant at the .01 level.

Petzold (1966, pp. 184–251) conducted a one-year pilot study of elementary school children's rhythmic abilities. Children were asked to reproduce common rhythm patterns found most frequently in seven elementary basal music series published between 1953 and 1959. Patterns were about two measures in length and were in three common meters: 2/4, 3/4, and 6/8.

In addition, children were asked to respond to a "Periodic Beat Test," which involved a series of beats at four different tempi. Each beat was presented twice and arranged so that the respondent moved from a fast tempo through three successively slower tempi; the order was reversed for the second part of the test. Usable data were obtained for 331 children on the "Rhythmic Patterns Test" and for 241 on the "Periodic Beat Test." Petzold summarized his results with respect to differences in grade level responses:

> The ability to respond accurately to the aural presentation of rhythmic patterns does not change substantially after the child has attained third grade. The same plateau is reached by third grade when children are expected to maintain a steady tempo that is provided by a metronome.

Taylor's (1973, pp. 44–49) study of the musical development of children aged seven to eleven also revealed increases in rhythmic responsiveness for younger children and a lack of increase with age for the older children in his study. He reports statistically significant differences between the mean rhythm scores of the younger age groups but no significant difference between the means of his two oldest age groups.

Igaga and Versey (1977, pp. 23–27) employed a rhythmic perception test devised by Thackray (1968) to study the rhythmic behaviors of 655 Ugandan and 573 English school children aged between ten and fifteen years. The test battery allowed for administration in groups and included six types of responses to recorded stimuli: (a) counting the number of notes in an item, (b) after being given a tempo, counting the number of beats in a period of silence, (c) matching a given pattern with one of four series of long and short dashes (an elementary aural-visual test), (d) marking in a row of dots the pattern of strong and weak beats heard, (e) comparing rhythm patterns (same or different), and (f) counting the number of notes in a melodic phrase. Although no tests of statistical significance were applied to data between the groups or age levels, means were reported for each cultural group and age level. The mean scores for the Ugandan children increased with each age level between ten and fifteen, although some of these increases would appear negligible. The mean scores for the English school children, while higher at the first four age levels than those for the Ugandan children, showed increases only between ages eleven and twelve and twelve and thirteen. Mean scores for the fourteen- and fifteen-year-old English children were lower than those for the comparable Ugandan children. Although some subtests showed considerable increase with age, the data as presented are inconclusive regarding cross-cultural comparative increases in rhythmic abilities of children.

An examination of norms for children on some standardized rhythm aptitude tests provides another perspective on the development of rhythmic behaviors with age. Bentley (1966b, p. 116) reports a "fairly steady increase from year to year" on the rhythm memory portion of his *Measures of Musical Abilities* (1966a). The normative data for some 2,000 boys and girls aged seven through fourteen support his statement. There is a mean yearly increase from 3.9 for seven year olds to 8.8 for fourteen year olds. Normative data for the *Seashore Measures of Musical Talents* (1939,1960) and Gordon's *Musical Aptitude Profile* (1965) also reflect increases in score with age level, even though both tests purport to measure factors that are little influenced by training.

A series of studies by Pflederer and Sechrest (1968, pp. 19–36) testing Piaget's theories of conservation* tend to support the position that rhythmic behaviors (meter and rhythm) are a function of development. Foley (1975), however, reports data suggesting that conservation can be expedited through training.

Bamberger (1982), who was primarily concerned with how children conceptualized a rhythm pattern, asked children ranging from four to ten years of age to draw a picture of a familiar nursery rhyme so that they could remember it or another child could clap it. The youngest children (four and five) tried to duplicate the clapping motion, resulting in swirling scribbles. The six and seven year olds tended to draw figural representations of individualized claps, whereas the oldest children tended to group the claps in a metric fashion. The effect of learning was apparent in the oldest children's responses, but an important finding was how the young children tended to make the drawings as near like the clapping behavior as possible; they were not able to deal with the patterns as abstractions.

---

*Conservation refers to the invariance of a particular dimension of empirical objects even though change occurs in other dimensions. Piaget partially views concept development in terms of conservation, which is nothing more than the stabilizing of a particular concept in the child's thinking (Zimmerman, 1971, pp. 16–17). More material on conservation appears in Chapter Ten.

Grieshaber's (1987) critical review of research on children's rhythmic tapping also supports the view that rhythmic behaviors improve with age, but she notes many methodological problems in the research and observes that there are inherent problems in using tapping tasks as measures of rhythmic behavior for young children, because they lack the coordination to perform anything beyond the simplest tapping task.

In studying the development of rhythmic behaviors, it is apparent that developmental research does not provide any clear-cut answers. The issues are confounded by variables in research design and type of rhythmic behaviors studied, not to mention the validity and reliability of the various measures of rhythmic behavior. At best, it may be concluded that rhythmic behaviors generally increase with age, although there tends to be a leveling of abilities in older children. To accept unquestioningly, however, that increases in rhythmic abilities are solely a function of age or developmental level is to disregard both the body of research concerning the development of rhythmic behaviors through experimental learning experiences and the empirical knowledge of music teachers who "know" that rhythmic behaviors can be improved through instruction. The next section examines the research literature regarding the development of rhythmic behaviors through learning experiences.

Experimental Research

Most of the research discussed herein is "experimental" because it seeks to examine the effects of some learning experience on the development of rhythmic behaviors. Much of it, however, lacks the rigorous control of the variables that would enable it to meet contemporary standards for research design in the behavioral sciences as delineated by Campbell and Stanley (1963), and therefore interpretations must be made with great caution.

The scope and variety of experimental research regarding the development of rhythmic behaviors also make it difficult to reach definitive conclusions. While some studies are concerned with behaviors reflecting discriminations among rhythmic stimuli, many others involve complex motor behaviors. Some investigators study the development of rhythmic behaviors in young children whereas others are concerned with older children, adolescents, or adults.

Jersild and Bienstock (1935) studied the effects of practice on young children's ability to keep time with music. Fourteen subjects, ranging in age from twenty-five to forty-four months, participated in a training program distributed over a ten-week period. The training program used a variety of means to direct their attention to the act of keeping time; these included bodily movements, vocalizations, and hand clapping. Although the fourteen children receiving practice obtained a mean score higher than a matched control group, the difference was not statistically significant. Neither were their posttest scores significantly higher than their pretest scores.

Coffman (1949), however, in a study of the effects of training on junior high and college students' scores on the Seashore rhythm discrimination test, found that trained subjects made statistically significant gains in rhythm discrimination scores while control group subjects did not. The training program involved a variety of rhythmic activities, including eurhythmics.

Dittemore (1970) examined the effects of a one-week rote teaching program of chanting and clapping melodic rhythm patterns on first through sixth graders' ability to chant melodic rhythm patterns. For two of the four criterion exercises, there were no significant differences among the six grade levels; for the two exercises involving more complex patterns, however, statistically significant differences were observed. Because of the study's nature, it is difficult to draw definitive conclusions regarding either the effects of the training or abilities at the different grade levels.

DeYarmin (1972) compared the effects of training in singing songs in usual, mixed, and unusual meters with the effects of training in singing songs only in usual meter on kindergarten and first-grade children's ability to chant melodic rhythm patterns. As in the Dittemore study, children were taught the songs by rote, and chanting and clapping were part of the learning activities. Five minutes of five successive music classes were used for instruction for each song; a sixth music period was used for recording each child's chanting of the song's melodic rhythm. Results showed no significant differences in the scores of children receiving instruction with songs in usual meters and the scores of children receiving instruction with songs in usual, mixed, and unusual meters. DeYarmin concluded that music programs for young children should include more songs in mixed and unusual meters.

Zimmerman's (1971) recognition that Piaget's developmental sequence applies to the development of musical behaviors has led to some research testing the hypothesis that conservation is a function of developmental level and cannot be influenced by training. Research by Foley (1975) and

Perney (1976), however, suggests that training can facilitate conservation in certain musical tasks.

Foley's study dealt with the improvement of conservation in two areas: (a) conservation of tonal patterns under the deformation of rhythm patterns and (b) conservation of rhythm patterns under the deformation of tonal patterns. Six intact second-grade classes were subjects, three classes randomly designated as experimental, the others as control. The experimental training used a variety of musical activities to foster the development of conservation. The experimental group made a statistically significant increase in their scores on the test for conservation of tonal and rhythm patterns; the increase was significantly greater than that of the control group. The investigator concluded that improvements in the conservation of tonal and rhythm patterns can be accelerated through training. Further, the training program was believed to have much practical significance in that expenses, equipment needs, and training required of teachers were quite minimal.

Perney (1976) examined the relation of musical training, verbal ability, and the combination of sex and grade on second and third graders' development of conservation of metric time. Results indicated no difference in performance of children who played musical instruments and those who did not. The mean performance of the second graders was higher, though not significantly higher, than that of the third graders. The most important finding, however, was that the second graders had greater verbal ability than the third graders, and there was a statistically significant correlation between children's verbal ability and their ability to perform the musical tasks. Perney concluded that performance of the musical tasks is not determined by age alone; rather it is more closely related to verbal ability.

Although there is a clear need for more research before definite conclusions can be drawn regarding whether rhythmic development is a function of age or development or whether it can be fostered through training, there is sufficient reason to question the hypothesis that rhythmic development is solely a function of age.

Groves (1969) studied the effects of rhythmic training on first, second, and third graders' ability to synchronize body movements with rhythmic stimuli. The study also examined the effects of home musical background, motor ability, sex, and personal social adjustment. The experimental group received two thirty-minute lessons of basic rhythm patterns each week for twenty-four weeks. However, no significant difference was found in the ability to synchronize body movements with rhythmic stimuli between children who had and those who had not received rhythmic training. The study further shows the need for more research in order to gain a clearer understanding of the relationship between developmental factors and training on the development of rhythmic behaviors.

Reading rhythms also is an important rhythmic behavior, and the balance of the research discussed in this section focuses on ways of developing such behaviors.

Palmer (1976) compared the approaches to rhythm reading advocated by Richards (1967) and Gordon (1971). Subjects were 136 fourth-grade children, forty-eight in the two Richards experimental classes, fifty in the two Gordon experimental classes, and thirty-eight in two control group classes. In addition to an investigator-constructed measure of rhythmic performance achievement, written achievement was measured via the rhythm portions of three standardized music achievement tests. Results showed a statistically significant difference between the control and aggregated experimental classes in terms of rhythm reading achievement. However, no clear-cut differences were found between the achievement of the classes using the Richards approach and the classes using the Gordon approach.

The tachistoscope was employed in two studies concerned with the reading of rhythm notation. In a study using freshman music theory students as subjects, Christ (1953) devised a series of exercises which were flashed on a screen to be tapped, *en masse,* by the eleven students of his experimental group who had been randomly selected from a class of twenty-nine. The remaining eighteen students served as a control group. After ten hours of training, spread over a seven-and-one-half-week period, both experimental and control groups were tested on an individual rhythm performance test in which the task was to tap the notated rhythm pattern. Scores of the experimental group were significantly higher (.002) than the scores of the control group.

Wiley (1962) sought to determine the relative effectiveness of the tachistoscope and conventional techniques in developing the ability of fifth-grade students to sight read rhythms. He exposed two groups of fifth-grade students to the same material. One group used conventional methods of learning while the other incorporated tachistoscopic drill. The criterion measure was a specially constructed performance test. Both groups made significant gains in their scores during the training period, but scores of students in the experimental group were not statistically superior to scores of students in the control group. He concluded that tachistoscopic techniques are not superior to conventional techniques in developing rhythm sight-reading ability at the fifth-grade level.

Two approaches to teaching instrumental music reading to beginners were compared by Skornicka (1958). The experimental approach emphasized time and rhythm by requiring the playing of quarter notes at the beginning of training (rather than the traditional whole notes), tapping the foot to mark the beat, and counting time mentally. The control group used conventional band method books and no bodily movements. At the conclusion of the study, the experimental group achieved significantly higher sight-reading scores on the *Watkins-Farnum Performance Scale* than did the control group.

In a study designed to examine the effects of bodily movement, notably foot tapping the beat and clapping the melodic rhythm, on junior high school band musicians' ability to sight read rhythms both in isolation and in context with other aspects of notation, Boyle (1968) observed that subjects using movement made significantly (.01) greater increases in both rhythm reading scores and music reading scores than did subjects who did not employ movement while reading rhythms. Results were based on individual performance tests given to 191 subjects representing a proportional random sample of the students in twenty-four junior high school training bands. The *Watkins-Farnum Performance Scale* was the measure of music reading ability and the rhythm patterns of it, notated on a single pitch, served as the measure of rhythm reading ability. A high degree of relationship ($r = .81$) was found between the subjects' scores on the two measures.

Elliott's (1982) multiple regression analysis of factors influencing university music students' instrumental sightreading supports the contention that rhythm reading is an important component of general music reading. Of seven predictor variables examined (technical proficiency, rhythm reading ability, sight singing ability, cumulative grade point average, grade point average, and major instrument grade point average), Elliott concluded that "rhythm-reading ability is the single best predictor of instrumentalists' sight-reading scores" (p. 13).

Research employing principles of programmed instruction as the experimental variable in teaching rhythm reading also has been conducted. An important aspect of this approach is providing the subjects with feedback regarding their performance. Ihrke (1969), the first to report research of this nature, developed a rhythm monitor which accepted tape recorded impulses and triggered an "error" light unless responses were properly timed. He compared the performances of university students in a course called "Music for the Classroom Teacher" who used the monitor with the performance of students who did not use it. Students using the rhythm monitor made significantly greater gains (.001) in their scores on a rhythm reading test than did students who did not use the system.

Shrader (1970) also developed a program for teaching rhythm reading. He utilized a stereotape teaching machine, with one channel activating a counter which indicated the number of correct responses made on a given exercise. He administered ten forty-five minute lessons to thirty-four high school students. Results showed that students using the teaching machine made significantly greater gains in rhythm reading scores than did a control group. Shrader's teaching machine is now available commercially (TAP MASTER RHYTHMIC SIGHT READING SYSTEM) and appears to be receiving acceptance as an important teaching tool.

Placek (1974) employed computer-assisted instruction as a means for providing learning feedback in a series of rhythm lessons. While the study was essentially a feasibility study and did not provide any comparative data regarding the effectiveness of the lessons, the investigator reported that the system did function as a teaching device for basic rhythm notation and that such teaching systems for rhythm should be developed and utilized in the future.

The studies cited above represent the diverse experimental research related to teaching and learning rhythmic concepts and behaviors. As should be apparent, they reflect diverse purposes, hypotheses, samples, independent and dependent variables, and some contradictory results. As Sink (1983) contends, teaching and learning of rhythmic concepts and behaviors are complex and controversial tasks. Clearly, a need exists for well-defined, systematic research on teaching and learning rhythmic concepts and behaviors. The following examination of teaching practices for rhythmic development further reflects the diversity of opinion and approach.

Teaching Practices for Rhythmic Development

Practitioners' views regarding ways to develop rhythmic behaviors are generally the result of trial and error techniques; once approaches are found "successful," however, they are passed from teacher to student, and many have now become tradition. Most appear to work for their proponents, although, as Horner (1965, pp. 140–141) has noted and as the above review also suggests, there is little or no experimental evidence to provide a basis for comparison of the various methods. They are summarized here to provide the reader with an overview of teaching practices.

Jackson (1963) summarizes devices and techniques commonly used in rhythm training. They are (a) counting aloud, (b) tapping the underlying beat, (c) the metronome, (d) tapping or clapping the phrase rhythm, (e) use of words, (f) ensemble experience, and (g) conducting.

The advantage of counting aloud is that it clearly outlines the beat. Its danger, she contends, is that it emphasizes the beat's mathematical rather than rhythmic aspects. Tapping the underlying beat has two advantages over counting: (a) it involves more extensive muscular action and (b) it does not emphasize arithmetic.

The metronome is valuable for setting the tempo and preventing tempo vacillation. Because it is an entirely external criterion, its usefulness is limited. Certainly, the use of such a device while reading music with varying tempi is impractical.

Tapping or clapping the phrase rhythm and the use of words as a system of mnemonics are both helpful techniques in the learning of phrase rhythms. Conducting aids in making students aware of the underlying beat.

Ensemble experience is one method of making students conform to the underlying beat. However, Revelli (1955) maintains that ensemble experience has been a staff for students to lean upon, and that their ability to read suffers from the lack of a systematic procedure for analyzing the various rhythm patterns.

Basic to most of the rhythm teaching devices mentioned above is muscular involvement. That rhythm is best approached through bodily movement has indeed become the byword of the elementary school music program. Few references to elementary school music fail to support this view.

Jaques-Dalcroze (1921) was one of the first to explore the possibilities of bodily movement as an aid in developing a sense of rhythm. In his system, which is generally referred to as the Dalcroze Eurhythmics, students learned specific movements to different rhythm patterns. After the movements were learned, the students were to realize, i.e., express by movements of the body, the rhythms of the music. Much stress was placed upon the ability to improvise rhythmic movements to music.

An especially pertinent aspect of the Jaques-Dalcroze (1915, p. 33) method is the use of separate limbs of the body to mark the underlying beat and the phrase rhythms. Coordinated movements to music constitute the essence of the system.

The use of rhythmic syllables also has received much emphasis in recent years, perhaps because of the emphasis on the application of the various adaptations of the Kodaly approach (Richards, 1967; Bachman, 1969; Lewis, 1972). Each of these approaches makes extensive use of rhythmic syllables as aids in developing elementary aged children's rhythm reading skills.

Gordon (1971, pp. 72–75) also is an advocate of rhythm syllables in developing rhythm reading readiness as a prerequisite to rhythm reading, but he also recognizes that the development of rhythmic understanding has its basis in the feeling of rhythm patterns through movement.

In his final publication regarding teaching rhythm, Mursell (1956, pp. 265–278) summarized three essential approaches to the development of rhythmic behaviors. He believed the first and most essential approach to rhythm is by way of bodily movement. Secondly, he believed that rhythm instruments are extremely valuable tools. Their value is that they tend to sharpen rhythmic behaviors by requiring more precise, more definite, and more discriminating responses. Finally, he believed that the study of rhythm symbols allows children a new, deeper, more generalized understanding of rhythmic experience. Because of Mursell's extensive work in the psychology of teaching music, his recommendations should not be taken lightly.

Hood's (1970) publication on the teaching of rhythm essentially reflects the types of activities advocated by Mursell. Moving to music, study of rhythm notation, and the use of rhythm instruments are used as approaches for teaching rhythm.

Teachers of instrumental music tend to focus on teaching rhythm reading. Magnell's (1968) summary of systems for reading rhythm at sight essentially parallels Jackson's. He does, however, elaborate on some approaches. He views foot tapping as basic to counting, chanting, clapping, and conducting. He also advocates the "down-up" principle as a means for organizing rhythm patterns in relation to the beat. Another principle he notes is that of the "time unit." The eighth note is usually the time unit maintained throughout the piece being counted. The student must mark the beat with hand movement (it could be with the foot) and count the number of time units in each note. Many other teachers also advocate the use of foot tapping, e.g., Hoover, 1968; D'Angelo, 1968; Pizer, 1969; Kohut, 1973, pp. 19–23; Hoffer, 1973, p. 377.

In summary, there are commonalities among the approaches to rhythmic development advocated by practitioners. Most teachers advocate more than one approach. The relative merits of the respective approaches, however, have not all been verified under controlled conditions. Perhaps the most important issue is, as Palmer (1976) has noted, that teachers at least employ some systematic approach to rhythmic development rather than leaving it to incidental learning as part of a total curriculum.

Evaluation of Rhythmic Behaviors

Evaluations of rhythmic behaviors generally involve one of three types of behavior: (a) behaviors reflecting discriminations between aurally presented stimuli, (b) movement behaviors demonstrating an ability to keep time with the beat or to reproduce an aurally presented rhythm pattern, and (c) behaviors reflecting an ability to discriminate between or associate visual rhythm symbols with aurally presented rhythm patterns. The last category includes all music reading behaviors, although it could be argued that reproduction of rhythm patterns from notated rhythm patterns constitutes a fourth type of behavior. In addition, there are several rhythm tests that require behaviors which at best are only peripherally related to the three basic types of behaviors. This discussion, however, will be limited primarily to the rhythm tests employing aspects of the three basic types of behaviors.

Several issues are involved in the evaluation of rhythmic behaviors. One noted previously in this chapter was whether *reproduction* of patterns or steady beats is a legitimate indication of rhythmic perception. Research has provided no clear-cut answers regarding the question, although it probably is prudent for teachers to recognize that failure to reproduce or perform a pattern does not necessarily indicate failure to perceive the pattern. Researchers and test designers usually select the response mode on some philosophical basis or else they follow precedents in test design.

In selecting or developing a test of rhythmic perception or ability, the primary concern is to select a response modality which best demonstrates what one is concerned with measuring. Pilot testing should always be done to ascertain the test's validity and reliability, as well as its appropriateness for the group being tested. If the concern is for measuring discrimination, the response mode should not require movements that may introduce problems for some respondents. If the concern is for aural-visual discrimination, musical performance should not be involved, but if the concern is for reading music, performance most likely should be involved.

Andrews and Deihl (1967) found that several response modes might be necessary for gaining a clear understanding of children's musical abilities. Their *Battery of Musical Concept Measures,* which unfortunately is not generally available, employed two written group measures (verbal and listening) and two nonwritten individual measures (manipulative and overt).

Rainbow (1981) noted an issue in the evaluation of preschool children's rhythmic abilities. Traditionally, investigators have made inferences regarding young children's rhythmic perceptions on the basis of their movements, e.g. tapping, clapping, or marching. Rainbow's data, however, suggest that vocal chanting is a much better response mode than movement tasks, because three- and four-year-old children in his three-year longitudinal study had much more difficulty reproducing patterns through movement than through vocal chanting. Schleuter and Schleuter (1985) made similar observations for kindergarten and first-grade children's rhythmic responses. Grieshaber's (1987) review of the literature on children's rhythmic tapping yielded the same conclusion.

The question of group versus individual measurement is of practical significance to both researchers and music teachers. While individual testing may be desirable, it is often prohibitive in terms of time and cost. Group measures often must serve as a compromise, although certain performance situations necessarily cannot be so assessed.

The issue of whether to evaluate rhythmic behaviors in isolation from a total music context has concerned music psychologists since testing became of interest. Seashore's (1938) view, reflecting what has been termed the "theory of specifics" approach, was that given traits or abilities should be isolated for evaluation under highly controlled conditions. Mursell's (1937) view, termed the "omnibus" approach, reflected the view that musical behavior should be evaluated as a totality rather than breaking it into subparts. Most contemporary approaches to evaluating rhythmic behaviors attempt to incorporate at least some rhythmic behavior in a total music context, although many measures also include some breakdown of rhythmic behaviors. Older tests usually reflect one or more approaches, depending on the purpose for which the evaluation is made. The purpose of the evaluation and the nature of the data sought should determine the nature of the evaluation approach used.

Several particularly interesting approaches to evaluating rhythmic behaviors have come about as a result of technological developments, including computer analyses of performance, e.g., Shrader, 1970; Petzold, 1966; Ihrke, 1969; Thackray, 1968; Bengtsson & Gabrielsson, 1980, 1983. Such technological advances have greatly facilitated precision in analysis of rhythmic behaviors, but, as Grieshaber (1987) has noted, such developments pose their own types of problems. Most computer or other electronic analysis programs do not have the flexibility to allow for variability in performance. While it is beyond the scope of this discussion to examine the various approaches, the sophisticated computer analysis system developed by Bengtsson and Gabrielsson warrants special mention.

Their RHYTHMSYVARD computer program was designed to assess performers' systematic variation from a mechanical norm, i.e., how a notated pattern would be performed in a precise metronomic way. It enabled them to determine the extent to which musicians' performances varied from the mechanical norm. Not surprisingly, their data revealed that professional musicians systematically vary their performances from that which is notated, often changing the ratios between the durations of notes to a considerable degree. For example, the durational ratio between a half note and a quarter note is theoretically 2:1, but they observed that musicians tend to perform such patterns at ratios between 1.7:1 and 1.8:1.

Following is a brief overview of the approaches to assessing rhythmic behaviors in published standardized tests. Most tests are designed for children above the age of eight, adolescents, and adults, although two recently developed tests are designed primarily for young children.

Test Four of Bentley's (1966a) *Measures of Musical Abilities* is a ten-item rhythm test that requires subjects to indicate on which of four beats a second rhythm pattern differs from a first. The rhythm test is an aural discrimination task and is designed for children aged seven to eleven. Although normative data are available for the rhythm test, reliability and validity data are available only for the four tests as a whole.

The *Seashore Measures of Musical Talents* (Seashore, Lewis, & Saetveit, 1939, 1960) include two tests related to rhythm, both of which are aural discrimination tasks. The "rhythm test" presents two tapped rhythm patterns and asks the respondent to indicate whether they are the *same* or *different;* the other, called the "time test," presents two tones and asks the respondent to indicate whether the second is of *longer* or *shorter* duration than the first. Although Mursell and other proponents of the omnibus theory question whether these are valid measures of musical talent, there seems little question that they are valid measures of the two particular discrimination tasks. Reliability coefficients for the tests range from .63 to .72.

The "rhythm test" of the *Drake Musical Aptitude Tests* (Drake, 1957), really a measure of the ability to silently maintain a given tempo, has two nonequivalent forms. Reliabilities range from .83 to .95 for form A and .69 to .96 for form B. Validity coefficients, based on comparisons with teachers' ratings of rhythm aptitude, range from .31 to .85.

Gordon's (1965) *Musical Aptitude Profile* includes a "rhythm imagery" test as one of its three basic parts. This test has two subtests, each of which requires respondents to discriminate between two hearings of a musical example performed on a violin. The tempo test requires an indication of whether the ending of a second presentation of a melody has the same tempo as the ending of the first or whether it was changed. The meter test asks whether a second statement of a melody is like the first or whether it differs from it with respect to *accents* which determine the meter. Split-halves reliabilities for the subtests range from .66 to .85; for the "rhythm imagery" portion as a whole they range from .82 to .91. Validity coefficients, based on teachers' estimates of musical talent, range from .64 to .74.

The *Iowa Tests of Music Literacy* (Gordon, 1970) include two divisions, "Tonal Concepts" and "Rhythmic Concepts." Each division has three subtests, (a) "aural perception," (b) "reading recognition," and (c) "notational understanding." The subtests of the Rhythmic Concepts division require the following types of responses:

Aural Perception: differentiation between rhythmic patterns in which beats are subdivided into duplets and triplets.

Reading Recognition: determining whether given aural patterns match given notated patterns.

Notational Understanding: filling in noteheads, flags, and rests to make a notated pattern match an aurally presented pattern.

Reliability coefficients for the subtests generally range from about .70 to .80. The author maintains that the test has rational and content validity. Concurrent validity coefficients, based on comparisons with sight singing and dictation scores, range from .44 to .52 for the Rhythmic Concepts division. The tests have six levels and provide normative data for grades four through twelve.

More recently, Gordon has developed two additional music aptitude tests for use with children: The *Primary Measures of Music Audiation* (1979) and the *Intermediate Measures of Music Audiation* (1982). The primary measures are for children in kindergarten through grade three and the intermediate measures are for children in grades one through four. Each test has a tonal and a rhythm portion, and the tasks are essentially the same on both portions of both tests. On the rhythm portion, the child must indicate whether the second of two short rhythm patterns is the same as or different from the first pattern. The reliability coefficients are satisfactory for both measures, ranging from .60 to .92 for the various grade levels.

Colwell's (1969–1970) *Music Achievement Tests* provide measures of rhythm behaviors in a musical context. A "meter discrimination" subtest asks respondents to indicate whether a musical example moves in two's or three's, i.e., is it in duple or triple meter. An "auditory-visual discrimination" subtest asks respondents to indicate measures in which the rhythm of notated melodies differ from the rhythm presented aurally. The test-retest reliability coefficient for the rhythm items is .80. The tests are claimed to possess content validity in that they reflect the objectives of several basal music series.

Several measures of aural-visual discrimination also include rhythm as part of a total test, but most do not include separate scores for the rhythmic portions, e.g., Knuth, 1966; Farnum, 1953. Rhythm also is one of the criteria for scoring the *Watkins-Farnum Performance Scale* (1954), but neither does it provide a separate rhythm score.

Finally, Thackray's (1968) *Tests of Rhythmic Perception* and *Tests of Rhythmic Performance*, discussed previously, should be mentioned here, particularly since they represent a major effort toward gaining greater understanding of rhythmic abilities. However, to the authors' knowledge, the tests are not yet standardized or commercially available.

Researchers and teachers concerned with selecting or developing measures of rhythmic behaviors should first and foremost consider the nature of the rhythmic task they wish to evaluate and be certain that any measure selected or developed indeed measures that task in a manner appropriate for the level of student being evaluated.

Summary

The major points of this chapter include the following:

1. Rhythm provides structure to music and serves as its dynamic, energizing force.
2. Rhythmic structure in music has several basic aspects: (a) tempo, (b) beat, (c) meter, and (d) melodic or phrase pattern.
3. Traditional theories regarding human response to rhythm are of four basic types: (a) instinctive, (b) physiological, (c) motor, and (d) learning.
4. Initial development of rhythmic behaviors is inextricably related to movement.
5. Perceptual research related to rhythm may be categorized as it relates to perception of (a) tempo of beats, (b) meter, and (c) rhythm groups.
6. Although developmental research is inconclusive, rhythmic behaviors generally increase with age for younger children but level out for older children.
7. The development of rhythmic behaviors can be expedited through training.
8. Although the development of rhythm reading skills is a major concern to both researchers and teachers, neither research nor practice yields any consensus regarding a "best" way to facilitate rhythm reading.
9. Evaluation of rhythmic behaviors usually involves assessment of one of three basic types of behavior: (a) behaviors requiring discriminations between aurally presented stimuli, (b) movement behaviors demonstrating an ability to keep time with the beat or to reproduce an aurally presented rhythm pattern, and (c) behaviors reflecting an ability to associate visual rhythm symbols with aurally presented rhythm patterns.

REFERENCES

Allen, T.W., Walker, K., Symends, L., & Marcell, M. (1977). Intrasensory and intersensory perception of temporal sequences during infancy. *Developmental Psychology, 13,* 225–229.

Allport, F.H. (1955). *Theories of perception and the concept of structure.* New York: Wiley.

Andrews, F.M., & Deihl, N.C. (1967). *Development of a technique for identifying elementary school children's musical concepts.* Cooperative Research Project 5-0233, The Pennsylvania State University.

Apel, W. (1944). *Harvard dictionary of music.* Cambridge: Harvard University Press.

Bachman, T. (1969). *Reading and writing music* (Books 1 & 2). Elizabethtown, PA: The Continental Press.

Bamberger, J. (1982). Revisiting children's drawings of simple rhythms: A function of reflection-in-action. In S. Strauss (Ed.), *U-shaped behavioral growth.* New York: Academic Press.

Barela, M.M. (1979). Motion in musical time and rhythm. *College Music Symposium, 19* (1), 78–92.

Behrens, G.A. (1984). In search of the long assumed relationship between rhythm and movement. *Contributions to Music Education, 11,* 33–54.

Bengtsson, I., & Gabrielsson, A. (1980). Methods for analyzing performance of musical rhythm. *Scandinavian Journal of Psychology, 21,* 257–268.

Bengtsson, I., & Gabrielsson, A. (1983). Performance of musical rhythm in 3/4 and 6/8 meter. *Scandinavian Journal of Psychology, 24,* 193–213.

Benjamin, W.E. (1984). A theory of musical meter. *Music Perception, 1,* 355–413.

Bentley, A. (1966a). *Measures of musical abilities.* New York: October House.

Bentley, A. (1966b). *Musical ability in children and its measurement.* London: George G. Harrap.

Boisen, R. (1981). The effect of melodic context on students' aural perception of rhythm. *Journal of Research in Music Education, 29,* 165–172.

Boring, E.G. (1942). *Sensation and perception in the history of experimental psychology.* New York: Appleton-Century Company.

Boyle, J.D. (1968). The effects of prescribed rhythmical movements on the ability to sight read music (Doctoral dissertation, University of Kansas, 1968). *Dissertation Abstracts, 29,* 2290–2291.

Boyle, J.D. (1987). An exploratory investigation of meter perception. *Council for Research in Music Education, 91,* 10–14.

Bregman, A.S., & Campbell, J. (1971). Primary auditory stream segregation and perception of order in rapid sequences of tones. *Journal of Experimental Psychology, 89,* 244–249.

Bregman, A.S., & Dannenbring, G.L. (1973). The effect of continuity on auditory stream segregation. *Perception and Psychophysics, 13,* 308–312.

Brink, E. (1983). A look at E. Gordon's theories. *Council for Research in Music Education, 75,* 2–14.

Campbell, D.T., & Stanley, J.C. (1963). *Experimental and quasiexperimental designs for research.* Chicago: Rand McNally.

Chang, H., & Trehub, S.E. (1977). Infant's perception of temporal grouping of auditory patterns. *Child Development, 48,* 1666–1670.

Chomsky, N. (1957). *Syntactic structures.* The Hague: Mouton.

Chomsky, N. (1965). *Aspects of the theory of syntax.* Cambridge: MIT Press.

Chomsky, N. (1968). *Language and mind.* New York: Harcourt Brace Jovanovitch.

Christ, W.B. (1954). The reading of rhythm notation approached experimentally according to techniques and principles of word reading (Doctoral dissertation, Indiana University, 1954). *Dissertation Abstracts, 14,* 684.

Clynes, M., & Walker, J. (1982). Neurobiological functions of rhythm, time, and pulse in music. In M. Clynes (Ed.), *Music, mind, and brain* (pp. 171–216). New York: Plenum Press.

Coffman, A.R. (1949). *The effects of training on rhythm discrimination and rhythmic action.* Unpublished doctoral dissertation, Northwestern University.

Colwell, R. (1969–70). *Music achievement tests.* Chicago: Follett.

Cooper, G., & Meyer, L.B. (1960). *The rhythmic structure of music.* Chicago: The University of Chicago Press.

Creston, P. (1964). *Principles of rhythm.* New York: Franco Colombo.

D'Angelo, D. (1968). A new twist to teaching rhythm. *The Instrumentalist, 23* (2), 64–65.

Davies, J.B. (1978). *The psychology of music.* London: Hutchinson & Co.

Demany, L., McKenzie, B., & Vurpillot, E. (1977). Rhythm perception in early infancy. *Nature, 266,* 718–719.

Deutsch, D. (Ed.). (1982). *The psychology of music.* New York: Academic Press.

DeYarmin, R.M. (1972). An experimental analysis of the development of rhythmic and tonal capabilities of kindergarten and first grade children. In E. Gordon (Ed.), *Experimental research in the psychology of music* (Vol. 8, pp. 1–44). Iowa City: University of Iowa Press.

Dittemore, E.E. (1970). An investigation of some musical capabilities of elementary school students. In E. Gordon (Ed.), *Experimental research in the psychology of music,* (Vol. 6, pp. 1–44). Iowa City: University of Iowa Press.

Dowling, W.J. (1968). Rhythmic fission and perceptual organization. *Journal of the Acoustical Society of America, 44,* 369.

Dowling, W.J. (1973). The perception of interleaved melodies. *Cognitive Psychology, 5,* 322–337.

Dowling, W.J., & Harwood, D.L. (1986). *Music cognition.* Orlando, FL: Academic Press.

Drake, R.M. (1957). *Drake musical aptitude tests.* Chicago: Science Research Associates.

Duke, R.A. (1987). *Musicians' perception of beat in monotonic stimuli.* Unpublished research paper, MENC Southern Division Conference, Orlando, FL, May 1987.

Elliott, C.A. (1982). The relationships among instrumental sight-reading ability and seven predictor variables. *Journal of Research in Music Education, 30,* 5–14.

Farnsworth, P.R. (1969). *The social psychology of music* (2nd ed.) Ames: The Iowa State University Press.

Farnum, S.E. (1953). *Farnum music notation tests.* New York: The Psychological Corporation.

Flavell, J.H. (1963). *The developmental psychology of Jean Piaget.* Princeton: Van Nostrand.

Foley, E.A. (1975). Effects of training in conservation on tonal and rhythmic patterns on second grade children. *Journal of Research in Music Education, 23,* 240–248.

Fraisse, P. (1982). Rhythm and tempo. In D. Deutsch (Ed.), *The psychology of music.* (pp. 149–180) New York: Academic Press.

Gabrielsson, A. (1973). Studies in rhythm. *Acta Universitatis Upsaliensis, 7,* 3–19.

Gabrielsson, A. (1982). Performance and training of musical rhythm. *Psychology of Music,* Special Issue, 42–46.

Gardner, H. (1971). Children's duplication of rhythm patterns. *Journal of Research in Music Education, 19,* 355–360.

Gaston, E.T. (1968). Man and music. In E.T. Gaston (Ed.), *Music in therapy.* (pp. 7–29) New York: MacMillan.

Gordon, E. (1965). *Musical aptitude profile.* Boston: Houghton Mifflin.

Gordon, E. (1970). *Iowa tests of music literacy.* Iowa City: The Bureau of Educational Research and Service, The University of Iowa.

Gordon, E. (1971). *The psychology of music teaching.* Englewood Cliffs: Prentice-Hall.

Gordon, E. (1979). *Primary measures of music audiation.* Chicago: G.I.A. Publications.

Gordon, E. (1980). *Learning sequences in music: Skill, content, and patterns.* Chicago: G.I.A. Publications.

Gordon, E. (1982). *Intermediate measures of music audiation.* Chicago: G.I.A. Publications.

Grieshaber, K. (1987). Children's rhythmic tapping: A critical review of research. *Council for Research in Music Education, 90,* 73–82.

Groves, W.C. (1969). Rhythmic training and its relationship to the synchronization of motor-rhythmic responses. *Journal of Research in Music Education, 17,* 408–415.

Hargreaves, D.J. (1986). *The developmental psychology of music.* Cambridge: Cambridge University Press.

Hebb, D.O. (1949). *Organization of behavior.* New York: Wiley.

Hebb, D.O. (1958). *A textbook of psychology.* Philadelphia: Saunders.

Hoffer, C.R. (1973). *Teaching music in secondary schools* (2nd ed.). Belmont, CA: Wadsworth.

Hood, M.V. (1970). *Teaching rhythm and using classroom instruments.* Englewood Cliffs, NJ: Prentice-Hall.

Hoover, W. (1968). An approach to rhythm. *The Instrumentalist, 23* (2), 59–62.

Horner, V. (1965). *Music education, the background of research and opinion.* Hawthorne, Victoria, Australia: Australian Council for Educational Research.

Howell, P., Cross, I., & West, R. (Eds.). (1985). *Musical structure and cognition.* London: Academic Press.

Igaga, J.M., & Versey, J. Cultural differences in rhythmic perception. *Psychology of Music, 5* (1), 23–27.

Ihrke, W.R. (1969). *An experimental study of the effectiveness and validity of an automated rhythm training program.* Storrs: University of Connecticut. (ERIC Document Reproduction Service No. ED 032 790)

Jackson, S.L. (1963). Ear and rhythm training. *Music Educators Journal, 50* (1), 133–135.

Jaques-Dalcroze, E. (1915). *The eurhythmics of Jaques-Dalcroze.* Boston: Small Maynard and Company.

Jaques-Dalcroze, E. (1921). *Rhythm, music and education.* London: Chatto and Windus.

Jersild, A.T., & Bienstock, S.F. (1935). *Development of rhythm in young children.* New York: Bureau of Publications, Teachers College, Columbia University.

Jones, R. (1985). A dialectic analysis of selected contradiction among definitions of meter in music. *Council for Research in Music Education, 83,* 43–56.

Killian, J.N. (1985). The effect of differential feedback on tempo performance and perception. *Contributions to Music Education, 12,* 22–29.

Knuth, W.E. (1966). *Knuth achievement tests in music.* San Francisco: Creative Arts Research Associates.

Kohut, D.L. (1973). *Instrumental music pedagogy.* Englewood Cliffs, NJ: Prentice-Hall.

Kuhn, T.L. (1974). Discrimination of modulated beat tempo by professional musicians. *Journal of Research in Music Education, 22,* 270–277.

Kuhn, T.L. (1977). Effects of dynamics, halves of exercise, and trial sequences on tempo accuracy. *Journal of Research in Music Education, 25,* 222–227.

Lerdahl, F., & Jackendoff, R. (1983). *A generative theory of tonal music.* Cambridge: MIT Press.

Lewis, A.G. (1972). *Listen, look, and sing.* Morristown, NJ: Silver Burdett.

Lund, M.W. (1939). *An analysis of the "true beat" in music.* Unpublished doctoral dissertation, Stanford University.

Lundin, R.W. (1967). *An objective psychology of music* (2nd ed.). New York: Ronald Press.

Madsen, C.K., Duke, R.A., & Geringer, J.M. (1986). The effect of speed alterations on tempo note selection. *Journal of Research in Music Education, 34,* 101–110.

Magnell, E. (1968). Systems for reading rhythms at sight. *The Instrumentalist, 23* (2), 68–70.

McNally, K.A., & Handel, S. (1977). Effect of element composition on streaming and the ordering of repeating sequences. *Journal of Experimental Psychology: Human Perception and Performance, 3,* 451–460.

Moog, H. (1976). The development of musical experience in children of pre-school age. *Psychology of Music, 4* (2), 38–47.

Moog, H. (1979). On the perception of rhythmic forms by physically handicapped children and those of low intelligence in comparison with non-handicapped children. *Council for Research in Music Education, 59,* 73–78.

Morgan, C.T. (1965). *Physiological psychology* (3rd ed.). New York: McGraw-Hill.

Mursell, J.L. (1937). *Psychology of music.* New York: W.W. Norton and Company.

Mursell, J.L. (1957). *Music education, principles and programs.* Morristown, NJ: Silver Burdett.

Nielsen, J.F. (1930). A study of the Seashore motor-rhythm test. *Psychological Monographs, 40,* 74–84.

Osgood, C.E. (1953). *Method and theory in experimental psychology.* New York: Oxford University Press.

Palmer, M. (1976). Relative effectiveness of two approaches to rhythm reading for fourth-grade students. *Journal of Research in Music Education, 24,* 110–118.

Perney, J. (1976). Musical tasks related to the development of the conservation of metric time. *Journal of Research in Music Education, 24,* 159–168.

Petzold, R.G. (1966). *Auditory perception of musical sounds by children in the first six grades.* Madison: University of Wisconsin. (ERIC Document Reproduction Service No. ED 010 297)

Pflederer, M., & Sechrest, L. (1968). Conservation-type responses of children to musical stimuli. *Council for Research in Music Education, 13,* 19–36.

Pizer, R. (1968). Toward more accurate rhythm. *The Instrumentalist, 23* (2), 75–76.

Placek, R.W. (1974). Design and trial of a computer-assisted lesson in rhythm. *Journal of Research in Music Education, 22,* 13–23.

Povel, D., & Essens, P. (1985). Perception of temporal patterns. *Music Perception, 2,* 411–440.

Rainbow, E. (1977). A longitudinal investigation of the rhythmic abilities of pre-school aged children. *Council for Research in Music Education, 50,* 55–61.

Rainbow, E. (1981). A final report on a three-year investigation of rhythmic abilities of preschool aged children. *Council for Research in Music Education, 66–67,* 69–73.

Regelski, T.A. (1975). *Principles and problems of music education.* Englewood Cliffs, NJ: Prentice-Hall.

Revelli, W.D. (1955). To beat or not to beat? *Etude, 73* (6), 19, 48.

Richards, M.H. (1967). *Threshold to music.* New York: Harper and Row.

Rosenbusch, M.H., & Gardner, D.B. (1968). Reproduction of auditory and visual rhythm patterns by children. *Perceptual and Motor Skills, 26,* 1271–1276.

Ruckmick, C.A. (1913). The role of kinaesthesis in the perception of rhythm. *The American Journal of Psychology, 24,* 305–359.

Ruckmick, C.A. (1945). The nature of the rhythmic experience. *Proceedings of the Music Teachers National Association, 39,* 79–89.

Sachs, C. (1953). *Rhythm and tempo.* New York: W.W. Norton.

Schellenberg, S., & Moore, R.S. (1985). The effect of tonalrhythmic context on short-term memory of rhythmic and melodic sequences. *Council for Research in Music Education, 85,* 207–217.

Schleuter, S.L., & Schleuter, L.J. (1985). The relationship of grade level and sex differences to certain rhythmic responses of primary grade children. *Journal of Research in Music Education, 33,* 23–30.

Schenker, H. (1935). *Der freie satz* (E. Oster, trans., 1979). New York: Longman.

Schoen, M. (1940) *The psychology of music.* New York: Ronald Press.

Seashore, C.E. (1938). *Psychology of music.* New York: McGraw-Hill.

Seashore, C.E., Lewis, D.L., & Saetveit, J.G. (1939;1960). *Seashore measures of musical talents* (revised). New York: The Psychological Corporation.

Serafine, M.L. (1975). *A measure of meter conservation, based on Piaget's theory.* Unpublished doctoral dissertation, University of Florida.

Shrader, D.L. (1970). An aural approach to rhythmic sight-reading, based upon principles of programmed learning, utilizing a stereo-tape teaching machine (Doctoral dissertation, University of Oregon, 1970). *Dissertation Abstracts International, 31,* 2426. (University Microfilms No. 70–21, 576.

Sink, P.E. (1983). Effects of rhythmic and melodic alterations on rhythmic perception. *Journal of Research in Music Education, 31,* 101–114.

Sink, P.E. (1984). Effects of rhythmic and melodic alterations and selected musical experiences on rhythmic processing. *Journal of Research in Music Education, 32,* 177–194.

Skornicka, J.E. (1958). *The function of time and rhythm in instrumental music reading competency.* Unpublished doctoral dissertation, Oregon State College.

Sloboda, J.A. (1985). *The musical mind.* Oxford: Clarendon Press.

Sperry, R.W. (1964). Neurology and the mind-brain problem. In R. Issacson (Ed.), *Basic readings in neuropsychology*. New York: Harper and Row.

Sternberg, S., Knoll, R.L., & Zukofsky, P. (1982). Timing by skilled musicians. In D. Deutsch (Ed.), *The psychology of music* (pp. 182–240). New York: Academic Press.

Taylor, R. G. (Ed.). (1981). *Documentary report of the Ann Arbor Symposium*. Reston, VA: Music Educators National Conference.

Taylor, S. (1973). Musical development of children aged seven to eleven. *Psychology of Music, 1* (1), 44–49.

Thackray, R. (1968). *An investigation into rhythmic abilities*. London: Novello & Company Limited.

Wang, C.C. (1983). Discrimination of modulated music tempo by music majors. *Journal of Research in Music Education, 31*, 49–55.

Wang, C.C. (1984). Effects of some aspects of rhythm on tempo perception. *Journal of Research in Music Education, 32*, 169–176.

Wang, C.C., & Salzburg, R.S. (1984). Discrimination of modulated music tempo by string students. *Journal of Research in Music Education, 32*, 123–132.

Watkins, J.G., & Farnum, S.E. (1954). *The Watkins-Farnum performance scale*. Winona, MN: Hal Leonard Music.

West, R., Howell, P., & Cross, I. (1985). Modelling perceived musical structure. In P. Howell, I Cross, & R. West (Eds.), *Musical structure and cognition* (pp. 21–52). London: Academic Press.

Wiley, C.A. (1962). An experimental study of tachistoscopic techniques in teaching rhythm sight reading in music (Doctoral dissertation, University of Colorado, 1962). *Dissertation Abstracts, 23*, 3925.

Winick, S. (1974). *Rhythm: An annotated bibliography*. Metuchen, NJ: Scarecrow Press.

Woodruff, A.D. (1970). How music concepts are developed. *Music Educators Journal, 56* (6), 51–54.

Whitson, T.C. (1951). *A study of rhythmic perception at the junior high school level*. Unpublished master's thesis, University of Texas.

Yeston, M. (1976). *The stratification of musical rhythm*. New Haven, CT: Yale University Press.

Zimmerman, M.P. (1971). *Musical characteristics of children*. Washington: Music Educators National Conference.

Chapter Five

MELODIC AND HARMONIC FOUNDATIONS

An understanding of music's pitch structure has interested people since the beginning of recorded history. Weber (1958) maintains that a drive to rationalize pitch structure has shaped Western musical development to a large degree.

Pitch structure in Western music has both horizontal and vertical dimensions. While other musics have evolved with elaborate developments of the horizontal dimension, none has approached the sophistication of Western music's vertical dimension, harmony.

The horizontal dimension involves pitch sequences, while the vertical dimension involves structuring simultaneous pitches. Music theorists have been concerned primarily with deriving systems for codifying and explaining practices with respect to these structures. Systems of scales and harmony are outgrowths of theorists' efforts.

Because music is a social phenomenon, and therefore a changing phenomenon, theorists' work is never complete. Scales and harmonic systems based on melodic and harmonic practices of the eighteenth and nineteenth centuries are inadequate for explaining all pitch structure of twentieth century music; no doubt they will be even less adequate for music of the twenty-first century.

While theorists traditionally have focused on melodic and harmonic structures *per se,* theorists in recent years have dramatically increased their interest in understanding how people perceptually and cognitively organize melodic and harmonic structures and larger musical forms. Much of the research base for this "cognitive science" approach lies in psychology, linguistics, neurophysiology, philosophy, computer science, and music theory (Lerdahl & Jackendoff, 1983, p. 332). This concern for understanding music perception and cognition has given rise to much theoretical and empirical research regarding the nature of the cognitive processes or structures involved in interactions with musical stimuli.

This chapter examines the nature of melody and harmony in Western music in terms of both its tonal structure and people's interactions with and responses to the tonal structure. For convenience, the extensive and diverse literature related to melodic and harmonic behaviors is discussed under several broad headings: (a) definitions of melody, harmony, and tonality, (b) scale, modal, and other pitch structures, (c) psychological processes underlying pitch-related behaviors, (d) development of melodic and harmonic behaviors, and (e) evaluating melodic and harmonic behaviors.

Extended Definitions

For most listeners to Western music, melody is inseparable from harmony and rhythm. We tend to remember melodies rather than rhythms or harmonies. The overwhelming majority of melodies we hear are couched in tonal harmonic frameworks utilizing chord structures built in thirds and progressing toward somewhat predictable "resolutions."

Melody

Whether constructed within a tonal harmonic framework or not, two factors contribute to the individuality of each melody: *pitch relationships* and *durational relationships* among the tones. As noted in Chapter Three, pitch is a relative phenomenon concerning the placement of tones on a high-low continuum.

Constructing a melody involves selecting tones from this continuum and placing them in temporal sequence. Because pitch is a continuous variable, any pitch can conceivably be used in a melody. *Portamenti* and *glissandi* are examples of melodies in which minute pitch differences are used. Electronic music makes considerable use of these "sliding" pitches, but most melodies, Western and non-Western, utilize fixed pitches.

Sloboda (1985, pp. 24–28) suggests that the use of fixed pitches in music may be related to the "categorical nature of pitch perception."[*] He draws some analogies between the structures of language and music,

---

[*]According to Burns and Ward (1982, pp. 250–251), the term *categorical perception* was coined about 1970 by a speech-perception group to describe the results of their experiments in the perception of some speech tokens that varied along a single acoustic continuum. Burns and Ward cite a number of studies demonstrating that the concept of categorical pitch is also appropriate for nonspeech stimuli, especially musical intervals. With musical stimuli, the effect is more easily demonstrated with musically trained individuals who are able to readily label stimuli than with individuals without musical training (p. 252).

noting that basic speech-sound classes in language (*phonemes*), which reflect a *range* of sounds along a continuum, actually are perceived as given sound units. Similarly, he views the use of fixed pitches in music as a "phonology" of pitch, noting that pitches are perceived categorically, particularly by musicians. In Western music we are accustomed to hearing musical tones within given scale and tonal harmonic frameworks. Individual tones may be mistuned yet still be perceived as a certain pitch. Apparently there are "category boundaries," which may vary from listener to listener, and as long as these are not exceeded the tone is perceived as having the pitch of that category. This is somewhat analagous to the physiological phenomenon of the *critical band width* discussed in Chapter Three, but appears to be a function of experience with fixed pitches.

Particular fixed pitches for use in melodies usually are selected from within conventions and traditions of a given musical culture. In non-Western cultures, most of which have not developed a tonal system based on a tertian harmonic framework, the octave is divided in various ways. Some cultures use *microtonic* scales, dividing the octave into a greater number of pitches than the seven tones of the Western diatonic scale. Other cultures utilize fewer pitches per octave, and their scales are classified as *macrotonic* scales. Most Western melodies utilize tones of scales within the diatonic scale system and have an implied, if not accompanying, harmonic framework.* Regardless of the scale system used in selecting pitches for a melody or whether the melody uses sliding or fixed pitches, the sequence of pitch relationships contributes to a given melody's individuality.

As long as the relative pitch positions and rhythm of the tonal sequence remain constant, a melody remains the same. Changing either the relative pitch positions, i.e., any tones, or the rhythm, therefore, changes the melody *structurally* and may or may not change it *perceptually.* The melody notated in Figure 5-1 has the pitch relations of "America" (also "God Save the Queen"), but the rhythm makes it an entirely different melody.

Composers and some performers change tones and pitches of melodies for aesthetic or artistic purposes. The degree to which the tonal or rhythmic structure of a melody can be changed while still evoking a

---

*Twelve-tone, or serial, melodies are a notable exception to this practice. Such melodies essentially involve the use of each of the twelve tones of the chromatic scale in any order chosen by the composer, and each tone must be used before another can be repeated.

Figure 5-1. "America."

response of "sameness," naturally, is subject to many variables. Farnsworth (1969, p. 49) believes that once a melody is learned it can be changed considerably and still be recognized. The degree to which it can be changed and still be recognized appears to be a function of the listener's degree of familiarity with the melody, particularly any *expectations* developed regarding it. Dowling's (1973) comparison of listeners' responses to simultaneous pairs of familiar "interleaved" melodies supports the contention regarding expectations. When subjects knew which tunes to listen for, they were able to recognize them, but when they had no such expectations, they were not able to recognize them.

Melody may be defined either in terms of its structural characteristics or people's responses to it (Lundin, 1967, p. 76). Music theorists traditionally have examined melodies in terms of structural characteristics, while psychologists have been more interested in response to or perception of melody. Melody also has been examined from a philosophical perspective, although Hickman (1976) questions whether "aesthetics of melody" has any meaning today. The present discussion examines melody only from structural and perceptual perspectives. Farnsworth (1969, p. 48) classifies descriptions of melody in terms of structural characteristics as *formalistic* and those involving perceptual or psychological variables as *relativistic*.

Structural Characteristics of Melody. In its broadest sense, melody means any succession of single tones (Ortmann, 1926), and as noted above, both pitch and durational relationships contribute to each melody's individuality. The particular pattern of ups and downs of pitches in a series of tones provides a constant *melodic contour*. The uniqueness of a melodic contour is strengthened by its particular rhythmic configuration. As demonstrated in Figure 5-1, change in rhythmic configuration may change a melodic contour perceptually, depending on the extent to which it is changed. Melodic contour serves as a *Gestalt* or holistic pattern to which a listener responds.

Melodies may be performed at different tempi and at different pitch levels, but unless the tempo is changed radically, there is a "sameness" about them and they tend to be perceived as the same. More will be said later of the variables affecting melodic recognition.

Lundin (1967, pp. 77–79) see three particular melodic attributes: (a) *propinquity*, (b) *repetition*, and (c) *finality*. The tones of most Western melodies are propinquous, that is, close together. Analyses of intervals by Ortmann (1937) and Radocy (1977) both revealed a preponderance of smaller successive intervals (conjunct) over larger intervals (disjunct).

Melodies are repetitious in that certain tones tend to be repeated with considerable frequency. Radocy's examination of randomly selected melodies from *The Norton Scores* (Kamien, 1972) and from *357 Songs We Love to Sing* (1938) supports Lundin's view. In the *Norton* sample, the tones *do*, *mi*, and *so* accounted for 45 percent of all the tones; when *ti* and *re* were added the percentage increased to 69. The corresponding songbook percentages were 67 and 81. Clearly there is a tendency in most Western melodies to return to certain tones with great frequency.

Lundin's third attribute, finality, refers to a tendency for melodies to end according to certain conventions of *cadence*, which convey an impression of momentary or permanent conclusion. Cadences in melodies constructed within a Western tonal harmonic framework often have an implied harmonic accompaniment, although not necessarily. Final tones of melodies often are ones which have been repeated frequently or emphasized in the body of the melody.

Ortmann (1926) believed that melody's structural characteristics could be understood best by examining the pitch relationship of the melodic contour in isolation from harmony and rhythm. His analysis revealed several *static* (his term) attributes of melody that are inherent in all melodies and tend to attract a listener's attention. They include: (a) *first and last tones*, (b) *highest and lowest tones*, (c) *repeated tones*, (d) *interval size*, (e) *pitch direction*, (f) *pitch proximity*, (g) *emphasis in tone groups*, (h) *interval relationship*, and (i) *degree of emphasis*. The first three attributes are termed *absolute*, while the balance are considered *relative*. Ortmann maintains that the relative attributes are more important than the absolute attributes. Melodic memory, which involves *relative pitch* recall, is common among listeners to Western music, while *tone memory*, i.e., absolute pitch, is relatively rare.

As may be apparent, the above discussion does little to delimit the type of tone sequences that may be called melody. It is consistent with Mursell's (1937, p. 103) view that "melody need have no unified structure." It does, however, reveal that Western tonal melodies frequently use small intervals between tones, repeat some tones with great frequency, and incorporate some type of convention to establish finality. Further, it suggests that a tone's emphasis within a melody depends on its structural relationship to other melodic tones.

The answer to "What constitutes a melody?" is not solely a function of its structural characteristics; the answer also must be considered in terms of the listener.

Perceptual Organization of Melody. Perhaps Mursell's (1937, p. 104) statement best answers the question "What constitutes a melody?": *"A sequence of tones constitutes a melody when it is apprehended in terms of a unified and single response,"* but then a more important question arises: "What psychological factors influence an individual's perception and apprehension of a sequence of tones as a melody?"

A traditional (and still generally accepted) explanation of melodic perception is in terms of the perceptual laws of Gestalt psychology. A melody is perceived as a Gestalt according to some fundamental organizational laws derived from the study of visual perception, the laws of proximity, similarity, common direction, and simplicity (Bower & Hilgard, 1981, pp. 302–310). Tones that are close together are more likely to be perceived as a melodic unit than tones that are not close together. Similar or repeated tones tend to be perceived together. Melodic perceptions proceed in a common direction toward completion, and the tendency is to perceive the Gestalt or tonal pattern in its simplest form.

The organizational laws of Gestalt psychology are reflected in the structural characteristics discussed above. Tone series tend to be perceived more readily if their tones are close together, involve a certain amount of repetition, and proceed toward a finish in a somewhat direct manner.

The authors do not, however, intend to suggest, as do some proponents of Gestalt psychology, that capacity to perceive patterns in melody is an inborn capacity that requires no learning. As Hebb (1949, pp. 17–59) both argues and carefully documents, the perception of *relative* phenomena, of which melody is one, involves the ability to perceive patterns and develops only as result of prolonged experience (learning), whether formal or informal, with the particular phenomenon. To recognize a given tonal sequence as a melody requires experience with tonal sequences of a similar style.

Thus, familiarity with a melody or melodic style is an important variable in influencing what an individual perceives as melody. As an individual interacts with music of his or her culture, he or she learns and comes to accept the conventions used in melodies. Experience with melodies in a given scale system enables an individual to develop certain *expectations.* When new tonal sequences in similar style are encountered, the individual recognizes the new sequence as conforming or not conforming to expectations for that which he or she has learned as melody.

More recent accounts of melodic perception have examined it in terms of cognitive processes and structures.* Indeed, the burgeoning research literature in the "cognitive psychology of music," as research in the field is termed, focuses primarily on the perception of pitch and melody.

Dowling and Harwood (1986, pp. 124–144) describe the pattern of expectations a listener has regarding a melody as a *melodic schema.* (*Schemata* are "knowledge structures," developed from prior experience, with which an observer may organize perceptions into cognitions.) Such schemata are developed through immersion in one's musical culture from early childhood. Employing context-dependent information beyond the specific ordering of specific pitches, melodic schemata apparently reflect melodic contour, intervals, pitch chroma (the circular dimension of pitch), and tonality.

Premising much of the theoretical base on the seminal work of Chomsky (1957; 1965; 1968) regarding deep structures of language and Schenker's (1935/1979) theoretical system for conceiving surface musical structures as outgrowths of an underlying musical core or *Urtext*, music psychologists have drawn analogies between cognitive structures underlying music and language behaviors, suggesting that the surface structures of music (notes and rests) are subsumible into larger "deep" hierarchical structures based on combinations of melodic, harmonic, rhythmic, and extramusical information. Sloboda's (1985) excellent text is both an introduction to and a detailed treatment of the cognitive organization of music on the basis of abstracted structures.

---

*The reader should remember that *structures* discussed in research in cognitive psychology refer to theoretical cognitive constructs rather tonal structures *per se.*

Many attempts to model hierarchical perceptual structuring exist; West, Howell, and Cross (1985) provide an excellent review. (More will be said of hierarchical structures later in this chapter.) Common to development of many of the models are examinations of melody's *phonology, syntax,* and *grammar.* Sloboda (1985, pp. 11–52) provides clear, authoritative definitions and descriptions of these concepts. Essentially, phonology concerns the way in which pitch sounds (*phonemes*) are divided into discrete sound (perceptual) categories. Syntax is concerned with the combination of sound units into sequences, and grammar is concerned with the "rules" for using, or processing, syntactical sequences.

Many model tonal hierarchies are built, either explicitly or implicitly, upon *generative grammars,* organizational rules that underlie musical structures. This approach is similar to that exemplified in Chomsky's work with language. Sloboda (1985, pp. 34–47) argues that "the *structures* embodied in such grammars have psychological reality" (p. 34). He uses Sundberg and Lindblom's (1976) generative grammar for eight-bar nursery tunes to demonstrate how a musical grammar resembles the generative phonology of language grammars. Of particular importance to the present discussion is the fact that many accounts of perception and cognition of melody are couched in terminology reflecting grammatical structures as psychological reality.

Whether one speaks of schemata, rules of generative grammar, or expectations regarding melody, there seems to be general agreement that the Gestalt laws of perceptual organization noted earlier in this discussion still have validity. The melodic expectations, or schemata, of an individual growing up in a Western culture most likely are for tonal Gestalts and probably are couched within a tonal harmonic framework, utilize tones of the diatonic scale, generally have small intervals between tones, return with considerable frequency to certain tones, and usually end with some implied conventional cadence.

When an individual is confronted with a melody in an unfamiliar style, and hence has no particular expectations, the probability of responding to it as a melodic entity is greatly lessened (Meyer, 1967, p. 277). The failure of total serial music to achieve wide acceptance is in part because listeners have not learned the structural premises of the style. Meyer also maintains that the nature of serial melodies, which requires each chromatic tone within the octave to appear before another may be repeated, does not allow sufficient repetition or *redundancy* for listeners to perceive them as a whole. The melodic pattern, while structurally *logical,* lacks sufficient *psychological* unity for perception by the casual listener. Further, Meyer suggests that there is no homogeneous core of style to serve as a reference point for serial music; the stylistic diversity within the idiom is too great.

In conclusion, Lundin's (1967, p. 84) position that melody is a function of both a listener's previous experience and certain sequential characteristics appears to provide the most viable basis for defining melody. An individual learns his or her culture's melodic idioms. Familiarity with these idioms provides a basis for developing expectations (or for formulating schemata) regarding unfamiliar tonal sequences, thus enabling response to a new sequence as a melodic entity. However, a culture's melodic idioms are the product of a musical development which has recognized that melodies must incorporate some unifying structural attributes that will enable listeners to perceive and remember them. Tonal series that provide bases for perceptual organization in accordance with the Gestalt laws of organization appear to be the most readily accepted, and therefore are most likely to be perceived as melodies. Ultimately, only the perceiver can judge whether a tonal sequence functions as a melody: If it does, it *is* a melody.

Harmony

The development of harmony is a particular achievement of Western music. It has become such an important aspect of Western music that people often respond to isolated melodies in terms of harmonic expectations as much as in terms of melodic expectations. As Sloboda (1985, p. 52) notes, "when listeners hear a melody, their processing of it normally involves the attempt to retrieve implicit harmonic and rhythmic structure." Apel (1969, p. 372) maintains that "from the beginning of the eighteenth century on, the beauty of melodic lines depended largely on the effective arrangement of the harmonies underlying them."

In its broadest sense, harmony refers to music's vertical pitch structures as opposed to its horizontal pitch structure, melody. Apel (1969, pp. 371–374) has summarized its development. Early combinations of melodies, *organum,* generally involved parallel motion between two or three melodies, but as judgments developed that certain intervals between melodies "sounded better" simultaneously than others, there was increased concern for the resultant sounds of the multiple voices. It was not until about the mid-sixteenth century that harmony gained acceptance as a primary structural concern in music. Apel categorizes the era between

900 and 1450 as the period of *pretertian harmony*. (Music prior to this era was essentially melodic.) Harmony of this era is characterized by much parallel motion, open spacing among voices, and some use of triads at the beginning and ending of phrases.

The years between 1450 and 1900 are considered the era of *tertian harmony*.[*] Western music of this era resulted in the development of triadic harmony from triad movement in essentially modal sequence, through the strong tonic, subdominant, dominant music of the late baroque and classical periods, to harmonies of the romantic period that exploited the triadic system to its extremes with extensive use of chromatic alterations and distant modulations.

While the preponderance of twentieth-century music still is constructed within a tertian harmonic framework, Apel considers the era beginning in 1900 through the present as the period of *posttertian harmony*, because it has seen the development of vertical structures that deliberately violate the triadic harmony system. Debussy's "parallel chords," Scriabin's quartal harmony, Schoenberg's serial techniques, aleatoric music, *musique concrete*, and many of the developments of electronic and avant-garde music reflect efforts to organize the vertical dimension of pitch in manners different than tertian harmony.

Because harmony in its various forms is such an integral component of most Western music, and therefore a factor to be considered when examining musical behavior, it will be examined in terms of both its structural and perceptual characteristics.

Structural Characteristics of Harmony. Simultaneous pitch combinations generally are classified as one of two basic textures, *polyphonic* or *homophonic*. (Melody alone is classified as *monophonic*, i.e., it involves only a single pitch at a time.) Polyphonic texture involves combining two or more melodies and may or may not be concerned with "how good" the resultant simultaneous pitch combinations sound. The extent to which polyphonic music is concerned with "how good" (the consonance-dissonance character) the simultaneous pitches sound varies to a large degree with the era in which it was composed. Generally, polyphonic music of the pre- and posttertian eras reflects less concern for the character of the simultaneous sounds than polyphonic music of the tertian harmony era. Homophonic texture combines melody with a tertian

---

[*]"Tonal harmonic framework" as used in the previous section refers to the tertian harmony system. As will be noted in the discussion of tonality, the tertian harmony system elicits a strong feeling for a tonal center; hence, the expression "tonal harmonic framework" applies to music constructed according to the practices of tertian harmony.

harmonic framework and considers *both* the resultant horizontal and vertical dimensions of the musical sound.

Most references to harmony in music are to homophonic music constructed in a tertian harmonic framework. Harmony in this narrower and more common sense refers to the highly developed system of triadic chords and relations between chords that characterize most Western music, notably that of the baroque, classical, and romantic periods. While differences in harmonic practices of the three periods are evident, there is a common structural base to the harmony of the three periods.

Music of these periods, which comprises the predominant styles of "classical" music performed today, is constructed around a key center, or tonic. Music constructed around a key center possesses *tonality*, or "loyalty to a tonic." (The next section provides a more detailed discussion of tonality.) The triads or chords constructed on the first, fourth, and fifth degree of the scale, respectively called the tonic, subdominant, and dominant, serve as the primary structural mechanism for maintaining emphasis on the tonal center. Once this mechanism became firmly established as the vehicle for focusing attention on the tonal center, thus providing harmonic unity or repetition, composers then could develop departures from the harmonic framework and then return to the tonic. Harmonic conventions were developed through which functional chord progressions, structured around the tonic, subdominant, and dominant but also extending through chords built on other scale tones as well as through modulations into other keys, served as a primary unifying force. Harmonic practices of the romantic period carried this system to its extremes.

Twentieth-century developments of ways for combining pitches simultaneously have resulted in a variety of styles. This is not to suggest, however, that tertian harmony is no longer used a compositional device. To the contrary, it is still the primary structural mechanism for combining pitches simultaneously, particularly in popular music.

Perceptual Organization of Harmony. Music's harmonic structure has been studied and analyzed by theorists since its inception, and harmony continues to be a major area of study for students preparing for careers in music. Until recently, however, there has been relatively little study of harmony in terms of people's responses to it or their ability to comprehend it.

Traditionally, attempts to explain response to harmony have been in terms of mathematics. Beginning with the work of the Greek philosopher Pythagoras in the sixth century B.C., and promulgated by the medieval church scholars, response to music, which was melodic during those times, had been examined and explained in terms of simple mathematical ratios. With the development of music constructed in a tonal harmonic framework, mathematical explanations continued to be offered, but because of the compromises of equal temperament,* convenient explanations in terms of simple mathematical ratios were no longer applicable. Consequently, attempts to explain harmony in terms of psychological characteristics must look beyond music's "scientific" or mathematical aspects.

A view advocated by both Farnsworth (1969, pp. 37–41) and Lundin (1967, pp. 88–89) is that response to harmony *is a cultural phenomenon.* Just as individuals' experiences with music of their culture enable them to develop melodic expectations, the experiences also foster harmonic expectations. Music in which the harmony does not conform in a general way to the harmonic practices with which a listener is familiar sounds "strange" or "different." Even though most listeners cannot verbalize *what* sounds strange or different, the effect is disturbing, because the listener's general expectations are unfulfilled.

Harmony, just as melody and rhythm, also is comprised of patterns and is perceived in terms of "wholes" (Mainwaring, 1951). Individuals respond to harmony in terms of its totality rather than its individual tones or chords. (It is only during formal musical training that most individuals attempt to analyze harmony into its constituent parts.)

There are three primary "holistic" attributes of harmonic structure toward which individuals respond and develop expectations: (a) tonality, (b) harmonic movement, and (c) finality. The laws of perceptual organization noted under the discussion of melody also appear basic for perceiving harmonic attributes. Tonality, with its tonal center, provides an underlying repetition or redundancy which helps a listener respond to a complex sequential series of multiple sounds bombarding the central nervous system via the auditory sensory mechanisms. As Meyer (1967, pp. 288–293) has noted, experience with music constructed in a tonal harmonic framework provides the basis for perceiving redundancy, in this case the tonality, which enables a listener to "make sense" of music heard in relation to expectations.

Response to harmonic movement appears to occur in a manner similar to the response to melodic contour. Harmonic movement or progression

---

*The equal tempered scale is discussed later in this chapter.

is a *relative* phenomenon, as is melody. We respond to harmonic movement in *relation* to tonality. Practices in functional harmony become a standard or model for listeners' harmonic expectations. As harmonic practices change, listeners learn the new harmonic styles and develop expectations accordingly. Meyer (1967, p. 292) believes that a primary difficulty composers face in having contemporary music, particularly serial music and other music not structured within a tonal harmonic framework, accepted by a large number of listeners is that it lacks the unifying harmonic attributes that provide the redundancy necessary for meaningful perception. Music constructed in a tonal harmonic framework has an inherent redundancy through its tonal center and harmonic movement in relation to that center.

Finality has been examined more in terms of melody than harmony, but finality effects are rooted in harmony as well as melody. The direction of the melody line at cadence points is readily predictable for melodies constructed in relation to a tonal harmonic framework, and the conventions of cadence used during the eighteenth and nineteenth centuries still provide the basis for most Westerners' finality expectations. Few listeners would not expect a dominant-seventh chord to resolve to a tonic chord, even though few could label the chords. Experience in hearing harmony provides the basis for such expectations, even without any formal training in music.

Contemporary music psychologists have not studied the perception of harmony nearly as much as they have studied melody. An examination of the contents of three recent collections of articles related to theory and research in cognitive music psychology reveals a virtual void of information on harmonic perception (Deutsch, 1982; Clynes, 1982; Howell, Cross, & West, 1985), whereas articles on aspects of rhythmic and melodic perception abound. Nevertheless, there appears to be at least a tacit acceptance of the view that, just as for melodic perception, experienced listeners possess internalized cognitive structures or schemata of music keys, key relationships, and functions of chords within keys. While theory and research on harmony is limited, three recent studies especially related to harmonic perception offer principles suggesting how experienced listeners organize harmonic information.

Krumhansl, Bharucha, and Castellano (1982) identified three *context-dependent* principles of harmonic organization, all of which are supported by experimental evidence. One principle is *contextual identity:* When a chord occurs in an established key context, it is heard as more closely related to *itself* than when it is out of the context of key. This means that the chord will be recognized more easily in the context key or a closely related key than in a distant key.

A second principle is *contextual distance:* Two different chords are more closely related (perceptually similar) when they are in the same key than when they are not both in the same key. The closer the keys, the less extreme is the difference. For example, the C and G major triads, which contain tones found in both the C major and G major diatonic scales, are quite closely related. The C major and D major triads are not so closely related, although since D major is the dominant of G major, a closely related key to to C major, the C–D relationship is closer than, say, the relationship between the C major and Db major triads.

The third principle, related to the order in which chords occur in a particular musical example, is *contextual asymmetry:* Two successive chords are more closely related when the first chord is out of context and the second chord is in context than when the first chord is in and the second chord is out. The strength of contextual asymmetry is a function of the context key and the keys of which the chords could be a part. Perceptual distance decreases as the second chord moves closer to the context key and the first chord moves further from it. As an example, in C major, movement of a D major triad to a G major triad results in a greater perceptual similarity between the two triads than the opposite movement, G–D. If, in the second case, the chords are made parallel *minor* chords so that a G–Bb-D chord moves to a D–F–A chord, the distance decreases.

Krumhansl, Bharucha, and Kessler (1982) identified a "core" of eight chords on the basis of how well the chords from the keys of C major, G major, and A minor seemed to follow each other in paired combinations. The "core" included the I (tonic), II (supertonic), III (submediant), IV (subdominant), V (dominant), and VI (mediant) chords from C major, the I, II, IV, V, and VI chords from G major, and the I, IV, V, and VI chords from A minor. Those chords reduce to eight triads: C major (C–E–G), D minor (D–F—A), E minor (E–G–B), F major (F–A–C), G major (G–B–D), A minor (A–C–E), D major (D–F#–A), and E major (E–G#–B). The I, IV, and V chords were particularly close in each key. Chords unique to G major or A minor were relatively remote. Subjects perceived C major as the dominant tonality; they had a strong preference for sequences ending on the C chord. There was a lesser preference for sequences ending on the G chord; no regular pattern existed for A minor.

Bharucha and Krumhansl (1983) gathered further evidence that the principles of contextual identity, contextual distance, and contextual asymmetry governed harmonic organization in tonal contexts. On the basis of their experimental data obtained from musically experienced subjects who evaluated how "well" one chord seemed to follow another or how "well" a chordal sequence differed from another due to one altered chord, the investigators reconfirmed the "context" principles and identified three additional "key" principles that govern harmonic organization *independently* of context: *key membership, intrakey distance,* and *intrakey asymmetry.*

The "key" principles are not surprising in view of the traditions of Western music theory, but the investigators helped give the principles a research basis. According to the key membership principle, chords from the same key are more related than chords from different keys. For example, the G major and E minor triads, I and VI from G major, are more related than the G major and Eb major triads. The intrakey distance principle says that a key's I, IV, and V chords (the key's "harmonic core") are related more closely than the key's "non-core" chords. In D major, for example, the relationships among the D, G, and A major triads are stronger than the relationships among the triads built on the remaining scale degrees, E, F#, B, and C#. Intrakey asymmetry means that paired chords from the same key are more closely related if the first chord is not in the "harmonic core" and the second chord is than they are if the first chord is in the "core" but the second is not. The II–V relationship, exemplified in C major by a D minor chord moving to a G major chord, is closer than the V–II relationship, exemplified in C major by the G–D chordal movement.

Together the "key" principles and the "context" principles summarize the organization of harmonic information, according to Bharucha and Krumhansl. The "key" and "context" principles reflect how experienced listeners abstract underlying structures from complex musical stimuli. The principles also suggest that harmonic perception involves the perception of *relationships* among patterns, particularly those related to chordal sequences and keys. It can also be argued that the principles provide further support that the perceptual organization laws of Gestalt psychology are operating during music perception; they certainly do not refute them.

Tonality

Implicit in the discussions of both melody and harmony has been the recognition of tonality as a unifying device in the perception of music constructed within a tonal harmonic framework. Many developments in twentieth-century music, however, are not constructed in a tonal harmonic framework; some specifically are designed to be atonal. Yet Temko's (1972, p. 33) study of pitch predominance in twenty avant-garde compositions revealed agreement among subjects concerning a predominant pitch in each of the compositions. Apparently even atonal and electronic music not designed with an *a priori* tonality may evoke listener response in terms of some central or focal pitch. Considering tonality from this perspective, most music could be said to reflect a "loyalty to the tonic" (Apel, 1969, p. 855), perhaps the most generally accepted broad definition of tonality.

This tonic is the *tonal center* and serves as the tone to which other tones ultimately return; the tonal center is the basic musical expectation to which most other expectations relative to melodic and harmonic perception are related.

Implicit in most discussions of tonality in Western music is the application (and limitation) of the term to music constructed in a tonal harmonic framework, using essentially the tones of either a major or minor diatonic scale. As is noted in the next section of this chapter, Western tertian harmony is built with the scale and chord tones of diatonic scales, and references to tonal music and tonality usually refer to music constructed of scale and chord tones from diatonic scales.

Melodic movement in tonal music includes both conjunct and disjunct motion. Conjunct motion is essentially scalar, although chromatic and/or altered scale tones may be used. Disjunct motion involves skips or leaps, usually on tones outlining chords underlying the implied harmonic framework. Melodies of the baroque and classical period tend to outline scale and chord patterns more clearly than music of the romantic period, much of which involves chromaticism and frequent key modulations.

Taylor (1976) reports that pitch structure of melodies is one determinant of tonality. The more the melodic movement conforms to the scale and chord structure of the key in which a melody is constructed, the greater the tonal strength, or tonality, of the melody. Melodies not using the scale and chord tones of the key have less tonal strength, and melodic contour alone does not appear to be a significant factor in the determination of the tonal strength of a melody.

Cuddy's (1982) research on the perception of tonality yielded similar results. Subjects in her study rated melodies ending on the tonic and whose structures used diatonic scale tones in patterns based on tertian harmony traditions as having a higher degree of tonality than melodies whose structures did not closely follow the diatonic scale and chord patterns of tertian harmony. Subjects for Cuddy's study included both trained musicians and people without formal training in music; the results were virtually the same for both groups.

Melodies of the baroque and classical periods tend to have greater tonal strength than romantic melodies. In turn romantic melodies elicit a stronger feeling for tonality than melodies that are not written within a tonal harmonic framework.

Krumhansl and Bharucha's "context" and "key" principles suggest that the perception of harmonic movement in tonal music also is intertwined with and dependent upon the chord patterns of tertian harmony. With the development of functional harmony in the seventeenth and eighteenth centuries, the basic patterns of harmonic movement and relationships among chord roots were established. The consistency of harmonic progressions in eighteenth-century music provides sufficient redundancy for listeners to develop and maintain strong feelings for tonality. Music of the romantic period, which also is essentially constructed within a tonal harmonic framework, extends harmonic practices far beyond those of the baroque and classical periods. It would be interesting to see the extent to which Krumhansl and Bharucha's context and key principles, which were derived under carefully controlled (perhaps "stereotypical") conditions, apply to music reflecting harmonic practices of the romantic period.

To date, most examinations of the psychological structures and processes related to perception of tonality have been in terms of Western music constructed within a tonal harmonic framework. Erickson (1982), however, suggests the need to expand the definition to the "tonal" music of all times and places. The particular definition he recommends "has the additional merit of leaving the relation between system and perception ready for research" (p. 522). The recommended definition:

> Tonality may be broadly conceived as a *formal system in which pitch content is perceived as functionally related to a specific pitch-class or pitch-class-complex of resolution,* often preestablished and preconditioned, as a

basis for structure at some understood level of perception....(The terms *pitch class* and *pitch-class-complex* are used to denote pitch independent of specific registral occurrence, or a complex of such pitches generically understood.) (Berry, 1976, p. 27)

Scales and Modes

Definitions of *scale* and *mode* are many and varied. In a narrow sense each has a particular meaning, but in a broad sense they both refer to the same phenomenon: the basic tones of a composition arranged in order of pitch from lowest to highest (or highest to lowest). Most Western music divides the octave into a basic number of discrete fixed pitches, which psychologists now recognize as being perceived as members of *pitch classes* or *categories*, hence the increasing number of references to fixed pitches as *categorical pitch.* The number and particular arrangement of pitches in a scale or mode may vary, although convention suggests that only a limited number of pitch arrangements have gained widespread acceptance.

Usage implies acceptance. Particular pitch arrangements that continue to be used by at least some cultural or subcultural group apparently have gained a certain acceptance; pitch arrangements that are not used apparently are not acceptable.

Conventional practice in today's Western music divides the octave into twelve equal semitones, i.e., a *chromatic* scale. Virtually all standard musical instruments have the capability for producing the chromatic scale. However, the chromatic scale is not the predominant scale; the *diatonic* scale, a designated order of tones and semitones which preceded the chromatic scale historically, remains the predominant pattern. Even though ancient Greek and medieval church scholars recognized chromaticism, dividing the octave into twelve equal semitones did not occur until the development of equal temperament, which is discussed later in this chapter. Chromaticism is very much evident in romantic and some contemporary music, but the chromatic scale *per se* has not become the predominant scale of Western music, even though virtually all musical instruments can produce it.

Essentially a scale is diatonic if the octave includes seven fixed pitches, usually creating five whole-tone intervals and two semitone intervals, with an eighth pitch doubling the lowest at the octave and eliciting a response of functional "equivalence" with the lowest tone. (The term "mode" often refers to a particular sequence of intervals, as in a major mode being two whole-tones, a semitone, three whole-tones, and a semitone.)

The phenomenon of the functional equivalence of octaves, sometimes referred to as octave generalization or examined in terms of perceptual similarity, is intriguing for persons concerned with understanding music perception. It appears to be related to a property of pitch termed *tone chroma*, which is an outgrowth of a "two-component" theory of pitch that recognizes two dimensions, *tone height* and *tone chroma* (Revesz, 1953). For Western music, generally, tones of different pitches (and usually pitch names), i.e. tones other than at the octave, are said to have differences in pitch height; tones at the octave (and usually having the same pitch name) are said to have the same tone chroma.

The phenomenon of tone chroma is complex and often is represented graphically by a helix or torus in which tone height is represented as a circular dimension and tone chroma is represented as the vertical dimension. Several excellent accounts of the phenomenon are available (Deutsch, 1982; Shepherd, 1982; Sergeant, 1983), and readers interested in examining the perceptual bases of tone chroma may want to consult them. Deutsch (p. 272) notes that contemporary music theorists make an analogous distinction between *pitch* and *pitch class*. Tones at the octave, the functional equivalents, are considered members of the same pitch class.

In common usage, the arrangement of tones and semitones within the octave determines whether the pitch arrangement is considered a scale or mode. The two predominant pitch arrangements for Western tonal music are called major and minor scales, although many consider scales to be particular modes. Following is a discussion of the functions of scales, scale tuning systems, major and minor scales, and other modal and scale structures.

Functions of Scales

According to Mursell (1937, p. 107), musical scales are social phenomena that allow for exploration of tonal relations. He maintains that scales are *not* manifestations of some mathematical idea. Neither, he says, are there *natural* scales; otherwise all cultures would use the same scales.

Musical systems are creations of man's efforts. As a system is developed, changes are made in terms of human feelings and perceptions rather than to fulfill any order of goodness in terms of frequency ratios. Evolved scale systems reflect attempts to codify and make the system available for use by others. If music were not a sociocultural phenomenon, there would be no need for musical scales; each person could develop a private scale system.

The tempered diatonic scale system is probably the most far-reaching and authoritative standardization of music for social purposes the world has ever known (Mursell, p. 107). Musical instruments, notation, and practices of Western cultures are so integrally bound to this system that new systems which are incompatible with the diatonic scale system appear unlikely to gain widespread acceptance. Even in electronic music, the type of compositions that are meeting with greatest acceptance generally involve the use of some traditional instruments or timbres and melodies and harmonies based on the diatonic scale.

Musical scales also provide a basis for establishing definite tonal relationships. Together with rhythm they provide the consistency which people need to deal with the infinite range of sounds from which music is comprised. Without a predominant scale system, it is unlikely that music ever would have become the potent force it is today. Scales make it possible for people to create from sounds a construct (music) that has functional and aesthetic value for significant proportions of most cultural groups.

Scale Tuning Systems

Throughout music history there have been changes in both the frequency standard, an absolute phenomenon, and the tuning of scales, a relative phenomenon. Backus (1977, pp. 150–151) notes that the frequency of A^4 (the present A 440) has varied from somewhere in the range 415 to 428 Hz during the mid-eighteenth century to as high as 461 Hz in the late nineteenth century. Standards also have varied from country to country. It was not until 1953 that A 440 officially was recognized by the International Standards Organization as the frequency standard for music.

Scale tuning systems have been subject to much debate by mathematicians, acousticians, and music theorists since the time of the ancient Greeks. While the tempered diatonic scale is today's standard for Western music, there still is much controversy regarding performance practices with respect to it and other tuning systems (Barbour, 1951, pp. 196–201; Farnsworth, 1969, pp. 26–27; Ostling, 1974).

Tempered means that the scale tone which have been changed so that, with the exception of the octave, intervals resulting from simultaneous combinations of tones within the scale are not in simple, i.e., whole number, mathematical ratios among the frequencies of the respective tones as are the intervals in some other tuning systems. *Equal temperament* is the name given to the tuning system which divides the octave into twelve equal semitones.

Equal temperament was developed along with, and indeed made possible, the development of Western tonal harmony. Tuning systems developed prior to equal temperament were adequate for monophonic music and to a degree for polyphonic music, but as polyphony developed and there became increased emphasis on the sonorities resulting from the vertical structure of music, previous tuning systems proved inadequate. While discussion of the various tuning systems perhaps is more appropriately a concern of musical acoustics or history books, a brief discussion of the most prominent tuning systems is necessary here, particularly since there is still controversy regarding tunings used in performance today. Readers interested in studying tuning systems in greater depth should consult the excellent presentations by Backus (1977) or Barbour (1951).

The diatonic scale has its roots in the tetrachords which were the basis of the Greek "Greater Perfect System." Tetrachords were series of four descending tones, the range of which was a perfect fourth. Depending on the arrangement of the two inner tones, the tetrachords were one of the three *genera: diatonic* (two tones and one semitone), *chromatic* (a minor third and two semitones), or *enharmonic* (a major third and two quarter tones). The diatonic genus apparently was the most popular among theorists at the time. Combinations of tetrachords, primarily in conjunct arrangement and with an added tone at the bottom, formed the Greek Greater Perfect System from which the present day diatonic system evolved. The pattern *do, re, mi, fa, so, la, ti, do,* although originally conceived in inverse order, has been basic to Western music ever since.

Tuning of Greek scale intervals apparently was based on the system developed by Pythagoras (c. 550 B.C.). His tuning system, now called the Pythagorean scale, derived frequency of all tones from the interval of a pure, i.e., beatless, fifth which has the simple ratio of 3:2 between the respective frequencies of the upper and lower tones. Theoretically, the Pythagorean diatonic scale frequencies are obtained by forming a series of successive ascending fifths which then are lowered to the correct octave to form the scale. In practice, as Backus (1977, pp. 137–139) and Roederer (1975, p. 156) have described, the tuning of the scale is derived by tuning a beatless ascending fifth, a beatless descending fourth, a beatless ascending fifth, etc. The result is the same, a scale that has beatless perfect fourths, fifths, and octaves. (See Table 5-1.)

Table 5-1

RATIOS AMONG INTERVALS OF THE PYTHAGOREAN DIATONIC SCALE ON C

Freq. ratios from *do*		$\frac{9}{8}$	$\frac{81}{64}$	$\frac{4}{3}$	$\frac{3}{2}$	$\frac{27}{16}$	$\frac{243}{128}$	$\frac{2}{1}$
Freq. ratios adjacent tones	$\frac{9}{8}$	$\frac{9}{8}$	$\frac{256}{243}$	$\frac{9}{8}$	$\frac{9}{8}$	$\frac{9}{8}$	$\frac{256}{243}$	
Frequency*	256	288	324	341.3	384	432	486	512
Pitch name	*do*	*re*	*mi*	*fa*	*so*	*la*	*ti*	*do*

*Scientific pitch, which has middle C = 256 Hz, as opposed to standard pitch, which has middle C = 261.3 Hz, is used for convenience.

As long as melodic music is performed without transposing, modulating, or using chromatic tones, the Pythagorean scale works well. However, its small semitone is a problem for instrument makers. Further, when the tuning system is extended to include chromatic tones, it results in nonequivalent enharmonic tones, thereby yielding different sizes of semitones. Also, since a Pythagorean scale must be formed in relation to a given starting tone, identical letter names may have different frequencies in different keys; e.g., F will be slightly different in the keys of C, Eb, and A. Clearly, the Pythagorean scale is inadequate for Western tonal harmony.

Just intonation, according to Barbour (pp. 89, 105), appears to have evolved during the fifteenth and sixteenth centuries as theorists sought to improve upon Pythagorean tuning. Just intonation has some advantages over Pythagorean tuning in that it uses more simple ratios between tones and accommodates the building of triads using simple ratios among the tones. Just intonation is so to named because its intervals conform to the ratios between the tones of the overtone series; i.e., the fifth has a 3:2 ratio, the fourth a 4:3, the major third a 5:4, and the minor third a 6:5. Table 5-2 shows the ratios among adjacent frequencies and in relation to *do*.

Although having the advantage of simple ratios, just intonation also has a number of disadvantages which for all practical purposes render it useless in Western tonal music: (a) the scale has two different ratios for whole tones (8:9 and 9:10), (b) the fifth, D–A (in reference to the key

Table 5-2

RATIOS AMONG INTERVALS IN JUST INTONATION

Freq. ratios from *do*		$\frac{9}{8}$	$\frac{5}{4}$	$\frac{4}{3}$	$\frac{3}{2}$	$\frac{5}{3}$	$\frac{15}{8}$	$\frac{2}{1}$
Freq. ratios adjacent tones	$\frac{9}{8}$	$\frac{10}{9}$	$\frac{16}{15}$	$\frac{9}{8}$	$\frac{10}{9}$	$\frac{9}{8}$	$\frac{16}{15}$	
Frequency	256	288	320	341.3	384	426.6	480	512
Pitch name	*do*	*re*	*mi*	*fa*	*so*	*la*	*ti*	*do*

of C), is not the same as the other fifths (27:40 versus 2:3), and (c) it does not accommodate modulation to other keys. The farther away from the reference key and the more use of accidentals, the more untenable the system becomes. Just as the Pythagorean system, just scales have tones which require different frequencies in different keys. In short, it is of little value for instruments of fixed pitch such as keyboard and wind instruments, which must accommodate chromaticism and modulation or transposition to all keys. It has been claimed, however, that instruments of variable pitch (string and voice) can accommodate the difficulties of modulation by adjustment and hence play thirds "better in tune," i.e., with "purer" or beatless intervals.

As efforts were made to accommodate harmony and modulation in Western music, two other systems evolved: *meantone* and *equal temperament*. Both involved the altering or tempering of some tones. It is not clear when meantone temperament was first used, but Barbour (p. 25) suggests that it was being used as early as the beginning of the sixteenth century. There are several variations of meantone tuning, but the essential aspect of the system is that it alters (flats) some of the fifths of the Pythagorean scale, thus allowing a limited degree of modulation. Its name was derived from the fact that the whole tone C–D was half the size of the major third resulting from the alterations of the fifth. Meantone temperament was used extensively in Europe throughout the seventeenth century and well into the eighteenth century until the acceptance of equal temperament.

Equal temperament is so named because it divides the octave into twelve equal semitones. (Other divisions are possible; technically, division of the octave into any number of equivalent units is "equal temperament.") Each adjacent pair of tones has the same ratio of frequencies, 1:1.05946. Although the octave is the only simple ratio (2:1), there is a consistency among each of the other intervals regardless of key. Equal temperament overcomes the limitations on transposition, modulation, and use of chromaticism that are inherent with Pythagorean, just, and meantone tunings.

The equal tempered semitone has been divided into 100 equal parts called *cents*. A semitone therefore equals 100 cents, a whole tone 200 cents. An equal tempered fifth is 700 cents, i.e., it encompasses seven semitones, while the octave, made up of twelve semitones, equals 1200 cents. Cents for a given interval may be computed with the formula $n = 3986.31 [\log (\frac{f_2}{f_1})]$ in which n = number of cents, f_1 = lower tone frequency, and f_2 = upper tone frequency.

Cents are a convenient way for comparing the size of intervals in the various tuning systems. Table 5-3, adapted from Farnsworth (p. 25), compares the size of intervals in the four tuning systems discussed above. As is apparent, the equal tempered fifth is slightly (two one-hundredths of a semitone) smaller than the beatless Pythagorean and just fifths; conversely, the equal tempered fourth is slightly larger than the Pythagorean and just fourths.

Table 5-3

COMPARISON OF PYTHAGOREAN, JUST, MEANTONE, AND EQUAL
TEMPERED TUNINGS

	do	re	mi	fa	so	la	ti	do
Pythagorean	0	204	408	498	702	906	1110	1200
Just	0	204	386	498	702	884	1088	1200
Meantone*	0	204	386	503	697	890	1083	1200
Equal	0	200	400	500	700	900	1100	1200

*This is the tuning used by Pietro Aron around 1523.

The major discussions regarding tuning tendencies in contemporary performances, however, center on tuning the major third, *do–mi*, and the size of the interval between the leading tone (*ti*) and *do*. Although equal temperament is the recognized standard, some performers insist that triads are "better in tune" if they approximate the tuning of the just triad, which has a major third 14 cents lower than the equal tempered major third. This would be possible for performances of a cappella choirs and string quartets, which are not bound by the constraints of keyboard or wind instruments. It also is claimed and supported by research (Greene, 1937; Nickerson, 1949) that soloists on string instruments that can adjust intonation tend to approximate Pythagorean tuning when performing leading tones.

Barbour (1951, pp. 192–202) and Ostling (1974) review much of the rhetoric regarding the issue and in addition cite the limited research on the matter. Apparently no research has been conducted regarding the tuning tendencies of choirs, but Barbour suggests that even if choirs did attempt to adjust to just intonation, the overall pitch would probably fall if the harmonic progressions are traditional diatonic progressions. He does concede, though, that such adjustments might be possible in modal progressions such as used by Palestrina. He maintains, however, that choirs singing with wind instruments quickly adapt to the intonation of the accompanying instruments.

Perhaps the classic study of intonation tendencies in performance is by Nickerson (1949), who analyzed performances of individual members of string quartets, both in isolation and in ensemble. He concluded that (a) performances do not conform completely to just, Pythagorean, or equal temperament, (b) performances of melodies both in solo and ensemble approach Pythagorean tuning, and (c) factors that cause this pattern appear to dominate both ensemble demands and presumed experience with equal temperament.

Roederer (1975, p. 159), however, cautions against concluding that soloists have a particular preference for Pythagorean intonation. He notes that other studies (Terhardt & Zick, 1975) have shown a tendency for performers to play or sing sharp the upper tone of all successive intervals.

While research is inconclusive regarding intonation practices in contemporary performances, it is apparent that much deviation from equal temperament does occur and is still perceived as "acceptable." Perhaps Ostling (1974, p. 18) best summarizes the current state of the matter:

> Research agrees that good intonation is not any one basic tuning system used exclusively. Beyond that, it seems to this writer that a basic minimum standard of at least equal temperament should be expected — the norm — from which artist-performers will depart for melodic gravitation and/or harmonic reinforcement, as the situation requires, and that is about all one can conclude, at least to date.

Meanwhile, we still have directors of a cappella choirs who insist that their choirs are able to sing in just intonation; further, string players consistently report that they must adjust their intonation differently when playing in a string quartet and when performing with (an equal tempered) piano accompaniment. Clearly there is need for much more research.

Major and Minor Modes

Major and *minor* are terms used to describe size of intervals and type of scales, triads, or keys. With intervals the term simply denotes differences in intervals of a second, third, sixth, or seventh; minor intervals in each class contain one less semitone than the major interval in each class.

When used to distinguish between types of scales, triads, and keys, the basic distinction between major and minor is in the size of the third: the third of the major scale (key, triad) is four semitones while the third of the minor scale (key, triad) contains only three semitones.

The basic interval pattern of the major scale is TTSTTTS, where T stands for a whole tone and S stands for a semitone. The minor scale has three variations: natural, melodic, and harmonic. All three forms have the lowered third, thus beginning TS for the intervals between the first three tones, but vary in the intervals between the highest three tones. The interval patterns for the three forms, respectively, are natural— TSTTSTT, melodic—TSTTTTS (ascending) and TSTTSTT (descending), and harmonic—TSTTSAS, with A standing for an augmented second.

The establishment of major and minor as the tonal bases of Western music appeared to evolve with the establishment of equal temperament and the development of harmony. In equal temperament, major and minor scales may be constructed on each of the twelve tones of the chromatic octave, and the interval and chordal relationships within the scale built on each degree of the octave, i.e., in each key, are functionally identical. The fact that music built on major and minor scales (and their harmonic patterns) has dominated Western music of the past three hundred years so completely suggests that major and minor scales and their concomitant systems of tonality and harmony provide an intelligible tonal harmonic framework for Western man's music.

Other Modes

While major and minor scales are the predominant scale systems for Western music, many other scales have been developed both within Western cultures and in other cultures. No other scale system, however, has been developed into a harmonic system that in any way approaches that of Western tonal harmony based on the major and minor scales, although some scale systems are in many respects compatible with Western tonal harmony.

The traditional narrow sense of the term *mode* refers to the *church modes* devised by scholars of the medieval church. They consist of eight diatonic scales, using the same names of earlier Greek modes but different in organization and structure, that are the tonal basis of Gregorian chant. Apel (1969, p. 165) describes the system as follows:

> Each [consists] of the tones of the C-major scale (white keys) but starting and closing on d, e, f, or g and limited to the range of an octave. For each of these four notes, called a final (*finalis*), there exists two modes distinguished by the different position of the octave range (*ambitus*) and called respectively authentic and plagal. In the *authentic modes* the ambitus extends from the final to the upper octave; in the *plagal modes,* from the fourth below the final to the fifth above it.

In the sixteenth century two scales on A and two on C, which essentially were the natural minor and major scales, were added to the system, bringing the total to twelve. The four authentic modes are the Dorian, Phrygian, Lydian, and Mixolydian. The plagal modes use the same four names but with the prefix "hypo," and the added minor and major modes are called the Aeolian and Ionian respectively. Some also recognize a Locrian mode. Following are the church modes, their ranges, and final notes, in reference to the white keys. (In actuality, each mode is found by its characteristic interval relationship; a modal scale could start on any tone.)

Mode	Final	Range
Dorian	D	D–D
Hypodorian	D	A–A
Phyrgian	E	E–E
Hypophrygian	E	B–B
Lydian	F	F–F
Hypolydian	F	C–C
Mixolydian	G	G–G
Hypomixolydian	G	D–D
Aeolian	A	A–A
Hypoaeolian	A	E–E
Locrian	B	B–B
Hypolocrian	B	F–F
Ionian	C	C–C
Hypoionian	C	G–G

Some of the church modes still are used in the traditional chants in the liturgy of the Catholic Church. Some also are found in folk and contemporary popular music, reflecting considerable rejuvenation of interest in them in the past couple of decades.

Many other modes have been developed in Western cultures, but only a few have gained much lasting acceptance. Perhaps Debussy's *whole-tone* scale is one of the most successful. It divides the octave into six whole tones, and there are only two basic scales: (a) C, D, E, F#, G#, Bb, C and (b) C#, D#, F, G, A, B, C#. The purpose of the whole-tone scale was to break away from the strong feeling for the tonic which traditional tonal harmony elicits. Omitting the three fundamental intervals of tonal harmony—perfect fourth, perfect fifth, and leading tone—was designed to accomplish this.

Pentatonic scales have five tones to the octave and have been developed in other cultures as well as in Western cultures. The pentatonic scale commonly used in Western cultures has no semitones and in the key of C uses the following tones: C, D, E, G, A, C. Pentatonic scales can be built on any tone of the chromatic scale; within each pattern they also can use any of the five tones as a tonic, thus having five different modes in a manner similar to the church modes. In practice, however, only two modes are used to any extent: the authentic mode, using C as the tonic, and the plagal mode, using G as the tonic.

The *chromatic* scale represents another modal system that has received a certain amount of use in Western cultures. It has been most used in terms of serial music. *Quarter-tone* scales also have been developed. They divide the semitone in half, hence, dividing the octave into twenty-four parts.

Backus (1977, pp. 148–149) notes three other scales which have been suggested; these scales divide the octave into nineteen, thirty-one, and fifty-three parts respectively. He notes that some combinations of the resulting small intervals closely approximate the semitones, thirds, and fifths of the just intervals. Von Hoerner (1975) has developed an elaborate scheme of chords, intervals, and chromatic properties of the nineteen and thirty-one tone scales.[*] Perceptually, tiny adjacent intervals become difficult to distinguish.

With developments in computers, synthesizers, and other electronic equipment it is possible to construct many other varieties of scales. Such scales, sometimes called *synthetic* scales, however, are intended to be unique and therefore of little general interest other than in relation to the particular compositions in which they are used.

---

[*]Theoretically, a person may divide the octave into any number of equal intervals. A division into n intervals uses the nth root of 2 as a multiplier or ratio symbol. With a division into 12 steps, 1.05946 ($\sqrt[12]{2}$) : 1 is the ratio between any two adjacent scale steps. With a division into n steps, $\sqrt[n]{2}$:1 is the ratio between any two adjacent scale steps. (The 2 is due to the 2:1 octave relationship.)

Modal organization in music of other cultures offers a great variety of additional modal patterns. Description of even the most common of these is beyond the scope of this discussion, although some are mentioned as examples.

Farnsworth (1969, pp. 23–25) notes that equally tempered scales also were developed in the Orient. The Siamese divided the octave into seven equal parts. Pentatonic scales, somewhat approximating the authentic mode of the Western pentatonic, have been used in nearly all ancient cultures—China, Polynesia, Africa, and American Indian (Apel, 1969, p. 653). Chinese music also uses six-tone (sexatonic) and seven-tone (heptatonic) scales, while scales of India and the Middle East are characterized by the use of microtones, i.e., intervals smaller than a semitone.

The possibilities of modal organization in music are infinite, but it is apparent that only a few modal systems have gained any wide-spread acceptance. Reasons for this are primarily cultural, although the compatibility of a scale structure with laws and principles of perceptual organization also appears to be a factor.

Other Types of Pitch Organization

Earlier in this chapter it was mentioned that the twentieth century has given rise to new ways for organizing pitch structure. Lest other discussions in this chapter suggest that pitches can only be organized within certain conventional frameworks, the present discussion seeks to provide a brief overview of twentieth-century developments in pitch organization of Western music.

The use of chromaticism and the resultant dissonance of the late romantic composers, particularly Wagner, led to a search for pitch organization beyond that which could be provided by triadic harmony. Chromaticism and modulation had evolved to the point that many composers no longer ended compositions in the original tonic key as had been the practice during the baroque, classical, and early romantic periods of music history.

Three distinct developments regarding harmonic practices evolved during the late nineteenth and early twentieth centuries. Some composers continued to compose within the broad outline of a tonal harmonic framework while at the same time utilizing chords of far greater complexity than traditional triads. A second group of composers continued to use chords from earlier harmonic practices, but sequenced them in such ways that expected progressions and resolutions were not forthcoming. Whole-tone music and polytonality were two results of this development. The third development was the abandoning of tonality for Schoenberg's serial techniques, which are intended to disrupt any feeling for tonality. Serial techniques, often called twelve-tone techniques because each of the twelve semitones in the octave must be used before another may be repeated, have provided the impetus for renewed interest in structuring the vertical dimension of pitch polyphonically, i.e., in terms of combinations of independent melodic lines. Twentieth-century polyphony, however, differs from the contrapuntal writing of the baroque, classical, and romantic periods in that there is little or no concern for the vertical sonorities of traditional tertian harmony.

Three other developments of twentieth-century pitch organization also deviate from the practices of tertian harmony. *Aleatoric* or *chance* music introduces an unpredictability regarding either its composition or performance. Such music leaves some of the pitch, duration, and loudness structure to chance, thus making it very difficult for listeners to develop any melodic or harmonic expectations other than uncertainty itself.

Musique concrete is the name given to the development in which traditional sound sources (instruments and voices) are replaced by sounds of various kinds—environmental noises, sounds of nature, or most any other conceivable sound source. These sounds can be recorded, combined, and modified at the composer's will. It may utilize fixed or changing pitches as well as sounds of indefinite pitches to create a collage of sounds. As might be expected, the pitch structure need have no confining framework such as tertian harmony, although it may be assumed that most composers creating music of this type do have some underlying organizational structure in mind.

A final and perhaps most important development in pitch organization of twentieth-century music is electronic music, which with computers, synthesizers, and sound samples has given composers a new vista not only for organizing pitches, but also for creating and modifying new timbres and textures. Composers using an electronic medium can generate and combine electronically pitches in an infinite variety of ways. No longer are the fixed divisions of an octave the basis for all music. The implications of electronic developments are staggering from a standpoint of music perception, not only because of possible stimulus arrangements but also because of possible limitations in human respondents.

Developments in serial music, aleatoric music, *musique concrete*, and electronic music have created ambiguities for listeners accustomed to hearing only music constructed in a tonal harmonic framework. At present, the acceptance of such developments in "classical" music appears to be only among a relatively small musical subculture of composers, theorists, musicians, and other listeners. Electronic music is being incorporated more and more in music of various popular subcultures. The general population of Western cultures, including many people who profess to have "considerable interest" in music, however, are not flocking to the concert halls or buying recordings of music that deviates too radically from tonal harmony. Whether this is just a normal slowness to accept new musical styles or whether it is because the music of these new developments lacks an organizational structure that allows listeners to perceive and cognitively organize the tonal structures is subject to conjecture.

Psychological Processes

The processing of individual pure and complex tones was examined in Chapter Three; this section, however, examines the psychological processes related to pitch structures in *music*. Much of the theory and research has sought to determine the internal higher level cognitive representations and strategies for processing musical stimuli. Most of this theory and research has been in relation to melodic organization of Western tonal music, although some work has extended to other aspects of music—rhythmic and harmonic structures. Also, several attempts have been made to establish more extended, elaborate hierarchical models of musical perception.

The impetus for this surge of interest in the cognitive structures of music is an outgrowth of a major shift in psychology toward focus on "higher level, more cognitive aspects of human behavior" (Krumhansl, 1983, p. 29) and several other developments. According to Krumhansl, the primary influences were Chomsky's (1965, 1975) linguistic theory, with its insistence that language behavior is dependent on abstract mental representations of the structure of language, and developments in computer technology, which allowed the development of models and terminology for characterizing complex mental behavior as well as greatly facilitating precision in controlling research variables and analyzing data. Other influences, also noted by Krumhansl, are that two seemingly contradictory approaches for examining music perception provide important bases for research on cognitive processes. These include (a) the "reductionistic approach," reflected in the early work of Helmholtz (1863/1954) and Seashore (1919, 1938), which broke down complex auditory perceptual stimuli for examination in terms of sensory response to basic units of the stimuli, and (b) the work of Gestalt psychologists (Wertheimer, 1923/1955; Koffka, 1935) in developing laws of perceptual organization. Other important influences cited by Krumhansl were from music theory, where (a) principles of organization for tonal music had been identified, (b) a terminology for characterization of pitch development had been developed, and (c) a number of music-theoretic accounts of the nature of the psychological processes involved in music perception also had been postulated.

Psychological processes are examined here as they relate to (a) hierarchical perceptual structures, (b) empirical studies of perception and memory, (c) melodic and harmonic expectations and information theory, and (d) pitch-related behaviors.

Hierarchical Perceptual Structures

A number of hierarchical perceptual models for music have been developed, and West, Howell, and Cross (1985) provide excellent reviews of some of the more influential ones. They also remind us that models are *analogues* that attempt to portray the psychological processes of music perception, and as such involve the making of inferences about how subjective experiences of musical sound stimuli in our senses and imagination may affect musical judgments and other behavior. Essentially, *models are descriptions of inferred internal psychological events*. They also are generalized, usually not accommodating individual differences. Nevertheless, most of them offer valuable insights into music perception, cognition, and behavior.

West, Howell, and Cross's (1985) observations and principles regarding hierarchical cognitive structures in music, noted previously in Chapter Four, are briefly reiterated here, because of the important perspective they provide regarding hierarchical perceptual structures. Essentially, they observed that persons developing models should recognize that (a) all perceptible dimensions of musical experience are reflected and accommodated, (b) each listener brings a unique history of music experience to each new music experience, (c) not all music is immediately perceived, organized, and classified in a well-ordered hierarchy, even by sophisticated listeners, (d) the theory should be verifiable in terms of behavior of particular listeners, and (e) extramusical or historical context may influence structural grouping. Their three modelling principles are that (a) models must account for both vertical and horizontal structures, because music involves patterning over time, (b) grouping principles of Gestalt psychology—good continuation, proximity, similarity, regularity, symmetry, and common fate—reflect global perceptual factors that operate in the context of cultural expectations, and (c) groups formed from Gestalt principles may form larger groups at higher hierarchical levels.

It is beyond the scope of this discussion to review the various perceptual hierarchies that have been proposed; however, for illustrative purposes, two are briefly examined here: (a) Krumhansl's (1979) *tonal hierarchy* for melodic patterns and (b) two aspects of Lerdahl and Jackendoff's (1983) model that pertain to pitch structure, *time-span reduction* and *prolongation reduction*. The aspects of Lerdahl and Jackendoff's model related to rhythmic structures were examined in Chapter Four. Readers interested in examining these models in detail are referred to the original sources.

Krumhansl's theory evolved from a series of experiments on the processing of pitch patterns in a tonal context. In one experiment, musical subjects listened to a C major scale or triad, followed by paired tones. Subjects rated the similarity of the stimuli within each pair on a 1–7 scale. Generally, tones from the C triad were quite similar, other tones from the C major scale were somewhat less similar, and nondiatonic tones (tones other than the scale tones) were less similar yet. The second tones tended to have larger similarity effects; i.e., the pair was more similar when the second tone was related more closely to the tonal context than the first tone.

In the second experiment, subjects heard patterns comprised of a standard tone, followed by eight interpolated tones and a final comparison tone, which either was the same as the standard or differed by a semitone. The task was to indicate on a 1–6 scale the certainty that the comparison tone matched the standard. Interpolated tones were either tonal, i.e., the standard was in the tonal context suggested by the interpolated tones, or atonal, i.e., the standard was nondiatonic in relation to the interpolated tones. In general, it was easier for subjects to remember diatonic standard tones when the "interference" was caused by diatonic interpolated tones. It was easier to remember nondiatonic tones when the interpolated tones were also nondiatonic. A similar third experiment in which the interpolated sequences were free of test tones gave similar results. In a fourth experiment, subjects judged tonal sequences to be more "musical" than atonal sequences.

Krumhansl applied multidimensional scaling to the similarity ratings and described a *tonal hierarchy.* The multidimensionality is represented by a three-dimensional cone, with the components of the tonic triad lying closely together near the vertex. The next level, farther from the vertex, is a less closely related subset consisting of the remaining diatonic scale tones. Still farther from the vertex is a widely dispersed grouping of the nondiatonic tones which remain from the chromatic octave. In other words, in a tonal context the tonic triad (e.g., C–E–G in C major) has a perceptual similarity among its components which is greater than any other similarity; the similarity among remaining scale tones (D, F, A, B in C major) is greater than that among nondiatonic tones (e.g., Bb, Db, G#). Perceptual similarities arising from experience with tonal contexts may be critical in guiding the perceptual tracking of a melody.

Lerdahl and Jackendoff's (1983) elaborate hierarchical model of tonal structure is based more in theory than research. Two of its hierarchical components, *time-span reduction* and *prolongation reduction,* concern pitch structures. As the name implies, the time-span reduction hierarchy seeks to formalize the way in which pitch events are perceived at different levels of structural importance within a given time-span. It involves examination of pitch within various levels of the hierarchical "tree" for that time-span, seeking to determine which pitch is most stable. That pitch is called the "head" of the time-span. The process is repeated hierarchically for groupings of time-spans, until the highest level of grouping is reached.

Two types of rules are applied in forming structures according to Lerdahl and Jackendoff: *well-formedness* rules, which specify possible structures, and *preference* rules, which designate the probable structures that are likely to conform to the way experienced listeners organize the music. Well-formedness rules may answer the question "What's possible?" Preference rules may answer the question "What corresponds to expectancies?" Well-formedness rules for time-span reduction are concerned with specifying the nature of time-span heads; preference rules for time-span reduction specify principles according to which time-span head is chosen.

Essentially, time-span reduction "is intended to account for the distribution of structural and ornamental [pitch] events in a piece, and to give a clear picture of the network of interconnected regions governed by these events" (Clarke, 1986, p. 6). Clarke notes that time-span reduction presents an essentially static and primarily spatial perspective on pitch organization in tonal music and that it ignores the dynamic properties operating within and beyond the boundaries of the time-span units.

Prolongation reduction attempts to overcome this problem. Whereas time-span reduction works from small groupings to larger, more abstract groupings, prolongation reduction works just the opposite. Showing some Schenkerian influences, prolongation reduction begins with a single pitch event, perhaps representing an entire piece or section, and "elaborates this single event until a level of detail close to the musical surface is reached" (Clarke, p. 6). Prolongation reduction essentially assigns pitches hierarchical positions based on tension-relaxation and continuity. Prolongation reduction also has a hierarchical tree structure, and well-formedness rules for prolongation reduction are similar to those for time-span reduction. Preference rules select a hierarchy in terms of melodic and harmonic stability and principles of harmonic progression derived from music-theoretic considerations.

As West, Howell, and Cross (1985, p. 39) state, the "model attempts to provide a symbolic representation of music that elucidates its structure as perceived by a listener." Lerdahl and Jackendoff suggest that the model provides a musical "grammar," which includes innate aspects arising from inherent cognitive organization. Just as people are "naturally" predisposed to acquire language, although the language they acquire is a function of learning, people may be "naturally" predisposed to acquire musical cognition, although the cognitized musical idioms and forms will depend on cultural experience and learning. Variation is possible in language and music, but there are limits to that variation.

Empirical Studies of Perception and Memory

Most of the recent research on music cognition has focused on perception and/or processing of melodic patterns, primarily ones presented in a tonal context. Serafine (1983) notes that this focus contrasts with earlier traditional research in music psychology that tended to dwell on response to single pitches, durations, or chords. Contemporary concerns in music cognition "focus on the structure and relationships *among* elements" (Serafine, p. 5).

Serafine sees three categories of cognitive processes for music: (a) *global, field-defining processes* that facilitate characterization of the general nature of a piece of music, (b) *temporal processes* that involve groupings of both successive, horizontal events and simultaneous, vertical events into units and groups of units, and (c) *nontemporal processes* that include more abstract processes such as *motivic* or *rhythmic abstraction, transformation, closure,* and *hierarchical structuring.* The research examined herein generally fits into the third category.

Serafine (1983) examined hierarchical structuring of compound melody, testing the assumption that, in certain types of melodic passages, listeners abstract from a single melody line "an underlying structure that embodies two or more simplified or more basic melodies" (p. 9). Subjects were presented three musical examples, (a) a short piece of music, (b) a *reduction* of the piece to its "more basic structural tones," and (c) a similar but "wrong" reduction, i.e, with tones not basic and structural. Both the "correct" and "wrong" reductions were presented at different levels of structure, i.e., at *foreground* and *middleground* levels. Subjects (adult nonmusicians) were able to select the "correct" over the wrong reduction at the foreground level, but not at the middleground level. Serafine concluded that her data provide evidence of an initial level of structuring for untrained listeners and that, perhaps even more importantly, the data provide evidence that hierarchical structurings are legitimate cognitive processes rather than just theoretical constructs.

Dowling and Harwood (1986, pp. 130–144) summarize a series of studies suggesting that contour, interval size, and tonal scale system are important features in adults' perception of and memory for melodies and that these features may have different importance, depending on the demands of the task. Contour is a particularly important feature for short-term memory tasks, but for long-term memory, where many melodies may share similar contours, interval size plays a much more important role in helping adults differentiate among melodies. Dowling and Harwood also recognize the importance of individual differences in musical experience for music cognition, particularly with respect to reliance upon learned melodic features, such as the tonal scale system, for processing melody.

Idson and Massaro (1978) conducted a series of experiments involving structural transformations of melodies to evaluate the effects of interval size, contour, tone height, and tone chroma on melodic recognition. In two transformations the component tones of a melody were displaced by octave intervals, either preserving or violating the patterns of change in pitch direction (melodic contour). When contour was violated, perception of the melody was severely disrupted, but when contour was preserved, the melodies were identified as accurately as the untransformed melodies, suggesting that contour, as well as interval size, provides essential information for melodic perception.

Cuddy, Cohen, and Miller (1979) provide evidence that diatonic conditions and cadential relationships are important information for maintaining melodic structures and recognizing deviations from those structures. Forty-eight subjects with "general interest in music" indicated which one of two transpositions of standard melodies was correct. Each transposition was either to the dominant (e.g., G in relation to C) or tritone (e.g., F# in relation to C) tonality in relation to the standard's diatonic context. Altered tones, which made particular melodies "wrong" in relation to their standards, were a semitone up or down from where they should have been in a totally accurate transposition. Subjects' performance deteriorated when the "core" of three tones containing the alteration was embedded in a nondiatonic context; it improved when a cadence was provided. The most accurate recognition occurred when (a) there was a diatonic and cadential context, (b) the altered tone was nondiatonic, and (c) the transposition was to the dominant level. The worst recognitions occurred under nondiatonic conditions. Essentially, the investigators provided important evidence that musical structures provide aids which people who are sensitive to those structures may employ in recognizing alterations in a tonal sequence.

Cuddy, Cohen, and Mewhort (1981) asked 120 undergraduates to rate short melodic sequences in terms of tonality or tone structure, with highest ratings for sequences with "musical keyness" or "completeness" and lowest ratings for sequences that contained "unexpected" or "jarring" notes. The seven-tone melodic sequences reflected five levels of harmonic structure; in addition, they varied on two other dimensions: contour and excursion. Essentially, contours were simple or complex, depending on the number of direction changes, and excursion was either zero or nonzero, depending on whether the final tone of the sequence was the same as the first or whether it differed from the first. In a second experiment, 60 undergraduates were asked to select the position of the correct transposition of the test sequence. A third experiment employed procedures similar to the second, but used on-line computer generated sequences. Results of experiment one revealed that, as the rules of diatonicism were violated, i.e., as the harmonic structure was changed from the highest level of tonal structures to sequences that deviated radically from diatonic tonal structure, there was a dramatic change in ratings. Both highly trained musicians and subjects with little formal training rated the sequences consistently according to the harmonic structure. Experiments two and three revealed that subjects were able to identify correct transpositions of melodies with greatest accuracy for melodic sequences with the highest level of harmonic structure and with the simplest contour and excursion. In a subsequent experiment using a similar but more difficult task, Cuddy (1982) confirms that the variables of structure, contour, and excursion held even when mistunings were introduced in the melodic sequences.

Implicit if not directly suggested in each of the above studies is the dependence of perception and memory on the tonal harmonic framework of the melody pattern. Apparently melodies that conform most closely to the rules or grammar of Western tonality are the most easily recognized and remembered. Such finding are consistent with Krumhansl's tonal hierarchy discussed in the previous section.

The dependence of Western music and the Western listener on harmonic structure and tonality for remembering melodies apparently carries over into performance. Sterling (1985) examined the effects of stylistically diverse harmonizations on 25 college singers' performance of an unfamiliar tonal melody that had been learned to a specific criterion level. The harmonizations included traditional tonal, chromatic, dissonant, quartal, and chords with extensions. Results revealed a higher degree of vocal accuracy when the melody was accompanied by traditional tonal harmonic accompaniment, suggesting that the structure provided by the tonal harmony affects singers' reproduction of melodies.

The potential of research on music perception and cognition for understanding and facilitating musical behavior appears to be great, although few efforts have been made to "apply" the results as part of a structured pedagogy of music. Perhaps the research base is as yet insufficient for such application, but the challenge remains for both psychologists and educators to interpret and apply such findings.

Expectations and Information Theory

The mass of aural stimuli comprising melody and harmony, with their inherent attributes of tonal and rhythmic structure, timbral variations, and dynamic change, presents listeners with a complexity of stimuli that, without some mechanism for rendering a sense of order in an individual's perceptual system, would appear to be unintelligible cacophony. Indeed, to some individuals, much of what is called *music* by others *is* unintelligible cacophony! The question under consideration here, therefore, is "How do individuals create musical meaning out of the mass of sounds called melody and harmony?"

From a psychological perspective melody and harmony are highly complex phenomena, but it appears that most individuals are able to receive a certain amount of musical *meaning* from them.* Many individuals who appear to gain meaning from music, however, have no extensive or intensive formal musical training. On the other hand, even some highly trained musicians apparently perceive little meaning from some avant-garde music. Members of a Western culture also can listen to a given Oriental melody and have great difficulty in recognizing any semblance of organizational structure. Still, some individuals within a Western culture can listen to Brahms' *D Major Symphony* and marvel at its structure while others perceive it as unintelligible cacophony. Such observations beg the question, "Why does some music hold meaning for some individuals and not for others?"

One approach to the question has been in terms of information theory (e.g., Broadbent, 1958; Moles, 1966; Meyer, 1956, 1967). This approach recognizes that a central problem in dealing with complexity is an individual's *capacity* for such. Capacity for perception and cognition of complex stimuli is limited for everyone, although each individual's limits are not the same. We do not know how to assess the limits of perceptual capacity except under somewhat artificial conditions for some isolated tasks. Information theory provides a construct for examining perceptual capacity for music.

Information theory basically is a system for quantifying the amount of *uncertainty* involved in a sensory stimulus or *message*. "A message is a finite, ordered set of elements of perception drawn from a repertoire and assembled in a structure" (Moles, 1966, p. 9). Messages may be spatial or temporal; music, like dance, is a time art and provides temporal messages, whereas painting, sculpture, and photography provide spatial messages.

If the circumstances surrounding the reception of a particular sensory event are such that only one possible symbol *could* have been transmitted, then the amount of information conveyed by the correct identification of that symbol (or message) is zero. If the message is one chosen from

---

*As used in the present discussion musical meaning refers to perceptual and conceptual meaning; Chapter Six examines musical meaning as aesthetic meaning.

two equally likely alternatives then the amount of information acquired through a correct reception of it is one *bit,* or one binary decision's worth. (Watson, 1973, p. 293)

The greater the amount of *information* conveyed via the sensory *message,* the greater the *uncertainty of meaning or response.* In theory, a mathematical formula can be used to predict the probability of a response, but the complex nature of melody and harmony, coupled with the human variable in terms of previous experience with melody and harmony, makes absolute accuracy of prediction virtually impossible.* The authors concur with Meyer (1967, p. 20) that our inability to measure precisely the amount of information in a musical message does not weaken or invalidate information theory as a basis for examining musical meaning; the theory still provides a useful construct for examining musical expectation as well as a framework for studying musical perception.

The amount of *information* an individual receives when listening to melody or harmony, and hence the individual's *expectations* regarding them, is a function of two basic variables: (a) the extent to which the *structural* characteristics of melody and harmony conform to fundamental laws of perceptual organization and (b) the individual's previous experience with the given style of melody or harmony. As should be apparent from previous discussions, melodies and harmonies that conform most closely to the rules and grammar of Western tonal harmonic structure generally conform to the fundamental laws of perceptual organization; the tonal harmonic framework provides the structural unity, and the melody or harmony is received as a Gestalt or holistic pattern.

The expectations an individual develops from melody or harmony are related to its perceptual *redundancy.* While information theory *per se* holds that the redundancy of a message is characteristic of the stimulus alone, Meyer (1967, pp. 277–279) maintains that redundancy in a musical message depends on both the extent to which structural characteristics conform to the laws of perceptual organization and the degree to which the individual has learned the syntactical-formal premises of the musical style.

Redundancy is never total, even in a musical style with which an

---

*Specific quantification of information in music is also complicated considerably by conflicts regarding what the basic *unit* of musical information is. Is it the individual tone, a chord, a phrase, or a period? It probably varies with the listener and the music.

individual is familiar; melody and harmony in Western tonal music have disorder, ambiguity, and unpredictability.

> Were a composition totally redundant, the result would be completely predictable and, consequently, total tedium.... The relative disorder or randomness that necessarily complements redundancy may be called *perceptual information.* (Meyer, 1967, p. 278)

Perceptual redundancy, which will vary with the individual listener, relies heavily on memory of previous experiences (long-term memory) with the style and allows the individual listener to create psychological order out of the melody or harmony, thus developing expectations and meaning or understanding. If redundancy is too low, the perceptual information is too great for the melody or harmony to be understood. If redundancy is too high, the music will be so predictable as to become quickly boring.

As may be apparent to the reader, the harmonic framework of Western music, with its melodies and harmonies using a familiar scale system and constructed in such ways that tonality and melodic and harmonic movement are built in, provides the stimulus for redundancy. Regardless of the historical period and its stylistic pecularities, tonality and scales provide strong *structural redundancy.*

When an individual with his or her lifetime of experience with Western tonal music, which Meyer calls *cultural* redundancy, listens to unfamiliar tonal music which has *structural* redundancy built in through its tonal harmonic framework, the *perceptual redundancy* is high, thus delimiting the amount of new or extraneous *information* in the music. Hence, the individual more readily can "make sense" of the unfamiliar music than he or she could if it were in a style which did not have structural redundancy and for which he or she had developed no cultural redundancy.

This does not mean, however, that everyone maturing in a Western culture automatically will be able to understand all tonal music, because within Western culture the variety of musical style is great; further, the range of experiences individuals within a Western culture have with music also is great. It does suggest, however, that if given adequate experiences with tonal harmonic music, an individual should have a strong psychological basis for interacting with it.

To recapitulate, perceptual redundancy limits the amount of information a listener receives from a musical message. The greater the redundancy, the more accurate the listener's expectations. Perceptual redundancy enables a listener to conceive melody and harmony as patterns or Gestalten even though he or she obviously may not perceive and remember each constituent tone or chord of the pattern. The expectations complement the tones and chords actually perceived to create the musical pattern.

When a listener encounters melodies or harmonies which do not have structural redundancy built in and for which he or she has not developed cultural redundancy, there is increased information. With the increased information, the accuracy of the individual's expectations decreases. When information is so great that the individual cannot develop expectations regarding the melodic or harmonic patterns, the music holds little meaning. Meyer (1967, pp. 283–293) suggests that the *lack* of perceptual redundancy, with its constituent aspects of structural and cultural redundancy, is most likely the reason serialism has failed to gain widespread acceptance. The authors submit that some avant-garde electronic music that does not provide structural redundancy to facilitate the perception of patterns or Gestalten also will be unlikely to gain widespread acceptance, particularly since few individuals are developing any cultural redundancy for such music.

Pitch-Related Behaviors

Expectations are fundamental to both receptive and production behaviors. While their role in receptive behaviors should be apparent from the preceding discussion, their role is perhaps less clear regarding production behaviors. In reception of melody and harmony, expectations are essentially a function of memory of previous experiences with melody and harmony which facilitate perception of new melodies and harmonies. Woodruff (1970) calls these memories of previous experiences *concepts* (see also Chapter Ten) and suggests that they provide the basis for musical behavior. Regelski (1975, p. 11) has elaborated on the view that concepts are general thought tendencies and suggests that they result from (a) perception and cognition of many particular personal experiences with the learning or skill to be mastered, (b) the transfer of certain learnings from these particular personal experiences to other particular but somewhat different situations, and (c) a gradually evolving tendency toward increased frequency of behavior.

Expectations, therefore, are basic to the conceptualization of music. Musical concepts, recognized as cumulative tendencies toward response resulting from cognitive musical organizations, are the product of memories and classifications of previous experiences with musical stimuli. While musical concepts involve covert cognitive activity, they form the basis for both receptive and production behaviors. Receptive behaviors are essentially perceptual and therefore covert in nature; productive behaviors involve production or reproduction of pitches in music.

Receptive Behaviors. The basic problem in studying receptive behaviors is that they are essentially covert, and to gain some understanding of them, investigators must devise some overt manifestation of them, a task which often creates as many questions as it answers. Investigators do not always agree regarding the appropriateness of certain overt behaviors as valid reflections of certain covert perceptual or conceptual activity. For example, investigators studying "perception of melodies" might devise musical tasks to serve as evidence of melodic perception, which range from simply recognizing a melody or discriminating between two melodies to singing or notating an aurally presented melody. Some "melodies" used in research are limited, contrived tonal sequences that may or may not be reflective of melody in Western music. While some investigators operationally define their terms and delimit their generalizations, others apply vague labels to their studies and sometimes generalize far beyond what the data warrant, thereby leaving the reader with a mass of seemingly contradictory information regarding receptive behaviors. The situation is compounded when theoretical considerations are intermixed with presentations and discussions of empirical data. Unfortunately, there appears to be no neat and tidy solution to the problem.

The reader should keep in mind, however, that receptive behaviors are essentially perceptual and involve *recognition of,* and *discrimination between,* musical stimuli. Both processes are fundamental to reception of melody and harmony. While listening to music an individual is constantly, and usually without any particular awareness, separating the familiar from the unfamiliar and comparing new patterns with memories of previously learned patterns. The better the new melodies and harmonies match the expectations based on memories of previous experiences, the more comprehensible they are.

Two additional classes of receptive behaviors also should be noted: *analytical* and *aural-visual discrimination.* Essentially these are extensions of recognition and discrimination, but each goes beyond the basic receptive processes. Analytical behaviors reflect efforts to consciously categorize melodic and harmonic patterns into their constituent parts. Aural-visual discrimination involves associating aural stimuli, melodic and harmonic patterns, with their symbolic (notational) representations.

As may be apparent to the reader, receptive behaviors are difficult to isolate entirely from performance behaviors; there is always an element of "performance" in any overt manifestation of receptive behaviors. Failure to produce does not necessarily mean failure to perceive or receive.

Production Behaviors. Production behaviors are of three basic types: singing, performing with an instrument, and creating music. It is recognized that the ability to make musical discriminations underlies all production behaviors. Without the ability to discriminate among pitch patterns, an individual would be unable to produce his or her musical intentions in any tonal manner. While the concern of the present discussion is production of melodies and harmonies, the principle is the same for all aspects of music, be they dynamics, rhythm, or timbre. If the individual cannot discriminate among the tonal attributes, the production efforts are hindered.

Each of the three types of production behaviors are subdivided according to whether the behavior is a *re*production or *pro*duction of music. Singing and instrumental performance may involve production of musical patterns not previously produced, i.e., improvisation. In improvisation the performer is combining new melodic and harmonic patterns within a given conceptual framework. Most improvising today, be it by the jazz musician or church organist, is conceived within a tonal harmonic framework. Singers and instrumentalists also are involved in the reproduction of melodies and harmonies. They may reproduce pitch patterns learned "by ear," i.e., by rote procedures, and patterns read or memorized from notation. At the risk of overgeneralization, it appears that most music performed in Western cultures involves reproduction rather than production.

Creation behaviors also can involve either production or reproduction of musical patterns. The apparent favorite pastime of music theory teachers, melodic and harmonic dictation, requires music students to reproduce in notation aurally given melodic and harmonic patterns. Production of notation, however, involves what some consider to be the ultimate musical behavior, composition.

Development of Melodic and Harmonic Behaviors

As may be apparent, the types of receptive and production behaviors are sufficiently broad that they could be divided into many sublevels or categories of musical behavior. While it might appear that a developmental taxonomy of melodic and harmonic behaviors could be developed, the uniqueness of each child's musical experiences is such that any attempt to set forth such a taxonomy would immediately encounter difficulties. Each child's developmental sequence, while subject to general laws of maturation, is necessarily unique, because musical development is greatly influenced by environment (Phillips, 1976; Sergeant & Thatcher, 1974). Nevertheless, some generalizations can be made regarding musical development and this section will examine them from two particular perspectives: research-based studies of musical development and music teachers' views.

Research-Based Findings

Research related to development of melodic and harmonic behaviors is primarily developmental research, i.e., studies of children's abilities to accomplish certain musical tasks at various age or developmental levels. A major problem with this approach is the gap between the various musical tasks children are asked to perform and the implications drawn from the performance of the tasks. Many varieties of tasks, including ones requiring musical performance, loosely are labeled as melodic perception, even though it is obvious that performance tasks involve production behaviors in addition to receptive behaviors. Loose application of labels to assessment of receptive and production tasks tends to confound the study of musical development, and the reader is cautioned to consider the nature of the behavioral task required in any given study and to draw any conclusions only with due consideration of the nature of the tasks.

Another difficulty in drawing conclusions from studies of young children is the notorious *un*reliability of measuring instruments. Often conclusions are drawn on the basis of investigators' observations of a very limited number of cases or on the basis of responses to tests of questionable validity and reliability. These difficulties, coupled with the uniqueness of each child's musical experiences, make sweeping generalizations about children's musical development extremely hazardous. Nevertheless, there is a growing body of research that reveals an increasing consensus regarding the development of melodic and harmonic behaviors, and some of the more significant studies are noted here.

A series of studies by Trehub and her colleagues (Chang & Trehub, 1977; Trehub, Bull, & Thorpe, 1984; Trehub, Thorpe, & Morrongiello, 1987) indicates that response to melody begins in infancy. Chang and Trehub monitored five-month-old babies' "startle" response to changes in six-tone melodic patterns and observed change of heart rate (deceleration) when a pattern with a different contour was played after the infants had become habituated to another pattern. Such response, however, was not evident when contour was maintained but transposed up or down a minor third. The 1984 study (Trehub, Bull, & Thorpe) examined the effects of additional melodic transformations (transposition to other keys, altering intervals while preserving contour, altering octaves of individual notes while preserving contour, and altering octaves with accompanying contour changes) on six- to eleven-month-old infants. Using the "operant head turn procedure" as the response measure, the investigators observed that the subjects responded to new melodies or tone sequences as *familiar* if the sequences had the same melodic contour and frequency range as a previously heard sequence, while sequences with either different contour or range were responded to as *novel*. The 1987 study (Trehub, Thorpe, & Morrongiello) tested nine- to eleven-month-old infants for their discrimination of changes in melodic contour in the context of variations in key or interval size. Results revealed that infants could detect changes in both variable contexts, lending further support to conclusions from previous studies that infants categorize sequences of sounds on the basis of global, relational properties such as melodic contour. The investigators noted that the absence of response to differences of key and key-plus-interval conditions suggests that infants encode contour, rather than interval, information.

Nearly all research on infants' and young children's development of melodic discrimination reveals an increase in skills with an increase in age; however, various studies do not always agree regarding the exact ages at which given skills are developed. According to Hargreaves (1986, pp. 68–69), "vocal play," the precursor of spontaneous song, begins during the first year, suggesting that even six-month-old infants possess the prerequisites of music making: the ability to vocalize, vary and imitate pitch, and detect changes in melodic contour.

Sloboda (1985) observes that the first striking change in overt musical behavior after the first birthday comes at about 18 months of age when spontaneous song singing begins to occur. "The main characteristic of spontaneous singing is the use of discrete stable pitches (rather than the microtonal glides of the earlier 'song babbling')" (p. 202). Such singing usually does not include words, leading Sloboda to suggest that musical development at this age occurs along a separate "stream" from speech. Spontaneous singing at this level does not appear to reflect efforts to imitate particular songs, although the singing begins to include short melodic patterns using intervals that approximate the seconds and thirds of tonal music.

Most accounts of children's singing during the latter half of the second *18+mo* year suggest that there is a gradual change toward use of melodic patterns reflecting tonal, or culturally "correct," structures in spontaneous singing, as well as an "emerging ability to select melodic fragments from an increasingly large repertoire [of standard songs], and to match these with increasing accuracy to the components of standard models" (Hargreaves, 1986, p. 72). Apparently children begin to borrow certain aspects of songs they have heard and assimilate them more and more into their own spontaneous songs.

During the third year, children's spontaneous songs appear to become longer and reflect a definite trend toward use of diatonic scale intervals. Davidson, McKernon, and Gardner (1981, p. 305) suggest that children appear to develop a set of song-related expectations that in essence provide a "song frame" which structures their performance of songs. As Sloboda (1985, p. 204) notes, "by two-and-a-half, the child seems to have assimilated the notions that music is constructed around a small fixed set of pitch intervals, and that repetition of intervallic and rhythm patterns is a cornerstone of music." However, the child as yet seems to lack any grasp of hierarchical structures governing groups of patterns that might prescribe direction and closure. Sloboda observes that songs of children of this age usually have an "aimless" quality, with little or no sense of "finishing."

Toward the end of the third year, children's singing begins to reflect less spontaneous song and more imitation of songs they hear in their environment. Moog's (1976) extensive study of children's musical development revealed that children in the early phases of this stage are able to imitate melodic contour more easily than they imitate exact pitch. However, during the third and fourth years, many children's capacity to imitate songs develops greatly, to the point that "most children can accurately reproduce the familiar songs and nursery rhymes of their culture by the age of five" (Sloboda, p. 205). Spontaneous song is no longer the predominant song style for the five year old. Apparently, children at about age five become much more concerned with accuracy of imitation, reflecting a general developmental trend toward precision and mastery of detail. Five year olds are able to maintain the key of a song much better than four year olds, apparently reflecting some higher order "knowledge" of key and tonal center that most four year olds have not yet developed.

The ability to maintain a key or tonal center is not necessarily the same as the ability to learn a song at a given pitch level. Sergeant and Roche's (1973) study of children's ability to learn to sing songs at specific pitch levels suggests that younger children may focus more on the absolute pitch when learning a melody than do older children. Over a three-week period they taught 36 children (13 three- to four-year olds, 10 five-year olds, and 13 six-year olds) to sing three melodies. Each melody was taught on an invariant pitch level. One week after the completion of the study, each child's singing of the melodies was recorded. Results revealed an inverse relationship between accuracy of pitch level and accuracy of the melodic pattern. The youngest group sang at the most accurate pitch level, but the oldest group sang the melodic pattern most accurately. The results support the investigators' hypothesis that younger children tend to focus on pitch *per se,* while with increased age and conceptual development they focus more on the attributes of melodic pattern. Sergeant and Roche suggest that absolute pitch ability appears to decrease with age; further, they suggest that absolute pitch skills could be developed if children were given training on fixed pitch instruments during a critical period, common to all children, before their preconceptual perception of pitch has been transcended by higher-order conceptual thinking. Michel (1973) also recognizes a critical period in musical development, but suggests that the critical period is between the ages of five and six, whereas Sergeant and Roche's data suggest that it might come earlier.

McDonald and Ramsey (1979) sought to replicate Sergeant and Roche's study with American preschool children. Seventy-six two through five year olds were taught to sing four songs at invariant pitch levels in six 30-minute training sessions over a three-week period. Their data partially supported Sergeant and Roche's results: There was a positive relationship between age and conceptualization of melody; however, their data did not yield the inverse relationship between age and pitch level, perhaps due to a more stringent scoring system for pitch level than that used by Sergeant and Roche.

A subsequent study by Ramsey (1983) examined the effects of age, singing ability, and instrumental experience on three-, four-, and five-year olds' perception of melody as indicated by song vocalization. Five aspects of melody were evaluated: (a) absolute pitching, (b) melodic rhythm, (c) melodic contour, (d) tonal center, and (e) melodic interval. Her data revealed (a) significant differences in the performance of three-, four-, and five-year olds on melodic rhythm, melodic contour, and melodic interval, (b) high ability singers scored higher than low ability singers on perception of melodic rhythm, melodic contour, tonal center, and melodic interval, and (c) instrumental and noninstrumental treatment groups did not differ significantly in perception of the melodic components. Surprisingly, the data yielded no significant age level effects on either absolute pitch or tonal center.

Zimmerman (1971, p. 28) notes the ages of six to eight are marked by rapid development of melodic perception. Petzold (1966, p. 254) and some other researchers, however, report a leveling effect following the third grade, or around the age of nine. Taylor (1973) notes that there is a marked development of harmonic awareness around the age of nine, but Thackray (1973) maintains that results of his harmonic perception test provide positive evidence that many children develop a considerable degree of harmonic awareness well before the age of nine. Bridges' (1965) study of harmonic discrimination ability of children in kindergarten through grade three also suggests a gradual development in harmonic discrimination ability. Moog (1976), however, maintains that his research shows unequivocally that preschool-aged children do not experience any sort of harmony at all.

Shuter-Dyson and Gabriel's (1981, pp. 147–149) review of several studies examining children's harmonic discrimination in terms of consonance and dissonance (essentially requiring the selection of which version sounded "better" or "correct" in paired comparisons) revealed great improvement between the ages of five and ten in selecting "better" or "correct" versions. Such findings lend support to the view that basic harmonic awareness is developed as part of children's enculturation with Western music.

Imberty's (1981, pp. 108–115) comprehensive study of the development of tonality reveals four stages in the tonal enculturation process: (a) before the age of six, a period of perceptual *undifferentiation* with respect to cadence, (b) six and one-half and seven years, characterized by a *cadential perceptive scheme;* a musical phrase without a cadence is considered unfinished, but there is no clear differentiation among differing cadential movements, (c) eight years, the child can differentiate between a perfect cadence and absence of cadence; interrupted cadences are responded to less clearly, and the primary characteristic of this stage is the "beginning of *perceptive decentration* which makes it possible for the subject to connect what precedes the cadential formula with the formula itself" (p. 113), and (d) ten years, which is characterized by the establishment of a *relation of order;* the perception of the dominant leads to anticipation of the tonic; *reversibility* is evident in the perception of tonal functions and the syntactic elements of the musical phrase makes possible the precedence of order and logical anticipation. Imberty's research with older children did not reveal continued development, leading him to recognize a sort of "ceiling effect" that apparently cannot be forced higher. Imberty's "ceiling effect" for tonality occurs at about the same age level as the plateaus for melody and rhythmic development observed by Petzold (1966).

In summary, melodic discrimination skills are apparent in infancy and continue to develop through about the age of eight, with a critical period for development somewhere around the age of five or six. Perhaps this critical period is reflected in the child's shift from the use of spontaneous song to imitation of songs heard in the child's cultural environment. Harmonic discrimination skills appear to develop later, with earliest awareness of harmony appearing around the age of five or six and with a marked increase in harmonic discrimination occurring about the age of nine. Whether the leveling in melodic skills around the age of nine is due to increased harmonic awareness, however, is subject to conjecture.

Music Teachers' Views

The research-based findings discussed above primarily reflect attempts to study children's melodic and harmonic development as a part of their enculturation process with Western music. As children reach school age, musical development becomes much more dependent on formal instructional experiences than during early childhood.

Music teachers naturally are concerned with more than developing melodic and harmonic behaviors, but the present discussion is limited to examination of some commonly used methods for developing melodic and harmonic behaviors. A general sequence for emphasis at the various levels of the elementary school appears to be that rhythm is emphasized at the earliest levels, nursery school, kindergarten, and early primary grades; melody appears to receive greater attention in grades two through four, and harmony begins receiving greater attention in grades four through six. Nye and Nye (1985, p. 272) note that this is the general order in which children develop musical concepts.

The major musical activities through which melodic and harmonic behaviors are developed include singing, listening, and playing instruments. While movement sometimes is used to reinforce melodic behavior, it primarily is used to develop rhythmic behaviors.

Music teachers also recognize that much musical development occurs outside of school, but for most children school music represents the first formal learning experiences with music. The initial pitch-related concept that teachers try to have children develop is that of *high* and *low* pitch, or more properly, *higher* and *lower* pitch, since pitch is a relative phenomenon.

Aronoff (1969, p. 42) notes that behaviors related to melodic direction and shape should be developed by young children. Melodic direction and shape are developed and reinforced through a variety of musical activities—singing, listening, and playing instruments. Children learn that melodies move up, move down, or repeat tones; once direction is established, children's discrimination can be refined to the point that they can describe how a melody moves—by steps or skips, repeated tones, sequences, etc.

While music reading is recognized as a developmental process ranging from the following of simple line notation to reading of actual notation, music teachers do not all agree as to how best to teach music reading. Many, of whom Mursell is a particularly strong advocate, maintain that reading is best facilitated through instrumental experiences in which the visual symbol stands for a particular sound and set of movements. Others advocate a system to foster *relative* pitch reading within a scale or key. The predominant system of this type is the movable *do* syllables, although some teachers use a number system for the eight tones of the major scale. A fixed *do* system is used primarily in Europe. Gordon (1971, pp. 100–103) cites the advantages and disadvantages of syllables and numbers and concludes that the moveable *do* system is best.

Just as research shows that harmonic behaviors develop following melodic behaviors, music teachers have determined empirically that the teaching of harmony should follow the teaching of melody. Whether there is any cause and effect relationship here is unsettled. Nye and Nye (1985, pp. 353–377) provide an extensive discussion of strategies for developing children's harmonic behaviors.

While this brief sketch of music teachers' views on the development of melodic and harmonic behaviors is limited both in scope and depth, it does indicate that the teaching sequence generally recognizes and follows the developmental sequence observed by researchers.

Evaluating Melodies and Harmonies

While an examination of the "goodness" of melody or "appropriateness" of harmony perhaps is more appropriate in a discussion of aesthetics, it also is relevant to the psychological foundations of melodic and harmonic behaviors. The present discussion, while recognizing that "good" and "appropriate" can reflect value judgments and therefore are legitimate concerns from an aesthetic perspective, focuses on "goodness" and "appropriateness" from a perceptual standpoint.

Earlier discussions in this chapter suggest that melodies and harmonies may be considered structurally as well as psychologically. Perception necessarily involves both structural and psychological characteristics.

What is "Good" Melody?

The fundamental problem in determining the goodness of a melody rests with the relative emphasis one places on its structural and psychological characteristics. If one evaluates solely on structure, such characteristics as propinquity, repetition, and finality might be important evaluative criteria. On the other hand, explanations in terms of psychological characteristics might concern the extent to which melodies are perceived as patterns or the degree to which a given melody is perceived as being within a familiar style.

Mursell (1937, pp. 105–106) notes that essentially all that is needed for an authentic melodic experience is "a tonal sequence held together and unified by a unity of response." He notes that "inferior" melodies lack unity in both structure and response.

Hickman (1976) reviewed a number of accounts of melody, including ones which variously treated melody from technical, educational, musicological, and sociological perspectives among others, and concluded that order and pattern are essential constituents of good melodies. He then offered a model with four criteria against which melodies can be evaluated:

(a) the melody must manifest a pattern of elements, (b) the melody must be a product of a person or persons, (c) the melody must do more than adhere to specifications previously laid down, and (d) the melody must be worth having in itself apart from any purpose it may serve.

Lundin (1967, pp. 84–85) offers a behavioral or cultural interpretation of melody in which melody is viewed as a function of both the listener's previous experience and certain structural characteristics. He maintains that what have come to be perceived as melodies are a result of many centuries of musical development. As scales changed, the new patterns were accepted gradually as people became familiar with them.

Sloboda (1985, pp. 52–55) views the goodness of a melody in terms of the extent to which it conforms to the rules of its underlying generative grammar. If the melody conforms totally to the structural rules of Western tonal music, he suggests that the melody is likely to be dull; on the other hand, if the melody violates basic structural rules in an extreme manner, it may be unintelligible to listeners. Sloboda's view presupposes that listeners are enculturated in the grammatical rules of Western tonal music.

Smith and Cuddy (1986) examined the effects of repetition and rule familiarity on the "pleasingness" of 20 melodic sequences which varied in complexity of contour and harmonic structure. (The more complex the melodic sequence, the more it violated the rules of tonal harmonic structure.) Their data indicated that the more complex the underlying harmonic structure of the melody, the *less* pleasing the subjects rated it. Whether such *affective* responses reflect a measure of perceptual "goodness" may be debatable, but it certainly seems to support Sloboda's contention that as a melody deviates from the basic grammatical structures of tonal harmony, listeners respond to it differently.

Reimer (1970, pp. 103–105), while concerned with musical goodness rather than just melodic goodness, cites two aspects of goodness: *excellence*, which has to do with the syntactic or structural refinement in the music, and *greatness*, which has to do with the level of profundity of the music's expressive content. The two aspects are based respectively on Leonard Meyer's (1967, pp. 22–41) theories of value and greatness in music, which are discussed in Chapter Six. While the criterion *greatness* is more properly discussed under aesthetics, the criterion *excellence* has its roots in the meanings of musical messages an individual receives while listening to music.

The meaning an individual receives when listening to a melody is a function of the uncertainty reflected in the information present in the melody. The amount of information an individual receives is dependent on both the structural and cultural redundancy of the melody, i.e., the extent to which the melody reflects a particular melodic style and the degree to which the individual is familiar with and has developed expectations within that style. The greater the perceptual redundancy, the combined effects of structural and cultural redundancy, the more likely the melody is meaningful, and hence "good" for the individual.

Goodness of a melody may vary from individual to individual. A good melody for kindergarten children is different from what is good for an adolescent. Similarly, a good melody for the musically sophisticated is different from that which is good for an untrained listener. A melody in unfamiliar style also would most likely lack goodness for a listener. However, the greater the number of individuals who find meaning in a melody, the more it would appear that the goodness status of the melody should be elevated in some manner.

What is "Acceptable" Harmony?

"Acceptableness" of harmony has received considerably less attention than either melody or music as a whole. What attention there has been is related to one of two basic approaches: (a) studies of the age at which children become cognizant of harmony, e.g., Bridges (1965), and (b) individuals' preferences for harmony of traditional tonal compositions (Wing, 1961; Long, 1968). (Wing has a separate test for harmony whereas Long asks individuals to select the "better" of two musical renditions and tell whether it was better in terms of melody, harmony, or rhythm.)

The latter approach is particularly relevant to our discussion because in essence it seeks to assess individuals' preferences in terms of appropriateness of the harmony for given examples of Western tonal music in what is loosely called classical style. To the extent that an individual's preferences conform to what musically trained judges agree is appropriate, the individual exhibits knowledge of harmonic style for Western music. While the "agreement with the experts" approach can be criticized as somewhat snobbish, the particular mode for evaluating has merit and offers many possibilities for examining views of "acceptable" harmony.

Ultimately the acceptableness of harmony, just as the goodness of melody, is an individual matter and is a function of an individual's experience with harmonic styles. The meaning an individual receives from harmony is related to the expectancies he or she has developed for the given style. The information theory framework noted in the discussion of goodness of melody also can be applied in the discussion of harmony. Appropriateness of harmony, therefore, also is an individual matter; the degree to which groups of individuals find given harmonies acceptable reflects a cultural or subcultural acceptance.

Evaluation of Melodic and Harmonic Behaviors

Evaluations of melodic and harmonic behaviors generally involve one or more of several basic types of behavior: (a) behaviors reflecting recognition of tonal patterns, (b) behaviors reflecting discriminations between aurally presented tonal patterns, (c) behaviors associating aural and visual stimuli, and (d) production behaviors. The preference tests mentioned above conceivably could be considered a fifth type of behavior, although the authors view them as essentially requiring discriminations between tonal patterns. Also, production behaviors possibly could be subdivided into notation and performance behaviors.

Some of the same concerns noted under the discussion of the evaluation of rhythmic behaviors also are apparent in the evaluation of melodic and harmonic behaviors. The nature of the response mode selected for measuring discrimination could affect the assessment; group versus individual measurement also is an important consideration, both in terms of economy and accuracy. Failure to perform does not necessarily indicate failure to perceive. Finally, the specifics versus global measurement question is reflected in the approaches used in some of the tests. The value of a particular approach depends ultimately on the purpose of the evaluation and the nature of the data sought.

While the bulk of this discussion is devoted to selected published standardized music tests, it should be recognized that the most commonly used measures of melodic and harmonic behaviors involve performance, usually from notation. Performance of both prepared pieces and sightread pieces is used for evaluative purposes at all levels, ranging from primary school through professional levels. Melodic and harmonic dictation also are much used, particularly in high school and college music theory classes. The evaluative criteria for performances are usually in terms of a teacher's or panel of judges' perceptions of what is "correct" performance. While the pitfalls of this are many, the system apparently works to the satisfaction of many musicians; otherwise, there would be greater demands for refinements in the system.

Common to many published music tests is a *tonal memory* test, of which there are two basic approaches. One plays a melody or series of tones as a model and then in subsequent hearings, which range from two to six in number, the testee is asked to indicate *how* the melody was changed, usually to be selected from options such as key, rhythm, or pitch of some individual tone. The *Test of Musicality* (Gaston, 1957) and the *Drake Musical Aptitude Tests* (1957) use this type of tonal memory test.

The other type of tonal memory test also provides a model, but in subsequent hearings the testee is required to indicate *which tone* has been changed. The number of subsequent hearings also varies, usually from two to seven. Tests using this type of tonal memory include the *Seashore Measures of Musical Talents,* (Seashore, Lewis, & Saetveit, 1960), *Standardised Tests of Musical Intelligence* (Wing, 1961), and *Measures of Musical Abilities* (Bentley, 1966).

Gordon's (1965) *Musical Aptitude Profile* measures tonal memory, or imagery as it is labeled in the test, by providing a model melody and then a second melody which is either an embellished rendition of the model or an entirely different melody. This approach appears to assess the respondent's ability to discriminate tonal patterns at different structural levels, since the testee must determine whether the second melody would be like the model if the embellished tones were not present. The "harmony" portion of the Gordon test also is unique. It involves essentially the same process, although the changes are in a bass line. The upper part remains the same for both the model and the second hearing.

Gordon (1979; 1982) has developed two additional tests that include measures of tonal aptitude. The tonal subtest of the *Primary Measures of Music Audiation* is designed to assess the ability of children in kindergarten through grade three to discriminate between pairs of two- to five-tone aural patterns. One tone in the second of each pair is changed. The *Intermediate Measures of Music Audiation* has a similar subtest that follows the same format, but is designed for children in grades one through four. More will be said of these tests in the discussion of musical ability in Chapter Nine.

Thackray (1973, 1976) has devised measures of tonality and harmonic perception which appear to be useful. The tonality test measures tonality in melodies and has four subtests. Part I introduces modulations in some melodies and asks respondents to indicate whether the melodies sound "right" or "wrong." Part II uses short unfamiliar melodies, some of which are diatonic and clearly adhere to tonality while others do not. Testees are asked to determine whether each melody is "ordinary" or "peculiar." Part III asks testees to determine whether the melodies sound "finished" or "not finished," and Part IV asks testees to determine whether the concluding tone is the same as the beginning tone of a melody. Although the test is not standardized, it appears to be potentially very useful in assessing children's perceptions of tonality.

Thackray's harmonic perception test, also not standardized, has three parts. Part I presents a series of sounds played on the piano, some of which are single tones and some of which are chords. The testee is asked to indicate which are chords. Part II presents three- or four-tone harmonized melodies. The testee is asked to indicate which tone (if any) in a second hearing is harmonized differently. Part III presents a chord followed by a pause and then a progression of three, four, or five chords, and the respondent is asked to indicate where the given chord appears in the progression.

Colwell's (1969–1970) *Music Achievement Tests* measure a variety of behaviors related to melody and harmony. Some of the behaviors measured include determination of whether a pattern or phrase moves scalewise or in leaps, whether chords and phrases are in major or minor mode, whether notated melodies match aurally presented melodies, which among three tones following a cadence or phrase is the keytone, and what is the style period of aurally presented musical excerpts.

The *Iowa Tests of Music Literacy* (Gordon, 1970) measure three aspects of tonal concepts: aural perception, reading recognition, and notational understanding. Essentially the aural perception tests measure the ability to discriminate between major and minor tonality and some extensions thereof. The reading recognition tests ask testees whether given notated melodies match aurally given melodies, and the notational understanding is a quasi-dictation test.

Several aural-visual discrimination tests measure melodic aural-visual discrimination, but separate scores are not provided for melody and rhythm, e.g., Knuth (1966) and Farnum (1953). Melodic performance also is a major criterion in the scoring of the *Watkins-Farnum Performance Scale* (1954), but neither does it provide a separate score for melody.

The same recommendations offered at the conclusion of the discussion of rhythm tests apply here. Researchers and teachers concerned with selecting and developing measures of melodic and harmonic behaviors should first and foremost consider the nature of the behaviors they wish to evaluate and be certain that any measures selected or developed indeed measure those behaviors in a manner appropriate for the level of student being evaluated.

Summary

Following are the major points discussed in the chapter:

1. The vertical structure of Western music is considerably more highly developed than that of other cultures.
2. Most Western music is constructed within a tonal harmonic framework.
3. Changing either the relative pitch positions or tones or the rhythm of a tonal sequence changes the melody structurally, although not always perceptually.
4. Melodies can be defined as both structural and psychological entities.
5. Recent accounts of melodic perception are descriptions of the cognitive processes and structures developed from experience with melodies.
6. Model tonal hierarchies are based either explicitly or implicitly on generative grammars, the organizational rules that underlie musical structure.
7. Most models of melodic perception acknowledge the perceptual laws of Gestalt psychology.
8. Harmony in Western music is primarily tertian harmony.
9. There are three primary "holistic" attributes of harmony: (a) tonality, (b) harmonic movement, and (c) finality.
10. Melodic and harmonic movement are relative phenomena.
11. Perceptual organization of harmony is context dependent.
12. Tonality is an underlying unifying device in the perception of Western tonal music.
13. The diatonic scale is the basic scale of Western music.
14. Scale systems are codifications of musical practices.
15. The tempered diatonic scale is the most far-reaching standardization of music in the world.
16. The diatonic scale evolved from the Greek "Greater Perfect System."
17. Equal temperament is the most satisfactory tuning system for Western music.

18. Major and minor scales comprise the basic tonal patterns for most Western music.

19. Other modes include the church modes, the whole tone scale, the pentatonic scale, the chromatic scale, the quarter tone scale, synthetic scales, and scales of other cultures.

20. While most music uses fixed pitches in a tonal harmonic framework, some contemporary music uses sliding and indefinite pitches and is designed without an intended tonality.

21. Hierarchical perceptual models essentially are descriptions of inferred psychological events.

22. Important hierarchical models regarding the perceptual organization of pitch structures are Krumhansl's tonal hierarchy for melodic patterns and Lerdahl and Jackendoff's time-span reduction and prolongation reduction models.

23. Recent research in melodic perception confirms the dependency of perception and memory on the tonal harmonic framework of a melody.

24. Musical meaning is a product of expectations a listener develops.

25. Expectations are a function of the information a musical example provides.

26. Information decreases as redundancy increases.

27. Redundancy is a function of the structural characteristics of the music and a listener's previous experiences with music of that style.

28. Basic receptive behaviors include recognition and discrimination.

29. Production behaviors are of three basic types: singing, performing music with an instrument, and creating music.

30. Children generally develop melodic behaviors before harmonic behaviors.

31. Practices of music teachers generally reflect the sequence in which melodic and harmonic behaviors develop.

32. The "goodness" of a melody and "acceptableness" of harmony in the psychological sense are functions of an individual's previous experience with melodies and harmony in given styles.

33. Evaluation of melodic and harmonic behaviors involves one or more of several types of behavior: (a) recognition of tonal patterns, (b) discriminations between aurally presented tonal patterns, (c) associations between aurally presented and visually presented patterns, and (d) production behaviors.

REFERENCES

Apel, W. (1969). *Harvard dictionary of music* (2nd ed.). Cambridge: Belknap Press.

Aronoff, F. W. (1969). *Music and young children.* New York: Holt, Rinehart and Winston.

Backus, J. (1977). *The acoustical foundations of music* (2nd ed.). New York: W.W. Norton.

Barbour, J.M. (1951). *Tuning and temperament.* East Lansing: Michigan State Press.

Bentley, A. (1966). *Measures of musical abilities.* New York: October House.

Berry, W. (1976). *Structural functions in music.* Englewood Cliffs, NJ: Prentice-Hall.

Bharucha, J.J., & Krumhansl, C.L. (1983). The representation of harmonic structure in music: Hierarchies of stability as a function of context. *Cognition, 13,* 63–102.

Bower, G.H., & Hilgard, E.R. (1981). *Theories of learning* (5th ed.). Englewood Cliffs, NJ: Prentice-Hall.

Bridges, V.A. (1965). An exploratory study of the harmonic discrimination ability of children in kindergarten through grade three in two selected schools (Doctoral dissertation, The Ohio State University, 1965). *Dissertation Abstracts, 26,* 3692. (University Microfilms No. 65-13, 206)

Broadbent, D.E. (1958). *Perception and communication.* New York: Macmillan.

Burns, E.M., & Ward, W.D. (1982). Intervals, scales, and tuning. In D.Deutsch (Ed.), *The psychology of music* (pp. 241–269). New York: Academic Press.

Chang, H.W., & Trehub, S.E. (1977). Auditory processing of relational information by young infants. *Journal of Experimental Child Psychology, 24,* 324–331.

Chomsky, N. (1957). *Syntactic structures.* The Hague: Mouton.

Chomsky, N. (1965). *Aspects of the theory of syntax.* Cambridge: MIT Press.

Chomsky, N. (1968). *Language and mind.* New York: Harcourt Brace Jovanovitch.

Chomsky, N. (1975). *Reflections on language.* New York: Pantheon.

Clarke, E.F. (1986). Theory, analysis and the psychology of music: A critical evaluation of Lerdahl, F. and Jackendoff, R., *A Generative Theory of Tonal Music. Psychology of Music, 14,* 3–16.

Clynes, M. (Ed.) (1982). *Music, mind, and brain.* New York: Plenum Press.

Colwell, R. (1969–70). *Music achievement tests.* Chicago: Follett.

Cuddy, L.L. (1982). On hearing pattern in melody. *Psychology of Music, 10,* 3–10.

Cuddy, L.L., Cohen, A.J., & Mewhort, D.J.K. (1981). Perception of structure in short melodic sequences. *Journal of Experimental Psychology: Human Perception and Performance, 7,* 869–883.

Cuddy, L.L., Cohen, A.J., & Miller, J. (1979). Melody recognition: The experimental application of musical rules. *Canadian Journal of Psychology, 33,* 255–270.

Davidson, L., McKernon, P., & Gardner, H. (1981). The acquisition of song: A developmental approach. In R.G. Taylor (Ed.), *Documentary report of the Ann Arbor Symposium* (pp. 301–315). Reston, VA: Music Educators National Conference.

Deutsch, D. (Ed.). (1982). *The psychology of music.* New York: Academic Press.

Dowling, W.J. (1973). The perception of interleaved melodies. *Cognitive Psychology, 5,* 322–337.

Dowling, W.J., & Harwood, D.L. (1986). *Music cognition.* Orlando, FL: Academic Press.

Drake, R.M. (1957). *Drake musical aptitude tests.* Chicago: Science Research Associates.

Erickson, R. (1982). New music and psychology. In D. Deutsch, (Ed.), *The psychology of music* (pp. 517–536). New York: Academic Press.

Farnsworth, P.R. (1969). *The social psychology of music* (2nd ed.) Ames: The Iowa State University Press.

Farnum, S.E. (1953). *Farnum music notation tests.* New York: The Psychological Corporation.

Gaston, E.T. (1957). *Test of musicality.* Lawrence, KS: O'Dell's Instrumental Service.

Gordon, E. (1965). *Musical aptitude profile.* Boston: Houghton Mifflin.

Gordon, E. (1970). *Iowa tests of music literacy.* Iowa City: The Bureau of Educational Research and Service, The University of Iowa.

Gordon, E. (1971). *The psychology of music teaching.* Englewood Cliffs: Prentice-Hall.

Gordon, E. (1979). *Primary measures of music audiation.* Chicago: G.I.A. Publications.

Gordon, E. (1980). *Learning sequences in music: Skill, content, and patterns.* Chicago: G.I.A. Publications.

Gordon, E. (1982) *Intermediate measures of music audiation.* Chicago: G.I.A. Publications.

Greene, P.C. (1937). Violin intonation. *Journal of the Acoustical Society of America, 9,* 43–44.

Hargreaves, D.J. (1986). *The developmental psychology of music.* Cambridge: Cambridge University Press.

Hebb, D.O. (1949). *The organization of behavior.* New York: Wiley.

Helmholtz, H. von. (1954). *On the sensations of tone as a physiological basis for the theory of music* (A.J. Ellis, ed. and trans.). New York: Dover. (Originally published, 1863).

Hickman, A. Some philosophical problems of melody. *Psychology of Music, 4* (1), 3–11.

Howell, P., Cross, I., & West, R. (Eds.). (1985). *Musical structure and cognition.* London: Academic Press.

Idson, W., & Massaro, D. (1978). A bidimensional model of pitch in the recognition of melodies. *Perception & Psychophysics, 24,* 551–565.

Imberty, M. (1981). Tonal acculturation and perceptual structuring of musical time in children (trans. from original French) (pp. 107–130). In *Basic musical functions and musical ability,* Publication No. 32. Stockholm: Royal Swedish Academy of Music.

Kamien, R. (Ed.) (1972). *The Norton scores* (rev. ed.). New York: Norton.

Knuth, W.E. (1966). *Knuth achievement tests in music.* San Francisco: Creative Arts Research Associates.

Koffka, K. (1935). *Principles of Gestalt psychology.* New York: Harcourt, Brace & World.

Krumhansl, C.L. (1979). The psychological representation of pitch in a musical context. *Cognitive Psychology, 11,* 346–374.

Krumhansl, C.L. (1983). Perceptual structures for tonal music. *Music Perception, 1,* 28–62.

Krumhansl, C.L., Bharucha, J.J., & Castellano, M.A. (1982). Key distance effects on perceived harmonic structure in music. *Perception & Psychophysics, 32,* 96–108.

Krumhansl, C.L., Bharucha, J.J., & Kessler, E.J. (1982). Perceived harmonic structure of chords in three related musical keys. *Journal of Experimental Psychology: Human Perception and Performance, 8,* 24–36.

Lerdahl, F., & Jackendoff, R. (1983). *A generative theory of tonal music.* Cambridge: MIT Press.

Long, N.H. (1968). *The Indiana-Oregon music discrimination test.* Bloomington, IN: N.H. Long. (originally developed as the *Oregon Music Discrimination Test* by K. Hevner in 1935)

Lundin, R.W. (1967). *An objective psychology of music* (2nd ed.). New York: Ronald Press.

McDonald, D.T., & Ramsey, J.H. (1979). A study of musical auditory information processing of preschool children. *Contributions to Music Education, 7,* 2–11.

Mainwaring, J. (1951). Psychological factors in the teaching of music. *British Journal of Educational Psychology, 21,* 105–121, 199–213.

Meyer, L.B. (1956). *Emotion and meaning in music.* Chicago: The University of Chicago Press.

Meyer, L.B. (1967). *Music, the arts and ideas.* Chicago: The University of Chicago Press.

Michel, P. (1973). Optimum development of musical abilities in the first years of life. *Psychology of Music, 1* (2), 14–20.

Moles, A. (1966). *Information theory and esthetic perception* (J.E. Cohen, trans.). Urbana: University of Illinois Press.

Moog, H. (1976). *The musical experience of the pre-school child* (C. Clarke, trans.). London: Schott.

Mursell, J.L. (1937). *Psychology of music.* New York: W.W. Norton and Company.

Nickerson, J.F. (1949). Intonation of solo and ensemble performances of the same melody. *Journal of the Acoustical Society of America, 21,* 593–595.

Nye, R.E., & Nye, V.T. (1985). *Music in the elementary schools* (5th ed.). Englewood Cliffs, NJ: Prentice-Hall.

Ortmann, O. (1926). On the melodic relativity of tones. *Psychological Monographs, 35* (1), 1–35.

Ortmann, O. (1937). Interval frequency as a determinant of melodic style. *Peabody Bulletin,* 3–10.

Ostling, A., Jr. (1974). Research in Pythagorean, just temperament, and equal-tempered tunings in performance. *The Journal of Band Performance, 10* (2), 13–20.

Petzold, R.G. (1966). *Auditory perception of musical sounds by children in the first six grades.* Madison: University of Wisconsin. (ERIC Document Reproduction Service No. ED 010 297)

Phillips, D. (1976). An investigation of the relationship between musicality and intelligence. *Psychology of Music, 4* (2), 16–31.

Radocy, R.E. (1977). *Analysis of three melodic properties in randomly selected melodies.* Unpublished research report. The University of Kansas.

Ramsey, J.H. (1983). The effects of age, singing ability, and instrumental experiences on preschool children's melodic perception. *Journal of Research in Music Education, 31,* 133–145.

Regelski, T.A. (1975). *Principles and problems of music education.* Englewood Cliffs, NJ: Prentice-Hall.

Reimer, B. (1970). *A philosophy of music education.* Englewood Cliffs, NJ: Prentice-Hall.

Revesz, G. (1953). *Introduction to the psychology of music* (G.I.C. de Courcy, trans.). London: Longmans, Green.

Roederer, J.G. (1975). *Introduction to the physics and psychophysics of music* (2nd ed.). New York: Springer-Verlag.

Schenker, H. (1979). *Free composition* (E. Oster, ed. and trans.). New York: Longman. (Originally published, 1935)

Seashore, C.E. (1919). *The psychology of musical talent.* New York: Silver Burdett.

Seashore, C.E. (1938). *Psychology of music.* New York: McGraw-Hill.

Seashore, C.E., Lewis, D.L., & Saetveit, J.G. (1939; 1960). *Seashore measures of musical talents* (revised). New York: The Psychological Corporation.

Serafine, M.L. (1983). Cognitive processes in music: Discoveries and definitions. *Council for Research in Music Education, 73,* 1–14.

Sergeant, D. (1983). The octave—percept or concept. *Psychology of music, 11,* 3–18.

Sergeant, D., & Roche, S. (1973). Perceptual shifts in the auditory information processing of young children. *Psychology of Music, 1* (2), 39–48.

Sergeant, D., & Thatcher, G. (1974). Intelligence, social status and musical abilities. *Psychology of Music, 2* (2), 32–57.

Shepherd, R.N. (1982). Structural representations of musical pitch. In D. Deutsch (Ed.), *The psychology of music* (pp. 344–390). New York: Academic Press.

Shuter-Dyson, R., & Gabriel, C. (1981). *The psychology of musical ability* (2nd ed.). London: Methuen.

Sloboda, J.A. (1985). *The musical mind.* Oxford: Clarendon Press.

Smith, K.C., & Cuddy, L.L. (1986). The pleasingness of melodic sequences: Contrasting effects of repetition and rule-familiarity. *Psychology of Music, 14,* 17–32.

Sterling, P. (1985). The effect of accompanying harmonic context on vocal pitch accuracy of a melody. *Psychology of Music, 13,* 72–80.

Sundberg, J., & Lindblom, B. (1976). Generative theories in language and music descriptions. *Cognition, 4,* 99–122.

Taylor, J.A. (1976). Perception of tonality in short melodies. *Journal of Research in Music Education, 24,* 197–208.

Taylor, S. (1973). Musical development of children aged seven to eleven. *Psychology of Music, 1* (1), 44–49.

Temko, P.M. (1972). The perception of pitch predominance in selected musical examples of avant-garde composers, 1945–1961 (Doctoral dissertation, Florida State University, 1971). *Dissertation Abstracts International, 32,* 5275. (University Microfilms No. 72-0918)

Terhardt, E., & Zick, M. (1975). Evaluation of the tempered tone scale in normal, stretched and contracted intonation. *Acustica, 32,* 268–274.

Thackray, R. (1973). Tests of harmonic perception. *Psychology of Music, 1* (2), 49–57.

Thackray, R. (1976). Measurement of perception of tonality. *Psychology of Music, 4* (2), 32–37.

357 songs we love to sing. (1938). Minneapolis: Schmitt, Hall, and McCreary.

Trehub, S.E., Bull, D., & Thorpe, L. (1984). Infants' perception of melodies: The role of contour. *Journal of Experimental Psychology: Human Perception and Performance, 12,* 295–301.

Trehub, S.E., Thorpe, L.A., & Morrongiello, B.A. (1987). Organizational processes in infants' perception of auditory patterns. *Child Development, 58,* 741–749.

Von Hoerner, S. (1975). The definition of major scales, for chromatic scales of 12, 19, and 31 divisions per octave. *Psychology of Music, 4* (1), 12–23.

Watkins, J.G., & Farnum, S.E. (1954). *The Watkins-Farnum performance scale.* Winona, MN: Hal Leonard Music.

Watson, C.S. (1973). Psychophysics. In B.B. Wolman (Ed.), *Handbook of general psychology* (pp. 275–306). Englewood Cliffs, NJ: Prentice-Hall.

Weber, M. (1958). *The rationale and social foundations of music* (D. Martindale, J. Reidel, & G. Neuwirth, ed. and trans.). [n.p.]: Southern Illinois University Press.

Wertheimer, M. (1955). Laws of organization in perceptual forms. In W.D. Ellis (Ed.), *A source book of Gestalt psychology.* London: Routledge & Kegan Paul. (Originally published in German, 1923)

West, R., Howell, P., & Cross, I. (1985). Modelling perceived musical structure. In P. Howell, I. Cross, & R. West (Eds.), *Musical structure and cognition* (pp. 21–52). London: Academic Press.

Wing, H.D. (1961). *Standardised tests of musical intelligence.* The Mere, England: National Foundation for Educational Research.

Woodruff, A.D. (1970). How music concepts are developed. *Music Educators Journal, 56* (6), 51–54.

Zimmerman, M.P. (1971). *Musical characteristics of children.* Washington: Music Educators National Conference.

Chapter Six

AFFECTIVE BEHAVIORS AND MUSIC

In recent years psychologists have become increasingly concerned with affective behavior in its various manifestations, and with this increased interest several issues have surfaced. For example: What is meant by *affect* and *emotion?* Is *aesthetic* behavior the same as *affective* behavior? Are changes in physiological rates affective responses? Can the affective and aesthetic be examined from a behavioral perspective? Or, are philosophical explanations of aesthetic experience sufficient?

The purpose of this chapter therefore is to examine some of these basic questions. Discussed are (a) extended definitions of central terms, (b) the range of behaviors which are considered affective, (c) some approaches to the study of affective responses to music, and (d) musical meaning and the variables that contribute to musical meaning.

Extended Definitions

visible

By and large, affective responses to music are covert, and many of the difficulties inherent in studying cognitive responses to music also are encountered in the study of affective responses. Terms used to describe affective response essentially reflect psychological constructs inferred from behavior. The terms and the various implied constructs used to denote affective response to music are not discrete; discussions of them are confounded further by seemingly loose and indiscriminate applications of the terms.

Three terms central to this discussion are *affect, emotion,* and *aesthetic.* While the terms perhaps are encountered more often in philosophical discussions, the intent here is to examine them from a psychological perspective. The distinction between psychological and philosophical use of the terms is not clear-cut, although traditional usage does recognize their subjective and personal connotations. Other terms to be

195

defined briefly include *attitude, interest, taste, preference, appreciation,* and *sensitivity.*

Affect

For hundreds of years students of human behavior have recognized three basic categories: thinking, feeling, and acting. Psychologists today refer to these as cognitive, affective, and psychomotor behaviors respectively. Affective behaviors include those which have a significant *feeling* component.

As used in everyday life, feeling has a variety of meanings, e.g., tactual perception (to *feel* a piece of cloth), cognitive belief (he *feels* something to be true), emotion, or simply whether an experience is pleasant or unpleasant. Psychologists do not use the term in a consistent way. To clarify matters, Young (1973) has summarized eight classes of affective processes: (a) *simple feelings* of pleasantness or unpleasantness in response to sensory stimuli, (b) negative and positive *organic feelings* such as hunger, thirst, dietary satisfaction, or physical well-being, (c) *activity feelings,* including appetitive states such as hunger or sexual desire as well as other activity feelings such as enthusiasm or aversion, (d) moral, *aesthetic,* religious, or social sentiments and attitudes based upon previous experiences, education, and training, (e) persisting *moods* such as cheerfulness, elation, anxiety, or grief, (f) pathological *affects* of deep depression, apathy, or hostility, (g) *emotions* such as fear, anger, laughing, agony, or embarrassment, and (h) *temperaments* such as vivaciousness, cheerfulness, or moodiness.

As should be apparent, affect is a broad term applied to a wide variety of human feeling behaviors. The problem is exacerbated by the fact that affective processes are related to virtually everything that is psychological —perception, memory, learning, reasoning, and action. Therefore, any discussion of affective behavior in relation to music must be defined in terms more definitive than just whether or not it is affective.

Emotion

One school of thought regarding music's import is that it conveys or expresses emotion. Proponents of this position, however, appear to be using the term *emotion* in a broader sense than contemporary psychologists use the term. Today emotion is considered only one type of affect. Young (p. 750) defines emotion as a disturbed affective process or state *"which originates in the psychological situation and which is revealed by marked*

bodily changes in smooth muscles, glands, and gross behaviors." This definition suggests that emotional behavior is a relatively temporary state—a
departure from the normal state of composure. Emotions involve perception and memory and always include an environmental factor, present or
past.

Meyer (1956, pp. 13–32) has theorized how emotion is aroused by
music. Central to his theory is the view that emotion is aroused when a
tendency to respond is arrested or inhibited. An individual's tendency to
respond is a result of previous experiences with music of the style to
which he or she is listening. From the previous experience the individual has developed expectations (tendencies to respond) regarding what
types of patterns might come next in the music. To the degree that the
anticipated patterns are not forthcoming, i.e., they are delayed or do not
come at all, *tension,* or *emotion,* is aroused.

Listeners to Western music, for example, learn that certain chords or
"sound terms" imply certain other musical entities. When the expected
musical consequent is delayed, suspense is aroused. However, Meyer
maintains that the mere arousal of tension via the inhibition of musical
expectations is of little import in itself. To have *aesthetic meaning* the
tension must be followed by a fulfillment of the expectation and hence
resolution of the tension.

More recent descriptions of the application of theories of emotion
such as Meyer's to musical experience essentially are elaborations and/or
refinements of a basic theory of emotion, but reflecting language and
refinements consistent with the authors' theoretical perspectives (e.g.,
Dowling & Harwood, 1986, pp. 214–219). More will be said of these
theories later.

The important point here is that theories of how emotion is created
in music are consistent with the contemporary psychological viewpoint
that emotion is a relatively temporary disruption of a normal state.
Further, emotion is seen as an essential component of aesthetic meaning,
although emotion alone is, in Meyer's words, "aesthetically valueless"
(p. 28).

Aesthetic

Aesthetic feeling is a particular type of affective behavior and is the
outcome of aesthetic experience. The term *aesthetic* usually is used in
relation to art and its value or meaning, although it is recognized that
aesthetic feeling may result from interactions with phenomena of nature

or from interactions with nonart objects or events. What makes some interactions *aesthetic* and others not has been subject to much discussion by philosophers, even to the point that aesthetics traditionally has been viewed as a branch of philosophy. While it is recognized that philosophical theory and discussion have provided many valuable insights regarding the nature and value of aesthetic feeling and experience, the present discussion also recognizes aesthetic feeling and experience as psychological behaviors which are subject to study via the same methods that are used to examine other forms of human behavior. Psychologists only recently have begun to study aesthetic behavior, while philosophical examination of the aesthetic has a long history. To the extent that psychologists will be able to substantiate philosophical theory regarding aesthetic behaviors, theory will be strengthened.

Common to most discussions of aesthetics is the concern for beauty, and it is with definitions of beauty that difficulties arise. When one says something is beautiful, he or she is reflecting a value. What causes this something to be valued as beautiful is subject to much debate. Some would hold that the beauty is inherent in the object or event due to its structure or form. In other words, beauty is a property of the object or event and remains so regardless of what an individual respondent might "feel." An opposing view is that "beauty is in the eyes of the beholder." Perhaps Saint Thomas Aquinas, as cited by Rader and Jessup (1976, p. 20), stated it best: "Let that be called *beauty*, the very perception of which pleases." The statement has two implications: First, beauty gives pleasure, and second, not everything that gives pleasure is beautiful, but only that which gives pleasure in immediate perception. Which position reflects the final truth regarding the determination of beauty has been and will continue to be subject to debate and conjecture. The point here is that beauty is the subject matter and stimulus for aesthetic experience and feeling.

Aesthetic experience is the term most often used to describe subjective, personal response to beauty or the aesthetic qualities of an object, event, or phenomenon. Hargreaves (1986, p. 108) argues that the term is applicable to "more or less any reaction that any person might have to any work of art, defined in the broadest possible terms." For Hargreaves, a schoolgirl's like-dislike reaction to a current pop record and a music critic's critique of a performance of a Beethoven symphony are both reflections of aesthetic experience. Other writers, however, are more delimiting in what they consider aesthetic experience.

The following discussion is based primarily on the descriptions of aesthetic experience offered by two advocates of aesthetic education, Bennett Reimer (1970, pp. 72–87) and Gerard L. Knieter (1971, pp. 3–20). Both recognize aesthetic experience as human experience, and while they also recognize beauty in nature and other objects and events that are not primarily intended to be art, they generally discuss aesthetic experience in relation to artworks.

Kneiter cites five characteristics of an aesthetic experience: (a) focus, (b) perception, (c) affect, (d) cognition, and (e) cultural matrix. *Focus* suggests that an individual must devote his attention to the artwork and respond thereto. *Perception* is viewed as the process through which sensory data are received and through which the individual becomes aware of the artwork. Knieter see two basic types of *affect* occurring during the aesthetic experience, physiological change and feelingful reaction. Concomitant with aesthetic experience are changes in blood pressure, respiration, and electrodermal response. The feelingful reaction may vary from simple feeling to complex emotional sets. *Cognition* is a particularly important attribute of aesthetic experience, reflecting the intellectual processes involved: analysis, synthesis, abstraction, generalization, and evaluation. Knowledge and learning regarding the stylistic attributes of a musical work contribute greatly to the quality of an aesthetic experience. Finally, the *cultural matrix* is reflected in an aesthetic experience. Aesthetic values are learned within a cultural context.

Reimer emphasizes that an individual's interest and reactions must be absorbed by or immersed in the aesthetic qualities of the music being attended to; the feelingful reaction must be to the expressive aesthetic qualities rather than to any symbolic designation. For Reimer, the aesthetic qualities of music conveyed by melody, harmony, rhythm, tone color, texture, and form are "expressive of or analogous to or isomorphic with the patterns of felt life or subjective reality or the conditions of livingness" (p. 74). The individual must be involved with the *embodied* meaning of music rather than with any symbolic designations it might have.*

Reimer also maintains that aesthetic experience is valuable in and of itself, is not a means toward non-aesthetic experience, and serves no

---

Embodied musical meaning results from expectations *within* the music, whereas *designative* meaning refers to meaning *symbolized* by the music. The differences are discussed in more detail later in the chapter.

utilitarian purpose. Taken at face value this might suggest a contradiction with the authors' view that aesthetic experience serves a human function and that music also serves other functions. This is not the case. While aesthetic experience may appear to have no purpose or *use*, it still serves a valuable *function*, providing an individual an opportunity for feelingful experience above and beyond the meeting of basic human needs. Maslow (1970, p. 51) contends that aesthetic experience is a human need, albeit one with which people become involved only when their physiological, safety, and certain psychological needs have been met. Therefore, an aesthetic experience is valuable in and of itself to the experiencing individual; however, the very fact that the experience holds value for the individual suggests that it is functional to his or her well-being.

Reimer's final characteristic of an aesthetic experience is that it must involve the qualities of a perceptible "thing." The "thing" is the sensuous element, the "formed substance," containing the aesthetic qualities which an individual perceives and responds to.

Implicit in both Knieter's and Reimer's descriptions is that aesthetic experience requires psychological *involvement* with the aesthetic stimulus, *perception* of interacting events within the artwork, *cognition* of the interplay among the events within the aesthetic stimulus, and *feelingful* reaction thereto. Aesthetic experience differs from most affective experience in that it must involve perception and cognition of an aesthetic stimulus. Without the immediacy of the aesthetic stimulus, the affective behavior cannot be an aesthetic behavior.

For an experience to be an aesthetic experience, it must result in feelingful reactions to perceived interactions of those aesthetic qualities contributing to the beauty of an artwork or other stimulus in which an observer (listener in music) is involved perceptually. Such a definition of aesthetic experience does not deny, however, that music and other aesthetic stimuli elicit many other significant affective responses. Certainly the hearing of a composition with which one has had previous associations may elicit feelings regarding those associations. For example, hearing a theme song of a movie which one has seen generally elicits thoughts and feelings regarding the movie. To say, however, that this feeling is aesthetic feeling is questionable. On the other hand, the feelings elicited may be very meaningful to the individual. In the authors' view, such feelings reflect another type of affective response to music.

Other Definitions

Several additional terms will be mentioned briefly, because they each suggest a psychological construct with a substantial affective component. Essentially these constructs are covert and therefore inferred from an individual's behaviors (including verbal) relative to the objects, events, or phenomena that are the stimulus for the affective response. While the definitions are neither discrete nor exhaustive, they are believed to reflect the general meanings of the terms as used in the literature. The definitions are essentially those the authors have offered elsewhere (Boyle & Radocy, 1987, pp. 195–199).

Attitude, the most general term, connotes a predisposition toward mental or psychomotor activity with respect to a social or psychological object, event, or phenomenon. The predisposition may be either positive or negative, that is, reflecting either approach or avoidance activity. Kuhn (1979) notes that an attitude is relatively long-term and stable and that any real changes in attitude necessarily take place over a considerable period of time.

Interest suggests feelings of concern, involvement, and curiosity. A clear demarcation between "attitude toward something" and "interest in something" is difficult to make, but it appears that in common usage interest is more often manifested through active participation or involvement with the object, event, or phenomenon, while attitude is considered more covert and suggests more of a value judgment.

Taste, as applied to music, usually suggests an element of connoisseurship, reflecting some agreement with the "experts" regarding quality and excellence. Kuhn equates taste with attitude, because both essentially imply covert predispositions, both are developed as a result of experience, and both appear to be long term in nature. However, all affective responses appear to develop through experience.

Preference perhaps is considered more overt, or behavioral, than taste or attitude in that preferences usually involve the act of making choices and indicating them in some overt manner. Abeles (1980) suggests that preference and taste actually represent a continuum from a short-term (preference) to a long-term (taste) commitment.

Price (1986) recognizes *behavioral preferences* and *behavioral intentions* as two important modes for expressing preference. A behavioral preference involves demonstration of choices through nonverbal actions such as concert attendance or record purchase, while a behavioral intention requires the verbal expression of a choice one would make in a specific decision-making context.

Appreciation with respect to music appears to be used in both a narrow and broad sense. Lehman (1968, p. 25) notes that in the broad sense appreciation includes a major knowledge component—knowledge of musicians, notation, literature, instruments, history, and so forth. The narrower sense appears to place more emphasis on sensitivity to aesthetic qualities of music and feeling response to them.

Sensitivity usually implies perception of and responsiveness to sensory stimuli and reflects both cognitive and affective dimensions. In common usage it implies making both subtle discriminations and subtle feeling responses. Considering these connotations, it is not surprising that the term *aesthetic sensitivity* is much used in the literature.

Types of Affective Responses to Music

To suggest that aesthetic experience is the only important feeling response elicited by music is to deny the value of a broad spectrum of affective behaviors related to music. The present discussion does not purport to consider relative value of the respective types of affective behaviors in relation to aesthetic experience per se, but it does recognize that various affective experiences are important to greater or lesser degrees for many individuals. The relative values of the various affective modes differ for *individuals,* and it is unlikely that any given affective mode, even the aesthetic mode, is of greater or lesser value for all individuals.

The variety of affective responses to music is great. Concomitant with all types are *physiological reactions* of the autonomic nervous system. Hector Berlioz's descriptions of his reactions while listening to a piece of music, as reported by Schoen (1940, p. 103), included increased blood circulation, violent pulse rate, muscle contractions, trembling, numbness of the feet and hands, and partial paralysis of the nerves controlling hearing and vision. While it is doubtful that many individuals' physiological mechanisms are affected to the extent that Berlioz claimed, there is objective evidence that changes in certain physiological rates do accompany affective behaviors. Whether these changes themselves are affective behaviors is subject to interpretation. The behaviorist might insist that they are because they can be observed (via certain measuring instruments); another view, however, is that they are merely physiological correlates of affective behavior, because feelings by definition are psychological rather than physiological.

A common affective behavior is the *mood* or *character* response. In Western cultures certain musical sound patterns have come to be reflective of different psychological states. Certain music is soothing or relaxing, other music makes an individual feel happy or sad, while still other music may elicit feelings of frustration or agitation. The range of moods that may be characterized by music is as great as the range of moods people can feel. There is no question but what music can elicit mood response; further, within a given cultural context there tends to be agreement among many individuals as to the mood elicited by certain types and examples of music. While the variables underlying this are many, it should be noted that whatever mood response is elicited by music is much more than a response to any inherent mood or character of the music. Mood responses to music, just as virtually all other responses to music, are essentially determined by an individual's previous experience with music. *Learning underlies all musical behavior, affective or otherwise.*

Affective responses to music also may be the result of *associations* an individual makes with music. The most common example of this is when an individual responds to the programmatic content of music. Feelings of this type are in relation to an event or story with which they have previously associated the music. The popularity of movie soundtrack recordings suggests that many people want to reexperience the occasions through listening to the music. The same type of associations are made with opera and musical comedy. The feeling response is to much more than the music itself. Listening to music of one's childhood or adolescence evokes feelings of childhood and adolescence associated with that music. Lovers recall special occasions through "their song." The power of music to elicit strong feelings of experiences associated with it provides individuals with a mechanism for reexperiencing many significant events of their lives. *Reminiscence*

While philosophers and aestheticians have been greatly concerned with the wordless meaning of music, there has been relatively little study of the feelings evoked by the words of songs. One only has to listen to the words of folk music, popular music, and art music, however, to realize that the verbal messages of music are primarily affective. Feelings of love, frustration, and virtually every deep-seated and persisting type of human feeling that individuals hold toward one another have been verbalized through song. Feelings expressed or elicited through blues, country-western, and rock music are primary examples of the affective impact of combined word meanings and music.

Words and music also have been combined to express and elicit affective reactions to all types of social, political, and religious issues. Music has been used as a persuasive tool throughout the history of mankind. As noted in Chapter Two, many of the basic functions of music are to sway feelings. There is little doubt that patriotic, social protest, and religious songs can arouse strong affective response. Such songs are symbols, are perceived and reacted to accordingly, and serve a legitimate and important function (Reimer, p. 92).

Many additional human behaviors related to music have an affective component in greater or lesser degree. Musical *preferences* (discussed in Chapter Seven), musical *interests,* musical *values, attitudes* toward music in general and various styles of music, and *appreciation* of music all reflect affective components. While these behaviors also are dependent in many respects on knowledge, their importance to music educators is great. Appreciation, values, and preferences are of essence to music education. Interests and attitudes are central to both the process and outcomes of music education.

Approaches to Studying Affective Responses to Music

Approaches to the study of affective responses to music traditionally have been through (a) physiological response, (b) adjective descriptors, and (c) philosophical inquiry. A fourth approach, which follows the work of Berlyne (1971; 1974), reflects a growing interest in examining empirical human response to musical stimuli. Termed *empirical aesthetics* in its broader sense, or *experimental aesthetics* in its narrower sense, this approach is seen as a major development in music psychology.

Although the four approaches to the study of affective responses to music overlap in several respects, they are discussed under four headings: (a) physiological measures, (b) adjective descriptors, (c) philosophical inquiry, and (d) psychological aesthetics.

Physiological Measures

Few musicians or psychologists deny that music can evoke changes in the rates of bodily processes, but there is little or no agreement regarding the degree to which these changes are reflective of affective responses to music. Affective behaviors are *psychological* behaviors, whereas measures of the rates of various bodily processes are *physiological* behaviors. The study of the interrelationships between physiological and psychological aspects of behavior is called *psychophysiology* (Sternbach, 1966, p. 3). If one is seeking to understand affective responses to music through study of changes in the rates of certain bodily processes, then one is engaged in psychophysiological research.

With the exception of a few studies, research on physiological responses to music stops short of actually examining interrelationships between the two types of behaviors, hence, providing little insight regarding affective responses to music. Generally, such studies involve the presentation of a musical stimulus as the independent variable and use polygraph data regarding various physiological rates as the dependent variables. The underlying hypothesis of most studies is that the frequency and/or amplitude of the various bodily processes controlled by the autonomic nervous system reflect affective response to music. The most frequently studied dependent measures include heart rate, respiration rate, respiration amplitude, and electrodermal activity (skin responses, formerly called psychogalvanic reflex, galvanic skin response, or GSR). Other measures which have been used include *electroencephalography* (EEG)—a technique for recording variations in brain wave rhythms, *electromyography* (EMG)—a measure of muscle tension, *electrooculography* —a measure of eye movement, *pupillography* —a measure of pupil size, *electrogastrography*—a measure of gastrointestinal response, *patellar reflex* —knee-jerk response, and the *pilomotor response*—movement of hairs on the skin.

Schoen (1927, 1940), Diserens and Fine (1939), Lundin (1967), and Farnsworth (1969) have summarized early research on physiological responses to music. A brief chronology of some of the research conducted prior to 1950 follows:

1880 Dogiel discovered that music influences blood circulation, heart rate, and respiration.

1888 Fere used music as a stimulus in studying galvanic skin response.

1895 Binet and Courtier measured pulse and respiration rate changes with changes in music.

1900 Fere discovered that isolated tones, scales, and tonal sequences energize muscles.

1906 Foster and Gamble concluded that music generally causes faster and shallower breathing regardless of loudness or mode.

1912 Weld recorded changes in pneumographic (breathing) and plethysmographic (blood supply) responses as a function of listening to music.

1918 Vescelius reported that music without abrupt key changes can relieve high fever, high pulse rate, and hysteria.

1924 Wechsler observed that subjects' GSR curves changed when music was played, although he noted that such curve changes were smaller than those elicited by direct sensory stimulation such as a pin prick.

1927 Hyde studied the effects of different kinds of musical selections on the cardiovascular responses of individuals fond of music, those indifferent or insensitive to music, as well as the effects of music on individuals of different nationality and training. She reported that people are psychologically and physiologically affected unfavorably by "tragic mournful tones" and favorably by "gay rhythmical melodies."

1932 Misbach studied the effects of isolated tonal stimuli on GSR, blood pressure, and pulse changes. He reported no significant pulse rate or blood pressure changes, although GSR changes were observed for tones of 512 HZ or higher and increased in magnitude as frequency became higher.

1933 Wascho observed changes in pulse rate and blood pressure when different types of music were played. More definite rhythms and melodies yielded more definite physiological changes.

1934 Phares reported a positive relationship between amount of GSR change and the strength of the verbally reported pleasantness of music. She also reported, however, that the GSR results were of little value in her analysis of music appreciation.

1947 Dreher compared subjects' verbal reports and GSR responses to various types of music. Musically trained subjects showed a relationship between GSR and mood as measured by adjectives checked on the Hevner Adjective Circle; data for untrained subjects revealed no relationship.

It should be recognized, however, that most of the studies noted above for the most part are merely descriptions of physiological responses to various musical stimuli and therefore cannot be viewed as true affective responses. They are indicative of the physiological concomitants of affective response, but with the exception of a few studies studies no attempts were made to examine relationships between these types of responses and affective responses.

Dainow's (1977) and Hodges' (1980b) excellent reviews and syntheses of the literature provide the basis for much of the following discussion. They review most of the studies noted above as well as some more recent research. Readers are encouraged to examine their excellent reviews and bibliographies.

For hundreds of years philosophers and musicologists have maintained and sought to substantiate the existence of a relationship between heart rate and music. Most "substantiation," however, has just been rhetoric. Dainow's review of studies of heart rate in response to music provides virtually no support to the hypothesis that heart rate varies with tempo of music. Of eight studies examining the effects of music on heart rate, all but one failed to elicit any statistically significant change in heart rate. Some other studies suggested that any music will increase heart rate, although it was not clear whether these changes in heart rate were statistically significant for any of the studies. Another group of studies cited by Dainow did not produce any effects on heart rate. Dainow concludes that, "despite considerable research the relationship between HR and music is still unclear" (p. 212). Even if clear-cut relationships could be established between heart rate and tempo, it would provide little insight into the affective response.

Dainow notes that summarizing research on respiration rate or amplitude is particularly difficult, because of the variety of experimental conditions. Some studies examine rate while others examine amplitude; further, some research has sought to examine respiration in relation to tempo, while other research has attempted to relate respiration to listeners' attention or enjoyment. Ries (1969), in one of the few studies which actually compared a physiological response to subjects' indicated enjoyment of musical examples, reports a .48 ($p < .01$) correlation coefficient between the two variables. Most of the other studies examined by Dainow, however, reported no clear-cut data regarding the relationship between respiration rate or amplitude and musical stimulus or response. They merely describe the responses to the musical stimulus. As was apparent for heart rate research, respiration research to date presents a confusing picture and provides little or no information regarding the affective response to music.

Dainow maintains that GSR experiments are even more incomplete and inconclusive than those for heart rate and respiration. He suggests that there is a general methodological "hodgepodge" in GSR research, noting that some studies measure magnitude and direction of response, some the number of deflections, and others the rising period or latency of response. Some have attempted to relate GSR to some ill-defined emotional response to music, while others have examined it in relation to stimulative versus sedative music or dissonant versus consonant sounds. Despite occasionally well-conceived studies such as Dreher's (1947) comparisons of verbal reports and GSR to different types of music, little can be concluded regarding GSR and affective response because of the many methodological problems involved in the various studies.

Hodges' (1980b) review corroborates Dainow's findings regarding contradictions in the results of research on heart rate, respiration, and electrodermal skin response. Focusing on studies of the effects of *stimulative* music, which reflects high rhythmic activity, and *sedative* music, which is characterized by sustained legato melodies and minimal rhythmic activity,* Hodges notes that, with respect to heart rate and pulse rate, (a) some studies resulted in increased rates for stimulative music but decreased rates for sedative music, (b) some resulted in increased heart and pulse rates for any music, whether stimulative or sedative, (c) some yielded changes in heart and pulse rates that were unpredictable, and (d) some yielded no change in heart rate or pulse rate for any music. Hodges noted similar contradictory results for studies of music's effects on respiration and electrodermal skin response.

Research on brain wave response to music has not focused primarily on brain waves as a measure of affect, but Hodges' conclusions regarding electroencephalographic (EEG) response should be noted. His review of EEG research revealed that (a) musicians produce more alpha brain waves than nonmusicians when listening to music, (b) children spend more time in alpha brain wave production during silence than during any of several conditions of aural stimuli, (c) musicians' and nonmusicians' brain waves are slightly more desynchronized during complex pitch discrimination tasks, and (d) there are significant variations in brain wave tracings both within and between musician and nonmusician groups.

The recent interest in hemispheric specialization and music has given rise to considerable research and much speculation regarding brain activity and musical processing. The research focus primarily has involved perceptual or conceptual responses to dichotic listening situations. Critical reviews of the research do not always interpret the research in the same way (Gates & Bradshaw, 1977; Hodges, 1978, 1980a; Radocy, 1978,

---

*See Chapter Eight for further discussion of stimulative and sedative music.

1979; Regelski, 1978; Webster, 1979), but two general conclusions appear to be receiving general acceptance:

> (1) hemispheric differences are to a considerable degree a function of the nature and complexity of the musical task, and (2) there are differences in the hemispheric activation on given musical tasks for musically trained and untrained subjects. (Boyle, Cole, Cutietta, & Ray, 1982, p. 10)

(Chapter Eleven provides a discussion of recent research on hemispheric specialization and music.)

While much of the research on hemispheric specialization and music purportedly was undertaken to gain a better understanding of the affective response to music, partially in response to Regelski's (1978, p. 13) strong assertation that aesthetic thinking is a right hemisphere activity, little research has actually examined hemispheric specialization systematically as either an independent or dependent variable in musical affect. Tucker's (1981) comprehensive review of hemispheric specialization and emotion, however, suggests that both hemispheres are involved. A recent exploratory investigation of right/left alpha wave ratios for liked and disliked music revealed no statistically significant differences in the ratios for liked and disliked music (Boyle, Cole, Cutietta, & Ray, 1982). In short, brain wave research, including that on hemispheric specialization and music, provides little or no insight regarding the affective response to music.

Electromyography, or muscle tension, perhaps holds more promise as a reflection of affective response to music than any of the other physiological measures. Western music appears to organize sounds in which tension-resolution patterns are developed, and Dainow suggests that "it might be expected that inherently tense music could induce a corresponding physical or muscular tension in the listener" (p. 214). He cites research by Sears (1957, 1960) which provides evidence that muscle tension can be altered by music. The potential of electromyography for evaluating affective response to music, however, has yet to be adequately explored.

Clearly, physiological research to date provides little insight into the affective response to music. Reasons for this are difficult to pinpoint, although Dainow and Hodges suggest that many methodological issues are involved. Particular concerns include instructions to subjects, loudness of the musical stimuli, subject attention, and possible suppression of response due to fear of disturbing electrodes. Another major difficulty involves measurement of the psychological variable affect. In addition, the sheer diversity of physiological variables themselves and the many aspects of each creates an overwhelming array of measurement and interpretation problems. Finally, even if all of the measurement and research design problems can be resolved, it may be that responses of the autonomic nervous system are sufficiently unique to each individual, who also brings a unique experiential background to the measurement situation, that making predictions or generalizations about affective response on the basis of physiological responses is inappropriate. As Hahn (1954, p. 11) states, "An investigation of the physiological response may offer a clue but not a solution to the individual's psychological reactions."

Adjective Descriptors

Laymen, musicians, psychologists, and philosophers agree that music can reflect moods and evoke mood responses in listeners. Mood response to music, as other psychological responses to music, involves learning. Individuals within given cultural groups *learn* that music with certain characteristics reflects certain moods while music with other characteristics reflects different moods. Moods have been described in various ways by psychologists and philosophers, but as used in research related to music, *mood* generally refers to "relatively transient states ... which can be cognized by individuals and designated with *words*" [Italics not in original] (Eagle, 1971, p. 19).

The traditional approach to assessment of mood response has been through the use of adjective descriptors, and most discussions of adjective descriptors as tools for assessment of response to music are labeled as discussions of mood response to music (e.g., Farnsworth, 1969, pp. 79–96; Lundin, 1967, pp. 160–172; Eagle, 1971, pp. 27–80). Eagle's discussion provides an exhaustive review of the traditional literature using verbal descriptors as a basis for studying affective response to music. He notes that three basic methods have been used for gathering verbal descriptions: (a) adjective checklists, (b) the semantic differential, and (c) various types of rating scales. The most commonly used of the three methods has been the adjective checklist, and following is a brief chronology and summary of the major research using adjective checklists.

1927   Schoen and Gatewood presented ten musical selections to 32 female subjects on two separate occasions under similar testing conditions. Although no statistical analysis was made beyond frequency count of the adjectives checked for each selection, the results were sufficiently similar for the researchers to conclude that "a given musical selection will arouse a certain definite reaction and will arouse the same reaction on different occasions" (Schoen & Gatewood, 1927, p. 151).

1927 Gatewood presented a list of twelve adjective descriptors to 35 female subjects who were asked to check the moods elicited by each of ten selections. The study sought to examine the influence of rhythm, melody, harmony, and timbre on stated mood effects. Again without statistical analysis, it was concluded that mood effects are dependent on definite musical elements.

1928 Heinlein studied adjectives checked in response to major and minor chords by 30 musically trained and untrained subjects. Two additional variables studied were intensity and pitch register. He found that mood effects were more a function of intensity than the chord per se. Further, pitch register also made a difference in which adjectives were checked. He concluded that "any fixity of feeling-tone in relation to a given mode is dependent upon training to react in a specified manner to a purely intellectual discrimination" (Heinlein, 1928, p. 140).

1935 Hevner (1935, 1936) developed an adjective checklist which has served as the basis for much subsequent research on mood response to music. She developed an adjective circle grouping 67 adjectives into eight clusters, each cluster containing adjectives of approximately the same meaning. (See Figure 6-1.) Listeners were asked to check the adjectives describing the mood of the music. The intent was that as one progressed around the circle from cluster one to cluster eight there would be eight more-or-less discrete moods, representing a general trend of mood change through the respective clusters. Her results revealed a general consistency among subjects in the adjectives checked. She conducted a series of follow-up studies in the late 1930s to ascertain the effects of various elements of music (modality, rhythm, tempo, harmony, melody, and pitch) on mood response. From her series of studies she concluded that the major mode is "happy, graceful, and playful"; the minor mode is "sad, dreamy, and sentimental"; firm rhythms are "vigorous and dignified"; flowing rhythms are "happy, graceful, dreamy, and tender"; complex dissonant harmonies are "exciting, agitating, vigorous, and inclined toward sadness"; simple consonant harmonies are "happy, graceful, serene, and lyrical"; and differences in expressiveness caused by rising and falling of melodic line are not clear-cut, distinct, or constant (Hevner, 1936, p. 268). Hevner (1937) reported that slow tempos express "dignity, calmness, and sadness"; fast tempos, "restlessness and happiness." High pitches are "sprightly and humorous," while low pitches reflect "sadness, dignity, and majesty." She observed that responses were generally the same for listeners of all kinds, intelligent and less intelligent, trained and untrained (Hevner, 1939).

1952   Capurso (1952) developed a list of 105 musical selections to match six mood categories. He then asked 1,075 "nonmusical" subjects to listen to the selections and categorize them according to mood. He found that sixty-one selections had listener agreement at least 50 percent of the time and thus suggested that the resulting list of musical selections may be suitable for creating a "desired emotional effect" on listeners and for selecting background music for television and radio programs.

1954   Farnsworth (1954) tested the internal consistency of the clusters of the Hevner Adjective Circle. He observed that several of the clusters did not describe internally consistent mood patterns and therefore did not justify the circle arrangement. He rearranged 50 of Hevner's adjectives into ten more consistent categories. (See Figure 6-2.)

1955   Sopchak (1955) developed a twelve-category adjective checklist which 553 college sophomores used in responding to fifteen compositions, five classical, seven popular, and three folk. Subjects also were asked to classify their own moods on a three-point scale: "cheerful" to "neutral" to "gloomy." It was found that a higher percentage of gloomy subjects responded to sorrow, joy, calm, love, eroticism, jealousy, wonder, and cruelty. Sopchak speculated that gloomy subjects have many tensions and thus more readily project into the music, while cheerful subjects may have less need to project into the music.

1960   Van Stone (1960) sought to ascertain mood differences associated with tone quality of music. Eight musical excerpts representing the eight clusters of the Hevner Adjective Circle were orchestrated and recorded by three ensembles: string, woodwind, and brass. Results indicated no significant differences among adjectival

6
bright
cheerful
gay
happy
joyous
merry

7
agitated
dramatic
exciting
exhilarated
impetuous
passionate
restless
sensational
soaring
triumphant

5
delicate
fanciful
graceful
humorous
light
playful
quaint
sprightly
whimsical

8
emphatic
exalting
majestic
martial
ponderous
robust
vigorous

4
calm
leisurely
lyrical
quiet
satisfying
serene
soothing
tranquil

1
awe-inspiring
dignified
lofty
sacred
serious
sober
solemn
spiritual

3
dreamy
longing
plaintive
pleading
sentimental
tender
yearning
yielding

2
dark
depressing
doleful
frustrated
gloomy
heavy
melancholy
mournful
pathetic
sad
tragic

Figure 6-1. Hevner Adjective Circle.

A	B	C	D	E
cheerful	fanciful	delicate	dreamy	longing
gay	light	graceful	leisurely	pathetic
happy	quaint	lyrical	sentimental	plaintive
joyous	whimsical		serene	pleading
bright			soothing	yearning
merry			tender	
playful			tranquil	
sprightly			quiet	

F	G	H	I	J
dark	sacred	dramatic	agitated	frustrated
depressing	spiritual	emphatic	exalting	
doleful		majestic	exciting	
gloomy		triumphant	exhilarated	
melancholic			impetuous	
mournful			vigorous	
pathetic				
sad				
serious				
sober				
solemn				
tragic				

Figure 6-2. Farnsworth's modification of the Hevner Adjective Circle.

responses to the three types of ensembles. Apparently timbre change had little or no effect on mood response.

While mood response in terms of adjective checklists has been subject to considerable study, the semantic differential technique is a more recently developed technique and therefore has been used less for study of mood response. Essentially the technique attempts to measure subjects' concepts by use of series of bipolar adjectives between which they make a response on a five- or seven-point continuum.* For example:

Concept: Mood

Happy	_____	_____	_____	_____	_____	Sad
Light	_____	_____	_____	_____	_____	Heavy
Humorous	_____	_____	_____	_____	_____	Solemn

Eagle (1971) used the semantic differential technique in a study which sought to answer three questions: (a) Does existing stated mood affect

*Readers interested in more information on the semantic differential technique should consult Osgood, C. E., Suci, G.J., and Tannenbaum, P.H., *The Measurement of Meaning.* Urbana: University of Illinois Press, 1957.

rated mood response to music? (b) Does presentation order of music affect rated mood response to music? (c) Do similarly rated mood responses hold true for both vocal and instrumental music? Subjects were 274 undergraduate and graduate music majors who were asked to rate their own present mood on a ten-step scale and then respond to twenty musical selections in terms of five pairs of bipolar adjectives (good-bad, pleasant-unpleasant, bright-dark, depressed-elated, and happy-sad. The ten vocal excerpts included rock, folk, country-western, popular ballad, and hymns; instrumental excerpts included jazz, march, semiclassical, and classical. Eagle found that existing mood of the listener does influence mood response to music, but order of presentation does not significantly affect mood response to music. In response to his third question, Eagle (p. 171) states that

> similar rated mood responses do not hold true for both vocal and instrumental music. A person responds differently to vocal music than to instrumental music, although both may seem to reflect the same mood qualities.

Eagle's (pp. 70–80) analysis of the literature using adjective descriptors as a measure of mood response revealed a number of research concerns. Only three studies mentioned the reliability of their testing instruments. Statistical analyses were not reported in more than half of the 43 studies he reviewed, and of the 20 reporting statistical data, nearly half used only frequency counts. Eagle did note, however, that eight of nine studies conducted since 1960 employed statistical analyses more sophisticated than frequency counts. Findings were not consistent regarding the importance of the elements in eliciting mood, although the review warranted the following broad generalizations:

> Rhythm seems to be the primary element in evaluating mood responses to music. "Happiness" was the term used most often to describe fast tempi, major mode, consonant harmonies, and tunes pitched in high registers. "Excitement" or "agitation" described dissonant harmonies. (p. 79)

The semantic differential technique also is useful for assessing responses to music other than mood or character per se. Crozier (1974) and McMullen (1976, 1980, 1982a) are the major proponents of the technique. Building on the work of Osgood, Suci, and Tannenbaum (1957), whose research demonstrated that the bipolar technique is a viable tool for assessing affective response and identified three principal factors or dimensions (*evaluative, potency,* and *activity*) that account for most of the semantic loadings in factor analyses of responses on semantic differential scales, Crozier and McMullen each have identified two dimensions of affective meaning based on their subjects' semantic differential responses to musical stimuli.

Crozier's (1974, p. 85) data suggest that these dimensions are reflected in *pleasingness* and *interestingness* ratings, which are "evidently close to Osgood's Evaluative and Activity dimensions, respectively." Both vary with *uncertainty* or information content (in information theoretic terms) of the musical sequences heard, but in different ways. The former is related curvilinearly, and the latter is related linearly.

This *dimensional approach* for relating verbal responses to musical stimuli, according to McMullen (1976), appears to be closely related to the adjective checklist approach in that both seek

> to define verbally the affective domain or stimulus variables that influence these response dimensions. The dimensional approach seeks a statistical grouping of adjectives that contain similar meaning for the response dimension, while the Hevner Checklist uses individual adjectives which collectively form a mood pattern. Additionally, both approaches seek to define the variables in the stimulus that influence such responses, the dimensional approach by defining general dimensions such as activity/uncertainty that conceivably could apply to many art forms, while the researchers employing the checklist primarily have used variables associated with the analysis of musical structure. (p. 2)

McMullen examined the relationship between responses to the Hevner Adjective Circle and some previously defined dimensions of *evaluation* (pleasing, beautiful, good), *potency* (interest, powerful, rugged), and *activity* (complex, clear, order). His data indicated that there is some merit in Hevner's concept of arranging her adjective checklist in a circle; two dimensions of semantic space, which he interprets as subfactors of the evaluative dimension, emerged. McMullen goes on to suggest that a third factor, associated with the activity dimension, might have emerged if additional activity-related adjectives had been used in the study.

Analysis of adjective descriptors into underlying dimensions holds much potential for assessing affective response to music and musical experience and has received increasing use. One of the most elaborate applications of the technique is Asmus's (1985) multidimensional instrument for the measurement of affective response to music. Called the

9-Affective Dimensions (9-AD), Asmus's technique yielded nine dimensions of affect, which he named *Evil, Sensual, Potency, Humor, Pastoral, Longing, Depression, Sedative,* and *Activity.* Others who have used the dimensional approach to assessment of affective response to music include Gabrielsson (1973, 1979), Hargreaves and Coleman (1981), and Hylton (1981). While the dimensional approach, whether involving basic factor analytic techniques or even more sophisticated multidimensional scaling techniques, holds much promise for analyzing adjective descriptor data, Hargreaves (1986, p. 125) cautions that "any dimensional model is ultimately restricted by the range of musical stimuli on which it is based, as well as on the subjects and response measures adopted." Further, the interpretation of the dimensions that emerge involves subjective judgments by the researcher. Hargreaves suggests that dimensional approaches to the study of musical responses are still in their infancy and do not yet provide an adequate basis for drawing any firm conclusions about the broad dimensions of responses to music (p. 128).

Philosophical Inquiry

Philosophical explanations regarding the value or meaning of artistic phenomena and experience have been a part of Western culture since the time of Plato, who is considered to be the founder of philosophical aesthetics (Hofstadter & Kuhns, 1964, p. 3.) The range and diversity of views that have been offered regarding the value and meaning of art (and music in particular) have resulted in a philosophical quagmire, often engulfing those who are not well schooled in aesthetics. While philosophical inquiry by nature arouses divergent viewpoints, it is believed that at least a cursory examination of some of the classical viewpoints will contribute to the understanding of the affective response to music, particularly since philosophical aesthetics represents the traditional and longest standing approach to the study of people's responses to arts phenomena.

Berlyne (1974, p. 2) suggests that *speculative aesthetics* is the most apt term for disciplines traditionally called philosophical.

They depend heavily on deduction—from definitions of concepts, from self-evident principles, from generally accepted propositions, from an author's own beliefs, intuitions, and experience. To a large extent, their method is "hermeneutic," i.e., they rely heavily on interpretive examination of particular texts, particular specimens of literary, musical, or visual art. Their ultimate criterion of validity is whether they leave the reader with a feeling of conviction.

Berlyne sees two divisions of speculative aesthetics: traditional *philosophical aesthetics,* usually taught in university departments of philosophy, and *art theory,* which is usually taught in the respective art, music, or literature departments. Philosophical aesthetics includes general statements regarding arts phenomena and their intent, value, or meaning, while art theory involves more examination of individual art works, art styles, and artists. In music, courses that concern art theory as defined by Berlyne are music history, music appreciation, music literature, and to a degree, form and analysis courses. As should be apparent, there is overlap among the various types of courses, and aesthetics comprises only one concern of a course. Speculative aesthetics generally is viewed as subjective in approach; other approaches to the study to the study of affective response are considered to be objective, although it is recognized that verbal descriptions of music may be subjective. The present discussion, however, examines only philosophical aesthetics.

Readers interested in examining some of the classic aesthetic theories should consult texts such as Morris Weitz's (1970) *Problems in Aesthetics* or Hofstadter and Kuhns' (1964) *Philosophies of Art and Beauty.* However, a sampling of some of the various theories' basic tenets suffices to illustrate the dilemma philosophical aesthetics holds for the uninitiated. Plato viewed art as *imitation* of an ideal—the beautiful and the good. Aristotle also viewed art as imitation, but in a different sense; for him imitation was the realization of form in a sensory medium and therefore art was a revelation of reality. Rousseau considered art an *expression.* French classicism turned art into arithmetical problems, while German romanticism sought explanations in metaphysical terms. Shiller viewed art as the most sublime form of play. Maritain suggested that all art begins for functional reasons and is a value of the practical intellect. Croce maintained that art is *intuition.* Schopenhauer saw music as the art *par excellence* because it "objectifies the world directly" and is "independent of the phenomenal world." Dewey viewed art as experience, reflecting the tension-release patterns of everyday life. Some other theories, as capsulized by Schwadron (1967, p. 33), are:

> Freud, desire and the unconscious; Santayana, reason; Langer, symbolic transformation; Garvin, feeling response; Stravinsky, speculative volition; Schoenberg, logical clarity; Leichtentritt, logical imagination; and Hindemith, symbolic craftsmanship.

To facilitate a modicum of order in dealing with aesthetic theories related to music, several writers have grouped aesthetic theories according to basic philosophical position (Meyer, 1956, pp. 1–3; Schwadron, 1967, pp. 34–47; Reimer, 1970, pp. 14–24). The basic viewpoints are summarized below.

The two most basic positions usually are classified as the *absolutist* and *referentialist* viewpoints, or in Schwadron's terminology, the *isolationist* and *contextualist*. Essentially, absolutist (isolationist) theories consider music's value or meaning to be the result of the musical sounds themselves and nothing more. For an absolutist, there is no musical meaning beyond that inherent in the sounds *per se*. Meyer (1956, pp. 2–3) sees an additional distinction within the absolutist framework. An absolutist may be a *formalist*, who contends that musical meaning is primarily intellectual based on perception and understanding of the formal structural relationships within a composition, or an *expressionist*, who views these structural relationships as capable of exciting feelings and emotions in the listener. The essential point regarding absolutist theories, however, is that any meaning or value derived from the music must be in terms of the musical sounds and nothing else. Eduard Hanslick (1891) is generally recognized as one of the earliest proponents of the absolutist position. For Hanslick and other absolute formalists, the value and meaning of music are derived entirely from musical structure.

Absolute expressionism has gained a certain acceptance in recent years. This view holds that the meaning of music must come not only from the music itself, but from its *expressive* or *aesthetic qualities* rather than its structure or form. Its major proponent, Bennett Reimer (1970), argues very eloquently that this philosophical position should be the basis for contemporary music education philosophy.

The other basic position, i.e., the view that the meaning of music involves more than the sounds themselves, including extramusical ideas, emotions, stories, and even spiritual states (Sullivan, 1927, pp. 27–37), is labelled the *referentialist* or *contextualist* position. Nearly all advocates of this position are expressionists; i.e., they view music as expressive of human experiences, although they also recognize that it can have other extramusical connotations.

A third position noted by Schwadron (1967, p. 42) is *relativism*. The relativist position allows for the development of personally derived value criteria, which consider that values are relative to and conditioned by cultural groups and historical periods. "For the relativist, musical meaning is a psychological product of expectation, an outgrowth of stylistic experience and cultural orientation" (Schwadron, p. 47).

Schwadron's (1984) recent review of research in music philosophy and aesthetics recognizes another direction of contemporary philosophical aesthetics: *phenomenology.* He cites thirteen doctoral dissertations completed between 1974 and 1983 that are concerned with "the phenomenology of music." Following, and borrowing metaphors from, philosophical trends in the aesthetics of visual arts, phenomenological examination of music focuses on sound *as perceived* rather than physical sound.

Smith (1979, p. 54) views phenomenology as "an overcoming of metaphysics" and argues the need to develop appropriate language for sound instead of continuing to depend on visual metaphors. The phenomenology of music is still an emerging and evolving aesthetic philosophy, but its underlying focus on music as a perceptual phenomenon is more in keeping with contemporary psychological persuasions than the positions of traditional philosophical aesthetics. Individuals concerned with understanding the affective response to music will gain an additional perspective by examining writings in the phenomenology of music.

Another contemporary philosophical position that recognizes the importance of auditory perception is Harrell's (1986, pp. 23–28) *theory of partial recall.* Concerned with explaining *depth metaphor* in music criticism, Harrell argues that ascribing qualities of profundity to a musical work in essence describes one's experiencing of it and reflects the value it holds for the individual. Harrell theorizes that music characterized as "deep" or "profound" may trigger memory for, or *partial recall* of, prenatal auditory experiences which most likely emanated positive emotional qualities and states. Because the fetus has a fully developed auditory mechanism from about the age of five months, but is devoid of visual and tactual sensory mechanisms and language as "ways of knowing" during these positive emotional experiences, the associated auditory experiences (sounds) hold increased importance. Harrell suggests that music to which the quality of *depth* is ascribed (and depth may be ascribed to music of any culture or style, *not just Western art music*) may enable a listener to "momentarily 'be in touch' with a [positive emotional] state that was pre-linguistic as well as pre-visual and pre-tactual" (p. 28). She goes on to argue that music requiring visual explication for artistic import, particularly film music, may lack the qualities of depth that music recognized as profound through auditory perception may hold.

From this cursory examination of philosophical aesthetics, no clear-cut answers emerge regarding the affective response to music. No position has been substantiated by empirical methods. Most information offered remains purely speculative and as a result leads many individuals concerned with understanding affective response to accept some other philosophical positions noted by Schwadron, (1967, pp. 34–35): complacency, eclecticism, skepticism, and agnosticism. Such philosophical positions, however, are not conducive even to attempting to understand affective response to music. The authors encourage those readers who find themselves reflecting one of the latter philosophical positions to examine not only the section immediately below, but particularly the subsequent section on meaning in music.

Psychological Aesthetics

Advocates of *psychological aesthetics* examine affective behavior in terms of human interaction with and response to musical sounds. Berlyne (1974, p. 4), the leading proponent of contemporary psychological aesthetics, equates psychological aesthetics with *empirical aesthetics,* which he defines as the study of aesthetic behavior through observation, using methods and objectives similar to empirical science. The bases for psychological aesthetics are drawn from several disciplines, especially psychology, physiology, and speculative aesthetics.

In contrast to philosophical aesthetics, psychological aesthetics has a relatively short history. Although Berlyne (1974, p. 5) traces its roots back to the work of Fechner in the 1860s and 1870s, he notes that its early products were relatively sparse and not very enlightening prior to 1960. Since about 1960, however, there has been a marked increase of interest in the discipline, which has been characterized by some new approaches, techniques, aims, and ideas.

Psychological aesthetics may involve any of three basic methodologies: (a) *correlational studies,* which examine how two or more factors vary in relation to one another, (b) *content analysis and description,* which involve measurement of artistic and other artifacts of specific social groups or historical periods, and (c) *experimental aesthetics,* which examines aesthetic response through experimental methods, i.e., seeking through systematically varying some factors to determine their causal effect on affective behavior. Berlyne maintains that experimental methodology offers the greatest potential for understanding aesthetic response to music and outlines basic criteria and premises that underlie what he terms the *new experimental aesthetics.*

For research to be identifiable with the new experimental aesthetics, it must possess one or more of four features: (a) a focus on the collative (structural or formal) properties of the musical stimulus, (b) a concentration on motivational questions, (c) study of nonverbal as well as verbally expressed judgments, and (d) efforts to establish links between aesthetic phenomena and other psychological phenomena. In addition, there are three basic theoretical premises of the new experimental aesthetics.

First, a work of art is analyzed in information-theoretic terms; i.e., it is comprised of elements, each of which can transmit *information* of four types: (a) semantic, (b) expressive, (c) cultural, and (d) syntactic. Berlyne recognizes some overlap among the four types of information, but notes that the four information sources also emit independent information, thus setting up a competition among them. More information from one generally allows less from other sources.

The second theoretical premise is that artworks are regarded as collections of symbols in accordance with the conception of signs and symbols in the semiotic movement.* Artworks have properties in common with objects or events that they signify, and they serve as symbols for communication of artists' values regarding which objects or events deserve attention.

The third theoretical premise is that an artwork serves as a stimulus pattern whose collative properties give it a positive intrinsic hedonic value. Variables for measuring "hedonic value" include degree of pleasure, preference, or utility, which usually are measured via verbal expressions, and such nonverbal variables as reward value and incentive value. An artwork that has "positive intrinsic hedonic value" is pleasurable or rewarding in itself and not because it serves as a means to an end. Berlyne hypothesizes that positive hedonic values are a function of *arousal*—through a moderate increase in arousal or through a decrease in arousal when arousal has reached an uncomfortable high. The "arousal potential" of an artwork's stimulus pattern for an individual depends on many factors, including intensity, association with, or resemblance to, experientially significant events, and collative properties.

McMullen (1982a), another strong proponent of psychological aesthetics, expanded on Berlyne's concept of arousal, or *activation* as some call it. He notes that the key concept of arousal—the degree of action or activity

---

*Readers interested in information on the semiotic movement should consult Chapter 6 of D.E. Berlyne's *Aesthetics and Psychobiology* (New York: Appleton-Century-Crofts, 1971).

by an individual—is the same whether viewed from a cognitive or behavioral perspective. He argues that the basic reason for including the concept of arousal at the core of psychological aesthetics is that it provides a bridge between what is perceived—the music—and the related feeling response.

When a person listens to and processes the acoustic properties of music, he or she is, according to McMullen, responding perceptually in terms of the "energy" and "structure" of the music, which in combination serve to arouse or activate the listener. Both McMullen and Berlyne suggest that this activation or arousal provides the framework for the aesthetic response to music.

Dependent variables for experimental aesthetics may include verbal ratings, psychophysiological measures, and behavioral measures. As noted in the earlier discussion of adjective descriptors, the semantic differential has become the predominant framework for verbal ratings, and much of the research using adjective descriptors is considered part of the contemporary psychological aesthetics movement. Three classes of scales are used: (a) *descriptive scales,* in reference to collative properties of stimulus patterns, (b) *evaluative scales,* reflecting hedonic value, and (c) *internal state scales,* for assessing subjects' reactions or mood while exposed to a stimulus. Psychophysiological measures generally are used as indicators of "arousal" rather than as attempts to measure "affect" as in much of the psychophysiological research cited earlier in this chapter. Behavioral measures generally are *exploration time* (in music, *listening time*) or *exploratory choice* (in music, *listening choice*). Exploratory time variously has been interpreted as a measure of the intensity of orientation time, the intensity of attention, or perceptual curiosity, while exploratory choice is viewed as an index of "incentive value" or "utility" (Berlyne, 1974, pp. 13–14).

Independent variables in experimental aesthetics generally reflect the *approach* to experimentation. The *synthetic* approach involves a more-or-less laboratory approach in which particular variables are isolated for manipulation and study, while the *analytical* approach examines reactions to art and other aesthetic stimuli taken from real life. While there are obvious advantages to the synthetic approach, McMullen (1978) argues that there is a great need for music psychologists to examine musical behaviors from the latter perspective. He maintains that the psychology of music reflects too much the one-sided position of psycho*acoustics* rather than psycho*music.* Berlyne (1974, p. 18) notes that both synthetic and analytical approaches are necessary, but he too recognizes that the synthetic approach has been the dominant approach for much research. Independent variables generally are structural or formal characteristics, i.e., the collative characteristics of the artwork, and their effects frequently are evaluated within an information theory framework.

Research in psychological aesthetics continues to develop in several directions. The psychophysiological approaches, using measures of various physiological rates as dependent measures, and the adjective descriptor approach, particularly the studies of dimensionality reflected in the descriptors, have received renewed emphasis and direction from the theory, methodology, and research of contemporary psychological aesthetics. The major developments in psychological aesthetics, however, seem to be emerging through research using experimental methodology that focuses on the collative variables of musical stimuli, "such as complexity, novelty/familiarity, redundancy/uncertainty, and orderliness, and various measures of 'aesthetic' response including liking, interestingness, and subjective familiarity and complexity" (Hargreaves, 1986, p. 110). The collative variables generally serve as independent variables, and the various measures of aesthetic response the dependent. Relationships within and between the two classes of variables obviously are highly complex, and examination of them is fraught with many semantic, measurement, methodological, and theoretical problems and issues. The present discussion is intended to serve as an introduction to the theory and issues and to provide an overview of some of the research directions using experimental methodology. Readers interested in more information on contemporary experimental aesthetics should examine Hargreaves' (1986, pp. 110–122) and his colleagues' (Sluckin, Hargreaves, & Coleman, 1982) thorough and lucid reviews of the literature and issues.

Research in music using the theory and methodology of experimental aesthetics appears to be spearheaded by one of Berlyne's associates, J.B. Crozier (Crozier, 1974, pp. 27–90; Bragg & Crozier, 1974, pp. 91–108). In the United States, Patrick McMullen seems to be the chief proponent (McMullen, 1976; 1977; 1982a; 1982b; McMullen & Arnold, 1976). Perhaps the strongest research thrust in recent years comes through the work of David Hargreaves and his colleagues in the Leicester Aesthetics Research Group in England (e.g., Hargreaves, 1982; 1984; 1986, pp. 110–122; Hargreaves & Coleman, 1981; Sluckin, Hargreaves, & Coleman, 1982).

Much of these scholars' research has been related to what Smith and Cuddy (1986) term the "classical model of aesthetic preference," the *optimal-complexity model.* At least some aspect of the theory pervades most research in experimental aesthetics. The theory's origin is generally attributed to Berlyne (1971), but it has been tested or modified over the years by a number of researchers, including Heyduk (1975), Davies (1978), and Walker (1981). Because many of the issues and problems central to research in experimental aesthetics are grounded in the assumptions of the theory, the balance of the present discussion will examine research in experimental aesthetics as it relates to the theory's assumptions, which Smith and Cuddy (pp. 17–18) have conveniently summarized:

1. The critical aspect of a stimulus that determines its hedonic, or positive affective value, is its complexity. Complexity is measured by the amount of variability or uncertainty associated with an event. In terms of information theory, it is directly related to the amount of information conveyed by an event and indirectly related to redundancy.

2. The relation between complexity and affective value may be described by an inverted U-shaped curve. In other words, an intermediate level of complexity elicits maximum positive affect; lower and higher levels of complexity elicit less positive affect.

3. The effect of stimulus exposure (repetition, training, practice) is to lower stimulus complexity and, by consequence, to alter the affective values of stimulus patterns. For example, a pattern whose preexposure complexity was on the high side of the optimal point of complexity would move toward the optimal point with repetition, and its attractiveness would increase. The pattern formerly at the optimal point would become lower than optimal complexity and its attractiveness would decrease. The result is that a higher level of complexity, as measured by the preexposure scale, is now required to elicit maximum positive affect.

Most of the general assumptions of the optimal-complexity model relate to the effects of the collative attributes of a stimulus. However, the collative attributes of a musical stimulus are not simple, isolated variables.

Complexity, which seems to be the central variable, may be either *objective,* a function of the stimulus attributes varied according to some systematic and objective procedure, or *subjective,* the apparent perceived complexity that is assumed to be a function of the interaction between the objective complexity of the stimulus and the listener's musical knowledge, experience with the musical style and/or idiom, and familiarity with the particular musical stimulus.* In reality, most collative variables are *relativistic;* i.e., their qualities are dependent on the interaction between the structural attributes of the musical stimulus and the prior musical experience of the listener with music in general, with the style and/or idiom, and with the particular piece. Subjective complexity is similar to the notion of *conceptual meaning,* discussed in Chapter Five.

If complexity is relativistic and is measured in terms of the uncertainty of the musical stimulus, as the optimal-complexity model assumes, then the uncertainty/redundancy continuum, another generally accepted collative variable, also must be considered relativistic, i.e., a function of both stimulus structure (*structural redundancy*) and the listener's experience with such music (*cultural redundancy*), with the net effect being *perceptual redundancy.*

Research tends to support the first general assumption. Crozier (1974) used a synthetic approach to examine the effects of uncertainty in melodic structure. He found that variations in information, i.e., varying levels of uncertainty, affected subjects' ratings of "pleasingness" and "interestingness." Further, he reported a "remarkably high degree" of interpredictability between mean verbal ratings and nonverbal measures of exploratory behavior.

McMullen and Arnold's (1976) study of the effects of distributional redundancy on preference and interest response for rhythmic sequences also suggests that redundancy influences both preference and interest. Preference tended to increase as redundancy decreased to a point, after which preference began to decrease; interest generally increased as redundancy decreased.

Smith and Cuddy (1986) examined the effects of (objective) harmonic complexity on 36 university psychology students' "pleasingness" ratings of 20 melodic sequences. The melodic stimuli had been previously classified into five levels of complexity, "according to rules defining tone sets and tone progressions in classical Western-European music" (p. 21). Essentially, the level of uncertainty or redundancy, as reflected by degree of tonality or tonal strength, was the variable of concern to the present discussion. Results indicated that pleasingness ratings varied with level

---

*The constructs *objective* and *subjective complexity* are borrowed and adapted from Hargreaves, 1986, pp. 116–117.

of objective harmonic complexity. Analysis of data according to subjects' level of musical training revealed that pleasingness ratings also varied according to level of musical training. They concluded that the data supported the first assumption of the optimal-complexity model.

The second general assumption of the optimal-complexity model, that the relationship between complexity and affective value may be described by an inverted U-shaped curve, suggests that a person will like more, prefer more, or be more pleased by music of an optimal-complexity level (i.e. moderately complex) for him or her than by music that is either very simple or very complex. Research testing this assumption includes both studies that attempt to vary the objective complexity (information or redundancy level) and studies that use subjective complexity (perceived or judged complexity).

Research examining the effects of both types of complexity generally is supportive of the inverted U-shaped curve hypothesis. Smith and Cuddy (1986) cite five studies using tone sequences with varied information content (i.e. complexity) as the independent variable that support the inverted U-shaped curve hypothesis (Berlyne, 1971; Crozier, 1974; Vitz, 1966a; Vitz, 1966b; and Walker, 1981). However, they also cite studies showing positive linear (monotonic) relationships between amount of information and judged preference (Vitz, 1962; Vitz, 1964).

Hargreaves' review of studies of subjective complexity and liking for musical excerpts is similarly supportive of the hypothesis. He notes the Crozier (1974) and McMullen and Arnold (1976) studies cited above, as well as some of the studies cited by Smith and Cuddy. Other studies cited as supportive of the inverted U-shaped curve hypothesis include Heyduk (1975), Radocy (1982), and Hargreaves and Castell (1986).

Heyduk (1975) varied the harmonic and rhythmic content of four brief piano compositions so that they reflected different level of objective complexity. Subjects' "liking" ratings of the resultant versions of varying objective complexity provided strong support for the inverted U-shaped curve hypothesis and the general assumptions of the optimal complexity model.

Radocy tested Walker's (1981) version of the optimal-complexity model, the "hedgehog" theory, so-named because Walker views the one central idea of the theory as being applicable in many situations, just as the European hedgehog has one response to fatigue, stimulation, or fright, namely rolling into a ball. Using 15 instrumental excerpts from Western art music as stimuli, Radocy asked college music and nonmusic majors to rate each excerpt in terms of complexity, familiarity, and preference. Results revealed that excerpts rated moderately complex were the most preferred, despite a strong positive linear relationship between familiarity and preference. It also was concluded that perceived complexity or lack thereof is more than just a matter of familiarity.

Hargreaves and Castell (1986) compared the preferences of subjects of different age levels, which were assumed to reflect different levels of enculturation with music, for four types of melodic sequences. The melodic sequences ranged from very familiar melodies of nursery rhymes and carols to some little-known English folk song melodies to "near" and "far" statistical approximations of music. Ratings of the familiar melodies and the unfamiliar folk song melodies yielded inverted U-shaped relationships with increasing age, but with a later peak for the unfamiliar melodies. The statistical approximations to music were preferred less as the age of the subjects increased. Data were interpreted as supporting the inverted U-shaped curve hypothesis, as well as Hargreaves' contention that *stimulus familiarity* serves as a key explanatory variable in tests of the optimal-complexity model.

Although research is generally supportive of the theory's assumption that complexity and affective value may be described by an inverted U-shaped curve, the role of familiarity is not quite as clear as Hargreaves suggests. Research related to the theory's third assumption, that repeated exposure to a stimulus (i.e., increasing familiarity) serves to lower stimulus complexity, has yielded contradictory results.

Hargreaves' (1984) study of the effects of repetition on "liking" of music examined the hypothesis that the liking curve would, with repeated hearings of the music, reflect a U-shaped curve. Using musical pieces in four styles, he conducted two experiments, one with adults and one with university students, asking them to rate the pieces on seven-point scales for liking and familiarity. Excerpts for the adult group were played three times, those for the other group four times. For the adult group, which heard easy listening and avant-garde jazz excerpts, familiarity ratings increased with repetitions, but results were different for the different styles. For the easy listening music, which appeared to be at about the listeners' optimal level of subjective complexity, liking ratings declined with repetitions, but for the avant-garde music, which was probably above the listeners' optimal level of subjective complexity, the liking ratings increased with repetition. For the university students, who heard avant-garde jazz, pop, and classical excerpts, liking curves also varied with style. Ratings for the avant-garde excerpts did not change, but those for the pop and easy listening generally supported the inverted U-shaped curve. Apparently the inverted U-shaped curve predicts preference well within a style but not between styles.

Smith and Cuddy (1986), whose study was discussed above in relation to the first assumption of the optimal-complexity model, also examined repetition effects. Their data revealed that for four of the five levels of complexity, subjects' "pleasingness" ratings increased with repetition. However, on a postrepetition test, which contained some repeated sequences and some nonrepeated sequences, the repetition effects did not carry over, leading the authors to conclude that "the degree to which we appreciate repetition depends in part on the initially perceived complexity of the repeated excerpt" (p. 31). They go on to suggest that "mere repetition does not necessarily lead to cognitive reorganisation; if it does not, the evaluation of rule complexity will be unaffected by repetition" (p. 31).

Hargreaves' (1986, pp. 118–122) excellent review of the literature on repetition and liking led him to conclude that "the results of approximately half of the studies seem to support the inverted-U hypothesis, whilst the other half show a positive monotonic 'mere exposure' relationship between familiarity and liking" (p. 119). He acknowledges that the contradictory results could be the result of differences in experimental design and procedures, but he argues quite convincingly that they may be due to the variations in the ranges of the familiarity variable sampled in the experimental stimuli. He maintains that studies showing linear relationships between repetition and preference could just be sampling the beginning or ending part of the U-shaped curve, depending on the initial complexity level of the stimuli for the subjects. He goes on to note that this view is in accord with Lundin's (1967) earlier review of the repetition literature in which it was noted that popular music tended to attain a maximal pleasantness level at an early repetition, while classical excerpts, which presumably were more complex, reached their affective maximum during later repetitions. Smith and Cuddy's (1986) discussion of the research on repetition effects essentially concurs with Hargreaves' explanation for the seemingly contradictory results from repetition studies.

As may be apparent, the experimental aesthetics approach to understanding the affective response to music has developed a workable research paradigm through which considerable data have been generated. However, it also is apparent that the research paradigm needs refinements so that more consistent data might be forthcoming. While a number of factors may contribute to the inconsistent data, future research should scrutinize some of the variables very carefully. The research appears to be overly dependent on verbal ratings as measures of liking, pleasingness, preference, etc., with little consideration given to the reliability of such ratings. Certainly, the assumptions of the optimal-complexity model and the complex interrelationships among the collative variables warrant further careful examination. The examination of familiarity has been almost solely in terms of particular pieces, whereas Meyer's (1956; 1967) application of information theory as a model for meaning in music, which is discussed in the next section, suggests that familiarity with style, idiom, or rules of musical grammar seems to be of even greater importance. The apparent relativistic nature of collative variables suggests that *individuals*, as well as groups, will differ greatly in their perception of and response to musical stimuli; consequently, there is great need to study individual differences in addition to the study of groups, which has been the primary concern of researchers to date.

While discussions of cognitive and affective responses to music generally are separated for convenience, there is need for more studies such as Smith and Cuddy's (1986) which seek to examine perceptual and cognitive underpinnings of affective behavior. Finally, researchers need to give greater consideration to the role of enculturation and the sociocultural context within which data are gathered. In short, there have been major developments in experimental aesthetics during the past few decades, but refinement of research variables and methodology is still necessary if psychological aesthetics is to provide satisfactory answers for those seeking to understand the affective response to music.

Meaning in Music

As may be apparent from the preceding section, there is a broad gap between philosophical and psychological aesthetics. Philosophers tend to talk to philosophers and psychologists tend to talk to psychologists. Philosophers tend to be concerned with whether music's value and import come from within the music or from its referents, while psychologists have examined the affective response to music in terms psychophysiological, verbal, or behavioral response to music. However, information theory, with its constructs related to redundancy, appears to offer a viable means for bridging the gap between aesthetic theory and musical response,* and Leonard B. Meyer's work toward this end provides some direction not only for philosophical aestheticians and psychological aestheticians, but for for anyone concerned with understanding the affective response to music.

Meyer (1956, pp. 1–42) espouses a theory of musical meaning based on a theory of emotion and expectation. The relationships between his theory of musical meaning and information theory are explored in another publication, *Music, the Arts, and Ideas* (Meyer, 1967). This section examines Meyer's theories of emotion and meaning in music as well as some of the parallels between his theories and information theory.

Meyer's theory of musical meaning is based on his *theory of emotion,* which has the same basic tenets as Dewey's *conflict theory of emotion.* "Emotion or affect is aroused when a tendency to respond is arrested or inhibited" (Meyer, 1956, p. 14). Emotional responses are dependent on the relationship between a stimulus (music) and a responding individual. A musical stimulus must produce a tendency for an individual to respond in a particular way. A stimulus that arouses no tendency to respond or that is satisfied without delay cannot arouse emotion.

Meyer differentiates between emotion *per se* and the emotional experience: the latter includes an awareness and cognition of a stimulus situation that always involves specific stimuli. Thus, affective experiences with music require *musical* stimuli.

Musical affective experience is distinguished from affective experience in everyday life. Tensions created by tendencies to respond in everyday life may go unresolved, whereas those aroused by music usually are resolved within a musical framework. Music can serve as both stimulus and as meaningful resolution to such tendencies; in life that which creates the tension usually cannot serve to resolve it.

Tensions, which may be either conscious or subconscious, are referred to as expectations. Music arouses expectations in various ways. Listeners to Western music *learn* (consciously or subconsciously) that certain "sound terms" (melodic, rhythmic, or harmonic patterns, phrases, etc.) imply certain other musical entities. When the expected musical consequent is delayed, suspense is aroused. In Meyer's (1956, p. 28) words,

---

*Besides the work of Berlyne, Crozier, et al., significant work has been conducted by Abraham Moles (1966, *Information Theory and Esthetic Perception,* Urbana: University of Illinois Press). In addition, much of Roederer's (1975) work in the psychophysics of music, previously noted in Chapter Three, utilizes information theory as a framework for examining responses to aural stimuli.

The greater the buildup of suspense, of tension, the greater the emotional release upon resolution. This observation points up the fact that
in aesthetic experience emotional pattern must be considered not only
in terms of tension itself but also in terms of the progression from
tension to release. And the experience of suspense is aesthetically
valueless unless it is followed by a release which is understandable in
the given context.

A musical consequent that will fulfill such expectations is dictated by
the possibilities and probabilities of the style of the musical composition
in question. When seen in this light, stylistic knowledge becomes essential;
without knowledge of a musical style or idiom, a listener's expectations
lack a basis for focus, other than the unexpected.

In summary, Meyer's theory of emotion is a theory of expectation,
which necessarily has certain cultural and stylistic presuppositions. He
states his central hypothesis as follows: Affect or emotion felt is aroused
when an expectation—a tendency to respond—activated by the musical
stimulus situation, is temporarily inhibited or permanently blocked"
(Meyer, 1956, p. 31).

While the question of musical meaning is centered on the opposing
views of the absolutists and the referentialists, much of the confusion
concerning it may be attributed to the different views regarding the
definition of meaning. The following definition suffices for Meyer:
"Anything acquires meaning if it is connected with or indicates, or refers
to something beyond itself, so that its full nature points to and is revealed
in that connection" (1956, p. 34). Meaning is defined in terms of the
relationship between a stimulus and the thing it points to or indicates,
but such a relationship must be perceived by the listener. Meaning thus
arises out of a triadic relationship among (a) a stimulus, (b) that to which
it points, and (c) the conscious observer.

Meyer maintains that music's meaning has been further muddled by
the failure of aestheticians to state explicitly that to which musical
stimuli point. He recognizes two types of musical meaning: *designative*
and *embodied.* The designative meaning of a musical stimulus may
indicate events or consequents that differ from itself in kind, i.e., nonmusical events. Embodied meaning refers to those in which the stimulus
and consequent are of the same kind, i.e., both musical. It is the embodied meaning of music with which Meyer is concerned. For Meyer, one
musical event has meaning because it points to and makes the listener

expect another musical event. Embodied musical meaning, therefore, is a product of expectations developed as a result of past experiences with music of the given style. Music that does not arouse expectations of a subsequent musical consequent is meaningless for the listener. Because expectation is so much a product of stylistic experience, music in a style with which a listener is totally unfamiliar is meaningless.

A knowledge of style implies that learning has taken place; thus, the perception of meaning cannot take place without involving cognition. The affective and intellectual responses to music cannot be separated. They both depend on the same perceptual processes, stylistic habits, and mode of mental organization. The same musical processes give rise and shape to both types of experience. Meyer maintains that the formalists' and the expressionists' conception of it seem to be complementary rather than contradictory. They are considered not different processes, but different ways of experiencing the same process. "Whether a piece of music gives rise to affective experience or to intellectual experience depends upon the disposition and training of the listener" (1956, p. 40).

Those people who have been taught that musical experience is primarily emotional will probably experience delay of expectations as affect. The trained musician will probably listen in more technical terms and will tend to make musical processes an object of conscious consideration. Regardless of the way in which one views the delay of expectations, Meyer's theory of expectation will suffice to explain it.

Meyer (1967, pp. 5–21) notes striking parallels between his theory of musical meaning and information theory and hypothesizes that "the psychostylistic conditions which give rise to musical meaning, whether affective or intellectual, are the same as those which communicate information" (1967, p. 5). Meyer specifically argues that it is the embodied meaning of music that is most consistent with information theory.

As discussed in Chapter Five, information theory is a system for quantifying the amount of uncertainty in a stimulus. The greater the amount of *information*, the greater the *uncertainty* of meaning or response. The amount of information a listener receives from a musical stimulus is a function of two basic variables: (a) the extent to which the structural characteristics of the music conform to fundamental organizational laws of Gestalt psychology and (b) the listener's previous experience with the given musical style. The greater the perceptual redundancy of the music, the more predictable the musical response.*

The relationship between Meyer's theory of musical meaning and information theory also has been examined by Trolio (1976). She notes that uncertainty created by the antecedent-consequent relationships provides both meaning and information. The relationships also arouse emotion. The relationship between information and emotion is further clarified with the recognition that uncertainty arising from when habit responses have been arrested is caused by a disturbance in the order and/or timing of a sequence of responses. Information is the measure of uncertainty, which also may arouse emotions.

Variables Contributing to Musical Meaning

Variables contributing to musical meaning may be classified under two broad categories: (a) those related to the structural (collative) characteristics of the musical stimulus and (b) those related to the listener, particular the experiential variables. McMullen (1978) conveniently has grouped the variables related to musical structure under three headings: *order, complexity,* and *energy.*

He notes that order is closely related to a traditional aesthetic principle of "unity in variety." Order within musical structure appears to be a function of the amount of structural redundancy in a composition; e.g., tonality and rhythmic redundancy appear to contribute greatly to musical meaning, but systematic investigation of the effects of order in musical structure had received little attention from researchers until recent years.

Complexity of musical structure, a construct not unrelated to order, is currently receiving considerable attention from psychological aestheticians, although much of the research examines it as a perceived or subjective variable rather than as an objective structural attribute of music. As discussed previously, the authors believe that complexity, as all collative variables, is relativistic and that responses to complexity are the result of the interaction between the structural attributes of the musical stimulus and the prior experience of the listener with music in general, with the given musical style and/or idiom, and with the particular music heard. Whichever way it is examined, structural complexity is a critical variable

---

*The relationship of perceptual redundancy to *structural* and *cultural* redundancy is discussed in Chapter Five.

in musical response, as demonstrated by its centrality to the optimal-complexity of music preference.

Energy is the musical quality that reflects stimulation or drive. Variables such as tempo and dynamics generally are recognized as primary contributors to energy, but other variables such as melodic and harmonic movement also appear to contribute. Some of the earlier work regarding mood response, as reported by Lundin (1967, pp. 160–177) and Farnsworth (1969, pp. 83–90), examined some of these variables, although it appears that many of the tentative conclusions reached were artifacts of the particular musical examples and evaluative measures employed.

More recently McMullen (1980; 1982a) has suggested that people's connotative verbal descriptions of music, traditionally mood response as indicated by adjective descriptors, have taken on greater import as reflections of musical meaning. Rather than just connoting some mood or other meaning external to the musical stimulus, he maintains that studies of dimensionality in these connotative labels (adjective descriptors) provide evidence for an *interpretive paradigm*. The proposed paradigm is relativistic in that it considers

> connotative vocabulary to be the result of a relationship between acoustical properties external to the human senses and the resultant perception as music, the human experience of and/or resulting from that perception and then, and only then, translating that human experience into overt form, in this case connotative vocabulary. (McMullen, 1982a, p. 49)

McMullen also offers a theoretical model, derived primarily from dimensional research, suggesting that the perceived dimensions of *energy* and *structure* are experienced as forms of *activation* or arousal. He hypothesizes that if the experience of perceiving music is related to activation (arousal), "when connotative labels (either in prose form or individual words) are used as descriptors of responses to music, these labels represent some combination of the two covert dimensions—activation and evaluation" (McMullen, 1982a, p. 52). In short, he argues that activation (arousal) and evaluation are the covert bipolar dimensions, reflecting respective continua from high to low activation and positive to negative evaluative judgments, that are operative in determining the *meaning* of a given connotative word.

Variables related to the listener are many and complex. Perhaps of greatest importance are the variables related to the listener's previous experiences with music. From infancy on, individuals have many varieties of experiences with music. They develop expectations regarding its structure (embodied meaning) as well as regarding its referents (designative meaning). In addition to expectations, formal musical training and the resultant learning, associations with particular musical examples and styles, as well as all of an individual's informal musical learning are variables that appear to affect musical meaning. Further, an individual's basic personality and state of motivation for interacting with music have received increased attention as potential variables affecting musical meaning.

In conclusion, the efforts of previous researchers in examining the effects of selected variables is acknowledged; they have contributed much to the understanding of musical meaning. However, it also is apparent that research efforts related to musical meaning, or the affective response to music, are still in their infancy, and much effort must be directed toward examining the effects of the variables noted here (as well as many others) before any "final truth" is reached regarding affective responses to music.

Summary

The major points of this chapter may be summarized as follows:

1. *Affect* is a broad term referring to a wide variety of human feeling responses.
2. *Emotion* is a particular type of affect reflecting a relatively temporary disturbance from a normal state of composure.
3. *Aesthetic* feeling results from certain types of experiences with artworks, natural phenomena, or other objects or events in which beauty or artistic value may be perceived.
4. *Aesthetic experience* requires perceptual involvement with interacting attributes within artwork (or natural phenomena or other objects or events), perception of beauty or meaning therein, and a feeling reaction thereto.
5. Other types of affective response to musical stimuli (besides the aesthetic) include, *mood* or character responses, *association* responses, *intrasubjective* responses, reaction to word meanings of songs, preferences, interests, attitudes, values, and appreciations.
6. Four basic approaches to study of the affective response to music have been through (a) psychophysiological research, (b) adjective

descriptor research, (c) philosophical inquiry, and (d) psychological aesthetics research.

7. Concomitant with affective responses are physiological reactions of the autonomic nervous system.

8. Although physiological reactions, particularly heart rate, respiration rate, and electrodermal responses, to music have been examined for nearly a century, such research provides little insight into the affective response to music.

9. Early research using adjective descriptors focused on assessment of mood response to music, but more recent research using dimensional analysis techniques on semantic differential data has sparked a renewed interest in adjective descriptors as tools for understanding affective behaviors.

10. Speculative aesthetics is of two basic types: *philosophical aesthetics*, which seeks to make general statements regarding arts phenomena and their intent, value, or meaning, and *art theory*, which in music is incorporated in such courses as music history, literature, and analysis and which involves examination of individual compositions, styles, and composers.

11. Basic philosophical aesthetic positions include the *absolutist*, which views the value or meaning of music as resulting from the musical sounds themselves, and the *referentialist*, which views music as reflecting more than sounds themselves; it may include extramusical ideas, emotions, stories, and even spiritual states.

12. Psychological aesthetics, particularly with the renewed emphasis on *experimental aesthetics*, utilizing methods of empirical science, focuses on the collative properties of aesthetic stimuli, examines motivational questions, studies nonverbal as well as verbal behavior, and seeks to establish links between aesthetic phenomena and other psychological phenomena.

13. Research in psychological aesthetics has focused on the optimal-complexity model of music preference, in which an individual's "liking," pleasingness," or "preference" response to a musical stimulus is hypothesized to reflect an inverted U-shaped curve with respect to complexity.

14. The collative variables of a musical stimulus (complexity, novelty/familiarity, uncertainty/redundancy) are relativistic.

15. There appear to be parallels between Leonard B. Meyer's theory of musical meaning, which views meaning in terms of expectations,

and information theory, which offers a promising model for examining affect resulting from musical uncertainty.

16. Variables contributing to musical meaning are of two broad classes: (a) those related to the structural (collative) characteristics of a music stimulus and (b) those related to the listener, particular the experiential variables.

REFERENCES

Abeles, H.F. (1980). Responses to music. In D.A. Hodges (Ed.), *Handbook of music psychology* (pp. 105–140). Lawrence, KS: National Association for Music Therapy.

Asmus, E.P., Jr. (1985). The Effect of time manipulation on affective responses to a musical stimulus. In G.C. Turk (Ed.), *Proceedings of the Research Symposium on the Psychology and Acoustics of Music* (pp. 97–110). Lawrence: University of Kansas.

Berlyne, D.E. (1971). *Aesthetics and psychobiology.* New York: Appleton-Century-Crofts.

Berlyne, D.E. (Ed.). (1974). *Studies in the new experimental aesthetics: Steps toward an objective psychology of aesthetic appreciation.* New York: Halsted Press.

Boyle, J.D., Cole, H.W., Cutietta, R., & Ray, W.J. (1982). Electrocortical responses to music: An exploratory study concerning affect and familiarity. In P.R. Sink (Ed.)., *Proceedings of the Research Symposium of the Psychology and Acoustics of Music 1981* (pp. 10–18). Lawrence: University of Kansas.

Boyle, J.D., & Radocy, R.E. (1987). *Measurement and evaluation of musical experiences.* New York: Schirmer Books.

Bragg, B.W., & Crozier, J.B. (1974). The development with age of verbal and exploratory responses to sound sequences varying in uncertainty level. In D.E. Berlyne (Ed.), *Studies in the new experimental aesthetics: Steps toward an objective psychology of aesthetic appreciation* (pp. 91–108). New York: Halsted Press.

Capurso, A. (1952). The Capurso study. In *Music and your emotions.* New York: Liveright Publishing.

Crozier, J.B. (1974). Verbal and exploratory responses to sound sequences varying in uncertainty level. In D.E. Berlyne (Ed.), *Studies in the new experimental psychology: Steps toward an object psychology of aesthetic appreciation* (pp. 27–90). New York: Halsted Press.

Dainow, E. (1977). Physical effects and motor responses to music. *Journal of Research in Music Education, 25,* 211–221.

Davies, J.B. (1978). *The psychology of music.* London: Hutchinson & Co.

Diserins, C.M., & Fine, H. (1939). *A psychology of music.* Cincinnati: College of Music.

Dowling, W.J., & Harwood, D.L. (1986). *Music cognition.* Orlando, FL: Academic Press.

Dreher, R.E. (1947). The relationship between verbal reports and galvanic skin response. Unpublished doctoral dissertation, Indiana University.

Eagle, C.T., Jr. (1971). Effects of existing mood and order of presentation of vocal and instrumental music on rated mood responses to that music. Unpublished doctoral dissertation, The University of Kansas.

Farnsworth, P.R. (1954). A study of the Hevner adjective list. *Journal of Aesthetics and Art Criticism, 13,* 97–103.

Farnsworth, P.R. (1969). *The social psychology of music* (2nd ed.). Ames: The Iowa State University Press.

Gabrielsson, A. (1973). Adjective ratings and dimension analyses of auditory rhythm patterns. *Scandinavian Journal of Psychology, 14,* 244–260.

Gabrielsson, A. (1979). Dimension analyses of perceived sound quality of sound-reproducing systems. *Scandinavian Journal of Psychology, 20,* 159–169.

Gates, A., & Bradshaw, J.L. (1977a). Music perception and cerebral asymmetries. *Cortex, 13,* 390–401.

Gates, A., & Bradshaw, J.L. (1977b). The role of the cerebral hemispheres in music. *Brain and Language, 4,* 403–431.

Gatewood, E.L. (1927). An experimental study of the nature of musical enjoyment. In M. Scheon (Ed.), *The effects of music.* Freeport, NY: Books for Libraries Press.

Hahn, M.E. (1954). A proposed technique for investigating the relationship between musical preferences and personality structure. Unpublished doctoral dissertation, The University of Kansas.

Hanslick, E. (1957). *The beautiful in music* (G. Cohen, trans.). New York: Liberal Arts Press. (Originally published 1854, translation, 1891)

Hargreaves, D.J. (1982). The development of aesthetic reactions to music. *Psychology of Music, Special Edition,* 51–54.

Hargreaves, D.J. (1984). The effects of repetition on liking for music. *Journal of Research in Music Education, 32,* 35–47.

Hargreaves, D.J. (1986). *The developmental psychology of music.* Cambridge: Cambridge University Press.

Hargreaves, D.J., & Castell, K.C. (1986). Development of liking for familiar and unfamiliar melodies. Paper presented at the Eleventh International Research Seminar of the International Society for Music Education, Frankfurt, West Germany.

Hargreaves, D.J., & Coleman, A.M. (1981). The dimensions of aesthetic reactions to music. *Psychology of Music, 9,* 15–20.

Harrell, J.G. (1986). *Soundtracks, A study of auditory perception, memory, and valuation.* Buffalo, NY: Prometheus Books.

Heinlein, C.P. (1928). The affective characters of the major and minor modes in music. *The Journal of Comparative Psychology, 8,* 101–142.

Hevner, K. (1935). Expression in music: A discussion of experimental studies and theories. *Psychological Review, 42,* 186–204.

Hevner, K. (1936). Experimental studies of the elements of expression in music. *American Journal of Psychology, 48,* 246–268.

Hevner, K. (1937). The affective value of pitch and tempo in music. *American Journal of Psychology, 49,* 621–630.

Hevner, K. (1939). Studies of expressiveness in music. *Proceedings of the Music Teachers National Association* (199–217).

Heyduk, R.G. (1975). Rated preference for musical composition as it relates to complexity and exposure frequency. *Perception and Psychophysics, 17,* 84–91.

Hodges, D.A. (1978). Split-brain research: A new frontier. In E.P. Asmus, Jr. (Ed.), *Proceedings of the Research Symposium on the Psychology and Acoustics of Music* (pp. 71–93). Lawrence: The University of Kansas.

Hodges, D.A. (1980a). Neurophysiology and musical behavior. In D.A. Hodges (Ed.), *Handbook of music psychology* (pp 195–224). Lawrence, KS: National Association for Music Therapy.

Hodges, D.A. (1980b). Physiological responses to music. In D.A. Hodges (Ed.), *Handbook of music psychology* (pp. 393–400). Lawrence, KS: National Association for Music Therapy.

Hofstadter, A., & Kuhns, R. (Eds.). (1964). *Philosophies of art and beauty.* New York: The Modern Library.

Hylton, J. (1981). Dimensionality in high school student participants' perceptions of the meaning of choral singing experience. *Journal of Research in Music Education, 29,* 287–304.

Knieter, G.L. (1971). The nature of aesthetic education. In *Toward an aesthetic education* (pp. 3–20). Washington, D.C.: Music Educators National Conference.

Kuhn, T.L. (1979). Instrumentation for the measurement of attitudes. Paper presented at the meeting of the College Music Society, San Antonio, Texas.

Lehman, P.R. (1968). *Tests and measurements in music.* Englewood Cliffs, NJ: Prentice-Hall.

Lundin, R.W. (1967). *An objective psychology of music* (2nd ed.). New York: Ronald Press.

McMullen, P.T. (1976). Influences of distributional redundancy in rhythmic sequences on judged complexity ratings. *Council for Research in Music Education, 46,* 23–30.

McMullen, P.T. (1977). Organizational and technical dimensions in musical stimuli. Paper presented at the MENC Eastern Division Conference, Washington, D.C.

McMullen, P.T. (1978). Music and empirical aesthetics: Present and future directions. Paper presented at the Symposium on the Psychology and Acoustics of Music. Lawrence: The University of Kansas.

McMullen, P.T. (1980). Music as a perceived stimulus object and affective responses: An alternative theoretical framework. In D.A. Hodges (Ed.), *Handbook of music psychology* (pp. 183–193). Lawrence, KS: National Association for Music Therapy.

McMullen, P.T. (1982a). Connotative responses to musical stimuli: A theoretical explanation. *Council for Research in Music Education, 71,* 45–57.

McMullen, P.T., (1982b). Empirical aesthetics: An overview. In P.E. Sink (Ed.), *Proceedings of the Research Symposium on the Psychology and Acoustics of Music 1982* (pp. 48–55). Lawrence: The University of Kansas.

McMullen, P.T., & Arnold, M.J. (1976). Preference and interest as functions of distributional redundancy in rhythmic sequences. *Journal of Research in Music Education, 24,* 22–31.

Maslow, A.H. (1970). *Motivation and personality* (2nd ed.). New York: Harper & Row.

Meyer, L.B. (1956). *Emotion and meaning in music.* Chicago: The University of Chicago Press.

Meyer, L.B. (1967). *Music, the arts, and ideas.* Chicago: The University of Chicago Press.

Moles, A. (1966). *Information theory and esthetic perception* (J.E. Cohen, Trans.). Urbana: University of Illinois Press.

Osgood, C.E., Suci, G.J., & Tannenbaum, P.H. (1957). *The measurement of meaning.* Urbana: University of Illinois Press.

Price, H.E. (1986). A proposed glossary for use in affective response literature in music. *Journal of Research in Music Education, 34,* 151–159.

Rader, M., & Jessup, B. (1976). *Art and human values.* Englewood Cliffs, NJ: Prentice-Hall.

Radocy, R.E. (1978). Cerebral dominance and music perception: Stop the fad, In E.P. Asmus, Jr. (Ed.), *Proceedings of the Research Symposium on the Psychology and Acoustics of Music* (pp. 120–130). Lawrence: The University of Kansas.

Radocy, R.E. (1979). Hemispheric specialization in music perception: It all depends. Paper presented at the national meeting of the National Association for Music Therapy, Dallas.

Radocy, R.E. (1982). Preference for classical music: A test for the hedgehog. *Psychology of Music, Special Issue,* 91–95.

Regelski, T.A. (1978). *Arts education & brain research.* Reston, VA: Music Educators National Conference.

Reimer, B. (1970). *A philosophy of music education.* Englewood Cliffs, NJ: Prentice-Hall.

Roederer, J.G. (1975). *Introduction to the physics and psychophysics of music* (2nd ed.). New York: Springer-Verlag.

Schoen, M. (Ed.). (1927). *The effects of music.* New York: Harcourt, Brace.

Schoen, M. (1940). *The psychology of music.* New York: Ronald Press.

Schoen, M., & Gatewood, E.L. (1927). An experimental study of the nature of musical enjoyment. In M. Schoen (Ed.), *The effects of music.* New York: Harcourt, Brace.

Schwadron, A.A. (1967). *Aesthetics: Dimensions for music education.* Washington, D.C.: Music Educators National Conference.

Schwadron, A.A. (1984). Philosophy and aesthetics in music education: A critique of the research. *Council for Research in Music Education, 79,* 11–32.

Sears, W.W. (1957). The effects of music on muscle tones. In E.T. Gaston (Ed.), *Music therapy 1957.* Lawrence, KS: Allen Press.

Sears, W.W. (1960). A study of some effects of music upon muscle tension as evidenced by electromyographical recordings. Doctoral dissertation, The University of Kansas.

Sluckin, W., Hargreaves, D.J., & Coleman, A.M. (1982). Some experimental studies of familiarity and liking. *Bulletin of the British Psychological Society, 35,* 189–194.

Smith, F.J. (1979). *The experiencing of musical sound: Prelude to a phenomenology of music.* New York: Gordon and Breach Science Publishers.

Smith, K.C., & Cuddy, L.L. (1986). The pleasingness of melodic sequences: Contrasting effects of repetition and rule-familiarity. *Psychology of Music, 14,* 17–32.

Sopchak, A.L. (1955). Individual differences in responses to different types of music in relation to sex, mood, and other variables. *Psychological Monographs, 69* (11), 1–20.

Sternbach, R.A. (1966). *Principles of psychophysiology.* New York: Academic Press.

Sullivan, J.W.N. (1927). Music as expression. In J.W.N. Sullivan, *Beethoven, his spiritual development.* New York: New American Library.

Trolio, M.F. (1976). Theories of affective response to music. *Contributions to Music Education, 4,* 1–20.

Tucker, D. M. (1981). Lateral brain function, emotion, and conceptualization. *Psychological Bulletin, 89,* 19–46.

Van Stone, J.K. (1960). The effects of instrumental tone quality upon mood response to music. In E. Schneider (Ed.), *Music therapy 1959.* Lawrence, KS: Allen Press.

Vitz, P.C. (1962). Preference for sequences of tones and the rate of information presentation. *Dissertation Abstracts International, 23,* 4440.

Vitz, P.C. (1964). Preference for rates of information presented by sequences of tones. *Journal of Experimental Psychology, 68,* 176–183.

Vitz, P.C. (1966a). Affect as a function of stimulus variability. *Journal of Experimental Psychology, 71,* 74–79.

Vitz, P.C. (1966b). Preference for differing amounts of visual complexity. *Behavioral Science, 11,* 105–114.

Walker, E.L. (1981). Hedgehog theory and music education. In R.G. Taylor (Ed.), *The documentary report of the Ann Arbor Symposium* (pp. 317–328). Reston, VA: Music Educators National Conference.

Webster, P.R. (1979). Music and brain asymmetry: Some basic concerns and thoughts toward a model. In *Proceedings report of the second annual Loyola symposium: Hemisphere laterality and music.* New Orleans: Loyola University.

Weitz, M. (Ed.). (1970). *Problems in aesthetics* (2nd ed.). New York: MacMillan.

Young, P.T. (1973). Feeling and emotion. In B.B. Wolman (Ed.), *Handbook of general psychology* (pp. 749–771). Englewood Cliffs, NJ: Prentice-Hall.

Chapter Seven

MUSICAL PREFERENCES

People vary in their preferences for any sensory experience in which they have a choice. Personal preferences for certain foods, paintings, home decor, clothing, and music are rooted in individual biological needs, cultures, training, and experience. Preferences are not always consistent, and they can be modified. What is preferred in one instance is not necessarily preferred in another.

The terms *preference* and *taste* occasionally are used interchangeably, as in the first edition of this text, but it may be useful to distinguish between the two terms on the basis of degree of commitment, as does Abeles (1980, p. 106). Taste implies a relatively long-term value for or commitment to a broad class of objects or events; preference implies a more immediate and specific choice within a set of possibilities. One might have a taste for white wines or Romantic orchestral music and preferences for a particular rhine or chablis, or particular works of Liszt or Strauss. The difference between preference and taste may be a matter of perspective, and, while semantically interesting, probably is of little consequence in studying factors which influence making musical choices.

A simple preference of one musical work to another may have meaning beyond the obvious musical evaluation. Expressed musical preferences sometimes are used to assess personality via deviations from population trends regarding musical choices. "Illogical" aesthetic reactions are believed to differentiate psychotics and paranoids from normals and alcoholics from other psychotics (Cattell and Anderson, 1953).

Hahn (1954) compared the clinical personality assessments of twelve students, randomly chosen from those seeking help at a university counseling center, with their musical preferences, expressed through musical choices and listening logs. He found that personality was reflected in individual musical choices, which also depended upon aesthetic values and individual needs for sensual pleasure. Aesthetic values in turn

243

depended upon cultural background, musical training, and the general attraction of music. Rhythm, staccato-legato, timbre, loudness level, and tempo influenced preferences. A large degree of idiosyncratic behavior was reflected in expressed preferences, and Hahn believed that musical preferences would continue to require study on an individual basis. Group preference tendencies perhaps are more obvious today, but prediction of individual musical preferences, particularly from personality information, remains tenuous.

This chapter examines determining what is "good" music, particular preferences, various musical, psychological, and social influences on preference, and alteration of preferences.

What is "Good" Music?

It is difficult to study artistic phenomena, particularly as they relate to preferences, in a scientific manner because of longstanding views of the arts as supernatural events (Berlyne, 1971). There are individuals who believe that music is a gift of (a) divine being(s), and people must hope to understand it through revelation. Others consider art as a personal experience, unopen to analysis.

Reasons for individual musical preferences include musical characteristics, such as tempos, orchestral colors, and lyrics, extramusical associations ("Darling, our song . . . "), and societal pressures. There are group preference tendencies; they are not solely a matter of individual choices. Group tendencies and differences arouse concern for what good music really is—what *should* be preferred?

One view of "good" music is that that which is good is good because of inherent aspects of the musical stimulus. In such a view there are melodic, harmonic, rhythmic, and formal ideals which are characteristic of good, even great music, and if the listener can be educated in such ideals, his or her preferences will conform to some aesthetic ideal. The view that good music owes its goodness to its structure is a manifestation of a formalistic (Meyer, 1956; Reimer, 1970), or *isolationist* (Schwadron, 1967) position regarding musical aesthetics: The value of music supposedly is inherent in the music itself.

All art has properties which are able to arouse people. The so-called "collative" variables of novelty, surprise, complexity, and ambiguity, related to form and structure, influence the response of one who observes art. Instability can lead to discomfort; incongruity may increase attention (Berlyne). The essence of Meyer's (1956) theory regarding musical enjoyment is that the delay of musical expectancy promotes pleasure through the ultimate dissipation of resulting frustration. Complex music, as long as it is not *too* complex, is more likely than simple music to be preferred over a longer period. McMullen and Arnold (1976) showed a tentative relationship between rhythmic redundancy and preference: the less the dominance of one rhythmic figure, the less the redundancy and the greater the preference, to a certain point.

Adorno (1976) classified musical listeners on the basis of how well they listen to what is in music's "objective" structure. His hierarchy suggests that structural awareness is of the greatest importance in listening; his highest classification is the *expert*, who can hear musical structures completely and properly order all formal nuances. The hierarchy then runs "down" through a *good listener*, who hears beyond musical details but lacks structural awareness, a *culture consumer*, mainly concerned with information about music, a nonintellectual *emotional listener*, a *protest listener*, an *entertainment listener*, and, finally, an *indifferent, unmusical*, or *antimusical listener*. Adorno believes that music is primarily an intellectual event, although he does state that one must understand music's social characteristics in order to understand music.

In contrast to the view that there is music which is "good" because of its structure, there is a view that music which is preferred is preferred because of its individual values and utilities rather than any inherent goodness. Whereas Adorno indicates that a criterion of individual taste would deprive "great" music of what makes it great, Chancellor (1974/1975) says that all art is ambiguous and acquires its values from subjective, pluralistic, and relative determinants. Hamm, Nettl, and Byrnside (1975) tie music to society and culture and allow for individual utility and personal identification. In its extreme, such a view is a manifestation of a *referential* (Meyer; Reimer) or a *contextual* (Schwadron) aesthetic position: Music is meaningless except to the extent that it communicates extramusical messages. There is a school of aesthetic *relativism* (Schwadron), which allows for different value systems for different musical styles and recognizes the importance of musical structure while allowing for cultural and functional variability in musical preference.

Individual critics, musicians, and listeners will continue to explain musical preferences on the basis of inherent musical properties, but it is more fruitful psychologically to study preference in terms of people's expressions of preference. "Good" music is good because it is *desirable* in terms of a person's mood, background, training, experience, prejudices, and beliefs. Some people want complexity. Some want simplicity. Some preferences are predictable; others are not. It all depends on the person making the choice.

Existing Musical Preferences

There is no formula for predicting individual musical preferences, although there are tendencies for particular groups to prefer particular musical styles. Most investigation has been directed toward preferences for classical music.

Investigations generally have relied on some sort of polling of representative groups and analyses of what is performed. A few studies have related listener characteristics to musical preferences.

Any measure of musical preference is risky. People may not respond honestly to questions regarding their preferences; reasons for attending performances selectively include nonmusical ones such as social visibility. Examining record collections may be useful, but individuals vary in the extent to which they can afford recordings. Possession of a recording tells little about how often it is heard. Analyses of what is performed or aired (over radio) are subject to biases of conductors and patrons of the arts. Scholarly discussions of music reflect musical preferences, but with editorial bias.

Regardless of what preference is based upon, it represents a subjective impression of musical desirability. As with sensory impressions, magnitude estimation (see Chapter Three) is a potentially viable measurement technique if one is willing to accept matching an impression with another as measurement (Radocy, 1986). Aesthetic judgments may be prothetic in nature; investigators have observed psychophysical phenomena, such as a tendency to hear the second member of a pair of ambiguous stimuli as having "more" of the property in question, in affective measurements (Koh, 1965; 1967). Perhaps magnitude estimation or some other technique which does not require counting units may enable quantification of preferences in a meaningful way.

The studies discussed below are representative of preference investigations.

Surveys

Keston and Pinto (1955) investigated the musical preference of 202 college students in terms of relationships between preference, as indicated by preferential choices of musical excerpts, and eight variables: introversion-extroversion, masculinity-femininity, age, educational level, sex, formal musical training, music recognition ability, and intelligence. Musical training, music recognition, and introversion were related significantly to preference. In scoring their preference measure, Keston and Pinto equated a choice of the classical music excerpt (rather than the "pop" concert, "dinner" music, or popular music excerpt) with a "correct" answer. The study showed that people with greater amounts of musical training and experience who were willing to spend the time required for concentrated listening tend to prefer classical music. It must be stressed that this is *correlational* evidence, an indication that there are tendencies for people scoring highly on one variable to score highly on others. Correlation means relationship, not causality. Training, recognition, and introversion do not cause a preference for classical or any other music.

One cannot study musical preferences for long without encountering Farnsworth's (1966) famous eminence rankings. Based on polls of American Musicological Society members in 1938, 1944, 1951, and 1964, the rankings list composers of classical music in order of their perceived eminence. "Eminence" apparently is interpreted in terms of contributions to music history and worthiness of study. In 1964, the "top five" composers were, in order, Bach, Beethoven, Mozart, Haydn, and Brahms. The rankings, relatively stable across the sampling years, show a notable absence of twentieth century composers. The American Musicological Society is hardly representative of "typical" listeners, and Farnsworth's polls have been criticized, but they do show that musical preferences within one style have some degree of consistency—they are not solely a matter of the whimsey of individual scholars. Eminence and preference are not necessarily the same thing, of course. Farnsworth (1969) reports in his text polls showing less than perfect relationship between perceived eminence and enjoyment of particular composers. On one occasion, preference may be based on eminence; on another it may be based on enjoyment.

Poland (1970) analyzed three music history texts, two music theory texts, Farnsworth's rankings, and the then most recent issue of the Schwann catalog.* He noted the thirty composers cited most frequently in each text, Farnsworth's top thirty, and the thirty composers receiving the most space in Schwann. The seven sources yielded a total of only seventy-one composers, which indicates considerable agreement regarding whose music merits attention in the opinions of the various authors, the sample completing Farnsworth's surveys, and the recording industry.

Correlations among the individual sources' citations of works by the seventy-one composers showed that eminence and preference may be two different things. Farnsworth's rankings correlated −.31 with the Schwann catalog listings (the minus sign is an artifact of 1 being "high" in the rankings) while the Schwann listings correlated at least .76 with all other sources.

Poland counted the total number of citations for each of the seventy-one composers in the combined five texts. He listed the sixty composers who had at least one full column of Schwann listings. The two lists were not identical, but there were remarkable similarities when each list was analyzed by composer nationality and historical period. About 59 percent of the combined citations were works of German composers. Ten percent were French works, 9 percent were Russian, 7 percent were Italian, and slightly less than 3 percent were American. The remaining 12 percent accounted for the rest of the world, and all those citations were to European composers' works with the exception of Villa-Lobos, a Brazilian.

About 19 percent of the combined citations were baroque; 26 percent were classical, and 34 percent were romantic. Because one music history text gave more attention to prebaroque music than the other texts, the list based on the texts showed 0.3 percent for the period 500 BC to 1450, 3.8 percent for Renaissance, and 17 percent for "modern" (1915–1955) works. The corresponding percentages for the Schwann-based list were zero, zero, and 20.

Fifty-two percent of the text citations were to just eleven composers, nine of whom were German. Just five composers had one-third of all citations; in order, they were Beethoven, Bach, Mozart, Brahms, and Haydn. Poland's investigation suggests that the core of music study is

---

*The *Schwann Long Playing Record Catalog,* published monthly by W. Schwann, Inc. of Boston, lists available recordings by composer and title. The relative amounts of space required to list the works of various composers provide some indication of those composers' popularities as indicated by demands of the marketplace.

built around works of "the three B's" plus Mozart and Haydn. Perhaps preferences are perpetuated.

The apparent reverence for the past, which emerges in descriptive research such as that of Farnsworth and Poland as well as in analyses of orchestral programs, is troublesome to fans of contemporary music. People wonder whether there is a "gap" between composer and audience and to what it might be attributable.

J. Mueller (1967) believes that contemporary composers and audiences indeed are separated by an "aesthetic gap" which is a twentieth century phenomenon, not an event recurring throughout music history. The claim that "good" music never was appreciated initially is not substantiated. Mueller's evidence includes favorable initial criticism of the works of Beethoven and others and the rate of new works' appearances in European concert programs of the nineteenth century. New music never is equally new; novelties vary in their public interest and adoption. The contemporary composer often is more experimental and pays a price through nonconformity which strains the audience's ears. Mueller suggests that modern composers need to make more effort to understand society.

A group of Dutch orchestral concert subscribers generally were satisfied with the programs according to an analysis of survey findings (De Jager, 1967). Beethoven was the most popular composer; contemporary composers collectively were the most disliked. Modern music was more disturbing to older people who had lesser amounts of education and did not play an instrument.

Although inherent musical properties do not guarantee "good," "great," or "truthful" music, many people may prefer the lyric melodies, predictable tonal and harmonic patterns, symmetric rhythms, extensive repetitions, and orchestral colors available in the music of eighteenth and nineteenth century composers. The widespread availability of recordings of many styles and eras means that twentieth century composers must compete with the music of previous generations (Hamm, Nettl, and Byrnside, 1975).

Closed-Mindedness

People who are dogmatic, generally resistant to change, and rather authoritarian sometimes are labelled as *closed-minded*. Variability in acceptance and admiration of new music is more than a matter of degree of closed-mindedness, but closed-minded individuals may be less willing to accommodate new music because of their difficulty in forming conceptual systems. In one study (Mikol, 1960), open- and closed-minded listeners with similar musical backgrounds evaluated works of Schoenberg and Brahms. There were no differences in reaction to Brahms, but the closed-minded subjects reacted more negatively to Schoenberg than did the open-minded subjects. An attempt to replicate the results with music of Bartok did not succeed.

Zagona and Kelly (1966) studied the reactions of forty-four highly dogmatic and forty-four lowly dogmatic individuals to an abstract film featuring lines and colors in motion synchronized with jazz. Subjects' ratings showed that the highly dogmatic persons were less accepting of the film.

Convergence Toward One Popular Style

Preferences for popular music have not been assessed to the degree they deserve. The view that popular music appeals only to some broad undifferentiated mass, victimized by an inferior culture, simply is false; all people, including teenagers, have specific and individual tastes (Denisoff, 1976). With the onset of television, radio stations and their advertisers began to cater to particular audiences; stations now specialize in "Top 40," soul, country-western, rock, folk, "beautiful music," and other styles (Peterson and Davis, 1974). "Top 40" listeners tend to be younger than average while "beautiful music," i.e., "easy listening," listeners tend to be older.

A major musical preference phenomenon is the development of separate American popular music cultures. From roughly 1930 to the early 1950s, popular music was aimed predominantly at an adult white middle class culture. Music popular with one generation generally was popular with another. Country-western, black, and folk styles were alive and well, but they had only a regional appeal. From about 1955 on, popular music became more fragmented. Country, soul, and folk styles acquired national audiences; rock music became the music of youth. Each musical style has its own values and sociological bases (Hamm, Nettl, and Byrnside).

In visiting music classrooms, the writers have noticed that overt group musical preferences narrow with advancing grade level. First, second, and third graders generally will listen to brief excerpts of a variety of musical styles without undue protest. A trained soprano, ethnic musics, and ambiguous electronic sounds are accepted. In fourth grade and beyond, students will cover their ears, cringe, and look around to ascertain that sufficient numbers of peers are doing the same thing. The preferred music becomes rock.

An increasing preference for rock music with advancing grade level was demonstrated clearly by Greer, Dorow, and Randall (1974), who studied the rock versus nonrock listening of 134 children, nursery school through sixth grade. Each child spent ten minutes with a device containing keys which he or she could press to hear either rock music (eight 75-second excerpts of a local station's "top twenty") or nonrock music. Nonrock meant eight 75-second symphonic music excerpts for nursery school children, second graders, and third graders. Nonrock meant classical piano excerpts for first, fourth, and fifth graders; the sixth graders' nonrock excerpts were Broadway show tunes. Total listening time increased steadily with grade level, with significant increases between nursery school and first grade, second and third grade, and fifth and sixth grade. Listening time for rock increased steadily, with an especially large increase between third and fourth grades; other significant increases occurred between nursery school and first grade, and between fifth and sixth grades. Nonrock listening time increased significantly between nursery school and first grade, but it *decreased* significantly between third and fourth grades. There were no significant differences between rock and nonrock listening time at the nursery school and first grade levels, but beyond first grade, rock was preferred consistently. Although this study was limited to two schools in one metropolitan setting, additional studies (Greer, Dorow, and Hanser, 1973; Greer et al., 1973) suggest decreasing interest in nonrock music with advancing grade level.

The assessment of attitudes toward music, conducted as part of The National Assessment of Educational Progress,* supports the trend noted by Greer et al. It reveals an increased preference for rock from nine year olds to thirteen year olds to seventeen year olds.

Summary of Existing Preferences

Existing preferences for Western music, then, are such that there is a tendency to prefer music of the eighteenth and nineteenth centuries as

---

*The National Assessment of Educational Progress is a project of the Educational Commission of the States. It was developed in collaboration with the National Center for Educational Statistics of the Department of Health, Education and Welfare. Additional funding was provided by the Carnegie Corporation and the Ford Foundation's Fund for the Advancement of Education. The project surveyed the educational attainments of nine-year-olds, thirteen-year-olds, seventeen-year-olds, and adults between the ages of twenty-six and thirty-five. The first music assessment was conducted in 1971–72.

far as art music is concerned. Such preferences may result in part from contemporary composers' excessive deviations from compositional norms as well as personal qualities of the listeners. Popular music, often ignored when musical preferences are studied, requires more investigation. In the elementary school years preferences appear to converge toward rock music, which may make education in a variety of musical styles difficult.

Influences on Musical Preferences

Music preferences are more than interaction of inherent musical characteristics and individual psychological and social variables. There are societal pressures which influence preference. A person making a musical choice considers opinions of other persons who are significant in his or her life, as well as cultural messages in and about the music.

Two experiments by Greer, Dorow, and Hanser (1973) suggested that teacher approval may influence young children's preferences. Thirty-nine second and third graders changed from a pretest preference for rock to no posttest difference between rock and symphonic music in a study of instrument discrimination training. Twenty-four nursery school children changed from either lack of a pretest preference or a preference for rock to a posttest preference for symphonic selections in a similar study. Dorow's (1977) study of fourth and fifth graders replicated and extended the findings of the Greer et al. 1973 study.

Rigg (1948) attempted to alter preference by introducing propaganda associating certain music with Nazi Germany. Three compositions of Wagner, one of Beethoven, one of Franck, and one of Sibelius were played twice for three groups of listeners. Each group initially heard the compositions without comment. One group then was given favorable information about the German selections. Another group received unfavorable propaganda-based information; the third group received neither favorable nor unfavorable information. After the second hearing, all groups showed increased enjoyment of the compositions, as indicated by ratings on a five-point scale, but the largest gain was in the favorable comment group. The unfavorable comment group had the least gain.

Popular music of the mid-1950s was classified according to the relationship of the lyrics to five stages of adolescent lovemaking: prologue, courtship, a honeymoon period, a downward course, and an abandoned lonely stage. The lyrics, appropriate to a limited and predictable love cycle, provided a conventional language for formulating adolescent expectations and self-conceptions (Horton, 1957).

Johnstone and Katz (1957) found that teen-age girls' musical preferences were influenced by their peers. Highly popular girls conformed more closely to neighborhood norms regarding particular songs and disk jockeys than did less popular girls. In a higher socioeconomic neighborhood, the girls who dated frequently preferred songs suggesting "blues" and deprivation, while girls who dated infrequently preferred songs suggesting "happy" or "indulgent" love. In a lower socioeconomic neighborhood, all girls, regardless of dating frequency, preferred songs suggesting happiness and indulgence.

Inglefield (1974) found that eighteen ninth graders showed an overall tendency to alter their expressed musical preferences to conform to those of acknowledged peer leaders. Those subjects who were more otherdirected than innerdirected, more in need of social approval, and more dependent than independent, as identified by personality tests, tended to be the greater conformers. The most conformity was to expressed jazz preferences, next to folk music, thirdly to rock, and least to classical music. Inglefield believed that jazz elicited the most conformity because it generally is alien to adolescent musical environments, while classical music elicited the least conformity because of well-established negative judgments. Conformity studies must be interpreted cautiously because public expression of a preference in accordance with what a respected peer says does not guarantee private acceptance of the peer's judgments. Nevertheless, the pressures to conform in musical judgments are real; they are discussed more fully in Chapter Eleven.

A symposium on new patterns of musical behavior of the young generation in eighteen industrial societies sought to examine the phenomenon of "pop music" and its sociological implications (Bontinck, 1972). Although many of the symposium papers reflected personal observations, more or less informal surveys, and even speculation, it was apparent that popular music is associated with a particular youth subculture in most of the nations represented. The extent to which these subcultures influence the musical preferences of youth in the respective societies is unclear, but the authors suspect that such influences are great.

Abeles (1980) extensively reviewed literature regarding musical preference and taste. He concluded that personality factors and emotional states are related to preference, but further exploration of the specific nature of those relationships is necessary. Little evidence exists that gender has any consistent influence on preferences. Socioeconomic status and musical preference show diverse relationships; Abeles believes that a lack of standardized measures of socioeconomic status complicates such studies. Correlational evidence suggests uncertain and modest relationships between musical aptitude or achievement and preference.

In examining studies in which researchers manipulated variables to investigate their effects on preferences, Abeles noted that long-term musical training may result in increased preference for "classical" or "concert" music, but effects of short-term training are unclear. One variable which clearly does influence preference is *repetition:* Familiarity enhances preference—to a point.

Abeles's review of literature regarding longer-term commitments (i.e., musical taste) suggests that women generally attach more importance to "classical" music than do men, that racial differences in taste exist, and that social class and political views may interact to influence taste. Although no "standardized" taste exists, mass media, peer groups, and musical experience all may influence taste.

LeBlanc (1982) created a hierarchical comprehensive model of the many sources of variation in musical preference and taste. While much research remains necessary to ascertain the relative importance of and relationships among the variables, his classification is useful in sorting variables which influence the listener as well as variables resulting from the listener's actions in making preferential judgments.

The "bottom" level of LeBlanc's model includes nine classes of input variables which characterize the situation under which the music is experienced. Four classes are primarily properties of the musical stimulus: physical (acoustical) properties, complexity, referential meaning, and performance quality. Media, peer group, family, authority figures, and incidental conditioning complete the input variables. The relative importance of the input variables will vary with individuals; the model makes no suggestion that any one variable class is more or less important than any other.

The input variables and interactions among them lead into LeBlanc's seventh level, physiological enabling conditions. The listener's auditory pathway must be able to receive the musical input, his or her brain must recognize the extramusical variables as relevant to music, and he or she must be sufficiently free from pain or other physiological emergency.

When a listener encounters the input variables, he or she will receive them to the extent that physiological enabling conditions permit. However, without basic attention, no further meaningful musical awareness or judgment can occur. LeBlanc's sixth level, basic attention, thus is a crucial "gate." If the "gate" is closed, the music is largely meaningless. To give or not give "basic" attention to a musical stimulus is a conscious choice.

At the fifth level, the listener's current affective state "filters" the musical input to which the listener has elected to give basic attention. The individual's mood will influence his or her further musical processing and judgments. For example, "happy" music usually will interact differently with a "sad" mood than will "sad" music.

Auditory sensitivity (which here means sensitivity to particular aspects of musical sound, not basic reception), musical ability and training, personality, sex, ethnic group, socioeconomic status, and maturity are relatively stable personal characteristics which comprise LeBlanc's fourth level. A person may be especially sensitive to phrasing, particular timbres, or rhythms, perhaps overly so in relation to other aspects. Training in a particular instrument may sensitize the listener to music literature featuring that instrument; an experienced French horn player certainly has a different sensitivity to hearing Strauss's *Til Eulenspiegel* or the Mozart horn concerti than does a listener who is unfamiliar with the horn. Remembering what was heard formerly as a guide to what one is hearing now can be crucial for organization.

So, input variables characterizing the listening experience comprise a total stimulus. The listener attends to that stimulus to the extent that he or she is physiologically able and personally willing. After influence by the current affective state, the musical input is influenced by personal characteristics and interactions among them. Now comes a change from variables that influence the listener to variables that result from the listener's actions.

The change occurs at level three of the model, where the listener actively *processes* the input. Processing may include labelling stimulus aspects, such as the formal sections, instruments, style, and likely composer. The listener may consider extramusical aspects, including images of what the music may "say" or "mean." He or she may establish musical expectancies, which then are confirmed or disconfirmed.

After actively processing the input at the model's third level, the listener makes a decision at the second level: He or she either decides that a judgment is possible or decides that more information is necessary. When desired, further information, of a musical or nonmusical nature, is sought through repeated listening with heightened attention; new input passes "up" the hierarchy.

At the very "top" of LeBlanc's hierarchy is the preference judgment, a decision based on the combination of all the variables at the lower levels. The listener *accepts* or *rejects* the musical input. In the event of acceptance, the model assumes repetition until satiation. As stimulus conditions change, or as listener conditions change, the judgment may change.

People will vary in the relative importance of the model's variables and variable categories, but almost all individuals who are able to hear music will share many of the model's aspects. Even people who generally are considered "deviant" or "different" in some way—be it due to mental retardation, a physical, sensory, or motor impairment, or social deviation—are influenced by many of the variables, and do process the input in some way. While the *amount* of perceived stimulus complexity, authority figure influence, basic attention, or other influence variables may differ drastically (in either direction) from what most other people experience, there will be *some* amount.

Complexity, one of LeBlanc's input variables, may be an especially important influence on musical preference. As used here, complexity refers to how intricate, ornate, or confusing a stimulus appears; it is a matter of subjective judgment. In appearance, function, and operation, an automobile usually appears more complex than a toy wagon. To Western listeners, a Bach fugue usually appears more musically complex than a European or American folk song. In information theory terms, a lack of redundancy results in excessive information, which increases complexity. Complexity may be a function of uncertainty, unfamiliarity, and a resulting lack of expectancy. As is the case with other psychological constructs, complexity never can be measured directly, but it can be estimated and quantified by evaluating stimulus properties or people's behaviors.

One conceivably may analyze complexity multidimensionally through factor analysis and/or multidimensional scaling of semantic differential, Likert scale, or paired or triadic comparison data. Possible dimensions may relate to a melody's direction and ornateness, harmonic changes, rhythmic regularity, and the degree to which expectancies are met. A simpler approach to measurement may be based on observers' immediate impressions of apparent complexity. In such a *global* approach, *why* something is perceived as relatively complex or simple is not immediately important; it is enough to say that a stimulus has a certain amount of complexity because of the way people react to it. A global approach recognizes that people vary considerably in why they make particular complexity judgments. For some listeners, an overall impression of a piece of music may include a degree of apparent complexity which defies analysis. For others, rhythm, harmony, melody, or some other property may override other properties as a basis for complexity. The authors lean toward a global approach for measuring apparent complexity.

The concept of musical preference as a function of complexity is not new. Berlyne (1971), one of the founders of the "new" experimental aesthetics movement, spoke of musical pleasure as an inverted U-shaped function of "activation" due to structure. McMullen (1980) suggests that the affective response to music depends in part on stimulus structure, which in turn depends partly on complexity.

One of the most important developments regarding preference as a function of complexity is Walker's (1980) "hedgehog" theory, so named because the theory has one explanation for many situations, just as the spiny little European animal rolls into a ball in response to many stimuli. Walker (p. 1) states the theory in his own words as "Psychological events nearest optimum complexity are preferred. Occurrence produces simplification." The theory presumes an optimal complexity level for any stimulus class, including music. Preference is highest at that optimal complexity level and declines more-or-less symmetrically as complexity increases or decreases away from optimum. Preference thus is an inverted U-shaped (quadratic) function of complexity, with the highest point of the preference curve corresponding to optimal complexity. Near the right or high complexity end is a point at which the individual "gives up" or quits trying to process the stimulus because it is too complex. Near the left or low complexity end is a point at which the individual loses interest or "becomes bored." As a stimulus recurs, it theoretically simplifies. If it moves closer to optimal complexity, preference for the stimulus increases. If the stimulus moves further from optimal complexity, preference decreases. If optimal complexity changes, the curve shifts in one direction or the other, and a particular stimulus's relative position on the newly shifted curve may change.

Although optimal complexity levels vary among and within individuals, each individual has an optimal complexity level for a stimulus class at any particular time. A group of people can provide an average estimate of the complexity of each object in a stimulus set, such as a collection of musical examples. Heyduk (1975), employing four compositions specifically composed to vary in complexity and a 13-point rating scale, demonstrated the expected complexity-preference relationship as well as reduced complexity with repetition.

Using "real" examples of Western art music rather than contrived examples, Radocy (1982) investigated preference as a function of complexity, preference as a function of familiarity, and complexity as a function of familiarity. If preference is a quadratic function of complexity, the excerpts which subjects rate as moderately complex within the set should be the most preferred; this indeed was the case for both musical and nonmusical subjects. Both groups also showed that, in general, the more familiar the excerpt, the more it was preferred. Although familiarity is supposed to produce simplification (presumably familiarity is a function of repetition), the data suggested that complexity was not a simple function of familiarity. A systematic listening procedure featuring repetition within the confines of a designated time period may be necessary for occurrence to produce simplification.

Desired or optimal complexity of music may interact with the social situation in which the music is heard, as Konecni (1982) demonstrated. In one of his studies, the experimenter's accomplice repeatedly insulted certain subjects while they worked on a nonmusical task. Other subjects were allowed to work without insult. Later, all subjects were able to listen to either complex or simple computer-generated melodies. (Complexity was a function of manipulated uncertainty, in accordance with information theory, and of subjective ratings from pilot studies.) Uninsulted subjects had roughly equal preferences between the two complexity levels. Insulted subjects preferred the simpler melodies approximately 70 percent of the time. In another experimental condition, insulted subjects who were allowed to retaliate against the accomplice (and thereby reduce their arousal levels) before making musical choices showed preferences very similar to those of the uninsulted subjects. Influences on preference due to socially induced changes in emotional states are in accordance with "current affective state," the fifth level of LeBlanc's model.

In another study, Konecni divided the subjects into two groups according to task assignment. One group worked on relatively complex tasks, such as memorizing as many details of slides of paintings as possible. The other group worked on relatively simple tasks, such as tracing the contours of written symbols. Every 10 seconds, each subject pressed one of two buttons to hear either a complex or a simple melody. In general, the greater the task's information processing demands (i.e., the greater its complexity), the less frequent were choices of complex music. Since music may distract people working on an intellectual task, people who are forced to choose music to accompany complex tasks may prefer simpler excerpts.

In addition to his investigations of effects of arousal and task complexity on musical choices, Konecni investigated effects on following behaviors. In one experiment, the accomplice insulted some subjects but not others. All subjects then had the opportunity to administer supposedly painful electric shocks to the accomplice. A 10-second computer-generated melody accompanied each trial while subjects decided whether or not to shock the accomplice. Four listening groups were formed by the interactive combinations of simple or complex melodies and comfortable or excessively loud listening levels; a control group deliberated in silence. Uninsulted subjects generally were not aggressive toward the accomplice, with the major exception of uninsulted subjects who had been exposed to loud complex melodies: These subjects were statistically as aggressive as the insulted control group members! (Konecni suggests that people aroused by loud complex music may overreact to relatively mild annoyances that ordinarily would be ignored.) Insulted subjects who had heard loud complex melodies during deliberation periods were the most aggressive. Moderate aggression characterized insulted subjects who had heard relatively soft complex melodies or loud simple melodies. Insulted subjects who had heard softer *simple* melodies showed aggression that was significantly lower than insulted control group subjects and, in a few cases, lower than that of some uninsulted subjects who had heard loud complex melodies. Melodies varying in complexity apparently have different effects on antisocial behavior, both as functions of themselves and in combination with anger.

Altering Preferences

Musical preferences may be altered. One's less preferred style may become a more preferred style, and a listener's range of choices may be broadened. Much music requires learning through formal instruction before a listener can expect more than some sort of sound bath. K. Mueller (1970) stressed that listeners cannot hear accurately because they are not taught to hear musical details. The potential for developing and expanding preferences through education was noted by Duerksen

(1968), who, in an extensive study of thematic recognition ability, observed that the typical student, college and high school, indicated some positive response toward classical and jazz music as well as rock, popular, and folk styles.

Seventh graders who were encouraged to be creative in activities related to contemporary music outscored a control group who followed the existing curriculum guide on a test of musical understanding (Archibeque, 1966), although all seventh graders in the study developed an interest in contemporary music regardless of prior training, grades, or initial attitudes.

Repetition, a process for making the unfamiliar familiar, may be useful in altering and expanding musical preference. Mull (1940) played obscure piano pieces by Bach, Chopin, and Brahms to thirty undergraduate musicians. Each piece, one per composer, was played three times, and listeners reported "direct aesthetic responses" by raising their hands at "high spots." Of the fourteen regions found especially pleasant by fifteen or more listeners, nine were repetitions of thematic material. With repeated hearings, as the music became more familiar, the lengths of the "high spots" increased. Listeners became aroused by anticipation of newly familiar sections and raised their hands in anticipation.

Getz (1966) found that seventh graders' preferences for string ensemble excerpts increased over ten weeks as a result of familiarity through repetition. Faster tempos usually elicited greater preference.

Schuckert and McDonald (1968) asked twenty children, four to six years old, to choose between a classical example and a jazz example. Eight preferred the classical example, twelve preferred jazz. During four quiet play periods each child was required to hear his or her less preferred style. A retesting showed the choices altered to eleven for classical, nine for jazz—not statistically significant, but in the direction predicted by the researchers.

Familiarity through repetition will not guarantee an increase in preference. In Hornyak's (1966) study, 1300 elementary, junior high school, and high school students in a Midwestern city attended concerts which included four woodwind quintets by contemporary American composers. Attempts were made to familiarize student groups with the less traditional music by playing tapes of the music in advance. Familiarity increased the positive responses of elementary students to the contemporary compositions, but it made no difference for the junior high pupils. The high school students showed a *less* positive response as a result of preliminary hearing.

Musical preferences can be altered, but the direction of alteration as well as the means is not always predictable. The philosophical question of *should* preferences be altered is not answered satisfactorily. Music educators and critics should remember that musical preferences result from a complex interaction of personal and social factors, all of which are not under the control of any one institution. An expansion of preferences may be attempted in educational settings with reasonable chances of success, but a reordering of musical preferences in some arbitrary direction is questionable.

Summary

The major points of this chapter include the following:

1. Musical preferences result from a complex mixture of musical and human characteristics.
2. "Good" music may be "good" because of inherent structural aspects; it may be "good" because of what people say about it in context.
3. Preferences may be related to various personality aspects.
4. There are group tendencies in musical preference, particularly for certain predominantly German composers of Western art music.
5. The apparent reverence for the past observed in classical music is a new occurrence in music history; it probably is attributable to perpetuation of tradition through formal education and the widespread availability of music from different eras as well as radical creations of nonconforming contemporary composers.
6. Popular music exists today in several forms, each of which has its own cultural orientation and sociological base.
7. The preferences of many American school children focus increasingly on rock music with advancing grade levels.
8. Musical preference and taste are a function of many variables, including variables in the music, short-term and long-term variables in the listener, and variables in the conditions under which the music is experienced.
9. Musical preferences may be altered and expanded through education, but the results are not always predictable.

REFERENCES

Abeles, H. F. (1980). Responses to music. In D. E. Hodges (Ed.), *Handbook of music psychology* (pp. 105–140). Lawrence, KS: National Association for Music Therapy.

Adorno, T. W. (1976). *Introduction to the sociology of music* (E. B. Ashton, Trans.). New York: Seabury Press.

An assessment of attitudes toward music. (1975). Denver: National Assessment of Educational Progress.

Archibeque, C. P. (1966). Developing a taste for contemporary music. *Journal of Research in Music Education, 14,* 142–148.

Berlyne, D. E. (1971). *Aesthetics and psychobiology.* New York: Appleton-Century-Crofts.

Bontinck, I. (Ed.). (1972). *New patterns of musical behavior of the younger generation in industrial societies.* Vienna: International Institute for Music, Dance, and Theatre in the Audio-visual Media.

Cattell, R. B., & Anderson, J. C. (1953). The measurement of personality and behavior disorders by the I. P. A. T. music preference test. *Journal of Applied Psychology, 37,* 446–454.

Chancellor, G. R. (1975). Aesthetic value in music: Implications for music education from the classic literature of the field (Doctoral dissertation, Northwestern University, 1974). *Dissertation Abstracts International, 35,* 6493-A. (University Microfilms No. 75-7886).

DeJager, H. (1967). Listening to the audience. *Journal of Research in Music Education, 15,* 293–299.

Denisoff, R. S. (1976). Massification and popular music: A review. *Journal of Popular Culture, 9,* 886–894.

Dorow, L. G. (1977). The effect of teacher approval/disapproval ratios on student music selection and concert attentiveness. *Journal of Research in Music Education, 25,* 32–40.

Duerksen, G. L. (1968). A study of the relationship between the perception of musical processes and the enjoyment of music. *Council for Research in Music Education, 12,* 1–8.

Farnsworth, P. R. (1966). Musicological attitudes on eminence. *Journal of Research in Music Education, 14,* 41–44.

Farnsworth, P. R. (1969). *The social psychology of music* (2nd ed.). Ames: Iowa State University press.

Getz, R. P. (1966). The effects of repetition on listening response. *Journal of Research in Music Education, 14,* 178–192.

Greer, R. D., Dorow, L., & Hanser, S. (1973). Music discrimination training and the music selection behavior of nursery and primary level children. *Council for Research in Music Education, 35,* 30–43.

Greer, R. D., Dorow, L. G., & Randall, A. (1974). Music listening preferences of elementary school children. *Journal of Research in Music Education, 22,* 284–291.

Greer, R. D., Dorow, L. G., Wachhaus, G., & White, E. R. (1973). Adult approval and students' music selection behavior. *Journal of Research in Music Education, 21,* 345–354.

Hahn, M. E. (1954). A proposed technique for investigating the relationship between musical preferences and personality structure. Unpublished doctoral dissertation, University of Kansas.

Hamm, C. E., Nettl, B., & Byrnside, R. (1975). *Contemporary music and music cultures.* Englewood Cliffs, NJ: Prentice-Hall.

Heyduk, R. G. (1975). Rated preference of musical compositions as it related to complexity and exposure frequency. *Perception and Psychophysics, 17,* 84–91.

Hornyak, R. R. (1968). An analysis of student attitudes towards contemporary American music. *Council for Research in Music Education, 8,* 1–14.

Horton, D. (1957). The dialogue of courtship in popular songs. *American Journal of Sociology, 62,* 569–578.

Inglefield, H. G. (1974, March). Conformity behavior reflected in the musical preferences of adolescents. Paper presented at the meeting of the Music Educators National Conference, Anaheim, CA.

Johnstone, J., & Katz, E. (1957). Youth and popular music: A study of the sociology of taste. *American Journal of Sociology, 62,* 563–568.

Keston, M. J., & Pinto, I. M. (1955). Possible factors influencing musical preference. *Journal of Genetic Psychology, 86,* 101–113.

Koh, S. D. (1965). Scaling musical preferences. *Journal of Experimental Psychology, 70,* 79–82.

Koh, S. D. (1967). Time-error in comparisons of preferences for musical excerpts. *American Journal of Psychology, 80,* 171–185.

Konecni, V. J. (1982). Social interaction and musical preference. In D. Deutsch (Ed.), *The psychology of music* (pp. 497–516). New York: Academic Press.

LeBlanc, A. (1982). An interactive theory of musical preference. *Journal of Music Therapy, 19,* 28–45.

McMullen, P. T. (1980). Music as a perceived stimulus object and affective responses: An alternative theoretical framework. In D. E. Hodges (Ed.), *Handbook of Music Psychology* (pp. 183–193). Lawrence, KS: National Association for Music Therapy.

McMullen, P. T., & Arnold, M. J. (1976). Preference and interest as functions of distributional redundancy in rhythmic sequences. *Journal of Research in Music Education, 24,* 22–31.

Meyer, L. (1956). *Emotion and meaning in music.* Chicago: University of Chicago Press.

Mikol, B. (1960). The enjoyment of new musical systems. In M. Rokeach (Ed.), *The open and closed mind.* New York: Basic Books.

Mueller, J. H. (1967). The aesthetic gap between consumer and composer. *Journal of Research in Music Education, 15,* 151–158.

Mueller, K. H. (1970). The other side of the record. *Council for Research in Music Education, 21,* 22–31.

Mull, H. K. (1940). Preferred regions in music compositions and the effect of repetition upon them. *American Journal of Psychology, 53,* 583–586.

Peterson, R. A., & Davis, R. B. (1974). The contemporary American radio audience. *Popular Music and Society, 3,* 299–314.

Poland, B. W. (1970). The content of graduate studies in music education: Music history and music theory. In H. L. Cady (Ed.), *Graduate studies in music education* (pp. 9–28). Columbus, OH: Ohio State University School of Music.

Radocy, R. E. (1982). Preference for classical music: A test for the hedgehog. *Psychology of Music, Special,* 91–95.

Radocy, R. E. (1986). On quantifying the uncountable in musical behavior. *Council for Research in Music Education, 88,* 22–31.

Reimer, B. (1970). *A philosophy of music education.* Englewood Cliffs, NJ: Prentice-Hall.

Rigg, M. C. (1948). Favorable versus unfavorable propaganda in the enjoyment of music. *Journal of Experimental Psychology, 38,* 78–81.

Schukert, R. F., & McDonald, R. L. (1968). An attempt to modify the musical preferences of preschool children. *Journal of Research in Music Education, 16,* 39–45.

Schwadron, A. A. (1967). *Aesthetics: Dimensions for music education.* Washington: Music Educators National Conference.

Walker, E. L. (1980). *Psychological complexity and preference: A hedgehog theory of behavior.* Monterey, CA: Brooks/Cole.

Zagona, S., & Kelly, M. A. (1966). The resistance of the closed mind to a novel and complex audiovisual experience. *Journal of Social Psychology, 70,* 123–131.

Chapter Eight

FUNCTIONAL MUSIC

As noted in Chapter Two, music has served and still serves many basic functions in society. It is an important human behavior that is an integral part of all cultures. Besides aesthetic and expressive functions, music also serves many nonmusical functions.

> Indeed most music is performed for the express purpose of achieving aims wherein the aesthetic is not the primary goal. The *functional music* is far older and more abundant than music played or composed for aesthetic purposes. All primitive music is functional music...[and] even today a majority of the reasons given for school music ascribe to its functional goals. (Gaston, 1951/52, p. 60)

While music's general functions were discussed in Chapter Two, the present chapter examines some specific *uses* of music today.

Some of the uses discussed are traditional; i.e., they are similar to the uses of music throughout much of the history of Western civilization: in religious rites and ceremonies, to promote social conformity and interaction, to accompany dance, and generally to contribute toward the continuity and stability of a culture. Other uses are directed more specifically toward particular ends. They include industrial, commercial, therapeutic, and educational uses.

It long has been recognized that different types of music serve different purposes. While all of the factors that serve to influence any musical behavior are variables to be considered, it appears that functional music generally stimulates or suppresses activity. Prior to examination of music's uses is a brief discussion of some of music's structural characteristics that appear to cause it to stimulate or suppress behavior. It should be recognized, however, that individuals' responses to these structural characteristics also are influenced by previous experiences with music that reflects these characteristics. Within a cultural setting people learn to react in certain ways to certain types music. While the exact nature of the interaction between learning and the structural characteristics is not clear, observation of reactions to the two basic types of music suggests that differential response patterns are real, regardless of the degree of influence coming from learning or the structural characteristics themselves.

Stimulative and Sedative Music

All music exists on a continuum between highly stimulating, invigorating music and soothing, sedating music (Gaston, 1968, p. 18). As noted in Chapter Six, McMullen's (1982) theoretical model of the dimensions underlying musical meaning suggests that *energy* and *structure* in music are experienced as forms of activation or arousal. Music therapists and others concerned with using music to influence behavior essentially are concerned with arousing or suppressing activity, and the type of music selected for influencing the desired behaviors generally reflects different structural characteristics, particularly with respect to the dimension of energy.

Stimulative Music

Music which stimulates or arouses listeners has a strong energizing component. "For most people it is rhythm that provides the energy of music, be it great or small" (Gaston, 1968, p. 17). Lundin (1967, p. 172) and Farnsworth (1969, p. 83) both suggest that tempo, an important attribute of rhythm, is of primary importance in influencing mood response to music.

Rhythm characterized by detached, percussive sounds stimulates muscular action. March and dance music has definitive and repetitive rhythm that appears to stimulate physical movement. The more percussive, staccato, and accented the music, the greater the apparent physical response to it. Whenever the underlying beat is clearly defined, even a casual listener is likely to respond with some overt physical response.

While rhythm, and particularly tempo, appears to be the predominant energizing factor, dynamic level also appears to serve as a stimulator. Louder music seems to stimulate greater response activity than softer music. Other musical attributes such as pitch level, melody, harmony, texture, and timbre also may help energize music, but the extent to which these variables contribute toward the driving, energizing force of music is less clearly understood than for rhythm and dynamics.

Sedative Music

Music which soothes, calms, or tranquilizes behavior appears to rely on sounds that are nonpercussive and legato. Its melodic passages are sustained, legato, and generally have a minimum of rhythm activity. The most important rhythmic attribute of sedative music is the underlying beat, which is usually monotonously regular but subdued. Lullabies are the primary example of functional sedative music. They are comprised of sustained legato melodies, but with a quiet, steady underlying beat. They also reflect other characteristics of sedative music. The dynamic level usually is quite soft, the tempo is generally much slower than for stimulative music, and the melody's frequency range appears to be quite limited.

Differential Response to Stimulative and Sedative Music

Apparently individuals concerned with using music for functional purposes have long recognized the differential response to the two types of music, but they have not gone to great lengths to corroborate the effects through research.* Certainly music used by the military throughout history to incite troops into battle reflects the characteristics of stimulative music, as does music of today's school pep bands and marching bands. On the other hand, melodies used to soothe infants reflect characteristics of sedative music. March music reflects different characteristics than romantic music. Responses to adjective checklists, taken as indicators of mood or character response to music, reveal quite different lists of adjectives for stimulative and sedative music. Applause at concerts generally is louder for stimulative music than for sedative music.

The bulk of the limited research particularly focused on comparisons of responses to the two types of music was conducted in the 1940s and 1950s at The University of Kansas by some of Gaston's students. His (1952; 1968, pp. 18–19) reviews of this research revealed that nearly all studies found significant differences in response to the two types of music. Drawings and paintings by both children and adults while listening to the two types of music were readily classified by judges according to the type of music to which they were drawn. Postural response to the two types of music revealed that subjects sat more erect when listening to

---

*An exception to this might be some of the research conducted by consultants for the Muzak™ Corporation. This research is discussed later in the chapter.

stimulative music than when listening to sedative music. Clinical observation of the effects of sedative music on patients in a hospital ward resulted in "an observable sedative effect for the ward as a whole."

Hodges' (1980) review of the effects of stimulative and sedative music on physiological response to music generally revealed differential response for stimulative and sedative music, although there were inconsistencies among the results of the various studies. With respect to heart rate and pulse rate, (a) some studies resulted in increased rates for stimulative music but decreased rates for sedative music, (b) some resulted in increased rates for any music, whether stimulative or sedative, (c) some yielded rate changes that were unpredictable, and (d) some yielded no change in heart or pulse rate for any music.

Boyle's (1982) study of 145 university students' verbal descriptions of excerpts of stimulative and sedative music appeared to yield clear-cut evidence of differential response to the two types of music. Subjects were asked to respond to each of six musical excerpts (three stimulative and three sedative) on a five-point continuum between each of the following pairs of bipolar adjectives: happy/sad, restless/calm, joyous/gloomy, whimsical/serious, vigorous/quiet, majestic/soothing, playful/dignified, and exhilarated/dreamy. Each pair of adjectives was selected from clusters on opposite sides of the Hevner Adjective Circle. The mean difference in rating for the two types of music for each pair of adjectives was highly significant (p < .001). Such data

> lend support to the theory that affective response to music is related to the activation and energizing characteristics of the musical stimulus. Mood response, which seems to reflect a "disposition to action," apparently is intertwined somehow with response to stimulative and sedative music. Music therapists and Muzak-like corporations undoubtedly will continue to exploit these activation characteristics of music to influence human behavior. (Boyle, 1982, p. 115)

With the exception of the inconsistent results from physiological research, there appears to be strong evidence from a variety of sources to support the contention that people respond differently to stimulative and sedative music: Examples of music throughout history, in everyday life today, and in a limited number and variety of research studies reveal differential response to stimulative and sedative music. The application of this knowledge and the subtlety with which it is applied for particular uses comprises the balance of the discussion in this chapter. Some of these functions capitalize on music ability to stimulate, while others capitalize on its ability to soothe. These applications are discussed as they pertain to music in ceremonies; "background" music; commercial, industrial, and therapeutic uses of music; music to facilitate nonmusical learning; and music as a reward for behavior change.

Music in Ceremonies

Ceremonial music reflects one of the earliest functional uses of music. It is a part of primitive cultures today just as it has been throughout history. Apparently music is viewed as an integral part of ceremony and does much to lend to the formality of such occasions. Virtually all types of ceremony incorporate music in one way or another, be they religious, military, state, athletic, or commercial.

Musselman (1974, p. 129) notes that music has functioned more consistently and more positively in religious ritual than in any other area of life in Western civilization, even to the extent that religious music now comprises one of the longest and richest musical traditions. The specific function of music in religious ceremony tends to vary with its place in the ceremony, as evidenced by the principal sections of the highly formalized Mass of the Roman Catholic Church. Anglican and Lutheran services also have music as an integral part of their formal services.

Churches of a more evangelical tradition, such as the Methodist, Baptist, and Presbyterian denominations, also include music as part of the services, but they appear to place less emphasis on observance of corporate sacraments than do the Roman Catholic, Anglican, and Lutheran services; instead, they appear to involve the congregation much more directly. Hymn singing appears to be a direct way for drawing the congregation into the service.

Music in religious services appears to serve several functions: at times it serves as a signal to stimulate the congregation to respond in a certain way. At other times quiet organ interludes are used to help establish a mood of reverence or tranquility. Congregational singing serves to draw people together, while choir anthems appear to lead the worshipers to reflect on the beliefs and values of the religion and its implications for them as individuals. Special religious ceremonies are accompanied by special music. Certainly weddings, funerals, and special religious days are made more meaningful by music designed to enhance the significance of the occasion. Some of these uses of music in religious ceremony, however, are more "persuasive" than "ceremonial," attesting further to the importance of music in religion.

Perris's (1985, pp. 123–155) examination of music in major world religions focuses particularly on music's persuasive function.

> Music in all worship is expected to heighten the desired emotional effect in the listener, to emphasize the ritual text, especially certain significant words, and to focus the worshipper's attention on the rite. But the danger of so sensuous a phenomenon as music is that it may be more seductive than the rite itself, and that the musicians may evoke more interest than the priests. If the music in the worship service is "entertaining," is the religious ambience destroyed? How can the worshipper's attention be shielded from wandering? (Perris, 1985, p. 124)

Perris's juxtaposition of concepts from four major world religions— Judaism, Christianity, Islam, and Hinduism—revealed that, even though there are some obvious differences in the way music is used in the four religions, there appear to be six underlying factors to consider when using music in religious service: (a) the words must be comprehensible to the congregation, (b) traditional melody and performance practice should be observed, (c) the musical instruments used must be morally and socially acceptable, (d) music must be used for proper purposes and at proper places in the worship ceremony, (e) music in worship ceremony should not be misused, i.e., detract from the purpose of the ceremony, and (f) artistic goals of composers should not override theological concerns. Perris notes that this final consideration is a particular concern of Western religious music.

While music in religious ceremony may serve more than "ceremonial" functions per se, these other functions do not negate its importance in heightening the meaning and impact of the ceremony, and music will most likely continue to serve a major role in religious ceremonies throughout the world. Perhaps composers' artistic concerns, which may undermine its persuasive value, may ultimately enhance its ceremonial value.

Music also has been a traditional part of military and state ceremonies, and as in religious ceremony, it has served a variety of functions. Perhaps the traditional function of military music has been to inspire and heighten interest in the military cause and to stimulate troops to battle. That music for the military traditionally has been band music characterized by percussion and fanfare is more than coincidental. Such music appears to have a highly stimulative effect. Even today, the military and state ceremonies of most nations include music of the military band rather than string instruments.

Music in military and state ceremony not only is used as a signal to draw attention to a particular part of the ceremony, such as playing "Hail to the Chief" to signal the arrival of the President of the United States, but it also is used to create a feeling of patriotism and to commemorate particular occasions that are considered important. Music serves to heighten the immediate importance of the occasion as well as to contribute toward the memorableness of the occasion.

Many occasions other than religious and military also include ceremonial music. Major sporting events are a prime example. The opening and closing ceremonies of the Olympic Games always involve special music, and the medal ceremonies include the playing of the national anthems of the gold medal recipients' countries. Major high school, college, and professional sports open with ceremonial music. Music of marching and pep bands, while not always ceremonial music per se, serves an important function for sporting events.

Nearly any queen (or king) crowning ceremony, whether a high school homecoming event or a Miss World beauty contest, incorporates music into the ceremony. Folk festivals, while perhaps not ceremony in the ritualistic sense, usually rely on music as an integrative force as well as for heightening the memorableness of the occasion.

From this cursory review, it is apparent that music is an important part of many ceremonies. While the effects of ceremonial music have not been examined from a "scientific" perspective, the fact that music has been and continues to be a part of most important ceremonies attests to its functional value.

"Background" Music

Although "background" music has been used in both religious and secular settings for centuries, it has been with the advent of electronically reproduced music that background music has come to be so prevalent in society. The type of function background music serves varies greatly for individuals. Background music is used in a wide variety of settings, some of which will be discussed in subsequent sections of this chapter. In some settings it is used systematically, while in others music of various styles appears to be played informally and indiscriminantly.

Background music, often called "mood music," "easy listening," or "beautiful music," is any music played while the "listeners" are primarily engaged in some task or activity other than listening to music. Musselman (1974, p. 93) notes that it is "intended to be heard but not actively or purposely listened to." The function it serves varies not only with individual listeners but also with the nature of the task or activity with which they are involved.

In recent years the label "new age" has been applied to some background music. "New age" generally refers to music that is instrumental, using perhaps solo piano or guitar, quasi-chamber ensembles, synthesizers, or a mix of acoustic and electronic instruments. "Almost invariably the tempos are slow, the harmonies simple, the timbres rich, and the recording quality full-bodied and noiseless" (Pareles, 1987, p. 3C). Pareles attributes the rapidly growing interest in new-age music to the fact that "it eliminates the most complex, time-consuming, mentally draining part of the musical experience: paying attention" (Pareles, p. 3C). Whether new-age music is really a new style or just a new name given to beautiful music is not really clear, but its purpose appears no different than that of traditional mood, background, or beautiful music.

Individuals use background music informally and for various reasons. Often they select a favorite style of music, perhaps an easy listening or popular music (usually meaning rock) radio station or some tape or disc recordings, and let the music play continuously while they are engaged in reading, studying, driving, working in their home or on a job, or doing any number of various activities. Functions for this type of music appear to be more varied than for systematically applied background music; further, little or no thought appears to be given to the function the music is serving. The individual, if asked, often replies merely that he or she likes to have some background music while reading, driving, working, or whatever. However, it appears that such informally used background music may serve a variety of functions.

An individual may use the music to break the monotony while he or she is engaged in some task that requires little concentration; another might use the music to alleviate feelings of loneliness or to establish a particular mood, perhaps of reverie or relaxation. The music might also be used to mask unwanted sounds. When entertaining some people play background music to help establish an atmosphere conducive to stimulating conversation. Although the effects of such informal uses of music have not been studied to any extent, they apparently are considered valuable by the individuals involved; otherwise there would not be such widespread usage of music in this way.

The use of background music as a stimulant for verbal interaction has been examined to a limited degree, but the results are mixed. Some studies (Dollins, 1956; Sommer, 1957) suggest that music facilitates group conversation and interaction among psychiatric patients; Traub (1969), however, reported that music had no effect on the verbal interactions of low verbalizing patients. Studies of nonpsychiatric subjects also are mixed. Bonny and others (1965) reported that neither stimulative nor sedative music significantly influenced verbal interaction in social interaction classes, while Mezzano and Prueter (1974), Prueter and Mezzano (1973), and Stratton and Zalanowski (1984) report that soothing (sedative) background music promotes significantly more verbal interaction than either no music or stimulative music. While the results of the effects of soothing music are consistent with informal observations of the effects of traditional background, much more research is necessary before definitive conclusions can be drawn.

Aside from uses of music in therapeutic and educational situations, the most extensive and systematic application of background music for functional purposes has been by the Muzak Corporation. Established in the 1930s, the corporation has capitalized on music's effects as background music and developed a vast international business that transmits music into offices, businesses, industries, and many other types of public and commercial environments in more than twenty countries. Much of the background music heard in businesses, doctors' offices, and other public places is produced and programmed by the Muzak Corporation, although some such music may be from radios, privately developed tapes, or perhaps other companies. Because of its prevalence,* a brief discussion of the characteristics of Muzak's music follows.

Central to Muzak's programming is their concept of "stimulus progression" music, fifteen-minute segments of recorded music designed to provide a psychological "lift"; i.e., the musical segments reflect a "sense of forward movement and change, designed to mitigate tension, boredom, melancholy and fatigue" (Muzak, 1976). Depending on the nature of the tasks or environment for which the music will provide a background, these segments are played either in alternating periods of fifteen minutes

---

*Indeed, the trade name "Muzak" often is used generically in reference to any background music, just as people may call different brands of facial tissue "Kleenex®" or different colas "Coke®."

of silence or "continuously," i.e., with two-minute interludes of silence between each fifteen-minute musical segment.

Each fifteen-minute segment includes a sequence of five or six specially-recorded instrumental pieces with progressively increasing stimulus values. The "stimulus value" is a composite of the effects of four variables: tempo, rhythm classification of popular music, instrument groupings, and number of instruments used. Although the empirical basis by which the stimulus values were originally derived is not known, Muzak has published "stimulus progression charts" which show that increased tempo reflects increased stimulus value, certain meter and rhythm styles have greater stimulus values than others, certain instrument groupings are of greater stimulus value than others, and an increase in the size of the ensemble (texture change) results in increased stimulus value. Popular music is selected, arranged, performed, and recorded to meet certain characteristics for each of the four variables, after which it is sequenced into fifteen-minute segments with increasing stimulus value.

Whether it is Muzak or some other music, background music for groups of people has become a part of the contemporary environment, and a basic function of such music appears to be to "humanize the impersonal atmosphere of the environment" (Musselman, 1974, p. 96). Public places such as airline and bus terminals, restaurants, hotel lobbies, doctors' and dentists' offices, and public conveyances such as subways, buses, and airplanes provide music as a familiar and welcome relief to the aloneness, anxiety, or nervousness that individuals sometimes feel in situations with large crowds of strangers or when in anticipation of a somewhat unknown or threatening event.

The use of background music in industry also is becoming more prevalent. Where workers are involved in simple repetitive tasks, the music can serve to break the monotony. In situations called "vigilance tasks," which require alertness on the part of a worker, music can serve an "arousal" function. The onset of fatigue and decline in efficiency which occurs twice a day in the normal eight-hour workday routine, called the "industrial efficiency curve," can be combatted to a degree with appropriate background music.

The white-collar worker's environment also includes background music. In some relatively quiet offices, background music is used to raise the overall sound level to mask the effects of occasional sudden noises which are distracting. In some offices, the environment may be too quiet for maximum efficiency and comfort of the workers. The quietness might inhibit conversation. In these cases music may serve to provide privacy for conversations within a large open space. Musselman (1974, p. 96) notes that the acoustical factors alone may help this situation. Normal human speech covers an intensity range of between 30 and 75 decibels and a frequency range from 100 to 7500 Hz. Background music above the lower limits of these ranges but well below the upper limits tends to render speech inaudible beyond a few feet, thus providing a semblance of privacy for conversation. In other situations, however, where spoken communication is essential, background music may interfere if the music emphasizes the frequencies corresponding to that of consonants, which are between roughly 500 and 4800 Hz.

Systematic research on the variables underlying background music and its effect is both limited and fragmented. Much music therapy research has examined the effects of background music of various types on patients' behaviors. Some research has been conducted on background music's effects on a variety of verbal, behavioral, or cognitive tasks. Because the literature is so diverse and confounded by the varying nature of both the independent and dependent measures, no attempt will be made to review it here. However, two studies that appear basic to the application of background music for functional purposes warrant mention.

A particularly important variable in the use of background music in any setting is its loudness level. If background music were so soft that it was inaudible due to being masked by other sounds in the environment, the music could have little effect, whatever it might potentially be. However, if the music were too loud, it would not function as background music; it would be obtrusive.

Wolfe's (1983) comparison of the effects of music loudness level on college students' answering of math problems yielded no significant differences in the performances of students hearing music at three different loudness levels and no music; however, a significantly larger proportion of the students hearing music at the loudest level, 80 to 90 dB, indicated that the background music was distracting. While Wolfe's data are inconclusive, the matter of loudness level effects remains a primary concern in the use of background music.

Madsen's (1987, p. 324) examination and discussion of the effects of background music on a reading comprehension task for college students led him to conclude that background music may cause "conflicting attentiveness" that might distract a student from another academic task.

He suggests that attention to *changes* in the music's loudness, tempo, and instrumentation appear to be the most distracting influences. He goes on to note, however, that

> music played at a soft or moderate volume without any abrupt changes may provide a pleasant sound environment in such places as department stores, supermarkets, restaurants, and places of employment without disrupting primary functions of work tasks, decision making and/or interpersonal conversations. People seem to adapt to certain continuous, predictable noises, and this may be the case with the ongoing nature of background music. (Madsen, 1987, p. 324)

Although background music often is intended to serve some specialized function, perhaps its ultimate value in nearly all situations is to humanize the environment. Music in Western culture is essentially a nonthreatening, satisfying phenomenon. While scientific documentation of the effects of background music may be lacking, it is apparent that it is believed to be valuable by many individuals, including those who provide the money to make it available. Such beliefs lend validity to Musselman's (1974, p. 96) statement that background music has the "practical economic effect of improving efficiency, morale, and safety, and of increasing productivity among employees or satisfaction among customers."

Commercial Uses of Music

The range of musical enterprise which could be considered commercial is great. Conceivably concert artists, composers, performers, and teachers could be viewed as engaging in musical activity for commercial reasons. On the other hand, some musical enterprise appears to be more obviously concerned with using music for financial gain, and this section examines four particular uses of music that appear to have financial gain as a major concern: (a) background music in places of business, (b) music for commercials, (c) music for television and movies, and (d) music as entertainment.

One obvious commercial use of music is to enhance the likelihood that people who visit a store will make purchases. Background (or even relatively loud "foreground") music is employed in discount houses, supermarkets, boutiques, and various specialty stores, as a visit to many American shopping malls will verify. The musical style will vary with the clientele and the store management's preferences. A recorded program designed for the store or "live" reception of a local radio station may be the source. Despite the ubiquitous use of music to enhance the market place, there is a curious lack of well-documented research, although there is some evidence that music may have desirable (from the store's standpoint) effects on potential consumers.

One indirect way in which music may enhance the marketplace is to build a positive attitude toward a mutual selling-buying enterprise. Music therapists recognize that "pleasant" music may make an environment more attractive and clientele more receptive toward therapeutic uses of music and other therapies. Similarly, music may give people a more positive outlook toward cooperating with others. Fried and Berkowitz (1979) divided eighty university students (forty men and forty women) into four groups. Three groups listened to music for approximately seven minutes; the remaining group "sat still" and heard no music. One listening group heard stimulative music, "One O'clock Jump." Another group listened to sedative music (labelled as "soothing" music by Fried and Berkowitz), two of Mendelssohn's "Songs Without Words." John Coltrane's "Meditations" was played to the third group as "aversive" music. At the conclusion of their respective group's activities, subjects were asked to volunteer to help the experimenters with another alleged experiment as a measure of helpfulness. The sedative and stimulative music created positive moods; the aversive music tended to arouse negative feelings. Subjects who heard sedative music were most "helpful," with significantly greater helpfulness than the aversive music or no music subjects.

Music may enhance the potential customers' emotional states in a positive way, and emotion is involved in spur-of-the-moment or impulsive buying. Weinberg and Gottwald (1982) found that people who were likely to make impulsive purchases perceived themselves as more interested, enthusiastic, joyful, and emotionalized, and less astonished than relatively nonimpulsive buyers. Careful weighing of the product's virtues has some role in the purchasing decision, but, despite the possibility of information-based, postpurchase rationalizations, emotional engagement is more important than information processing for impulsive buyers.

In an experimental study regarding music's effects on choices between competing products, Gorn (1982) paired otherwise similar beige and blue pens with liked music ("Grease") and disliked music (Indian classical music). Beyond the .001 level of statistical significance, subjects tended to prefer the pen, regardless of color, which was paired with the preferred music. In a second experiment, under a "decision-making" condition, subjects saw the beige pen while they heard the liked music and saw the blue pen while they heard the alleged product information (e.g., the blue pen did not smudge). These subjects knew in advance that they would be rewarded by their choice of pens, and a majority (71%) selected the blue pen. Under a similar "nondecision-making" condition, a majority (63%) of other subjects, who did not know of the reward in advance, selected the *beige* pen. Gorn's study thus suggests that information has less impact in nondecision-making situations; perhaps music which can induce pleasant feelings or emotions is useful in "reaching" uninvolved potential consumers.

In a very realistic study, Milliman (1982) contrasted the effects of no music, slow music, and fast music on (a) in-store traffic flow, (b) daily gross sales, and (c) the number of shoppers expressing awareness of the music (after they left the store) in a medium-size supermarket over a nine-week period. Tempo classifications were based on earlier interviews with similar clientele: Slow tempi were MM $\leq$ 72 (mean tempo = 60); fast tempi were MM $\geq$ 94 (mean tempo = 108). The mean times for passage between two places in the store were 127.53, 119.86, and 108.93 sec respectively for the slow, no, and fast music conditions, with the slow and fast means differing significantly: Slow music slowed shoppers down. Gross sales were greatest for the slow music condition and least for the fast music condition; that difference was significantly different. There was no significant difference in awareness. So, a frequent belief that faster music can increase the speed with which customers move though a store (or restaurant) while slower music can make them linger longer and possibly buy more has some evidence behind it.

More systematic but realistic study of music's effects in stores is needed. As Milliman indicated in the introduction to the supermarket-tempo study (p. 86),

> Despite the widespread use of music in the marketplace, research documenting the effects of music is limited, and the results of existing research are inconclusive regarding its effects on consumer behavior. This is unfortunate because music is an atmospheric variable readily controlled by management.

The authors concur.

Music for radio and television commercial advertising has become a business in itself, even to the point that there are composers who specialize in writing such music. Writing *jingles,* the music for radio and television commercials, has become "a billion-dollar-a-year industry that's growing all the time." (Shea, 1988, p. 49)

Commercials usually last between 15 and 90 seconds. Radio commercials involve both verbal and musical sounds, while television commercials include verbal and musical sounds as well as visual-verbal information and visual images. The intent is to persuade the listener (and viewer) of the value of the product and to cause him or her to remember it. The fact that commercials are brief interruptions within or between some continuing programs calls them to the listener's attention. Toddlers playing in a room with television playing often will interrupt their play to listen to and view commercials.

The verbal message of a commercial often is via a song, the melody of which is "catchy." Depending on the nature of the product, the melody may reflect varying degrees of stimulative characteristics; other commercials, however, use music as a background to help create a particular mood relevant to the type of product being advertised.

Wintle's (1979) study of the dimensions underlying response to television commercials lends support to the contention that music does make a difference in a commercial. In a series of three studies in which college students were asked to respond to commercials with and without music, three factors emerged: activity, pleasantness, and potency. In the third study, which paired commercials respectively with a supporting musical excerpt, a counteracting excerpt, and an irrelevant excerpt, results showed that supporting background music "routinely intensified the dimension positively characterized by a commercial" (Wintle, 1979, 5115-A).

Recently, rock music of previous decades has been increasingly incorporated into commercials to provide an aura of familiarity and identity for the audience and potential buyers in their 30s and 40s. The idea is to get these listeners to identify with the song and in turn the product being advertised. This use of rock music in commercials is considered a causal factor in Lincoln-Mercury's recent increase in their share of the market (Shea, p. 49), and currently nearly all commercials for General Motors use rock music (Shea, p. 57).

It is clear that music is useful in creating interest in, identification with, and memory of products, and there appears little likelihood that this functional use of music will diminish in the future.

Musselman (1974, p. 103) maintains that one of the most important uses of music in Western culture is to enhance the emotional qualities of words, actions, or images in film and television dramas. While some might argue that this use of music is more "artistic" than "commercial," it is clear that television and film music in itself has become a huge commercial enterprise. Composing, scoring, and performing such music is a multimillion dollar business.

Television and film media are a theatre of illusion. The intent is to stimulate the viewer to perceive or imagine a sense of reality, something which appears to be substantially aided by music. The more successfully this is accomplished, the greater the commercial success of the production.

The function of music in film and television has been summarized by Musselman (pp. 103–106). The most basic uses are to fill silence, mask unwanted sounds, and encourage empathy for the figures on the screen. Music which fulfills these functions generally must be consistent with the mood and tempo of the story. Another use is to imitate or suggest sounds of natural phenomena. Perhaps the most important function of music in film and television is to lend to the continuity of the story. The traditional practice is to identify certain distinctive themes or motifs with particular persons, places, or ideas in the story and to use these themes with reappearances of the person, place, or idea or whenever they are to be remembered. Television serials or weekly shows also are readily identified by their distinctive musical themes. That such themes are readily recognized by the general public is reflected by the apparent popularity of marching band football shows based on themes from television shows. Music also provides continuity to film and television dramas by serving as a cushion or transition between scenes with quite different emotional implications.

The dependence on music to heighten the emotional impact of a scene represents another major use of music in film and television. Music usually is used to build suspense rather than dispel it. Musselman (p. 106) typifies this use of music in a television western:

> We are looking over the shoulder of a cowboy who is scanning the distant horizon. Suddenly a lone horseman appears there, silhouetted against the rising moon. Is he friend or foe? The cowboy cannot tell for sure, but a sudden loud (*sforzando*) dissonance warns us that danger is imminent.

Without question, background music has become a vital and functional part of the film and television industries, and the commercial success of the industries is due in no small part to the effects of music on audience response.

Perhaps the greatest commercial success with music is the field of entertainment, particularly the recording industry. According to recent information from the Recording Industry of America, sales from recordings of all sorts (tapes, LPs, CDs, singles, etc.) grossed nearly 2 billion dollars for 1985 (*Statistical Overview—Update '86*). Sixty percent of this gross was for rock and popular music; only five percent was for classical music.

While persons working in the popular music field are considered "artists," many appear to develop their art for commercial rather than artistic ends. The concern is to develop a style that "sells," even if artistic values have to be compromised. As Musselman (1974, pp. 141–42) notes, artists and composers of popular music are engaged in a commercial enterprise, resulting in music that can survive *intensive* exposure for a relatively short period of time, whereas art, or classical, music requires and survives *extensive* exposure.

As may be evident, commercial uses of music serve financial ends as well as other ends. Certainly the entertainment value of popular music and film and television music is great. The point of the present discussion, however, has been to bring to light perhaps the most prevalent functional uses of music in contemporary society.

Industrial Uses of Music

Although some might argue that industrial uses of music have their roots in work song of more primitive times, early uses of music in industry were primarily recreational. Industries in the early decades of this century sponsored bands, orchestras, choirs, ukulele clubs, harmonica bands, mandolin clubs, and various other types of musical performance organizations. Such organizations apparently were viewed as having a beneficial effect on worker morale, although as Lundin (1967, p. 292) notes, assessment of the actual value of such organizations was difficult.

Beginning in the 1930s, music began to be introduced into the actual work situation, and since then psychologists and industrial managers have been trying to assess its effects. A review of studies conducted during the 1930s and 1940s has been provided by Soibelman (1948, pp. 173–203). Other reviews of such studies have been provided by Uhrbrock (1961), Lundin (1967, pp. 291–303), and Farnsworth (1969, pp. 217–219).

A variety of criteria for "effectiveness" of music on industrial workers has been employed: worker output, attitudes, morale, absenteeism, safety, health, as well as feelings of tiredness and unpleasantness. Many of the studies reviewed, however, do not meet contemporary criteria for quality research, leading Farnsworth (p. 291) to caution that "claims made for industrial music can be generalized only with some hazzard. Perhaps the most promising area is that of worker morale." Soibelman (1948) was even more cautious: She made no generalizations from her review. Uhrbrock (1961) concluded that music's effectiveness in increasing worker production has not actually been proven. Also cautious in his generalizations, Lundin does venture several observations, one of which is contrary to that of Uhrbrock. Based on several studies conducted in the 1940s, he concludes that music does increase production for certain types of factory work, although he notes that the specific reasons for this are unclear. A second effect, he notes, is that music tends to relieve monotony, although there is an inverse relationship between the complexity of the work task and the effects in this regard. A third generalization Lundin makes is that worker attitudes are related to any beneficial effects music has in industry.

Studies by Konz (1964) and Devereux (1969) yield little additional insight into the issues. Konz studied the effects of background music on twenty noncollege women's performance of repetitive tasks. Using each subject as her own control, he found no significant effect on the productivity of the group as a whole. Devereux studied the effects of background music on both output and attitude of personnel working on both routine and complex activities. Subjects were 31 telecommunications operators. Music was played at a ratio of 24 minutes on to six minutes off. Results indicated no significant differences in either worker output or attitude.

Literature published by the Muzak Corporation, including research conducted by consultants, not surprisingly, reports a number of beneficial effects of music in industry. A 1974 Muzak publication (no author or editor) cites five selected case histories of the effects of music on workers. The studies were conducted at various times between 1958 and 1973 in the Black & Decker Manufacturing Company, Blue Shield/United Medical Services, Bulova Watch Company, Mississippi Power & Light Company, and an unnamed major appliance manufacturer. While the particular criteria for effectiveness, i.e., the dependent variables, varied from study to study, the common conclusions were that Muzak had a beneficial effect on both productivity and attitude. It should be noted, however, that statistical tests of the significance of the differences in "before-after" comparisons were not included in the reports of these studies, even though mean differences on productivity criteria appeared to be large. The conclusions appeared to be warranted, although the statistical rigor was inadequate.

A more recent study of the effects of Muzak in industry appears to have a stronger data base than some of the earlier studies. Wokoun (1979) reports the effects of Muzak on fatigue of workers on automobile rigging lines equipped with conveyors. Using checklist data, a "Symptoms of Fatigue" form developed by the Japanese Center for Science of Labor, data were gathered for 53 workers on 30 symptoms. Data were analyzed according to three categories of fatigue condition and by time of day. Results revealed that working with Muzak "reduced the percentage of workers experiencing 29 of the 30 fatigue conditions" (p. 12). Muzak's effects at alleviating these conditions were greater in the afternoon than in the morning.

Regardless of the lack of clear-cut statistical data to support the claims in their promotional literature, it is apparent that Muzak has been well received in the business world, which in itself attests that many believe that beneficial effects accrue from the use of Muzak's music.

To generalize regarding the effects of music in industry is difficult. When so many variables are involved, it is risky to make too specific claims regarding music's effects on productivity. On the other hand, virtually all studies that asked workers whether they liked having background music while working reported that a large majority did prefer to have the music. Apparently, music does have some positive effects, particularly in relieving boredom on certain types of monotonous tasks. Perhaps its greatest value, however, is in humanizing the work environment and thus alleviating some of the undesirable effects of monotony, tension, and fatigue.

Therapeutic Uses of Music

Although healing, soothing, and persuasive effects of music have been espoused throughout the history of Western civilization, it has been only within the past few decades that music has come to be systematically used toward therapeutic ends. Michel (1985, p. 5) notes that it has come into widespread use in the United States only since about 1946. The National

Association for Music Therapy (NAMT) was founded in 1950.* The development of music therapy as a profession has been coordinated and promoted primarily through the NAMT. Accreditation as a Registered Music Therapist (RMT) is awarded through the NAMT and requires a therapist to pass a national certification examination.** The designation RMT has been "adopted by many levels of government and by private employers as the standard for employment of music therapists" (Michel, p. 11).

The founding principles which underlie therapeutic uses of music, as stated by Gaston (1968, p. v), were that music in therapy should facilitate

1. *The establishment or reestablishment of interpersonal relationships,*
2. *The bringing about of self-esteem through self-actualization,*
3. *The utilization of the unique potential of rhythm to energize and bring order.*

While these principles are still valid, the potential of music therapy in contemporary society appears to have broadened in scope. Music therapists today are professionally trained individuals who use music as a medium to help influence desirable changes in their patients. Michel (p. 11) notes that today's therapist is no longer restricted to working with patients with specific behavioral, emotional, physical, or mental disorders; rather, today's therapist is viewed as a generalist with special *musical* tools that may be adapted to meet the professionally assessed needs of various patients. Michel notes two particular aspects of the therapist's musical tools: (a) the basic power of the musical stimulus to arouse or soothe activity and (b) music's traditional functional values as a socializing agent and as a symbol or vehicle for expressing patriotism, religion, or fraternity.

Although the uses of music in hospitals include a variety of specializations for patients with particular needs, music therapy is essentially an activity therapy. The RMT usually is a member of a professional team, most often headed by a psychiatrist, which outlines the therapeutic

---

*For a review of music therapy organizations in other countries see D.E. Michel's *Music Therapy, An Introduction Including Music in Special Education* (2nd ed.). Springfield, IL: Thomas, 1985, pp. 103–110.

**The national certification examination was first administered in November 1985 by the administratively independent Certification Board for Music Therapists.

program for the individual patient. Music therapy, as one of several activity therapies, may be selected as the particular activity, or one of the activities, through which behavioral changes will be sought. A particular value of activity therapy is that it requires an interpersonal relationship between the therapist and the patient.

The specific music activities selected for individual patients are determined by the music therapist who takes into consideration many factors, including the recommendations of the therapeutic team, the patient's disabilities and behavior disorders, the objectives for the therapy, and the patient's musical background and interests. While musical goals often are established, they are secondary to the behavioral and social goals established by the therapeutic team. The music therapist must select musical activities that capitalize on music's stimulative and socializing strengths to get the patient actively involved while at the same time subtly working toward effecting the desired behavioral changes.

That such an approach in a relatively young field has difficulty in documenting the effects of therapy via carefully controlled research is understandable. The clinical approach necessary in activity therapy lends itself more to case study research than experimental research. Further, since music therapy often is used in conjunction with other therapies and medications, it is difficult to attribute any effects solely to the music; also, the personality of the individual therapist is an important variable.

A review of the research literature on particular applications of music in therapy is far beyond the scope of the present discussion, but Standley's (1986) recent meta-analysis of empirical studies using music in actual medical/dental treatments warrants discussion. She identified 81 studies for possible inclusion in the meta-analysis, but only 30 were included. The others had (a) failed to report empirical data, (b) used simulated diagnoses, treatment, or pain stimuli, (c) used auditory stimuli other than music, or (d) reported results in formats not amenable to replicated data analysis. Using the statistic *Estimated Effect Size* (ES), which represents the proportion of a standard deviation that quantifies the experimental effect of the two conditions, i.e., the difference in the means of the groups receiving music treatment and the groups not receiving music treatment, Standley's data revealed that for 54 of 55 variables analyzed, "music conditions enhanced medical objectives whether measured by physiological ($\overline{ES}$ = .97), psychological/self-report ($\overline{ES}$ = .85), or behavioral observation ($\overline{ES}$ = 1.10)"* (Standley, p. 79).

Because of the comprehensive nature of the data from the 30 studies included in the meta-analysis, Standley (pp. 81–97) was able to identify seven types of music therapy applications and techniques for use in clinical medical settings. Following is a list of the techniques and the function the music is intended to serve for each technique. Readers interested in the therapeutic objectives, populations for whom the techniques are intended, and the procedures involved in application of the techniques should consult Standley's article. It represents a major contribution to the field.

    1. *Technique:* Music Listening and Anesthesia, Analgesia, and/or Suggestion

Music Function: To serve as an audioanalgesic, anxiolytic or sedative.

    2. *Technique:* Music Listening/Participation and Exercise

Music Function: To serve as a focus of attention and/or to structure exercise (tempo, repetition, duration, force, or fluidity).

    3. *Technique:* Music Listening/Participation and Counseling

Music Function: To initiate and enhance therapist/patient/family relationship.

    4. *Technique:* Music Listening/Participation and Developmental or Educational Objectives

Music Function: To reinforce or structure learning.

    5. *Technique:* Music Listening and Stimulation

Music Function: To stimulate auditorily and increase awareness of other forms of stimuli.

    6. *Technique:* Music and Biofeedback

Music Function: To serve as reinforcer or structure for physiological responses.

    7. *Technique:* Music and Group Activities

Music Function: To structure pleasurable and positive personal interactions.

While it is obvious that music therapy still is a relatively new application of music in functional ways, it appears to have a stronger research base than other functional applications of music. Its value as an activity

---

*An ES of 1.00 indicates that the experimental group (music condition) scored one standard deviation better than the control group (nonmusic condition). The number of variables analyzed was greater than 30 because some studies included more than one dependent variable.

therapy is recognized, and it appears that research, training, and other standards for the profession are high, thus strengthening the position of the profession within the medical and paramedical community. In conclusion, there is little doubt that the ideals and principles under which music is used in therapy make music therapy one of the most, if not *the* most, valuable applications of music in a functional way.

Music to Facilitate Nonmusical Learning

Many claims have been made regarding the effects of music on nonmusical learning. Many students of all ages claim that they study more effectively while listening to music. Music educators faced with program cutbacks in schools are seeking new ways to justify music's position in the curriculum, and some have begun to suggest that music facilitates learning in other curricular areas. An area for which perhaps the most claims have been made is in teaching language arts.

A solid research base for these claims appears to be lacking. While some isolated studies yield "significant differences" in favor of approaches using music, there are many more that yield "no significant differences." Whether these differences are real or are due to the approach or design of the experiments has been a concern of some comprehensive reviews of the literature, and this discussion relies heavily on those reviews, particularly that of Wolff (1978). Other reviews include those by Hanshumaker (1980; 1986); his reviews included studies regarding the effects of other arts besides music, and his generalizations therefore must be considered with this in mind.

Music has been used in a number of different ways in attempts to facilitate nonmusical learning. One method, which will be discussed in the concluding section of this chapter, is to use music or musical activities as a reward for having accomplished a given task. This method is a part of a behavioral approach advocated by Clifford K. Madsen and many of his former students. Much of their research is reported by Madsen, Greer, and Madsen (1975) and Madsen and Prickett (1987). While much of the research they report uses behavioral techniques to facilitate musical learning, much uses music as a reinforcer for nonmusical behavioral change.

Of the other approaches involving music to facilitate nonmusical learning, perhaps the most basic is that of examining the effects of musical experience and learning on achievement in other subject areas.

Wolff labels this approach as *general learning transfer* in which "the study of music serves as a mental discipline which expedites the learning of other subjects" (Wolff, 1978, p. 3). She also notes that the notion of training faculties of the mind had already been discredited by the time of Thorndike. Other studies have investigated *specific transfer learning* on certain tasks common to music and other subjects. An example of such a study is that by Madsen, Madsen, and Michel (1975) in which tonal cues were used to facilitate verbal auditory discrimination.

Another approach using music to facilitate nonmusical learning is through the use of background music. While few specific claims are made regarding the effects of this type of music on academic achievement, there appears to be enough interest in the approach that the Muzak Corporation has published a brochure on "how environment can affect the learning process" (Muzak, brochure, no date).

No attempt will be made to review the literature regarding the effects of music on nonmusical learning, but readers are encouraged to examine Wolff's excellent review and status report on the matter. She also reviews studies that examine the effects of music experience on self-concept, personality factors, and certain physical activities.

Hanshumaker examines the studies in his 1980 review under headings related to language development and reading readiness, reading and mathematics, learning behavior and attitude, creativity, socialization, and intellectual development and achievement. His 1986 review essentially is an update of the 1980 review. Generally, Hanshumaker concludes from his reviews that music has positive effects on language development, reading readiness, and student verbalization. He also notes that daily music instruction has a significant, positive effect on math scores and that creativity and perceptual motor skills are positively affected. A conservative but particularly important conclusion for music educators is that "school time spent on music and other arts activities has no negative effect on academic achievement" (Hanshumaker, 1986, p. 11).

Overall, Wolff is more cautious in her conclusions, although she agrees that there may be measurable effects of music education on the development of cognitive skills and understanding. She acknowledges that most of the research she reviewed reported positive results, but she maintains that the conclusions drawn generally remain unconvincing, primarily due to "obvious inadequacies in the experimental designs and also to the incomplete and equivocal descriptions of the experiments themselves" (p. 21). She concludes her review with the statement that "definitive evidence of the nonmusical outcomes of music education is yet to be provided" (p. 21). The authors concur.

Music as a Reward

As noted in the above discussion, there is a growing body of research in which music is used as a reward for behavior change or accomplishment of a given nonmusical task. Vance Cotter (1973) was a pioneer researcher in this area, but as noted above, Clifford Madsen and his students (and former students) have provided the bulk of the research.

The research in this area reflects a behavioral approach to learning. Learning is viewed as change in behavior and must be observable (see Chapter Ten). Most of the research reflects careful control and isolation of variables.

Cotter (1973) studied the effects of contingent and noncontingent music on the performance of manual tasks in a simulated workshop situation by 16 moderately retarded adolescent females. Subjects in the noncontingent group, i.e., the one receiving music regardless of their work performance, did not achieve a higher mean work rate, while subjects in the contingent group, for whom receiving of music was dependent on work rate, did increase their mean work rate.

Greer, Randall, and Timberlake (1975) compared the contingency effects of music listening, pennies, and no reward on improvement in vocal pitch accuracy and attendance. No significant differences were observed between the groups' vocal gain scores, although significant differences were found between the nonreinforcement group and the groups receiving music or pennies for attendance. No significant difference in attendance was found between the groups receiving music and pennies.

Madsen and Forsythe (1975) examined the contingency effects of individual music listening (via earphones), group music listening, math games, and no reward on sixth graders' mathematical achievement. Results revealed statistically significant differences in favor of the two groups receiving music. A subsequent study, in which the contingency for first graders' math achievement was the viewing of televised music lessons, also revealed greater achievement for the group viewing the music lessons than for a control group receiving no reward (Madsen, Dorow, Moore, & Womble, 1976).

Madsen and Geringer's (1976) study of the effects of choices of reinforcement indicated that televised music lessons were just as effective as free playing in increasing children's academic skills. Madsen's (1981) more recent study comparing the effects of televised music lessons and the receipt of books as reinforcement alternatives for achievement in math also revealed that both reinforcers were effective in promoting increased performance in mathematics. The study also examined the effects of the televised music on achievement in music. Results indicated that the televised music lessons had the added advantage of facilitating achievement in music.

The selected studies cited here all suggest that music can function as a reward for achievement of nonmusical tasks. The extent to which these results can be generalized and applied to other learning situations is subject to conjecture. Madsen and Forsythe (1975, p. 31) acknowledge that studies of this type have several problems, including "Hawthorne" and "halo" effects as well as all of the effects presumed to be operating in school settings.* The studies do, however, indicate that music as a reward is equally effective with other contrived classroom contingencies and perhaps has the additional effect of facilitating learning in music.

Summary

The major points of this chapter are:
1. Music that stimulates or arouses listeners has a strong energizing component.
2. The energizing component in music for most people primarily is rhythm, particularly its attribute of tempo,
3. Music that soothes, calms, or tranquilizes behavior is characterized by sounds that are nonpercussive and legato.
4. Reviews of the limited amount of research on the effects of stimulative and sedative music reveal differential response to the two types of music.
5. Music has been a part of ceremonies, particularly religious and military, throughout history.
6. Background music is used informally by individuals as well as for groups of people in public places.

---

*The "Hawthorne" effect refers to an increase in performance derived apparently because a group perceives itself as receiving special treatment; the "halo" effect refers to a bias in evaluations arising from the tendency of an evaluator to be influenced in ratings of specific traits by some general impression he/she may have of the person being rated.

7. The Muzak Corporation has been the most successful proponent and producer of background music.

8. Muzak's "stimulus progression" concept involves 15-minute segments of specially recorded instrumental music with increasing stimulus values from one composition to another as a result of changes in tempo, rhythm classification, instrument grouping, and number of instruments used.

9. Commercial uses of music include background music in places of business, music for radio and television commercials, music for television and movies, and music as entertainment.

10. Music in industry has been studied primarily in terms of its effects on employee productivity and morale.

11. Fundamental principles of music therapy are that therapeutic experiences should (a) enhance the establishment or reestablishment of interpersonal relationships between a patient and others and (b) help foster the patient's self-esteem.

12. Two basic "tools" of music therapists are music's (a) power to stimulate or soothe activity and (b) values as a socializing agent and as a symbol or vehicle for expressing patriotism, religion, and fraternity.

13. Standley's seven music therapy functions include the use of music to (a) serve as an audioanalgesic, anxiolytic, or sedative, (b) serve as a focus of attention and/or to structure exercise, (c) initiate and enhance therapist/patient/family relationships, (d) reinforce or structure learning, (e) stimulate auditorily and increase awareness of other forms of stimuli, (f) serve as reinforcer or structure for physiological responses, and (g) structure pleasurable and positive personal interactions.

14. There has been a surge in research examining the effects of music on nonmusical learning, but results are inconclusive.

15. It has been demonstrated that music can serve as a reward for completion of nonmusical tasks.

REFERENCES

Boyle, J.D. (1982). College students' verbal descriptions of excerpts of stimulative and sedative music. In P.E. Sink (Ed.), *Proceedings of the Research Symposium on the Psychology and Acoustics of Music 1982* (pp. 105–117). Lawrence: The University of Kansas.

Cotter, V.W. (1973). Effects of music on mentally retarded girls' performance of manual tasks. *Council for Research in Music Education, 27,* 42–43.

Devereux, G.A. (1969). Commercial background music—its effect on workers' attitudes and output. *Personnel Practice Bulletin, 25,* 24–30.

Dollins, C. (1956). The use of background music in a psychiatric hospital to increase group conversational frequency. *Music Therapy, 6,* 229–230.

Farnsworth, P.R. (1969). *The social psychology of music* (2nd ed.). Ames: Iowas State University Press.

Fried, R., & Berkowitz, L. (1979). Music hath charms . . . and can influence helpfulness. *Journal of Applied Social Science, 9,* 199–208.

Gaston, E.T. (1951/52). The influence of music on behavior. *University of Kansas Bulletin of Education, 6,* 60–63.

Gaston, E.T. (1968). Foreword. In E.T. Gaston (Ed.), *Music in therapy.* New York: Macmillan.

Gaston, E.T. (Ed.). (1968). *Music in therapy.* New York: Macmillan.

Gorn, G.J. (1982). The effects of music in advertising on choice behavior: A classical conditioning approach. *Journal of Marketing, 46* (1), 94–101.

Greer, R.D., Randall, R., & Timberlake, C. (1975). The discriminate use of music listening as a contingency for improvement in vocal pitch accuracy and attending behavior. In C.K. Madsen, R.D. Greer, & C.H. Madsen, Jr. (Eds.), *Research in music behavior.* New York: Teachers College Press, Columbia University.

Hanshumaker, J. (1980). The effects of arts education on intellectual and social development: A review of selected research. *Council for Research in Music Education, 61,* 10–28.

Hanshumaker, J. (1986). The effects of music and other arts instruction on reading and math achievement and on general school performance. *UPDATE, The Applications of Research in Music Education, 4* (2), 10–11.

Hodges, D.A. (1980). Physiological response to music. In D.A. Hodges (Ed.), *Handbook of music psychology.* Lawrence, KS: National Association for Music Therapy.

Konz, S.A. (1965). Effect of background music on productivity (Doctoral dissertation, University of Illinois, 1964). *Dissertation Abstracts, 25,* 4830. (University Microfilms No. 65-853)

Lundin, R.W. (1967). *An objective psychology of music* (2nd ed.). New York: Ronald Press.

McMullen, P.T. (1982). Connotative responses to musical stimuli: A theoretical explanation. *Council for Research in Music Education, 71,* 45–57.

Madsen, C.K. (1981). Music lessons and books as reinforcement alternatives for an academic task. *Journal of Research in Music Education, 29,* 103–110.

Madsen, C.K. (1987). Background music: Competition for focus of attention. In C.K. Madsen and C.A. Prickett (Eds.), *Applications of research in music education* (pp. 315–325). Tuscaloosa: The University of Alabama Press.

Madsen, C.K., Dorow, L.G., Moore, R.S., & Womble, J.U. (1967). Effect of music via television as reinforcement for correct mathematics. *Journal of Research in Music Education, 24,* 51–59.

Madsen, C.K., & Geringer, J.M. (1976). Choice of televised music lessons versus free play in relationship to academic improvement. *Journal of Music Therapy, 13* (4), 154–162.

Madsen, C.K., & Forsythe, J.L. (1975). The effect of contingent music listening on increases in mathematical responses. In C.K. Madsen, R.D. Greer, & C.H. Madsen, Jr. (Eds.), *Research in music behavior.* New York: Teachers College Press, Columbia University.

Madsen, C.K., Madsen, C.H., Jr., & Michel, D.E. (1975). The use of music stimuli in teaching language discrimination. In C.K. Madsen, R.D. Greer, & C.H. Madsen, Jr. (Eds.), *Research in music behavior.* New York: Teachers College Press, Columbia University.

Madsen, C.K., & Prickett, C.A. (Eds.). (1987). *Applications of research in music education.* Tuscaloosa: The University of Alabama Press.

Mezzano, J., & Prueter, B.A. (1974). Background music and counseling interaction. *Journal of Counseling Psychology, 21,* 84–86.

Michel, D.E. (1985). *Music therapy: An introduction including music in special education* (2nd ed.). Springfield: Thomas.

Milliman, R.E. (1982). Using background music to affect the behavior of supermarket shoppers. *Journal of Marketing, 46* (3), 86–91.

Musselman, J.A. (1974). *The uses of music: An introduction to music in contemporary American life.* Englewood Cliffs, NJ: Prentice-Hall.

Muzak Corporation. (1974). *Significant studies of the effects of Muzak on employee performance.* New York: Muzak Corporation.

Muzak Corporation. (1976). *Stimulus progression* (demonstration recording). New York: Muzak Corporation.

Muzak Corporation. (n.d.). How environment can affect the learning process. In brochure, *Muzak and schools.* New York: Muzak Corporation.

Pareles, J. (1987, December 3). Consumers are legitimizing new-age music in a big way. *The Miami News,* p. 3C.

Perris, A. (1985). *Music as propaganda: Art to persuade, art to control.* Westport, CT: Greenwood Press.

Preueter, B.A., & Mezzano, J. (1973). Effects of background music upon initial counseling interaction. *Journal of Music Therapy, 10,* 205–212.

Shea, G. (1988, January). Rock 'n' roll is here to sell. *Continental,* pp. 42–43, 49–50, 52, 57.

Soibelman, D. (1948). *Therapeutic and industrial uses of music.* New York: Columbia University Press.

Standley, J.M. (1986). Music research in medical/dental treatment: Meta-analysis and clinical applications. *Journal of Music Therapy, 23,* 56–122.

Statistical overview – Update ''86. New York: Recording Industry of America.

Stratton, V.A., & Zalanowski, A. (1984). The effect of background music on verbal interaction in groups. *Journal of Music Therapy, 21,* 16–26.

Traub, C. (1969). The relation of music to speech of low verbalizing subjects in a music listening activity. *Journal of Music Therapy, 6,* 105–107.

Uhrbrock, R.S. (1961). Music on the job: Its influence on worker morale and production. *Personnel Psychology, 14,* 9–38.

Weinberg, P., & Gottwald, W. (1982). Impulsive consumer buying as a result of emotions. *Journal of Business Research, 10,* 43–57.

Wintle, R.R. (1979). Emotional impact of music on television commercials. *Dissertation Abstracts International, 39* (8), 5115A. (University Microfilms No. 7901953)

Wokoun, W. (1979). *A study of fatigue in industry.* [New York: Muzak Corporation].

Wolfe, D.E. (1983). Effects of musical loudness on task performance and self-report of college-aged students. *Journal of Research in Music Education, 31,* 191–201.

Wolff, K. (1978). The nonmusical outcomes of music education: A review of the literature. *Council for Research in Music Education, 55,* 1–27.

Chapter Nine

MUSICAL ABILITY

Study of musical ability occupies a prominent place in psychology of music. Identifying ability and predicting the likelihood of musical success are traditional concerns of music educators as well as psychologists. Studying musical ability is complicated by lack of a definition, diverse criteria for musical success, and measurement uncertainties. This chapter discusses conflicting terms, differing views of musical ability, selected influences, and measurement and prediction.

Extended Definitions

Ability suggests being "able" to do something. A person with musical ability is able to perform, create, or, perhaps, analyze music if given the opportunity. Unfortunately, the terms *talent, musicality, capacity,* and *aptitude* are interchanged with ability, and opinions differ regarding the permissible degree of interchange. The following definitions represent the authors' views.

Talent is an imprecise term, designating some obvious indication of ability, usually in performance. A violinist who can perform the Mendelssohn concerto from memory after seeing the music once obviously is talented. A young child with an unusually accurate and extended vocal range may be talented. Talent implies something more than ability: While almost anyone has some musical ability, fewer people are talented. To say that someone lacks musical talent does not mean that that person is *unable* to have a satisfactory musical experience.

Musicality also is imprecise. It refers to a state of being "musical," of being sensitive to changes in a musical stimulus. For inexperienced performers, it may mean a tendency to taper phrases and vary dynamic levels without direction from a teacher. It may simply mean interest in music.

Capacity refers to a portion of a person's ability which he or she possesses as a result of genetic endowment and maturation. To the extent that musical capacity increases, it increases regardless of environmental influences. Superior auditory discrimination ability may be a matter of capacity.

Musical *aptitude* includes capacity plus the result of environmental influences other than formal musical education. It refers to what a person can do musically without regard for musical achievement. Since much concern for musical ability relates to predicting a person's musical success prior to opportunity for musical training, musical ability's measurement problems often are problems of measuring aptitude.

Musical *ability* is what a person is "able" to do musically as a result of capacity, environmental influences, and formal instruction. A person who already has profited from formal instruction may continue to profit. Ability is the broadest of the terms and allows for the greatest diversity of measuring techniques.

Musical Ability: Specifics or General?

Musical ability's multifaceted nature suggests questions regarding its constituent factors. What are they? Is there a loosely related cluster of relatively narrow abilities which comprise musical ability? Is there a general musical ability factor which pervades most specific musical tasks? Unfortunately, the answer to these questions is, "It depends."

Factor analysis is a technique for extracting common core variables or *factors* from a matrix of correlations among several tests which are believed to measure different aspects of the psychological property of interest. Various tests may measure the same thing in different ways; they will "load" on an identified factor to the extent that they are functions of that factor. Factor analysis condenses many observations to a few explanatory constructs. The results depend on the particular tests, the mathematical strategies employed, and the judgment exercised in naming the factors. Factor analysis is one logical tool for assessing the structure of musical ability, but results are inconsistent.

In one representative study, Wing (1941) administered seven measures of his own construction to over 2,000 children and approximately 300 adults. The tests required the subjects to (a) indicate how many tones a chord contains, (b) indicate which tone is changed in a repetition of a chord, and (c) in a repeated phrase, (d) select the member of a pair performed with more appropriate accentuation, (e) harmonization, (f) dynamic contrasts, and (g) phrasing. The test data yielded three factors: general musical ability, a judgment factor related to analysis and synthesis, and a judgment factor related to harmony and rhythm.

In a study of similar vintage, Karlin (1942) administered a total of thirty-three tests in pitch, loudness, timbre, time, auditory analysis and synthesis, auditory and visual memory, age, and intelligence to 200 high school students. Unlike Wing, Karlin found no general factor.* The thirty-three tests yielded eight identifiable factors, including (a) pitch-quality discrimination, (b) loudness discrimination, (c) "auditory integral for perceptual mass," (d) auditory resistance, (e) speed of closure, (f) auditory span formation, (g) auditory and visual memory span, and (h) incidental closure. Karlin concluded that auditory ability requires more than auditory acuity and that rhythm is not primarily an auditory factor.

In her review of literature regarding musical ability, Shuter-Dyson (1982) cites a 1971 University of London dissertation in which Whellams reanalyzed "many" earlier correlational and factor analytic studies of the Seashore, Gordon, or Wing tests (discussed below) or the long out-of-print Kwalwasser and Dykema (1930) tests. Whellams identified 15 significant factors, of which 11 were basically perceptual and four were basically appreciative or judgmental in nature. In order of importance (based on the number of studies in which the factors appear), Whellams arranged the 11 perceptual factors into eight interpretations: pitch imagery, a "dynamic" factor for developing pitch perception, harmonic ability, tonal separation, rhythmic ability, and two experience factors. Whellams's four ordered interpretations for the four appreciative factors were respectively a musical judgment factor and three factors peculiar to sections of the Wing test. The research Whellams examined obviously suggests that perception of pitch and rhythmic structures is important, but so is experience.

Two pioneering music psychologists engaged in a controversy that never has been resolved because of musical ability's elusive nature and varied criteria. Carl Seashore (1938) maintained that musical ability is a matter of inborn capacity in six loosely related areas involving sensory discrimination. His tests, discussed below, essentially are tests of psycho-physical skills. James Mursell (1937) believed in an "omnibus" theory of

---

*Farnsworth (1969) indicates that British factor analytic studies characteristically find a general factor while American studies do not. Wing is an Englishman; Karlin is an American.

musical ability. He never published a test of musical ability, but he later criticized Seashore's concept of loosely related specifics. Mursell insisted that musical ability is an all-pervasive ability which can be developed and improved through training. With time, it has become evident that musical ability is more than loosely related sensory skills, but the general musical ability factor remains elusive.

A person who is musically able can apply diverse skills to particular musical situations. Whether such skills are specific or general is a matter of perspective. How such skills may be nurtured, regardless of specificity or generality, is perhaps a more important question.

Selected Influences on Musical Ability

How, without formal instruction, does musical ability develop? Is it a matter of what is *in* or what is *around* the person? As with all nature vs. nurture questions, the answer is that *both* count in varying but unknown degrees.

Auditory Acuity

Music is an aural art form, so it appears logical that sufficient hearing is an essential part of musical ability. Hearing impaired individuals will have difficulty experiencing music in a normal manner. Various hearing ailments are viewed with alarm by musicians. However, musical ability bears little relationship to hearing acuity.

Sherbon (1975) administered tests of melody, harmony, visual music recognition, musical memory, pitch, loudness, and timbre to sixty undergraduate students, thirty music majors and thirty nonmusic majors. Each subject had his or her hearing threshold determined and was tested for diplacusis.* The music majors outperformed the nonmusic majors on all but the loudness and timbre tests. However, the two groups did not differ in acuity or diplacusis, and neither acuity nor diplacusis showed a significant relationship to any of the seven sets of test scores. From the standpoint of being "able" to accomplish the tasks Sherbon required, superior hearing ability made no difference.

The view that musicians have weak auditory skills and compensate for them with vigorous artistic effort is unsubstantiated (Farnsworth, 1941).

---

*Diplacusis, of the type Sherbon tested, is a condition in which a particular frequency sounds with a different pitch in each ear.

Genetics

Genetic endowment for musical accomplishment is unlikely except to the extent that genetic endowment may contribute to overall abilities. What Farnsworth (1969) calls "D.A.R.*-like studies," showing how Bach and Mozart were in "musical families," are as much evidence for a stimulating musical environment as they are for a strain of musically superior beings. No musical gene or chromosome has been found.

Belief that musical ability is largely innate and presumably genetically influenced does persist. Bentley (1966), basing his view in part on highly diverse levels of musical ability observed in relatively homogeneous groups of children, maintains that musical abilities are mostly a matter of innate capacity.

Scheid and Eccles (1975) hypothesized that the physical size of the right cerebral hemisphere's planum temporale is an indicator of genetically-coded musical ability. Their belief is based on hemispheric asymmetries, clinical studies of patients undergoing lobectomies or severance of the corpus callosum, and dichotic listening tests purporting to show more right than left hemisphere involvement in music processing.** The planum temporale is located just behind the primary auditory cortical area and can be observed without a microscope. Scheid and Eccles suggest postmortem examinations of brains from individuals of high and low musical ability. If the planum temporale can grow with environmental stimulation, such postmortem evidence would not be valid unless the cadavers had equal stimulation while alive.

There are differences in people which are not of an environmental nature, of course; it is silly to pretend that anyone can do anything, given the right opportunities and education. Someone whose adult height is 150 cm (about 4 ft 11 in) is not likely to play center in the National Basketball Association; a child born with Down syndrome (formerly called Down's syndrome or mongolism) is unlikely to become a professional musician, although such a child still may have satisfying

---

*The Daughters of the American Revolution (DAR) is an organization of American women who believe that their ancestors were involved in some way with the War of American Independence (1775–1783). Tracing ancestry may be especially important in such an organization, hence Farnsworth's pejorative use of the term. The authors intend no offense.

**One hemisphere, generally the left, is superior for sequential, analytic, time-ordered processing, such as speech, while the opposite hemisphere is superior for holistic, spatial processing, such as musical contours. This often is oversimplified and misinterpreted; hemispheric specialization is discussed in greater detail in Chapter Eleven.

experiences with music. Nevertheless, while differences in musical ability due to innate differences in people should be theoretically possible, the evidence for influence of the planum temporale or any physiological structure or neurochemical process presently is tenuous.

Physical Features

Physical features such as teeth alignment and lip, hand, and finger sizes may influence performing ability regarding particular instruments. The upper lip protrusion known as a Cupid's bow makes it difficult to form the characteristic flute embouchure. Children with tiny fingers have difficulty covering clarinet fingerholes, and a pronounced overbite makes a trumpet embouchure difficult. Specific instrumental ability is only a part of musical ability, however. If physical influences on musical ability are important, they must relate to many aspects of musical behavior.

Home

There are grossly insufficient data regarding the musical development of children: some are discussed in the next chapter. There obviously are influences of the home's musical stimulation on musical achievement and development of certain musical skills; absolute pitch acquisition via imprinting, discussed in Chapter Three, is an example. In an interesting descriptive study, Simons (1964) observed gross responses to musical stimuli, pitch and rhythm imitation, and free-play activities of twelve pairs of same sex twins (five male, seven female; aged 9 to 31 months) and twelve matched singletons (of similar sex and age) in their home environments. Both groups responded the most to rhythmic stimuli, less to melodic stimuli, still less to harmonic stimuli, and least to dissonant music. The older singletons generally showed greater amounts of response than younger singletons, but the older twins did not consistently respond more than the younger twins. The singletons as a group showed significantly more response to music than the twins. Evidently, constant companionship of a nearly identical child may have some detrimental relationship to musical response, but it is unwise to generalize that family size and age proximity of the children influence musical ability.

Creativity

Composition obviously requires creativity, in the sense of constructing a new arrangement of sounds. Performance may be a creative act (although some say it is more recreative), and a person can listen in creative ways.

Attempts to explain musical ability in terms of creativity have been unsuccessful because neither term is defined adequately.

In an often-cited study, Getzels and Jackson (1962) identified twenty-six Chicago area private school students as a high creativity group: They scored in the top 20 percent on the researchers' creativity measures, but they were below the top 20 percent in intelligence, according to school records. A high intelligence group, containing twenty-eight students from the same school, scored in the top 20 percent in intelligence but were below the top 20 percent in creativity. Among their findings, Getzels and Jackson reported: (a) both groups were superior to the school population in school achievement and did not differ in motivation to achieve, (b) teachers showed a preference for the high intelligence group, (c) the creative students were less success-oriented in an adult sense, (d) the creative students had more humor and were more prone to take risks, and (e) the creative students were more able to fantasize.

Of particular interest here is the view of creativity which the measuring techniques imply. Creativity was identified through tests requiring multiple associative responses to stimulus words, suggestions of novel and nonstereotyped uses for common objects, detection of simple geometric figures hidden within complex patterns, composition of endings for four fables, and composition of mathematical problems from four paragraphs containing numerical statements.

The two student groups were compared for fantasy via stories written about pictures and pictures drawn to portray given situations. Running throughout is the presumption that the creative student is inventive, nonconforming, and prone to unconventional and even bizarre ideas. For example, a creative student, when asked to depict children playing tag in a schoolyard, submitted a blank white paper and said that the children were playing during a blizzard. The student describing a picture of a man in an airplane seat as a scientist, travelling to the moon, who is about to be consumed by a mass of protoplasm, which he mistakenly believes is a pillow, also was creative. Or were they sarcastic? Any student with a sense of humor and ability to spot absurdities in daily life probably could be highly creative if creativity is synonymous with inventiveness.

Guilford (1957) stressed that creative ability is not uniform. It requires a number of factors, as does intelligence. Particularly important for the artist are fluency, flexibility, originality, and evaluative factors. Moore

(1966) concluded that creativity requires above average intelligence but is not synonymous with intelligence.

Creativity may be defined in terms of creation, divergent thinking, problem solving, or something mystical. In one opinion, creativity is in the eyes and ears of the beholder. If something is *judged* as "creative" rather than ordinary, unmusical, "wrong," or bizarre, it *is* creative (Radocy, 1971).

Musical ability may be related to creativity in many facets of music, but divergent thinking, inventiveness, and bizarre behavior are hindrances in the context of ordinary musical development and instruction. Creativity may characterize the musically able, but without discipline and direction creativity is insufficient to make a person musically successful.

Intelligence

Intelligence has been examined as an important influence on musical ability. It seems reasonable that an intelligent person is better able to cope with musical problems, if intelligence is defined as a means of coping with intellectual demands of the environment. As with creativity, definition problems have clouded the relationship of intelligence and musical ability. Different measurement tools imply different definitions.

One may cite cases of so-called idiots savant as evidence that intelligence is not requisite for musical ability. An idiot savant is a person of subnormal intelligence who displays remarkable ability in one or more narrow areas. Anastasi and Levee (1960) report a case involving musical talent in a thirty-eight-year-old man. The subject, brain damaged from encephalitis, walked at eighteen months and did not talk until his fifth year. He hummed tunes before he talked, and a speech therapist taught him to talk by using song lyrics. As an adult, the subject was sexually immature, unable to read beyond a fifth-to-sixth grade level, and generally lazy, except for his music. He disliked children and anything else that disrupted his schedule, and showed excessive, apparently nonintentional echolalia.* The man had exceptional keyboard ability. The only time he appeared to concentrate was when he played the piano, often from six to nine hours daily. He was an excellent sight reader and could play by ear. He had a preference for music of the classic period. Although he could not interpret abstract reading, he had a phenomenal verbatim

---

*A person with echolalia immediately repeats what another person just said to him or her.

memory for printed passages and events which were one month or more in the past.

Sloboda, Hermelin, and O'Connor (1985) described the case of NP, an idiot savant residing in a residential home for autistic persons. Although NP displayed bizarre behaviors, rarely produced spontaneous speech, avoided looking at people, and had minimal verbal intelligence, he was delighted to play the piano for people, and he had a phenomenal ability to memorize music. In a comparison with the memorization skills of a professional pianist, NP easily "outmemorized" the professional in the task of memorizing a piece by Grieg, but he did not do well at all in memorizing an atonal work of Bartok. The investigator's report error rates of 8 percent for NP and 63 percent for the professional on the Grieg; for the Bartok, the corresponding rates were 80 and 14 percent. NP's ability is apparently based in structures and relations of tonal music.

The existence of such idiots savant shows that intelligence in the ordinary sense is not required for musical ability. Gordon (1968) reported that musical aptitude scores often related only slightly to intelligence, although, in European studies, performance ratings related more highly to intelligence. He found (not surprisingly) that his own musical aptitude measures were better predictors of musical success, as measured by etude performance, teacher ratings, and a notation test after three years of instruction, than were intelligence tests. But the logic that intelligence *ought* to be related to musical success persists.

Sergeant and Thatcher (1974) demonstrated that apparent weak relationships between tests of musical ability and intelligence likely are a statistical artifact caused by the less-than-perfect reliability and validity of the tests. Correlation techniques, often used to relate musical ability and intelligence, are such that a relatively small change in absolute rank on one variable as compared with absolute rank on another variable can produce a spuriously low relation. The authors conclude, on the basis of three experiments employing various measures of intellectual and musical abilities, where data were analyzed via analysis of variance and trend analysis, that all highly musical people appear to be highly intelligent, but not all highly intelligent people are musical. Musical ability requires an interaction between intelligence and appropriate environmental stimulation. Phillips (1976) also suggests a close relationship between musical ability and intelligence, believed to result from a common environmental cause: A home promoting musical ability also is likely to promote intelligence.

Gardner (1983) developed a theory of loosely-related multiple intelligences which includes a *musical* intelligence as well as linguistic, logical-mathematical, spatial, bodily-kinesthetic, and personal intelligences. Gardner's criteria for an intelligence (pp. 60–67) include (a) potential isolation by brain damage, (b) the existence of idiots savant and prodigies (e.g., NP and Mozart), (c) identifiable core operations, such as sensitivity to pitch or rhythm relations, (d) a developmental history which leads to expert performance, (e) evolutionary history, (f) support from experimental psychological tasks, (g) support from psychometric findings, and (h) the ability to encode the information with which an intelligence deals in a symbol system. For Gardner, no person's intelligence may be measured adequately in one testing session, as is usually the case with studies comparing musical ability or aptitude scores with scores on a verbal intelligence measure. It might be better to measure the discrepancy between what a person can do now and a month later after instruction, in accordance with Vygotsky's (1978) *zone of proximal development.* In any case, the intelligences do not necessarily exist in anything approaching equal amounts; perhaps a concept of a separate musical intelligence will give new direction to assessing musical ability as the present stage in development of the intelligence.

Sex and Race

Sex presents an apparent paradox regarding musical ability. Girls dominate in many school musical organizations, which can be verified by examining membership lists and attending concerts and festivals. Many college music majors are females. Yet, except for certain types of vocalists, most professional performers and conductors are males. This is a result of sexual stereotyping and discrimination, not any inherent sexual differences in musical ability.

Gilbert (1942) administered musical aptitude measures to 500 male and 500 female college students in the Northeastern United States. In general the females outscored the males, but not when musically untrained females were compared with untrained males. Only 231 males had any musical training; their average amount was two years. Four hundred females had an average of three-and-one-half years of private lessons. The social stereotype of women being more "artistic" was a self-perpetuating one, in Gilbert's opinion, as a result of musical training being given more readily to females. (It must be recognized that most of his subjects, male and female, attended expensive private schools and were from high socioeconomic levels.)

On the basis of data gathered in the creation, design, and improvement of music aptitude tests for elementary school children, Bentley (1966) concluded that there are no inherent sexual differences in musical ability. At certain ages, many boys begin to associate musical activity, particularly singing, with feminine roles as a result of classroom social stereotypes.

Figgs (1976), reviewing literature on sexual discrimination and stereotypes, concluded that women have been encouraged to excel only to a certain degree, be dependent, and avoid specialization. Stigmas regarding who should play certain instruments and who should occupy certain roles in music education have not dissipated. Human differences in musical ability exist, but sexual differences are a cultural artifact.

Racial and ethnic characteristics influence musical ability only to the extent that particular cultures encourage musical development in designated directions. There are no inherent influences: Blacks do not necessarily "have rhythm," all Italians are not singers, and all Hungarians are not violinists.

Summary

Musical ability is not influenced significantly by hearing, genetics, and physical features, provided minimal perceptual and physical capacities are present. Sex and race are irrelevant psychologically, although not necessarily sociologically. Creativity is too ill-defined to be very helpful in the prediction of musical ability. It is difficult to be musically able without being intelligent (idiots savant to the contrary), although there are different forms of intelligence, with varying relationships among them. The constituents of musical ability vary with how they are conceptualized, defined, and measured. Although the major determinants of musical ability are not understood, it probably results from interaction of audition, physical coordination, intelligence, and experience. Attempts to measure and predict musical ability have yielded interesting descriptive information.

Measurement and Prediction

Lack of a clearcut definition of musical ability encourages varied measurement methods. Musical ability is defined operationally, rather than constitutively, by the particular means of measurement. (An operational definition specifies how a trait will be recognized in a specific instructional or research setting, while a constitutive definition is a dictionary-style definition.) Some tests stress basic discrimination skills; others require more "musical" tasks. Some measures require prior musical achievement. Instrument manufacturers have published "tests" on which almost anyone who is minimally literate may score well.

This book is not a measurement text; only three of the available measures are discussed below. Readers who wish to investigate other tests and necessary considerations in test development should consult Boyle and Radocy (1987) and scan *Dissertation Abstracts International,* as well as examine the older texts by Colwell (1970), Lehman (1968), and Whybrew (1971). Test development remains a common doctoral research project.

Some Approaches

Musical ability may be assessed, particularly by an experienced observer, by means of educated guessing. Children vary in the extent to which they actively seek to make and listen to sounds. Children with musically successful older brothers and sisters may be successful themselves. Any child who asks for musical experiences should be welcomed and encouraged. But educated guesses may be misleading, particularly if they stress overt indicators. Discovering "latent" musical ability requires a more formal assessment. Three representative tests are discussed in detail to illustrate approaches to formal measurement.

The *Seashore Measures of Musical Talents* (Seashore, Lewis, and Saetveit, 1960) appeared initially in 1919 and were revised extensively in 1939. Only slight changes have occurred since. The term "measures" rather than the singular reflects Seashore's view that musical ability consists of loosely related specific sensory capacities. Each particular measure must be interpreted as a measure of one narrow skill; the six measures together yield a musical profile, which shows a pattern of auditory acuity. There is no total score possible on the Seashore tests.

The Seashore pitch, loudness, time, and timbre tests all require judgments of paired tones. The subject respectively must indicate whether the second tone is higher or lower, stronger or weaker, longer or shorter, and same or different in comparison with the first tone. Pitch stimuli are based on a 500 Hz standard; the smallest difference is 2 Hz (a 9 cent interval), which approaches jnd for pitch discrimination. Loudness stimuli, all 440 Hz, vary in intensity level by as little as 0.5 db. The timbre stimuli are altered by varying the third and fourth partials of a 180 Hz complex tone; the smallest change from the standard is a simultaneous 0.7 db decrease and a 4.0 db increase in the third and fourth partials respectively. All the differences are subtle enough that the results may be influenced by the fidelity of the sound reproduction system and acoustical aspects of the testing environment. Plomp and Steeneken (1973) demonstrated the variability of sound pressure level in reverberant sound fields and the place dependence of sound sensations for steady-state tone.

The Seashore rhythm and tonal memory tests require pattern recognition and comparison. Short paired bursts of 500 Hz tones in five-note, six-note, or seven-note patterns comprise the rhythm test; the subject must indicate whether the second pattern is the same as or differs from the first. In the tonal memory test, paired three-note, four-note, and five-note organ sequences are presented; no difference between adjacent tones is smaller than a whole step. The subject must identify which tone differs in the two presentations.

Seashore believed that there was a physiological limit to auditory abilities, and that consequently, scores on his tests would not change appreciably over time except as a function of misunderstood directions and experience in test taking. Investigators attempting to improve Seashore-measured skills by training the subjects have obtained various results, but there is no question that many individuals can raise their scores after training. For example, Wyatt (1945) trained sixteen adults, eight musicians and eight nonmusicians, who did not score well on several administrations of the Seashore pitch test. Training procedures, adapted to each individual, featured the use of tunes, repetition, imitation, and feedback. Several post-training testings showed that the musicians gained, on the average, 49 percent of the maximum possible gain. The nonmusicians' average gain was 26 percent, but they nevertheless scored higher after training than the musicians did before training.

For the person who equates musical ability with the Seashore tests' perceptual tasks or believes that such tasks are an important part of musical ability, the *Seashore Measures of Musical Talents* are a useful tool. They are fairly reliable and are valid for what their creators claim to measure. There are other, more "musical" approaches, which, depending on the test user's philosophy, may be "better."

Wing (1961), whose factor analytic study was described above, developed the *Standardised Tests of Musical Intelligence*. Although the Wing is a battery of seven tests, there is a total score possible, which is appropriate because Wing found a general factor of musical ability. All of Wing's stimuli are piano tones; some of the subjects' tasks require a greater degree of memory.

The chord analysis and pitch sections of Wing's battery require the subject respectively to evaluate individual chords for the number of tones contained therein and to indicate whether the second of paired chords contains a tone higher or lower than the first chord.

The memory, rhythmic accent, harmony, intensity, and phrasing sections require comparisons of paired melodies, some of which are rather lengthy. In the memory section, the subject must indicate which one of three to ten tones is altered in the second rendition. The others require the subject to indicate if the second melody is the same or which he or she prefers regarding the property to question.

Wing tried to make his tests musical while psychologically adequate. He believed that musical ability, as measured by his tests, is largely innate, not necessarily related to intelligence, and not influenced by environment (Wing, 1954). This perhaps is going too far in light of other evidence.

Wing's test is amusing to many American listeners because of the characteristics of the recorded voice and some problems with the audio quality. However, the test is an interesting one for a person who believes in the importance of melodic, harmonic, and rhythmic discrimination.

Gordon's (1965a) *Musical Aptitude Profile* is one of the more recent published tests and is perhaps the most comprehensive prediction measure. Each of the seven subsections, each of the three major sections, and the total battery all yield a score. The subject's basic task is to evaluate paired phrases; the stress is on what Gordon calls *imagery* or *sensitivity*. All stimuli are played on string instruments.

The tonal imagery section contains a melody subsection, in which the subject must indicate whether the second phrase is an embellished melodic variation of the first ("same") or a different melody, and a harmony subsection, in which the subject labels the second phrase as having a lower voice the same as, or different from, the lower voice of the first.

One subsection of rhythm imagery requires the subject to indicate whether the second phrase's tempo accelerates, retards, or stays the same. The second rhythm imagery subsection asks for a same-different comparison regarding metrical accents.

Gordon's musical sensitivity section contains three subsections. In all, the subject must indicate which of two performances sounds better. In the phrasing subsection, musical expression is varied. Endings differ, rhythmically and melodically, in the balance subsection. In a so-called style subsection, tempo differences predominate.

Gordon's test is lengthy and expensive, but it is thorough and has an excellent manual. Gordon based the test on eight years of research and believes that it minimizes musical achievement (Gordon, 1965b). Several investigations, mostly by Gordon's students, attest to the *Musical Aptitude Profile's* predictive validity. The person who believes that sensitivity to tonal and rhythmic variation and nuance in a musical context is a vital aspect of musical ability would find Gordon's battery useful.

The Seashore, Wing, and Gordon batteries illustrate approaches to measuring musical ability. More precisely, they are measures of musical *aptitude*, intended to assess ability without requiring specific musical knowledge. In order for a person to use these or any other tests, he or she must be convinced of the tests' *validity*.

Validity

A test's validity refers to how well the test measures what it is supposed to measure. Validity must not be confused with *reliability*, the consistency with which a test measures. A test must be reliable in order to be valid, but a test may be highly reliable without being valid.

Any respectable published test is accompanied by a manual which includes reliability estimates and an explanation of how they were obtained. There are four common ways of estimating test reliability in classical test theory, which applies to nearly all the musical ability measures. Three ways rely on relating two sets of scores; the other is a matter of interitem consistency.

Parallel-forms reliability, in which scores from alternative forms of the same test administered to the same people are correlated, is one method. Test-retest reliability, in which the same test is administered twice to the same people and the scores are correlated, is another. When only one administration of one form is practical, two halves of the test may be correlated and the resulting correlation coefficient adjusted in accordance with a compensating formula; this is called split-halves reliability.

Kuder-Richardson reliability, computed in accordance with a formula, makes use of proportions of examinees answering each item correctly. Each reliability technique has its strengths and weaknesses. The most authoritative discussion of classical reliability techniques is in Stanley (1971); simpler discussions may be found in educational measurement texts such as Lindvall (1967) and Mehrens and Lehmann (1973).

Reliability estimates range, in theory, from -1.00 to $+1.00$, although negative estimates are rare. The closer to $+1.00$, the more reliable is the test. There is no magic criterion, but a published measure should have reliability in the .80s before it is considered especially useful, in the writers' opinion.

Given sufficient reliability, a test must have some satisfactory rationale for *why* it is a test of whatever it is supposed to test in order to be valid. Since musical ability is not defined clearly, no ability measure is completely valid.

If a measure of musical ability is valid as a predictor of musical success, a logical way to validate such a test is to administer it to a large representative sample, measure the sample's success later, and look for a strong positive relationship between test scores and musical success. This is called criterion-related or predictive validity, and the problem often becomes one of the criterion's validity. Musical success often means accomplishment in a formal music instruction setting. Children particularly may be "unsuccessful" musically because of organizational and personality problems rather than musical problems. Teacher ratings are influenced easily by nonmusical variables. Correlating a new with an old test presumes that the old test is sufficiently valid.

Validity may be a matter of how well a designated body of material is represented in the test. This is called content validity and is more readily appropriate for achievement than for ability measures. It requires a fairly complete specification of just what a musically able person should be able to do.

Construct validity, the extent to which a test measures ability in accordance with underlying theoretical constructs of ability, is difficult to establish. Invalidity may be a failure of the test or a failure of the theory.

The prospective test user must examine the validity claims for the test under consideration and determine whether such claims are personally acceptable.

Importance of Nonmusical Variables

Given the facts that musically able people may be able in other areas and that musical success may be judged with nonmusical criteria, it is reasonable to examine the idea that additional nonmusical variables might increase the accuracy with which musical success may be predicted.

Multiple regression analysis is a statistical technique for determining the amount of variance in a criterion variable predicted by two or more predictor variables and the degree to which each predictor bears a significant relationship to the criterion. Rainbow (1965) used teacher ratings of apparent student musical "talent" and "awareness" in a university laboratory school as a criterion variable for a multiple regression study. His fourteen predictor variables were:

(1) pitch discrimination
(2) tonal memory
(3) rhythm
(4) musical memory
(5) academic intelligence
(6) school achievement
(7) sex
(8) age
(9) musical achievement
(10) musical training
(11) home enrichment
(12) interest in music
(13) relatives' participation
(14) socioeconomic background

The first three predictors were measured by appropriate Seashore sections; the fourth predictor was measured by a section of the *Drake Musical Aptitude Tests* (Drake, 1957) in which the subject indicates whether repeated melodies are the same or change in key, rhythm, or individual tones. Variables five and six were assessed via combinations of standardized tests administered routinely in the school. Musical achievement was measured with the *Kwalwasser-Ruch Test of Musical Accomplishment* (Kwalwasser & Ruch, 1927), which primarily is a test of visual notation reading skills.

The upper and lower 20 percent ability groups, in accordance with teacher ratings, were compared for each variable. A significant difference existed between the groups for each variable except sex and age. The multiple regression analysis gave somewhat different results for different grade levels. For ninety-one elementary students (grades four through six), the significant predictors of teacher ratings were pitch discrimination, tonal memory, interest in music, and socioeconomic background. For 112 junior high school (grades seven and eight) students, academic intelligence, sex, musical achievement, and relatives' participation in music were the significant predictors. For eighty-eight high school (grades nine through twelve) students, the significant predictors were pitch discrimination, tonal memory, home enrichment, and interest in music. For the total group of 291, significant predictors were tonal memory, academic intelligence, musical achievement, home enrichment, interest in music, and socioeconomic background. Rainbow concluded that these last three significant predictors for the total group are important extramusical variables for prediction purposes.

Multiple regression analysis is an extention of correlation; the prediction-criterion relationships are not evidence of causality. Although Rainbow's choice of measures may be questioned, particularly for musical achievement and the criterion variable, the importance of his study is its evidence that musical ability in one operational definition is more than a matter of traditional facets.

Whellams (1970) used discriminant function analysis, a technique for assessing the relative strengths of variables which discriminate between two criterion groups. In one study, the number of terms in the Royal Marines School of Music was the strongest discriminator between a group of below and above average Junior Musicians, as identified by their grades. In another study, comparing buglers and Junior Musicians of two levels, strong discrimination weights were found for nonmusical variables, especially algebra scores. Whellams concluded that musical aptitude batteries need aural-musical and nonmusical tests.

Hedden (1982) employed multiple regression analysis to study the effectiveness of attitude toward music, self-concept in music, musical background, academic achievement, and gender as predictors of musical achievement by 144 fifth- and sixth-grade students in two schools. The most significant predictor, accounting for 25 percent of the variance in musical achievement in one school and 40 percent in the other, was academic achievement, measured via the *Iowa Tests of Basic Skills.* Addition of the self-concept measure in one school and the attitude measure in the other increased the respective amounts of accounted variance to 34 and

61 percent respectively. The other variables, including musical background, were not effective predictors. (Unlike the Rainbow study, Hedden's criterion variable was measured by a formal test, part of the Colwell (1969) *Music Achievement Tests,* not by teacher judgments.)

Particularly when the musically able person is viewed as a person capable of achieving musical success in some academic setting, the use of nonmusical variables as predictors of musical ability appears especially propitious. Variables of academic skills and home environment are the most promising.

What Should We Measure?

While formal measures of musical and nonmusical variables may aid in the measurement and prediction of musical ability, there is no one test that is likely to be adequate by itself. A reliable and valid battery which tests musical skills that the investigator deems important in combination with assessments of intellectual ability, academic achievement, prior opportunities for musical stimulation, and, where necessary, physical attributes probably offers the best approach to making judgments of musical ability on which to base decisions regarding student recruitment, selection, and counseling. There is no substitute for providing an *opportunity* for success, of course; the chance to do something usually is the best predictor of whether a person is able to do something. The zone of proximal development, mentioned earlier, conceivably could be assessed by requiring a series of ordered tasks in musical recognition, discrimination, and production, followed by instruction and then another series of tasks: Perhaps more musically able persons have wider zones of proximal development; i.e., they are more able to profit from musical instruction.

Sloboda (1985, p. 238) suggests that "musical expertise" consists of awareness of musical structures, such as melodies, harmonies, rhythms, and underlying "deep" structures; therefore, assessing where a person is in some sequential development of musical awareness and sensitivity may be a potentially useful approach to assessing some forms of musical ability. Of course, this would require a more detailed understanding of normative or "typical" developmental sequences.

Relation to Educational Philosophy

Blacking (1973) discusses at length the musical culture of the Venda people of South Africa. The Venda stress the functional effectiveness of music. Music is a social experience more than a technical experience, and the Venda, while recognizing that some people are better performers than others, do not consider the possibility of *anyone* being unmusical. The listener as well as the performer has an important musical function. A musical elite, by Western standards, does not exist in Venda culture.

Interest in selection and construction of a musical elite is natural in a competitive society, particularly when resources are limited. If there are only so many school instruments available for beginners, it makes sense to issue them to students who are likely to profit from instruction. If a conservatory can accept a limited number of students, it makes sense to admit those who demonstrate a strong possibility of attaining a musical career.

But the risk of allowing an "unmusical" person to try to play an instrument or develop sophisticated listening skills hardly is in the same class as allowing an apparently low ability potential pilot to fly an airplane. Pursuit of a musical career by a person lacking successful musical achievements is dubious, but a child who has had no musical training should not be denied musical opportunity. We know enough about musical ability to know that it has many facets. We do not know enough about it to use it as a barrier. And music educators should not be desirous of establishing musical barriers.

Summary

The major points in Chapter Nine include the following:
1. Musical ability is a broad term which includes capacity (whatever a person is born with that promotes musical ability), aptitude (capacity plus results of environmental stimulation), and results of previous instruction.
2. Musical ability has a number of components, but they have not been identified precisely.
3. Musical ability does not vary significantly as a function of hearing acuity.
4. Environmental influences probably play a greater part in determining musical ability than do genetic influences, but there are innate differences in people.
5. Physical features, such as teeth, lips, and hands, are related only to particular aspects of musical ability, generally regarding performance on particular instruments.

6. Creativity is ill-defined and its relation to musical ability, except for composition, is uncertain.
7. Intelligence, depending on how it is defined and measured, may relate strongly to musical ability; a separate musical intelligence may exist.
8. Sex and race have no bearing on musical ability except to the extent that social stereotypes hamper or promote particular persons' abilities.
9. Musical ability probably is an interaction of audition, physical coordination, intelligence, and experience.
10. There are numerous measures of musical aptitudes and abilities; three of the best known are the Seashore, Wing, and Gordon tests.
11. Some tests, such as Seashore, test basic sensory discriminations, while others, such as Wing and Gordon, test musical discrimination at a more contextual level.
12. A musical ability test's validity is critical and often uncertain because of varying standards and techniques.
13. To be valid, a test must be reliable.
14. The most logical way of establishing an ability test's validity is to show a relationship between test success and musical success.
15. Nonmusical variables such as academic achievement and home enrichment may enhance the likelihood of predicting musical success.
16. A combination of information sources is necessary in order to make judgments regarding musical ability; ability to profit from instruction needs consideration.
17. The use of musical ability to establish unnecessary educational barriers is not recommended.

REFERENCES

Anastasi, A., & Levee, R. F. (1960). Intellectual defect and musical talent: A case report. *American Journal of Mental Deficiency, 64,* 695–703.

Bentley, A. (1966). *Musical ability in children and its measurement.* New York: Random House.

Blacking, J. (1973). *How musical is man?* Seattle: University of Washington Press.

Boyle, J. D., & Radocy, R. E. (1987). *Measurement and evaluation of musical experiences.* New York: Schirmer Books.

Colwell, R. (1970). *The evaluation of music teaching and learning.* Englewood Cliffs, NJ: Prentice-Hall.

Drake, R. M. (1957). *Drake musical aptitude tests.* Chicago: Science Research Associates.

Farnsworth, P. R. (1941). Further data on the Adlerian theory of artistry. *Journal of General Psychology, 24,* 447–450.

Farnsworth, P. R. (1969). *The social psychology of music* (2nd ed.). Ames: Iowa State University Press.

Figgs, L. (1976). The ms. mess. *Kansas Music Review, 38* (3), 24–25.

Gardner, H. (1983). *Frames of mind.* New York: Basic Books.

Getzels, J. W., & Jackson, P. W. (1962). *Creativity and intelligence: Explorations with gifted students.* New York: Wiley.

Gilbert, G. M. (1942). Sex differences in musical aptitude and training. *Journal of General Psychology, 25,* 19–33.

Gordon, E. E. (1965a). *Musical aptitude profile.* Boston: Houghton-Mifflin.

Gordon, E. E. (1965b). The musical aptitude profile: A new and unique musical aptitude test battery. *Council for Research in Music Education, 6,* 12–16.

Gordon, E. E. (1968). A study of the efficiency of general intelligence and musical aptitude tests in predicting achievement in music. *Council for Research in Music Education, 13,* 40–45.

Guilford, J. P. (1957). Creative abilities in the arts. *Psychological Review, 64,* 110–118.

Hedden, S. K. (1982). Prediction of musical achievement in the elementary school. *Journal of Research in Music Education, 30,* 61–68.

Karlin, J. E. (1942). A factorial study of auditory functions. *Psychometrika, 7,* 251–279.

Kwalwasser, J., & Dykema, P. W. (1930). *Kwalwasser-Dykema music tests.* New York: Fischer.

Kwalwasser, J., & Ruch, G. M. (1927). *Kwalwasser-Ruch test of musical accomplishment.* Iowa City: University of Iowa Bureau of Educational Research.

Lehman, P. R. (1968). *Tests and measurements in music.* Englewood Cliffs, NJ: Prentice-Hall.

Lindvall, C. M. (1967). *Measuring pupil achievement and aptitude.* New York: Harcourt, Brace and World.

Mehrens, W. A., & Lehmann, I. J. (1973). *Measurement and evaluation in education and psychology.* New York: Holt, Rinehart, and Winston.

Moore, R. (1966). The relationship of intelligence to creativity. *Journal of Research in Music Education, 14,* 243–253.

Mursell, J. L. (1937). *The psychology of music.* New York: Norton.

Phillips, D. (1976). An investigation of the relationship between musicality and intelligence. *Psychology of Music, 4* (2), 16–31.

Plomp, R., & Steeneken, H. J. M. (1973). Place dependence of timbre in reverberant sound fields. *Acustica, 28,* 50–59.

Radocy, R. E. (1971). Thoughts on creativity. *Kansas Music Review, 33* (5), 16–17.

Rainbow, E. L. (1965). A pilot study to investigate the constructs of musical aptitude. *Journal of Research in Music Education, 13,* 3–14.

Scheid, P., & Eccles, J. C. (1975). Music and speech: Artistic functions of the human brain. *Psychology of Music, 3* (1), 21–35.

Seashore, C. E. (1938). *Psychology of music.* New York: McGraw-Hill.

Seashore, C. E., Lewis, L., & Saetveit, J. G. (1960). *Seashore measures of musical talents.* New York: The Psychological Corporation.

Sergeant, D., & Thatcher, G. (1974). Intelligence, social status, and musical abilities. *Psychology of Music, 2* (2), 32–57.

Sherbon, J. W. (1975). The association of hearing acuity, diplacusis, and discrimination with musical performance. *Journal of Research in Music Education, 23,* 249–257.

Shuter-Dyson, R. (1982). Musical ability. In D. Deutsch (Ed.), *The psychology of music* (pp. 391–412). New York: Academic Press.

Simons, G. M. (1964). Comparisons of incipient music responses among very young twins and singletons. *Journal of Research in Music Education, 12,* 212–226.

Sloboda, J. A. (1985). *The musical mind: The cognitive psychology of music.* Oxford: Clarendon Press.

Sloboda, J. A., Hermelin, B., & O'Connor, N. (1985). An exceptional musical memory. *Music Perception, 3,* 155–170.

Stanley, J. C. (1971). Reliability. In R. L. Thorndike (Ed.), *Educational measurement* (pp. 356–442). Washington: American Council on Education.

Vygotsky, L. (1978). *Mind in society* (M. Cole, ed.). Cambridge, MA: Harvard University Press.

Whellams, F. S. (1970). The relative efficiency of aural-musical and non-musical tests as predictors of achievement in instrumental music. *Council for Research in Music Education, 21,* 15–21.

Whybrew, W. H. (1971). *Measurement and evaluation in music.* (2nd ed.). Dubuque, IA: W. C. Brown.

Wing, H. D. (1941). A factorial study of music tests. *British Journal of Psychology, 31,* 341–355.

Wing, H. D. (1954). Some applications of test results to education in music. *British Journal of Educational Psychology, 24,* 161–170.

Wing, H. D. (1961). *Standardised tests of musical intelligence.* The Mere, England: National Foundation for Educational Research.

Wyatt, R. F. (1945). Improvability of pitch discrimination. *Psychological Monographs, 58* (2). (Whole No. 267)

Chapter Ten

MUSIC LEARNING

"Learning Music" is a major enterprise. Incidental learning occurs through radio, television, and films. Songs are conveyed within and across generations through oral traditions. Formal instructional programs are offered in most American school systems; private music teachers of varying statures work throughout the world. "Learning music" includes learning to perform, analyze, evaluate, create, and rearrange music through deliberately sought formal experiences. It also includes the development of musical expectations, based on the perceptions and cognitions that result from immersion in one's environment and musical cultures.

Teaching or instruction may be confused with learning. Elegant presentation of a musical concept or principle is not learning. No matter how attractive and expensive the instruments, books, or other instructional paraphernalia, they are not learning. Learning requires action on the part of the learner.

This chapter offers extended definitions of key terms which are particularly important in a rational discussion of music learning. After briefly describing relevant neurophysiological activity, the chapter overviews selected learning theories. Tentative sketches of musical development in childhood are presented. A concluding section suggests applications of psychological principles to music learning.

Extended Definitions

The terms *learning, reinforcement, goal, motivation,* and *concept* are selected for definition because, in the writers' opinion, they have proved troublesome to musicians discussing learning. Other terms appear in context.

Learning

Learning is hereby defined as an observable change in behavior, due to experience, which is not attributable to anything else. This definition is patterned after that offered in Bower and Hilgard's (1981, p. 11) authoritative text.

Without a behavioral change between times A and B, no learning has occurred in that time span. Someone who already can recite major and minor key signatures cannot learn to do it, although he or she obviously learned the signatures in the past. Furthermore, learning, from the standpoint of someone who must ascertain learning in another individual, requires observable evidence. Showing a student how to produce a trumpet tone is insufficient; learning has not occurred until the student produces the tone. Some recognize so-called latent or hidden learning, i.e., the student "knows" but cannot or has not expressed what is "known." From the standpoint of anyone who requires tangible evidence of learning, latent learning is nonfunctional or even nonexistent: If a person "knows," he or she can demonstrate the knowledge.

The qualification of "not attributable to anything else" is necessary to exclude behavioral changes resulting from maturation or genetic programming. An infant does not learn to breathe; it happens "naturally." An adolescent boy does not learn to grow facial hair; such secondary sexual characteristics result from maturation. Beament (1977) believes that even a component of musical activity, called *musicality,* or the *potential* for musical activity is inherited. (Beament's "musicality" is analogous to "capacity" in Chapter Nine.)

With the possible exception of "automatic" perceptual subprocesses such as eardrum and basilar membrane movement and reflexive startle responses to sudden loud music, any musical behavior requires learning, even when "musical behavior" is conceived very broadly. The forms of particular behaviors are influenced by genetic and maturational processes or lack thereof; consider the qualities of men's and women's voices and the seventeenth century castrati. But people do not organize, analyze, or perform specific musical sounds as a result of instinct or secreted hormones. They learn to react to and with music.

Reinforcement

Reinforcement is both a process and an entity. While reinforcement's exact role and importance will vary with one's theoretical perspective of learning, it is viewed here as increasing the likelihood of a behavior, whether the increase is due to protecting the behavior from competing behaviors, confirming or clarifying cognitive organization through feedback, or strengthening an existing response to a stimulus. Reinforcement is *positive* when it is a *welcomed* (by the learner) consequence of the learner's behavior. Verbal praise from a teacher, a medal for a superior musical performance, and a decal or sticker attached to a young piano student's music all may function as positive reinforcement. Removal of an *undesired* (by the learner) situation is *negative* reinforcement; this may be exemplified by excusing a bored high school student from a study hall to go to the practice room or constantly chastising a student until a piece is performed correctly and then saying nothing. Negative reinforcement is not *punishment,* which is an *unwelcomed* consequence of behavior. Punishment is positive when the consequence is presentation of something the learner does not want, such as a reduction in a report card grade for missing a rehearsal or a slap on the hand for an incorrect fingering. Punishment is negative when the consequence is removal of something the learner wishes to keep, such as not allowing a student who enjoys playing an instrument to play because the student failed an examination in another class. Teachers may inadvertently reinforce when they intend to punish or vice versa: Scolding a student for turning left when the rest of the band turned right may provide positively reinforcing attention; praising a student in front of his or her peers may provide punishing embarrassment. Reinforcers may be primary, in the sense of meeting some immediate biological need, or secondary, in the sense of virtually anything of momentary or future utility to the organism. An action may be reinforcing in itself.

Although individuals will vary greatly in what they perceive as reinforcing and how often reinforcement is necessary, *everyone,* teachers as well as students, requires reinforcement occasionally. One of the most difficult, perhaps impossible, tasks in music or any other education is to arrange optimal reinforcement situations.

Goal

A goal is something toward which an organism directs its behavior. It may be long-term and elegant, such as desiring to become the conductor of the Philadelphia Orchestra; it may be short-term and mundane, such as desiring to leave rehearsal in time to reach the supermarket. Goals may be related to biological survival or psychological needs. All *purposeful* behavior is directed toward a goal, which is not necessarily obvious, spiritually uplifting, or "important."

Word games regarding *objectives* vs. goals may have some appeal to curriculum writers. An objective generally is a desired result of instruction and is more specific than a goal. Objectives require more formal specification.*

Motivation

Someone who "wants" to reach a goal is motivated toward that goal. Motivation represents some need or desire. People (and other organisms) have biologically based drives to quell appetites, quench thirsts, seek shelter from temperature extremes, and attain sexual gratification; they are "motivated" in various ways to preserve and protect themselves and their species. In a civilized society, individual needs and desires usually must be channeled into socially appropriate avenues. Many civilized people desire music and musically related behaviors, which generally are not based on immediately apparent biological concerns. The music teacher who wishes to instill in students a long-standing desire to "learn music" or the music therapist who wishes to instill in clients a desire to change maladaptive behavior clearly needs to build a desire to attain a goal which may have no immediate importance to the student or client but potentially has considerable importance regarding the future quality of life. Arousing and maintaining motivation to attain that which is not immediately attainable is a major pedagogical concern.

Motivation traditionally is dichotomized into extrinsic and intrinsic forms, which depend on whether the motivation arises from without or within the individual. In the authors' opinion, E.L. Walker's (1981) classification is more useful; it recognizes different forms of intrinsic motivation.

Autarkic motivation, in which the motivation arises from some desired object or state in and of itself, is the first of Walker's three categories. It certainly is intrinsic and is due to the particular appeal of that toward which it is directed. A person who practices the piano for the sheer joy of practicing may be motivated autarkically.

Idiocratic motivation, also intrinsic, is due to an individual's personal-

---

*Readers desiring more information regarding *objectives* of musical learning should consult the following: J.D. Boyle (Comp.), *Instructional objectives in music*. Vienna, Va.: Music Educators National Conference, 1974.

ity characteristics; it may be directed toward various objects and states. A learner may be motivated toward a personal concept of "success," so activities that provide successful feelings will arouse further motivation. A student may be motivated to avoid failure, so he or she avoids unfamiliar activities which appear threatening. Biological needs may be met in a variety of ways, as when hunger is alleviated and the particular means of alleviation is relatively unimportant. A child's need for self-esteem may be met through successful musical performance, but it also could be met through athletic competition, scholastic performance, fearful respect from peers, and a variety of other ways. Idiocratic motivation, then, arises from within but may be directed toward widely varying goals.

Extrinsic motivation, Walker's third category, is aroused by some reward or threat and presumably disappears when the rewarding or threatening contingency disappears. Realistically, much human behavior *is* motivated by the possibility of rewards or punishment. At all levels of formal education, students work for grades. In music schools and conservatories, auditions and jury examinations may motivate extra practice. A client undergoing music therapy may be motivated partly by the potential for receiving various tokens of achievement from the therapist. Extrinsic motivation occasionally is considered less desirable than the intrinsic forms because it may (a) not be as "lasting" or as strong as autarkic and idiocratic motivation, (b) disappear when the immediate goal is attained, and (c) be interpreted as surrender of internal control.

The different forms of motivation may interact, as when a music therapy client simultaneously feels an inner idiocratic drive to enhance well-being, an autarkic attraction to a particular musical activity, and an extrinsic desire for rewarding comments and tokens from the therapist. A student memorizing a piece for public performance may anticipate meeting some inner idiocratic need for public recognition by performing on stage and be motivated extrinsically to memorize rapidly in order to avoid the teacher's wrath.

Deci (1980), in a "metatheory" of human behavior, suggests that human behavior results from the interactions of three motivational subsystems (intrinsic, extrinsic, and amotivational), three personality orientations (beliefs in internal, external, and impersonal causality), and three perceived environments (responsive informational, controlling, and capricious). People have innate needs for competence and self-determination, so opportunity to exercise free choices and see the consequences of those choices is critical in building intrinsic motivation. Indeed, excessive reliance on extrinsic motivation through reward may have a detrimental effect on performance, as McCullers (1978) notes in *The Hidden Costs of Reward* (Lepper & Greene, 1978).

Concept

A concept is an internal organizational creation which enables a learner to classify objects and events with sufficiently similar attributes into one category. Concepts may be highly specific, such as an instrumentalist's concept of a German bassoon sound, or vaguely broad, such as a young child's concept of music. Concepts are unique to an individual; no one person's concept of Beethoven, periodicity pitch, hearing, or turkey dinners is exactly like any other's. Attempts to promote conceptual learning are attempts to facilitate formation of categories in accordance with relevant classification cues.

Neurophysiological Activity

The brain and central nervous system are vital to human learning, as are the neurochemical processes involved in message transfer and memory storage. Only a few basic aspects of neurophysiology are discussed here; readers desiring more extensive and intensive information may consult *Scientific American*, volume 241, no. 3 (1979) and the neurophysiology chapter in Bower and Hilgard (1981). The standard texts of Pribram (1971) and Deutsch and Deutsch (1973) also may be useful, as well as various encyclopaedic treatments.

The basic neural message is in the form of variations in electrical voltage transmitted between and among neural cells or *neurons*. The brain, which weighs about three pounds, contains about one hundred *billion* (10^{10}) neurons (Hubel, 1979). No two neurons are completely identical, but most contain a *cell body* or *soma*, an *axon*, and *dendrites*. The soma is responsible for the cell's basic life processes. The axon, a relatively long structure which branches near its end, is a pathway for electrochemical signals emitted by the neuron. Dendrites are the main receptors for incoming signals; they tend to branch in clusters near the soma. A simplified diagram of a neuron appears in Figure 10-1.

Synapses are small gaps across which information is transferred between neurons. According to Stevens (1979), a neuron may contact about one thousand other neurons across anywhere from one to ten thousand synapses. A synapse generally occurs between a transmitting neuron's axon and a receiving neuron's dendrite, but axon-axon, dendrite-dendrite, and axon-soma synapses also are possible. A chemical neural transmitter substance squirts across the tiny synaptic cleft to transmit information; a neutralizing chemical then normally clears the synapse for further action. Synapses may be either *excitatory*, where they tend to stimulate firing of receiving neurons, or *inhibitory*, where they cancel signals. The brain contains about thirty known transmitter substances, each of which has characteristic excitatory or inhibitory effects (Iversen, 1979). All stimulation, including sounds from Handel's *Messiah*, a beginning oboe class, and chirping crickets, may result in squirts of transmitter substances.

The overall neural network includes sensory, motor, and interconnecting neurons (Nauta & Feirtag, 1979). Most of the brain's neurons are interconnectors; they may be considered as part of a gigantic interrelated computational network. Learning must involve enhancing the meaning and efficiency of communications among functional units of neurons.

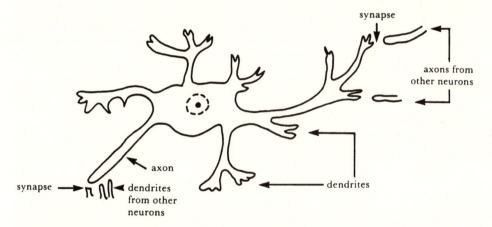

Figure 10-1. A diagram of a neuron. The dendrites are receivers, the axon is a transmitter.

Musical inputs, as all sensory inputs, stimulate neural structures. During such stimulation, deoxyribonucleic acid (DNA), the genetic memory molecule, produces ribonucleic acid (RNA), which appears in the glia (nonneural cells embedded in neural tissue) after stimulation. This *consolidation* process may be the basis for long-term memory (Pribram, 1971, pp. 37–38). Current sensory information may be compared with the stored representative record of prior experience, thereby guiding the organism's musical behavior (Pribram, p. 49).

Vital to neural transmission and memory consolidation is sensory inhibition, as described comprehensively by Von Bekesy (1967), who noted that (pp. 133–134) "a good observer is one who has the ability to inhibit the unnecessary phenomena." Sensory inhibition, more pronounced for stronger stimuli, eliminates unwanted information. Chapter Three noted the ear's reduced sensitivity to low frequency sounds. This prevents hearing one's own heartbeat and blood circulation sounds loudly. The eye's insensitivity to infrared light prevents people from seeing light resulting from self-radiation. A sensation of vibration does not extend along the skin as far as the actual physical disturbance. Inhibition of basilar membrane activity is necessary in order to obtain the relatively precise pitch sensations characteristic of human hearing. Sensory inhibition results in a funneling and sharpening of neural information without which human learning, as it exists currently, would be impossible.

The brain is the major control center of human learning. It may be roughly categorized into the *hindbrain, midbrain,* and *forebrain.*

Within the hindbrain are the *cerebellum,* which is an organizer and coordinator of muscle movements, and the *brain stem,* which includes the *pons* and the *medulla.* The pons's nerve fibers connect the two halves of the cerebellum and aid in movement coordination. The medulla, involved in direct control of many involuntary muscular and glandular actions, is a type of interface with the spinal cord.

The relatively small midbrain serves as a switching station within the *reticular activating system,* which is a type of "early warning system" that the brain can use in vigilance tasks, such as awaiting return of a theme or listening for a particular instrument.

The forebrain is the largest of the three sections. It includes the *diencephalon,* which in turn includes the *thalamus,* a switching center for sensory impulses, and the *hypothalamus,* a regulator of certain vital functions and conditions as well as a pleasure-pain center. The forebrain also includes the *cerebrum,* comprised of the two cerebral hemispheres linked by the corpus callosum. Analysis of sensory data, origination of many motor impulses, and most "master control" of the human body occur in the deeply grooved and highly intricate cerebral cortex.

Although useful conceptions of human musical learning and pedagogical principles may exist without detailed understanding of the brain and related biochemical bases of behavior, one should remember that the brain is "in charge" of an individual's learning. Educators can do much to enhance learning and therapists can do much to promote well-being, but biochemical difficulties cannot be eliminated by psychological means.

Basic Learning Theory

The major classifications of learning theories are the *behavioral-associationist* (stimulus-response) and the *cognitive-organizational* theories. Distinctions are not always clearcut, but, essentially, behavioral-associationists tend to take an empirical approach to the study of learning and view it in terms of behavioral sequences, habit acquisition, and trial-and-error. Cognitive-organizational theorists, often employing a more rational approach, are more concerned with central brain processes, structuring and restructuring of perceptual and cognitive fields, and "insightful" problem solving (Bower & Hilgard). No one learning theory accounts for all learning phenomena; no theory which survives in the literature is completely without utility. As Lathrop (1970) noted during an earlier time when music educators were "discovering" learning theory, learning theory does not offer instant explanations and solutions to music learning problems. Nevertheless, theoretical frameworks can be quite useful in planning instruction, developing curricula, and questioning why particular professional practices occur.

Behavioral-associationist theories discussed below include those of Thorndike, Pavlov, Guthrie, Hull, and Skinner. The cognitive-organizational school is represented by Gestalt psychology, Piaget, Vygotsky, and, while his work may not be strictly a "learning" theory, the important "career path" theory of Raynor. Humanism, difficult to classify, is treated briefly. The authoritative bases for the discussions include, in addition to the theorists' works, Bower and Hilgard, Hilgard and Bower (1975) (an older edition), Bugelski (1971), LeFrancois (1982), and the Music Educators National Conference publication *Documentary Report of the Ann Arbor Symposium* (Taylor, 1981).

Thorndike

Edwin L. Thorndike (1874–1949) believed in an actual, albeit ill-defined, connection between a stimulus and a response. Such a connection or *bond* could be established and strengthened by following a desired stimulus-response connection by a satisfying state of affairs. Thorndike's *Law of Effect* originally said that connections were weakened if followed by an annoying state of affairs, but the law was modified to stress the positive aspects. Reinforcement in the form of reward is critical in Thorndike's system.

Established connections may be strengthened through practice; this is the *Law of Exercise*. Thorndike saw no use in practice without reward, however. The student who has excessive amounts of unsupervised practice time between lessons likely is practicing without reward.

Much of Thorndike's theoretical construction was based on laboratory work using the puzzle box, a device for confining an animal, usually a cat, which can escape if it somehow pulls on a latch inside the box. Cats usually do not like confinement which is not self-imposed, and release from such a situation is a satisfying state of affairs which rewards the action(s) leading to release. Learning thus is a matter of mechanical trial-and-error attempts, although some responses are more likely than others.

Also part of Thorndike's system are the *Law of Readiness*, essentially stating that once an organism is ready to do something, doing it is rewarding, the *spread of effect*, in which responses close in time to a rewarded response also are learned to some degree, the concept of *belongingness*, saying that rewards should be perceived by the learner as part of the learned event, and the principle of *prepotency of elements*, stating that more vivid or salient stimuli are likely to lead to learning.

Thorndike's "bonds" are nonexistent physically, and his theory has a hard time accounting for varying degrees of learning difficulty. From the standpoint of promoting music learning, his positions regarding reinforcement and the need to specify just what is to be learned are important. Further information is available from Thorndike himself in *The Fundamentals of Learning* (1932).

Pavlov

Ivan Petrovich Pavlov (1849–1936) was a Nobel Prize-winning (1904) physiologist who turned his attention to studying reflexes. He is the father of the classical conditioning paradigm (ding-slurp), refined to a high degree in his famous dog experiments. Pavlov, limited by the technology available to him, was unable to refine his views regarding cortical irradiation, how incoming stimuli are represented in the cortex. But his conditioning techniques are and will remain contemporary.

The basic classical conditioning paradigm operates as in Figure 10-2. An existing linkage between an unconditioned stimulus and an unconditioned response is exploited by *preceding* the unconditioned stimulus, often by about three seconds, with a potential conditioned stimulus. The conditioned stimulus, signaling the onset of the unconditioned stimulus, eventually can elicit the response without benefit of the unconditioned stimulus. The response then is conditioned. Pavlov exploited the hungry dog's unconditioned response of salivation to the unconditioned stimulus of meat powder and was able to condition salivation to stimuli such as bells, time passage, tones, and combinations thereof by preceding meat powder with the desired potential conditioned stimuli. The precision of the conditioned response could be increased until a very slight difference in time or tonal frequency could prevent a response.

(1)   US → UR
(2)   (CS)   US → UR
(3)   CS → CR

Figure 10-2. Pavlovian or classical conditioning. (1) An unconditioned stimulus elicits an unconditioned response; (2) the conditioned stimulus precedes the unconditioned stimulus; (3) eventually the conditioned stimulus elicits the same response which now is a conditioned response.

Generalization of the conditioned response to similar stimuli is both a strength and a weakness. A Pavlovian cannot allow learners to "get by" or "pass" because they "have the idea" with rough approximation. Stimulus differentiation and discrimination must be forced by withholding the unconditioned stimulus except for the particular desired condition.

Conditioned responses will extinguish with continued omission of the unconditioned stimulus. They may, however, reappear suddenly or spontaneously recover.

One must not consider conditioning as limited to "lower" animals. Conditioned responses are common events in human life. Student fear of particular teachers, reaction to particular functional household objects at certain times of day, and special behaviors of trained troops or marching bands are possible examples of conditioning.

It is very difficult to apply Pavlov's system, because the requisite unconditioned stimulus-unconditioned response links are seldom apparent and extinction of undesirable stimulus generalization by withholding the unconditioned stimulus is not always practical. Nevertheless, the tremendous power of the conditioning paradigm and the opportunities for its occurrence, desirable and undesirable, should be of concern to anyone responsible for developing musical behaviors.

Details of many of Pavlov's experiments are presented vividly in his *Conditioned Reflexes* (1927).

Guthrie

E. R. Guthrie (1886–1959) stressed contiguity, as did Pavlov, but he found the classical conditioning paradigm too restrictive. Rather than substituting one stimulus for another, Guthrie conceptualized the stimulus as being conditioned to the response. The response that removes or significantly rearranges the stimulus ("shuts it off") becomes linked to that stimulus.

For Guthrie, responses were *movements,* covert as well as overt. The essence of his theory is that stimuli or a stimulus responded to with a movement will be followed by that movement in the future. The full associative strength of a stimulus and a responding movement is gained when the initial association is made. This one trial learning paradigm at first glance seems inapplicable to complicated tasks, such as playing an instrument, but Guthrie solved that problem by noting that complicated tasks require separately learned responses to myriads of stimuli.

Guthrie's one trial learning means that reinforcement is important because it protects behavior from new associations; strengthening of response in the Thorndike sense is nonexistent. Practice brings improvement because movements can occur in response to a greater variety of stimuli, not because of strengthening responses. Completely identical stimulus configurations never occur.

Learning, for Guthrie, was habit formation. Such habits, which are stimulus-response linkages, never can be broken. The cigarette smoker who stops smoking *replaces* his or her smoking with something else. The student who finally stops playing F sharp incorrectly as F in a particular piece replaces the wrong note with the right note. Guthrie's methods of replacing habits include presenting the stimulus ordinarily eliciting the "bad" habit at a faint level and gradually increasing its strength. This threshold method is used when a person conquers a fear of spiders by having caged hairy tarantulas and other spiders gradually brought closer and closer until the former spiderphobe can handle them. Another way to replace a habitual response is to fatigue the subject by having him or her respond repeatedly until the undesirable response is replaced by no response. Another method is to present the stimulus which elicits the "bad" habit in contexts where the person is unable to respond.

Guthrie was a fluent writer and speaker, not overly concerned with rigid scholarly inquiry or extensive quantification. His theories are criticized, but they are sufficiently flexible, in Bower and Hilgard's (p. 93) opinion, that they are hard to attack through experimentation. The utility of a Guthriean interpretation of learning probably lies in the concepts of habit replacement and the all-or-none occurrence of parts of a complex learning task at definite points in time.

Guthrie's *Psychology of Learning* (1952) may be consulted for further information regarding his system.

Hull

Clark Hull (1884–1952) attempted to construct a quantitative model of behavior. For Hull, learning proceeded in an incremental manner, small steps at a time, as an organism works toward a goal. The organism is motivated toward that goal by a drive. As the goal is approached, drive is reduced, and that reduction is reinforcing. Each response made as the goal is approached becomes a stimulus for another response. A chain of successive responses is used in reducing a drive and approaching a goal. Anticipation of reward is crucial in Hull's system; the closer the goal, the more active the learner's responses.

An organism learns many habits; they have various strengths and are arranged in *habit family hierarchies,* which are ordered patterns of response. The habit family closest to the particular need will perform the necessary function, and the individual habits with the greatest strengths will be utilized first.

Hull allowed for latent learning. Learning may occur as habits are established before the learning is observable.

Motivation is the basis for reinforcement, which in turn serves as both a drive and a reward. Performers may be motivated to perform well at some future date and be "driven" toward that goal. Successful rehearsals are reinforcing. All the while existing habits are used and new habits are formed, each to take its place in an appropriate habit family hierarchy.

Hull attempted to be very precise and systematic. He created many symbols and quantifications, which, with time, have been easy to fault, but he was a major inspiration to other theorists. The idea of gradual approach to a goal and, again, the importance of reinforcement are useful to someone planning a long-term musical learning experience.

The reader wishing to learn more about Hull should consult appropriate chapters in Bugelski and Bower and Hilgard prior to reading Hull's (1943) *Principles of Behavior.*

Skinner

B. F. Skinner (1904–19) is a strict behaviorist: That which is not observable is superfluous to understanding, predicting, and controlling human behavior. To understand the Skinnerian view of learning, one must understand operant conditioning and reinforcement schedules.

Operant conditioning is the basis for chaining behavior in the Skinnerian model. It differs from classical conditioning in that the organism *emits* a response rather than having it elicited by the stimulus. The emitted response is called an operant; the operant is strengthened and made more likely if reinforced.

If an encaged pigeon pecks at a particular spot and receives food as a consequence, the pigeon is more likely to peck at that spot again and can learn to do it whenever food is required. If a cat escapes from a cage by a certain combination of movements, that combination is more likely to occur when the cat is recaged; the cat can learn to escape. If a baby "discovers" that dropping a toy from the crib brings Mother's solicitous attention, the baby is more likely to drop the toy again; the baby learns to fetch Mother. In these and similar instances of operant conditioning, a behavior occurs "naturally" and is reinforced. Skinner chains behavior through a series of selective reinforcements with remarkable results.

Reinforcement may occur continuously or intermittently. In continuous reinforcement, each and every emitted response is reinforced, or, if extinction of the operantly conditioned stimulus-response connection is desired, no response is reinforced. Intermittent reinforcement occurs in two main classes, interval and ratio, each of which features reinforcement only for specified instances.

In a fixed interval reinforcement schedule, the first response occurring after a fixed amount of time is reinforced. Responses observed in laboratory animals often show time discrimination after a while; responses cease immediately after reinforcement and accelerate to a high rate just before the next reinforcement is due. Responses are more uniform under variable interval reinforcement schedules where the time spans vary at random. Bower and Hilgard (p. 180) indicate that responses developed under variable interval schedules are unusually resistant to extinction.

In ratio schedules, reinforcement is provided for the nth (n usually equals ten or more) response after the prior reinforcement. The ratio is *fixed,* so that every *n*th response is reinforced, or it is variable, so that *n* is continually changing.

The proper reinforcement schedule added to opportunities arranged in the proper sequence virtually guarantees the stimulus discrimination and response differentiation necessary for learning to perform clearly structured tasks. Skinner's work is a basis for linear programmed instruction, in which learning proceeds, relatively error-free, in small sequential steps according to a structured presentation of the material.

Skinner has been rather unsuccessful in accounting for verbal behavior, particularly regarding speech development. His description of emotions as a set of operations alarms "humanists." There is much to learn from his reinforcement schedules, however. Constant praise, as most experienced music teachers recognize, becomes ineffective; a variable praise schedule will, in the long run, motivate more students to higher goals. Secondary reinforcers, such as verbal praise, do work with human learners, and a careful structuring of reinforcement is a powerful learning aid. A useful review of manipulations of reinforcement contingencies in studies pertaining to music education appears in Greer (1981).

Skinner has many publications; his 1938 and 1953 texts are particularly useful for acquiring detailed knowledge of his system. His *Beyond Freedom and Dignity* (1971), in which he makes the point that people are not "free" because they always are controlled by the environment operating through the laws of behavior, has been criticized negatively. Skinner believes that systematic planned positive controls would be more beneficial to human beings than the quasi-random controls which presently exist. Some place faith in "human will" and regard Skinner's views as tyranny. Others merely wonder who will do the planning.

Gestalt Views

The German word Gestalt may mean shape or form as an attribute or as an entity in itself. The Gestalt psychologists, of whom Kohler, Wertheimer, and Koffka were the leaders, were interested primarily in perception. Perception extends to learning; in the Gestalt view, learning is a matter of perceptual organization. The clarity of past organization improves present organization.

For the Gestalt advocate, problem solving is structuring and restructuring relations. Insightful behavior, generally not considered by stimulus-response learning theory advocates, is recognized in Gestalt theory; insight requires the proper relations.

Learning requires coherence rather than association. The essence of Gestalt learning theory is the *Law of Pragnanz* (compactness), which states that psychological organization is toward "good" or "harmonious" figures. Just what a "good" or "harmonious" figure *is* is somewhat clarified by the four sublaws of the Law of Pragnanz.

The *Law of Proximity* states that grouping elements to make a figure is in accordance with the elements' nearness or proximity to each other. The pattern 11 11 11 11 is more likely to be grouped as four twos rather than two fours or one two and two threes.

If not overridden by proximity, objects or events with similar attributes, such as shape, color, or timbre, will be grouped together in accordance with the *Law of Similarity*. A musical idiom containing groups of four sixteenth notes, as in often is heard as a duet when played by one instrument such as a clarinet: The last three notes of each group are in a different register than the first and are within a semitone; they are "similar." (From a frequency standpoint they also are "proximate.")

The *Law of Common Direction* refers to grouping on the basis of extrapolated completion. The incomplete lower case cursive letter *d* easily can look like *cl*, but it can be read as a *d* from the context of the word. Incomplete notes and clefs abound on music manuscript, but experienced players generally have no difficulty interpreting them.

The *Law of Simplicity* refers to a perceptual preference for smoothness, regularity, and symmetry as compared with roughness, irregularity, and asymmetry; it relates to making perceptual order out of chaos.

People who do not care for the essentially mechanistic nature of stimulus-response theories may use the term Gestalt only in the sense of antibehaviorism and speak lovingly of insight, meaningful learning, and the whole being greater than the parts. This is unfortunate because a Gestalt view of learning is positive. Music learning can be promoted by facilitating perceptual organization; for example, music manuscript which violates the principle of rhythmic spacing is asking for trouble, especially with inexperienced performers, because of the Law of Proximity. The Law of Simplicity suggests that a teacher should begin "music appreciation" with novice listeners by using music with predictable and readily perceivable forms.

Kohler's (1929) text is a good source for exploring classic Gestalt viewpoints. Gestalt theories have a contemporary importance in theories about aspects of music perception; some melodies are just easier to organize than others. Phenomena mentioned earlier in this book, such as the tonal hierarchy and auditory stream segregation, are related to Gestalt considerations.

Piaget

Jean Piaget (1896–1980), trained as a biologist, was a developmental psychologist who founded a theory of *genetic epistemology,* a result of formal logic and psychology. Piaget observed children in their natural settings, often with a clinical rather than an experimental viewpoint, and hypothesized four developmental stages through which all children must pass. Movement from one stage to the next results from maturation and learning.

From birth to approximately two years of age,* the child is in the *sensorimotor* stage. Objects initially have no existence when they are not in the newborn child's immediate environment; by about age one an object acquires a permanence in the child's thinking. Piaget divides the sensorimotor stage into six substages; essentially, the child moves from a type of motor intelligence to a more symbolic intelligence as reflexive behavior is replaced by voluntary movements.

The *preoperational* stage, roughly ages two to seven years, is characterized by illogical and incomplete concepts and the lack of reversibility, i.e., ability to understand that a given operation can be undone by an inverse operation. This stage is dominated more by perception than reason. Children will say that a higher or wider container contains more beads than a lower or narrower container despite seeing equal amounts of beads placed individually in each container. The preoperational stage also is characterized by a peculiar transductive reasoning. As LeFrancois (pp. 228–229) indicates, transductive reasoning enables a child to go from particular instances to particular instances, as in assuming that two animals which give milk must belong to the same species.

---

*Children vary greatly in when they reach each stage and how long it takes to pass through them. The ages are only a rough approximation, and a child of a given age never should be tagged automatically as being in a certain stage.

The stage of *concrete operations,* roughly ages seven to eleven years, is when a child learns to conserve. Conservation is recognition that changes can occur in an object's form or spatial arrangement without changing the object's other attributes. If two identical shot glasses are filled to the same height (water is sufficient) and the liquid from one glass then is placed in a test tube while the liquid from the other is placed in a wide shallow pan, the amounts of water are still equal, but a nonconserving child will insist that one or the other container contains more liquid. When the liquids are returned to their corresponding original containers, the same child readily will agree that the amounts are the same, but he or she just as readily will insist that one container "has more" if the shot glasses are again emptied into the test tube and pan.

Conservation has interested some music researchers, partly because children in the concrete operations stage often are beginning formal musical training and conservation is necessary for form perception and musical analysis. Pflederer (1967), after intensive research, identified five types of musical conservation: (1) *identity,* when thematic material maintains its essential characteristics across various permutations, (2) *metrical groupings,* in which meter recognition and discrimination are maintained despite changes in note value distributions within measures, (3) *augmentation and diminution,* recognition that respective lengthening and shortening of a melodic passage's note values does not change the basic tonal relations, (4) *transposition,* where a change of frequency level does not alter perception of tonal configurations, and (5) *inversion,* in which an inverted simultaneous or successive interval is recognized.

On the basis of data from forty children, Rider (1977) reported acquisition of rhythmic conservation, as indicated by a child's ability to tell that an accompanying drumbeat remained constant (MM = 60) while a song was played at three different tempi (MM = 60, 120, 240), at a mean age of 6.1 years. Area conservation, as indicated by ability to recognize that four cubes occupy an identical area on a sheet of paper regardless of whether they are adjacent to each other or scattered across the paper, was acquired at a mean age of 7.6 years. Volume conservation, as indicated by a task similar to the above shot glass example, was acquired at a mean age of 8.1 years. Ability to tell that a drum and bell playing alternately on the odd beats and even beats in $\frac{4}{4}$ meter were at the same tempo as when they both were played only on the odd beats indicated tempo conservation; its mean age of acquisition was 8.3 years. Rider's data must be interpreted cautiously because he used children with developmental difficulties, as well as because of variable acquisition ages, but the *order* of acquired conservations is important: Tempo conservation may indicate the approaching end of the concrete operations stage.

Conservation's arrival time will vary greatly with individuals. All aspects of all the developmental stages must occur; attempts to accelerate conservation or any other aspect are highly questionable.

Concrete operations are characterized by thought processes dependent on a concrete framework. Once a child moves to more formal, propositional thinking and can combine various grouping operations, he or she is in the *formal operations* stage. This usually occurs from eleven to fifteen years of age. The adolescent can now consider diverse possibilities, make "what if" judgments, and organize principles into networks. In short, he or she can now reason as an adult.

Equilibration is the self-regulated process which is the basis for psychological development and learning in Piaget's system. It includes the functions of *assimilation,* in which a new environmental experience is accepted into the existing cognitive structure, and *accommodation,* in which the cognitive structure is altered to take cognizance of a new reality. Learning problems may result from assimilation occurring rather than accommodation because of ignored details in a "new" stimulus.

While Piaget may be a relatively "popular" learning theorist with music educators, as indicated by conservation research and other articles in music journals, there is question regarding the applicability of the theory in detail. Serafine (1980), in a rather negatively critical review, notes that Piaget sought to study how the "mind" becomes capable of thought, language, and knowledge; he was relatively unconcerned about learning and individual differences. She questions the validity of music conservation tasks because of possible confusion of lack of conservation with aural perception difficulties. More generally, Gardner (1983, pp. 20–22), while crediting Piaget with developing important broad guidelines to child development, believes that research shows that Piaget's stages are far more continuous and gradual in their transitions than Piaget indicated. Furthermore, Piaget's operations are more content specific than they might appear in theory; conservation, for example, might be exhibited with some materials but not others. Piaget's theory probably is most applicable in the development of "scientific" thinking in Western literate societies; it may be less applicable to the arts and other cultures.

Despite the danger of overcategorizing children in stages on the basis of ungeneralizable evidence and unwarranted concern with conservation, Piaget's work is valuable because it clearly shows that children are not miniature adults. Teachers must present material to children in ways in which the children are ready to handle it. Excessively hypothetical questions (what if . . .) without concrete referents are unsuited to a child in the stage of concrete operations.

The relevant Hilgard and Bower (1975) chapter provides a comprehensive overview of Piaget's theories. Piaget's *The Psychology of Intelligence* (1950) and *The Psychology of the Child* (1969), coauthored by Piaget and Barbel Inhelder, are detailed discussions of his work and views.

Vygotsky

Lev Semenovich Vygotsky (1896–1934) is relatively unknown in comparison with the other theorists discussed here, but the authors believe that he deserves some commentary because his work has relevance to cognitive aspects of learning. Vygotsky was especially interested in children's development of "inner speech" and thought as well as how formal instruction might expand the range of mental operations. In contrast to Piaget, who believed that thought precedes language, Vygotsky believed that language precedes thought; children should be allowed to freely "talk to themselves" as a prelude to inner speech and cognitive manipulations thereof.

For Vygotsky, higher cognitive processes were qualitatively different from fundamental sensory processes. Social interaction is critical for cognitive development; as Day (1983, p. 161) indicates, "His thesis is that intellectual functions are internalized from social interaction." The *zone of proximal development* (ZPD), mentioned earlier in connection with measuring musical ability and intelligence, could give special focus to carefully planned music instruction because it represents the difference between what a student can do while working independently and what that student could do as a result of instruction. Although in the sense of intelligence testing, greater ZPD's may indicate higher intelligence, it is also conceivable that more efficient or appropriate instruction may widen the ZPD. In any case, maintaining an instructional setting which features challenging but comfortable social interactions may enhance learning, especially in younger children.

Day's chapter, cited above, provides an excellent overview of Vygotsky's philosophical orientation and the theoretical and functional importance of the ZPD. Books by Vygotsky (1962; 1978), translated from Russian, provide more details of his developmental theory.

Raynor

Joel Raynor (1981), a contemporary psychologist studying motivation to achieve, has a theory of *psychological career paths,* which, while not really a "learning" theory, has important implications for learning and maintaining motivation over long periods of time. Many of its aspects apply to teachers and therapists who necessarily must work in less-than-ideal situations.

A psychological career path is a series of short-term or long-term activities. Most American adults function simultaneously on three career paths: occupational (related to earning a living), sexual (related to masculinity and femininity), and family (related to identity as a spouse or parent). The occupational career, with "occupation" broadly including careers as students, teachers, clients, and therapists, is of concern here.

Career paths have three dimensions: time, contingency, and goal fixation. On the *time* dimension, there are *past* steps, steps in the immediate *present,* and *future* steps. People who are just beginning a career tend to look ahead to an anticipated future; people who are approaching the end of a career tend to look back at a remembered past.

On the *contingency* dimension, paths may be *contingent, partially contingent,* or *noncontingent.* Contingency, a matter of subjectively perceived utilities of outcomes or "steps along the path," is best understood as interacting with the time dimension. In a future contingent path, an individual pursuing the path believes that an immediate positive outcome, such as passing an audition, is necessary for additional positive outcomes along that path. An immediate negative outcome, such as not being accepted into a major ensemble, is perceived as detrimental to future opportunities. The "pathwalker" could look back to a remembered past along the path and perceive a past event as having been crucial to what has occurred since, positively or negatively ("If only I had accepted that job in. . . . "). On a partially contingent path, a positive outcome guarantees further steps, but a negative outcome has no consequence for further steps. A noncontingent path may be travelled regardless of immediate outcomes, positive or negative.

Goal fixation makes the career path *open* or *closed.* An original final goal, such as becoming a music teacher or therapist or playing first chair in a band, remains fixed on a closed path. The "Is that all there is?"

feelings occasionally experienced when a person finally reaches a long sought goal may be a symptom of a closed career path. On an open path, an individual constantly revises the goal so that further opportunities continually appear. ("If I can play well enough for them, maybe I can play well enough for *them.*" "I don't always have to teach here; I could be a supervisor in a large system.")

Activities along a career path have five perceivable types of positive and negative values. *Intrinsic* value is the inherent value of some activity, regardless of its importance to pursuing a career path. (The intrinsic value of music and the ability to help others may be important in keeping music teachers and therapists on career paths which otherwise are offering little positive value.) *Difficulty* value is the appeal (or repulsion) arising from an individual's perceived likelihood of attaining an outcome; the less likely the outcome, the greater the difficulty value. Sequential importance along a contingent path is *instrumental* value: The greater the positive instrumental value, the greater the number of perceived future (or past) opportunities; the greater the negative instrumental value, the greater the number of apparent barriers to future (or past) travel along the path. (For a person on a closed path, future instrumental values decrease as the final goal is neared; the final step has no instrumental value.) There is *extrinsic* value, which comes from rewards that are contingent on steps toward a goal but have no systematic logical relationship to intrinsic or difficulty value, and *cultural* value, related to a person's belief that attaining some outcome is good or bad, right or wrong.

So, people pursue career paths, with the path's steps having various sources of value. They may take future, past, or present perspectives, and their paths may be open or closed. Motivation to continue along a path is enhanced when that toward which people are directed is seen as a source of positive value and self-identity.

One remaining important aspect of Raynor's theory is his dichotomy of *success-oriented* and *failure-threatened* individuals. He indicates that about 25 percent of the general population are clearly success-oriented: They are dominated by a general motive to achieve; they thrive on explicit standards, a contingent path, and a definition of an attractive future. About 25 percent are failure-threatened: *They* are dominated by a general motive to avoid failure or negative evaluation. Failure-threatened students can learn and succeed at various tasks, but they cannot handle explicit evaluation standards well. (Public performance, particularly as a soloist, may be inherently threatening to a failure-threatened student.) The remaining 50 percent of the general population are about equally disposed to attain success and avoid failure.

A Humanistic Approach

If one presumes that scientific study of learning in terms of an organism reacting to the environment dehumanizes people, an alternative approach may be humanism, as discussed by LeFrancois (Chapter Eight) and exemplified by Carl Rogers (1951; 1969). In a humanistic approach, the individual is the central focus of his or her own activity. The individual reacts as a whole to the world, as it is experienced, with goal-directed behavior. The basic goal is so-called *self-actualization,* a "becoming" of whatever one can become, a reduction of distance between a perceived and an ideal self. The "self" aspects of self-actualization—self-regulation, self-government, free choice—make such a view incompatible with behaviorism.

An individual evaluates the information which is received about himself or herself. Such information is organized and incorporated into self-perception, denied because of its perceived incompatibility with self-perception, or simply ignored because there is no perceived relevance or incompatibility.

Learning, in this view, requires promotion of a positive self-concept. Rogers advocates student-centered teaching, in which the teacher is a facilitator. Tait (1981) discusses the teacher's important role in facilitating a "sharing" of information and feelings about music and music's personal significance. Sharing becomes a means of giving students a vested interest in the mutual success of teaching and learning music. In any case, the "humane" teacher or student always must admire and respect a person because of that person's humanity.

Humanism may place excessive and naive faith in a questionable "basic good" in people, and student-centered teaching may be inefficient in many contexts. Most people *do* like to "feel good about themselves"; however, musical experiences can enhance an individual's life, regardless of the details by which music is learned. The teacher who uses the music class, lesson, or rehearsal to ridicule students is not practicing sound educational psychology from a humanistic, cognitive, or behavioristic standpoint.

Musical Development

Extensive normative data regarding the musical development of children are lacking, but there has been some interesting descriptive work.

Kresteff (1963) noted characteristic musical behaviors of children in their first four years. Children's early first-year interest in sound is no clue to future musical development. Free vocalization, with only approximations of up and down, and discrimination between low and high and loud and soft occur during the second year. The third year features more rhythmic movement (in general, rhythmic perception develops faster than tonal discrimination). Awareness of tonal relations, particularly the minor third, at the expense of tonal freedom occurs during the fourth year.

Then, according to Kresteff, comes a growth of tonality in seven stages, varying considerably in their time of appearance. The first stage, the only one constant worldwide, features the pattern *so-mi*,* a descending minor third.

In the second stage, the characteristic tonal pattern expands to *la-so-mi*, often with a stress on *la. Do* is added in the third stage, *la-so-mi-do*, although it does not function as a tonic.

A pentatonic scale, *la-so-mi-re-do*, appears in the fourth stage. There are no fixed tones, and there is no dissonance. The fifth stage adds the octave *do*, so the characteristic tonal relations are now based on *do-la-so-mi-re-do*.

A half-step is introduced in the sixth stage as the syllable *fa* extends the pentatonic scales to a hexachord, *do-la-so-fa-mi-re-do*. With the addition of the leading tone *ti* in stage seven, the diatonic scale is complete.

Petzold (1963) administered tests of tonal configurations, rhythm, and phrasing to children in the first six grades. The children were required to respond with some type of musical performance as evidence of the appropriate musical perception. Findings included a large improvement in musical perception at the sixth grade level, nonsignificant sex differences, and significant effects of musical training and out-of-school experience. Perception of short patterns preceded perception of long patterns, and rhythm had little influence on melodic perception. Consid-

---

*For the reader unfamiliar with solfeggio syllables, they are tone syllables attached to particular scale degrees. The syllable *do* goes with the tonal center. As an example, the C major scale tones have the following syllables, in *descending* order: *do* (C), *ti* (B), *la* (A), *so* (G), *fa* (F), *mi* (E), *re* (D), *do* (C).

erable variation in perceptual abilities existed within grade levels. Petzold recommended less rote learning of music and more "intelligent thought."

According to Bentley (1966), music's first appeal elicits a spontaneous response, varying from indiscriminate movements to a feeling for the beat. Rhythmic perception precedes concern for tonality. Spontaneous responses lead to what Bentley calls the "apprehension" of music. Tunes become more accurate, and children recognize and have a memory for melodies. One can enjoy music at this level, and some people never advance beyond this stage.

An analytic stage follows for those who do advance; the individual can isolate figures from a tune and learn to recognize intervals. Then come three developmental stages of melodic response: (a) rhythmic coalescence, in which individuals will sing as a group with nearly identical rhythm but not pitch, (b) an appropriate grasp of tonal configurations, and (c) a group coincidence of pitch. All this normally occurs, in Bentley's view, by the time a child is eight years old.

No one has identified an optimal music learning sequence which is influenced by curriculum as well as "natural" musical development. One study with a limited school population (Hufstader, 1977) suggested a learning sequence of timbre, rhythm, melody, and harmony. Timbre discrimination skills were evident at the first grade level. Rhythmic discrimination did not begin to reach criterion until seventh grade.

Gordon (1977) developed a music learning sequence which begins with "audiation," the ability to recall previously heard sounds, especially in comparison to presently heard sounds. ("Aural imagery" may be more suggestive for some readers than "audiation," but Gordon (p. 2) finds "imagery" inappropriate.) Then there are two learning sequences, *discrimination* and *inference*. The discrimination sequence, based upon and including perception, moves from aural/oral associations through verbal association, partial synthesis, and symbolic association to composite synthesis. The inference sequence, dependent on discrimination but emphasizing conceptualization, moves from generalization through creativity/improvisation to theoretical understanding. Gordon presents ordered sequences of tonal and rhythm patterns which may be a basis for detailed sequential learning objectives.

Using musically untrained children (aged 6–12), younger adults (18–37), and older adults (ages 50–70), Funk (1977) studied recognition of thematic variation, discrimination of variations from themes, and detection of modulation (in tonality). Recognition improved moderately into adulthood, but the older adults performed the most poorly of the three groups. Young children relied heavily on rhythmic cues for recognition. Discrimination was clearly superior in both adult groups; about 80 percent of the time children thought a variation was a theme. Modulation improved with age; tonality apparently is the last of the three skills to develop. Funk concluded that musical structure is largely "invisible" prior to age eight; perception is limited to awareness of rhythm and overall melodic shape. More stimulus attributes are detected and organized as development progresses.

In a study of very young children's vocalization, Ries (1982) studied, through taped performances, the "spontaneous" (creative "composed" singing) and "imitative" (imitation of "standard" songs) singing of 48 Canadian children. She employed naturalistic inquiry methods; the babies were observed in their homes and were able to perform before their parents and other people with whom they were familiar. Subjects ranged in age from approximately seven to thirty-two months. While there was considerable individual variation, Ries generally found that babies do sing in an expressive manner with style, articulation, and vocal quality. Prelanguage babies do not need words to be expressive vocally. The data suggested a developmental sequence of pitch or melody at seven months, articulation at eleven months, and very simple rhythms until nineteen months, when words are added. Pulse and meter are employed at thirty months. Standard song develops more slowly than spontaneous song. One particularly interesting finding because of research indicating that tonality is unstable until age five years (Dowling, 1982b) was that thirty-month children could sing spontaneous songs with definite tonality. While Ries's subjects were from a closely-knit family-centered subculture and may have been musically atypical, the findings do suggest that at least some very young children are capable of more advanced musical behavior than may have been thought previously.

Reviewing research in melodic and rhythmic perception, Dowling and Harwood (1986) suggest general developmental sequences. Four-month-old infants may notice changes in beat and tempo. Five- and six-month-old babies may respond to changes in melodic contour but not to transpositions to new keys. Such babies are unlikely to sing a melody in anything like an adult manner, but they can match individual pitches. By the time the young child is two, he or she may recognize specific tunes, sing individual phrases from melodies, invent phrases, and beat rhythm patterns. There is *considerable* variation among children, of course.

Dowling and Harwood suggest that the progress of the young child during roughly the ages of two to four is similar to learning to tell stories. Just as a child might focus on an isolated incident from a story, he or she might continually repeat one phrase or segment of a song. Later, phrases are ordered in a meaningful way, both for spontaneous and standard songs. Tonality is unstable until about age five or six. Rhythmically, children impose longer and longer steady beat patterns as they grow older; regular subdivisions of beats generally do not occur until ages three or four. Again, there is considerable variability, and the evidence of developing musical skills is inexorably connected with developing verbal, vocal, and motor skills.

Tonal Memory

Tonal memory (sometimes called musical memory) is the skill used in recalling a tonal sequence across time. It may require a relatively short time span, as in comparing a first and second version for melodic identity on a musical aptitude test, or a relatively long time span, as in "drop the needle" games dreaded by many music history students. Tonal memory probably involves both spatial and temporal aspects. The necessary degree of tonal memory will vary with the musical context and the necessary degree of discrimination.

Ease of tonal memory varies with tonality and sequential characteristics. Tonal melodies are easier to recall than atonal melodies; practice may bring improvement (Long, 1975/1976). Recognition of tonal patterns in altered forms improves with age (Larsen, 1973; Foley, 1975); a perceptual shift in which the salience of individual pitches declines while melodic contour, interval size, and tonality become more relevant occurs in many children between the ages of three and six (Sergeant & Roche, 1973). In a series of experiments requiring subjects to indicate whether comparison tones matched standard tones when interfering tones separated the standards from the comparisons, Krumhansl (1979) found that subjects tended to perform better when the interfering tones were from the same key as the standard than when the interfering tones were atonal. Conversely, when the interfering tones were in a clear tonality but the standards and comparisons were outside the key (atonal in relation to the interfering tones), subjects tended to do less well than they did when the task was to compare atonal standards and comparisons separated by atonal interfering tones.

Tonal memory in the sense of melodic recognition may not require exact recognition of pitches and intervals. Dowling and Fujitani (1971) found that the recognizability of distorted familiar melodies varied with the type of distortion; few recognition problems occurred when the melodic contour was the same as the original and relative (but not exact) interval sizes were preserved. Later research showed that interval recognition and the place of particular pitches in a tonal context (chroma) are more critical than contour for tasks involving less familiar melodies, especially over a long term (Dowling, 1982a; Dowling & Bartlett, 1981; Kallman & Massaro, 1979). Dowling and Harwood (1986, p. 144) conclude that contour, interval size, tonal context, and listener experience all interact in facilitating tonal memory.

Practical Applications

Consideration of learning theory, experience, and particular problems in music learning suggests specific recommendations in regard to encouraging learning. The following recommendations, while neither complete nor a recipe for successful teaching, are offered as practical suggestions.

Reinforcement

Whether they strengthen a stimulus-response connection, prolong a response, maintain goal-seeking behavior, prevent other responses, or promote a positive self-concept, positive reinforcements generally do *work.* Greer's (1981) review cites many instances of effective reinforcement in music instruction.

Positive comments, music listening, money, candy, stripes on band uniforms, and many other objects and processes may serve as reinforcers. Classically, if something desirable (to the learner) happens, the likelihood that the behavior which the learner perceives as eliciting the reward will reoccur is increased. Young, immature, and relatively unmotivated learners may require especially frequent rewards. Yet over reliance on rewards that have little intrinsic relation to the desired behavior may retard the development of intrinsic motivation toward musical goals.

Reinforcement needs to be timed appropriately. Constant reinforcement for a learned behavior generally is less effective than random or intermittent reinforcement. Excessive time between reinforcements promotes extinction. Opportunities for reinforcement should be a consideration in scheduling performances, auditions, evaluations for grades, and practice sessions.

Practice

Depending on one's theoretical position, one may regard practice as exercising or strengthening stimulus-response connections, applying a learned response to a new stimulus, anticipatory goal-seeking responses, or searching for insight. Regardless, practice is essential in developing musical skills in both performance and nonperformance areas.

The traditional weekly private lesson grossly ignores what is known about learning, particularly with younger students. During the time between lessons, mistakes may be practiced continually with no opportunity for correction until the next lesson. It often is difficult to maintain an incentive to practice without frequent reward. The "music as its own reward" is an unrealistic ideal when one is just beginning to develop musical skills. Frequent short instructional periods should have a higher priority than weekly concentrated instructional periods. Practice sessions are facilitated by comprehensive statements of objectives and models: It is easier to practice if one knows for what he or she is practicing.

The strange belief that the so-called *beta hypothesis* can enhance musical learning should not be taken seriously. Dunlap (1932) believed that negative practice could help a person "unlearn" persistent errors made in psychomotor tasks such as typewriting and piano playing. Negative practice involves the deliberate practice of an error, accompanied by self-admonishment, e.g., "This is wrong. I shouldn't do it this way." Attempts to apply negative practice to music learning, such as Reitmeyer's (1972/1973) attempt with clarinet fingerings, have not been successful.

One does not have to be a follower of Guthrie to advocate the importance of practice in varied situations. No two "stimulus conditions" —concert halls, performance dates, stadiums, audiences, adjudicators— are exactly alike.

Concept Formation

Children's confusion of labels may interfere with proper musical conceptualization (Andrews & Deihl, 1968); hence, descriptive use of adequate terminology is important in aiding concept formation. High, low, loud, soft, fast, slow, and other musical terms must be demonstrated.

It is said that many students are unable to tell what they like about music or compare and contrast two compositions because their relevant concepts are incomplete and they lack the necessary vocabulary. "It has a beat," a favorite evaluative comment of many junior high school students, is at best an obvious statement and at worst a gross musical oversimplification. Learners need to become explicit; it is not "enough" to "have the idea."

Concrete referents are important for younger learners. Overly abstract and symbolic language is beyond the processing capabilities of many (but not all) elementary school pupils.

Concepts are private, and there is an inherent difficulty in fully expressing an aurally experienced phenomenon orally. Clarity of presentation, explicit examples, models, and emphasis of important musical attributes will facilitate concept formation.

Summary

The major points in Chapter Ten include the following:
1. Learning requires an observable behavior change, nonattributable to anything else.
2. Teaching and instruction are not learning.
3. Reinforcement, as a consequence of behavior, is essential in most forms of learning, although theoretical explanations differ regarding why.
4. Purposeful behavior is directed toward a goal.
5. Motivation, which directs a learner toward a goal, may arise from within or without the individual.
6. Motivational states (intrinsic, extrinsic, or amotivational) may interact with personality states and environmental perceptions in determining behavior.
7. Concepts are individual categorization schemes which help to organize experience.
8. The brain includes an incredibly large and complex collection of interconnecting neurons.
9. Neurons exchange excitatory and inhibitory messages electrochemically across synapses; learning requires neural networks to function together.

10. Neural stimulation may promote memory consolidation via a permanent chemical change in adjacent nonneural cells.

11. Sensory inhibition serves to channel and funnel essential information while suppressing nonessential information.

12. Learning theories may be classified broadly as behavioral-associationist and cognitive-organizational.

13. For Thorndike, learning was a matter of establishing and strengthening stimulus-response bonds.

14. For Pavlov, learning was a matter of conditioning stimulus-response linkages and generalizing them.

15. For Guthrie, learning was a matter of connecting stimuli with movements on a one-trial basis.

16. For Hull, learning was establishing habit families as the organism works in small increments toward a goal.

17. For Skinner, learning is a matter of operant conditioning of desired responses through selective reinforcement.

18. In Gestalt theory, learning depends on perceptual organization through proximity, similarity, common direction, and simplicity.

19. For Piaget, learning results from assimilation and accommodation as the child progresses through developmental stages.

20. For Vygotsky, speech is a prelude to thought and higher cognitive processes.

21. Many activities of learners (and teachers) may be conceived as steps along a "career path" in accordance with Raynor's theory.

22. Humanism stresses self-actualization through promotion of a positive self-concept.

23. Several descriptions of musical development exist, but comprehensive normative data are lacking.

24. Rhythmic sensitivity precedes tonal sensitivity.

25. Tonal sensitivity is culturally based and proceeds from simple to complex patterns.

26. Tonal memory is a function of melodic contour, interval size and sequence, and tonal context; these factors' relative importance will vary with familiarity of the material and experience of the listener.

27. Learning can be promoted by judicious use of reinforcement, varied vocabularies and examples, and frequent instruction.

REFERENCES

Andrews, F. M., & Deihl, N. C. (1968). Development of a technique for identifying elementary school children's musical concepts. *Council for Research in Music Education, 13,* 1–7.

Beament, J. (1977). The biology of music. *Psychology of Music, 5* (1), 3–18.

Bentley, A. (1966). *Musical ability in children and its measurement.* New York: October House.

Bower, G. H., & Hilgard, E. R. (1981). *Theories of learning* (5th ed.). Englewood Cliffs, NJ: Prentice-Hall.

Boyle, J. D. (comp.). (1974). *Instructional objectives in music.* Vienna, VA: Music Educators National Conference.

Buckton, R. (1977). A comparison of the effects of vocal and instrumental instruction on the development of melodic and vocal abilities in young children. *Psychology of Music, 5* (1), 36–47.

Bugelski, B. R. (1971). *The psychology of learning applied to teaching* (2nd ed.). Indianapolis: Bobbs-Merrill.

Day, J. D. (1983). The zone of proximal development. In M. Pressley & J. R. Levin (Eds.), *Cognitive strategy research: Psychological foundations* (pp. 155–175). New York: Springer-Verlag.

Deci, E. L. (1980). *The psychology of self-determination.* Lexington, MA: D. C. Heath.

Deutsch, J. A., & Deutsch, D. (1973). *Physiological psychology* (2nd ed.). Homewood, IL: Dorsey.

Dowling, W. J. (1982a). Chroma and interval in melody recognition: Effects of acquiring a tonal schema. *Journal of the Acoustical Society of America, 72,* S11 (abstract).

Dowling, W. J. (1982b). Melodic information processing and its development. In D. Deutsch (Ed.), *The psychology of music* (pp. 413–429). New York: Academic Press.

Dowling, W. J., & Bartlett, J. C. (1981). The importance of interval information in long-term memory for melodies. *Psychomusicology, 1,* 30–49.

Dowling, W. J., & Fujitani, D. S. (1971). Contour, interval, and pitch recognition in memory for short melodies. *Journal of the Acoustical Society of America, 49,* 524–531.

Dowling, W. J., & Harwood, D. L. (1986). *Music cognition.* Orlando, FL: Academic Press.

Dunlap, K. (1932). *Habits: Their making and breaking.* New York: Liveright.

Foley, E. A. (1975). Effects of training in conservation of tonal and rhythmic patterns on second-grade children. *Journal of Research in Music Education, 23,* 240–248.

Funk, J. D. (1977). Some aspects of the development of music perception. (Doctoral dissertation, Clark University, 1977). *Dissertation Abstracts International, 38,* 1919B. (University Microfilms No. 77-20, 301)

Gardner, H. (1983). *Frames of mind.* New York: Basic Books.

Gordon, E. E. (1977). *Learning sequence and patterns in music.* Chicago: G. I. A. Publications.

Greer, R. D. (1981). An operant approach to motivation and affect: Ten years of research in music learning. In R. G. Taylor (Ed.), *Documentary report of the Ann Arbor Symposium* (pp. 102–121). Reston, VA: Music Educators National Conference.

Guthrie, E. R. (1952). *The psychology of learning* (Rev. ed.). New York: Harper & Row.

Hilgard, E. R., & Bower, G. H. (1975). *Theories of learning* (4th ed.). Englewood Cliffs, NJ: Prentice-Hall.

Hubel, D. H. (1979). The brain. *Scientific American, 241* (3), 44–53.

Hufstader, R. A. (1977). An investigation of a learning sequence of musical listening skills. *Journal of Research in Music Education, 25,* 184–196.

Hull, C. L. (1943). *Principles of behavior.* New York: Appleton-Century-Crofts.

Iversen, L. L. (1979). The chemistry of the brain. *Scientific American, 241* (3), 134–149.

Kallman, H. J., & Massaro, D. W. (1979). Tone chroma is functional in melody recognition. *Perception & Psychophysics, 26,* 32–36.

Kohler, W. (1929). *Gestalt psychology.* New York: Liveright.

Kresteff, A. D. (1963). The growth of musical awareness in children. *Council for Research in Music Education, 1,* 4–10.

Krumhansl, C. L. (1979). The psychological representation of musical pitch in a tonal context. *Cognitive Psychology, 11,* 346–374.

Larsen, R. L. (1973). Levels of conceptual development in melodic permutation concepts based on Piaget's theory. *Journal of Research in Music Education, 21,* 256–263.

Lathrop, R. L. (1970). Music and music education: A psychologist's view. *Music Educators Journal, 56* (6), 47–48.

LeFrancois, G. R. (1982). *Psychology for teaching* (4th ed.). Belmont, CA: Wadsworth.

Lepper, M. R., & Greene, D. (Eds.). (1978). *The hidden costs of reward: New perspectives on the psychology of human motivation.* Hillsdale, NJ: Lawrence Erlbaum Associates.

Long, P. A. (1976). Pitch recognition in short melodies. (Doctoral dissertation, Florida State University, 1975.) *Dissertation Abstracts International, 36,* 3840A–3841A. (University Microfilms No. 76-2664)

McCullers, J. C. (1978). Issues in learning and motivation. In M. R. Lepper & D. Greene (Eds.), *The hidden costs of reward: New perspectives on the psychology of human motivation* (pp. 3–17). Hillsdale, NJ: Lawrence Erlbaum Associates.

Nauta, W. J. H., & Feirtag, M. (1979). The organization of the brain. *Scientific American, 241* (3), 88–111.

Pavlov, I. P. (1927). *Conditioned reflexes.* London: Clarendon Press.

Petzold, R. G. (1963). The development of auditory perception of musical sounds by children in the first six grades. *Journal of Research in Music Education, 11,* 21–43.

Pflederer, M. (1967). Conservation laws applied to the development of musical intelligence. *Journal of Research in Music Education, 15,* 215–223.

Piaget, J. (1950). *The psychology of intelligence.* New York: Harcourt Brace Jovanovich.

Piaget, J., & Inhelder, B. (1969). *The psychology of the child.* New York: Basic Books.

Pribram, K. H. (1971). *Languages of the brain.* Englewood Cliffs, NJ: Prentice-Hall.

Raynor, J. O. (1981). Motivational determinants of music-related behavior: Psychological careers of student, teacher, performer, and listener. In R. G. Taylor (Ed.),

Documentary report of the Ann Arbor Symposium (pp. 332–351). Reston, VA: Music Educators National Conference.

Reitmeyer, J. W. (1973). The application of negative practice to the correction of habitual fingering errors in clarinet performance. (Doctoral dissertation, The Pennsylvania State University, 1972.) *Dissertation Abstracts International, 33,* 3403A–3404A. (University Microfilms No. 72-33, 201)

Rider, M. S. (1977). The relationship between auditory and visual perception on tasks employing Piaget's concept of conservation. *Journal of Music Therapy, 14,* 126–138.

Ries, N. L. L. (1982). An analysis of the characteristics of infant-child signing expressions. (Doctoral dissertation, Arizona State University, 1982.) *Dissertation Abstracts International, 43,* 1871A. (University Microfilms No. 82-23, 568)

Rogers, C. R. (1951). *Client-centered therapy: Its current practice, implications, and theory.* Boston: Houghton Mifflin.

Rogers, C. R. (1969). *Freedom to learn.* Columbus, OH: Charles E. Merrill.

Serafine, M. L. (1980). Piagetian research in music. *Council for Research in Music Education, 62,* 1–21.

Sergeant, D., & Roche, S. (1973). Perceptual shifts in the auditory information processing of young children. *Psychology of Music, 1* (2), 39–48.

Skinner, B. F. (1938). *The behavior of organisms: An experimental analysis.* New York: Appleton-Century-Crofts.

Skinner, B. F. (1953). *Science and human behavior.* New York: MacMillan.

Skinner, B. F. (1971). *Beyond freedom and dignity.* New York: Alfred A. Knopf.

Stevens, C. F. (1979). The neuron. *Scientific American, 241* (3), 54–65.

Tait, M. J. (1981). Motivation and affect. In R. G. Taylor (Ed.), *Documentary report of the Ann Arbor Symposium* (pp. 121–128). Reston, VA: Music Educators National Conference.

Thorndike, E. L. (1932). *The fundamentals of learning.* New York: Teachers College.

Von Bekesy, G. (1967). *Sensory inhibition.* Princeton, NJ: Princeton University Press.

Vygotsky, L. S. (1962). *Thought and language* (E. Hanfmann & G. Vakar, eds.). Cambridge, MA: M. I. T. Press.

Vygotsky, L. S. (1978). *Mind in society* (M. Cole, ed.). Cambridge, MA: Harvard University Press.

Walker, E. L. (1981). Hedgehog theory and music education. In R. G. Taylor (Ed.), *Documentary report of the Ann Arbor Symposium* (pp. 317–328). Reston, VA: Music Educators National Conference.

Chapter Eleven

FUTURE RESEARCH DIRECTIONS?

The future is speculative. No mortal knows what really will happen during the future decade and beyond. Those hardly are profound statements! Yet the near future will resemble the present, and informed observers may make educated guesses regarding trends in the psychology of music. Furthermore, the degree of "futureness" varies with particular areas and perspectives. Consequently, the authors are using this chapter to speculate about some issues which may, and in their opinion *should*, become the focus of especially significant research in the next few years.

The first edition of this text (1979) suggested that the limbic system, cerebral dominance (hemispheric specialization), perception's role in tone production, synesthesia, and conformity would be especially important for research in the then near future. As far as the psychology of music is concerned, the time which has elapsed since preparation of the first edition has not shown any particular interest in the limbic system, perception's role in tone production, or conformity. The limbic system, which includes the hypothalamus, the amygdala, the hippocampus, and the septal area, is the brain's dispenser of pain and pleasure, and, as Roederer (1975, p. 164) suggested, it *should* be involved in the enjoyment of music. People can perform some music on instruments even though they cannot sing it; perception can be manifested in various ways. The authors still believe that the expression of musical preferences and performance judgments often is partly a function of who previously has expressed similar preferences and judgments. Yet, researchers understandably have had other concerns.

The hemispheric specialization issue indeed did become an important research focus. The authors' original concern was due to their perceptions that overly zealous individuals were waging intracranial war in an effort to lead the forces of the heroic "musical" right hemisphere against

353

the stultifying "analytic" left hemisphere. The hemispheres are not exact duplicates of each other. Specializations *do* exist, but they are complicated by the interactions of task nature, training, and experience, as well as physiology. Gates and Bradshaw (1977) concluded, after reviewing 211 sources, that neither hemisphere should be considered musically dominant. Nothing has occurred since to suggest otherwise.

Many studies of hemispheric specialization in the processing of auditory stimuli obtain data through the technique of dichotic listening, where separate signals are sent to the two ears. Due to the neurological fact that most information from the left ear goes to the right hemisphere and vice versa, stimuli may be directed mainly toward one hemisphere or the other. A recent study by Deutsch (1985), in which musically experienced subjects listened to sequences of dichotic dyads (simultaneous intervals with the upper tone in one ear and the lower tone in the other ear) constructed from the first six tones of the F major scale, showed more accurate recognition (as indicated through notation) of dyads in which the *upper* tone was in the *right* ear and the *lower* tone was in the *left* than for the opposite pairing. Introspectively, subjects reported hearing mostly high tones from the right earphone and mostly low tones from the left, even though (a) subjects were instructed to attend to one ear or the other and (b) the assignment of highs and lows between the ears was balanced over the experimental stimuli. Deutsch suggests a basic anisotropy or "unsymmetricalness" between the respective perceptions of high and low tones such that "high-right low-left" pairs are easier to perceive than "high-left low-right" pairs. This confounds studies in which an assumption is made that the target ear variable will not interact with any other variable. Some of the observed ear advantages which earlier investigators believed resulted from hemispheric processing differences may in fact be due to Deutsch's anisotropy, the basis for which is unknown. Consequently, investigations of hemispheric specialization may require even more qualifications in the future.

Synesthesia, the multisensory response to a stimulus normally experienced in one sensory mode, has not had any noticeable stress, but phenomena where people see colors with tones or taste the sounds of certain words probably now are less likely to be viewed as merely bizarre. An individual described in the first edition as "one case . . . known personally to the authors" (p. 324) became the subject of an extensive case study (Haack & Radocy, 1981). Video-recorded presentations of popular songs (e.g., Music Television) and elaborate lighting effects accompanying certain rock concerts suggest quasi-synesthetic phenomena and may provide fertile areas for research.

What of the near future? Rather than be too specific, the authors have elected to suggest general areas where they expect increasing interest among researchers and the consumers of research. Their views naturally are biased by personal interests and their experiences as music educators.

A search for cognitive "maps" of musical behavior, suggested by work such as Krumhansl's tonal hierarchy and Lerdahl and Jackendoff's rules for generating tonal music (see Chapter Five), probably will expand. Most of the work likely will be done by cognitive psychologists, perhaps with assists from music theorists and computer scientists. Reliable descriptions of the cognitive frameworks for musical organization employed by experienced listeners and stages through which naive listeners go as they become experts would be especially valuable to music educators and therapists.

The psychology of music historically has not addressed musical performance in any comprehensive way. The concept of abstract "performance plans," which become more abstract with increasing expertise, is presented by Sloboda (1982; 1985, pp. 77–101). Study of the conceptualization, development, and implementation of performance plans by performers at various ability levels in diverse performance media certainly may enhance understanding of psychomotor aspects of musical behavior as well as be of practical benefit to music education.

In general, the study of expertise—in listening, composing, and musical analysis—may be a fruitful area of inquiry. Studies of individuals with exceptionally high abilities play a prominent part in Gardner's (1983) theory of multiple intelligences. Dreyfus and Dreyfus (1986) identify five stages through which learners in diverse fields go as they become experts: Novice, advanced beginner, competence, proficiency, and expertise. Commenting on the final stage, Trotter (1986, p. 36) notes "Experts don't apply rules, make decisions or solve problems. They do what comes naturally, and it almost always works." What are the organizational skills that enable the expert performer, composer, and listener to "do what comes naturally"? To what extent may they be developed?

Finally, there may be an attitudinal trend toward research which stresses ways in which people's musical behaviors differ, i.e., research which stresses atypical rather than typical musical behavior. The mentally retarded student who rarely can match isolated pitches but can sing flawlessly familiar melodies with words, the sophisticated academician who cannot seem to maintain a steady beat, the high school dropout who can sit at the keyboard and with little effort pick out melodies and harmonize them, and other individuals who defy logical expectancies and commonalities are worthy of extensive description and documentation through case study/ "naturalistic inquiry" methods. Normative data mean more when one can recognize abnormality. And, normality and abnormality are a matter of perspective: For those engaged in abnormal behavior, it may be perfectly normal.

REFERENCES

Deutsch, D. (1985). Dichotic listening to melodic patterns and its relationship to hemispheric specialization of function. *Music Perception, 3,* 127–154.

Dreyfus, H. L., & Dreyfus, S. E. (1986). *Mind over machine: The power of human intuition and expertise in the era of the computer.* New York: Macmillan.

Gardner, H. (1983). *Frames of mind.* New York: Basic Books.

Gates, A., & Bradshaw, J. L. (1977). The role of the cerebral hemispheres in music. *Brain and Language, 4,* 403–431.

Haack, P. A., & Radocy, R. E. (1981). A case study of a chromesthetic. *Journal of Research in Music Education, 29,* 85–90.

Roederer, J. G. (1975). *Introduction to the physics and psychophysics of music* (2nd ed.). New York: Springer-Verlag.

Sloboda, J. A. (1982). Music performance. In D. Deutsch (Ed.), *The psychology of music* (pp. 479–496). New York: Academic Press.

Sloboda, J. A. (1985). *The musical mind.* Oxford: Clarendon Press.

Trotter, R. J. (1986). The mystery of mastery. *Psychology Today, 20* (7), 32–38.

AUTHOR INDEX

Citations to jointly authored works are listed by the first author only. For example, the Getzels and Jackson study is listed here only as Getzels.

A

Abeles, 201, 243, 253–254
Adorno, 245
Allen, D., 51
Allen, T., 107
Allport, 92
Anastasi, 302–303
Andrews, 120, 347
Apel, 82, 139–140, 146, 157, 159
Archibeque, 260
Aronoff, 181
Asmus, 216–217
Attneave, 59

B

Bachem, 49
Bachman, 118
Backus, 47, 49, 67, 151, 151–152, 158
Bamberger, 110
Barbour, 148, 151, 152, 153, 155
Barela, 103
Beament, 18, 320
Beck, 58
Behrens, 90
Bengtsson, 121
Benjamin, 81–82, 83–84, 84, 86, 97
Bentley, 110, 121, 186, 299, 305, 343
Berlyne, 204, 217–218, 221–222, 223, 223–224, 225, 227, 244, 245, 257
Berry, 148
Bharuca, 46, 145
Blacking, 18, 19, 25, 313–314
Boisen, 105
Bond, 60

Bonny, 273
Bontinck, 253
Boring, 92, 93
Bower, 136, 320, 324, 327, 331, 332
Boyle, 99–100, 115, 201, 209, 268, 306, 322
Bragg, 224
Bregman, 104
Bridges, 179, 184
Broadbent, 169
Bugelski, 327
Bugg, 45
Burns, 132

C

Campbell, 111
Capurso, 212
Cardozo, 38
Cattell, 243
Chancellor, 245
Chang, 107, 176
Chomsky, 101, 137, 161
Christ, 114
Clarke, 164–165
Clynes, 84, 143
Coffman, 88, 112
Colwell, 123, 187, 306, 313
Cooper, 80, 81, 83, 87, 98
Corso, 48, 49
Cotter, 289
Creston, 83, 85, 86, 87, 98
Crozier, 215, 216, 224, 226, 227
Cuddy, 49–50, 147, 167, 167–168

SUBJECT INDEX